Syria

WORLD BIBLIOGRAPHICAL SERIES

General Editors:
Robert G. Neville (Executive Editor)
John J. Horton

Robert A. Myers   Hans H. Wellisch
Ian Wallace   Ralph Lee Woodward, Jr.

John J. Horton is Deputy Librarian of the University of Bradford and was formerly Chairman of its Academic Board of Studies in Social Sciences. He has maintained a longstanding interest in the discipline of area studies and its associated bibliographical problems, with special reference to European Studies. In particular he has published in the field of Icelandic and of Yugoslav studies, including the two relevant volumes in the World Bibliographical Series.

Robert A. Myers is Associate Professor of Anthropology in the Division of Social Sciences and Director of Study Abroad Programs at Alfred University, Alfred, New York. He has studied post-colonial island nations of the Caribbean and has spent two years in Nigeria on a Fulbright Lectureship. His interests include international public health, historical anthropology and developing societies. In addition to *Amerindians of the Lesser Antilles: a bibliography* (1981), *A Resource Guide to Dominica, 1493-1986* (1987) and numerous articles, he has compiled the World Bibliographical Series volumes on *Dominica* (1987), *Nigeria* (1989) and *Ghana* (1991).

Ian Wallace is Professor of German at the University of Bath. A graduate of Oxford in French and German, he also studied in Tübingen, Heidelberg and Lausanne before taking teaching posts at universities in the USA, Scotland and England. He specializes in contemporary German affairs, especially literature and culture, on which he has published numerous articles and books. In 1979 he founded the journal *GDR Monitor*, which he continues to edit under its new title *German Monitor*.

Hans H. Wellisch is Professor emeritus at the College of Library and Information Services, University of Maryland. He was President of the American Society of Indexers and was a member of the International Federation for Documentation. He is the author of numerous articles and several books on indexing and abstracting, and has published *The Conversion of Scripts and Indexing and Abstracting: an International Bibliography*, and *Indexing from A to Z*. He also contributes frequently to *Journal of the American Society for Information Science*, *The Indexer* and other professional journals.

Ralph Lee Woodward, Jr. is Professor of History at Tulane University, New Orleans. He is the author of *Central America, a Nation Divided*, 2nd ed. (1985), as well as several monographs and more than seventy scholarly articles on modern Latin America. He has also compiled volumes in the World Bibliographical Series on *Belize* (1980), *El Salvador* (1988), *Guatemala* (Rev. Ed.) (1992) and *Nicaragua* (Rev. Ed.) (1994). Dr. Woodward edited the Central American section of the *Research Guide to Central America and the Caribbean* (1985) and is currently associate editor of Scribner's *Encyclopedia of Latin American History*.

VOLUME 73

Syria

Revised Edition

Neil Quilliam

Compiler

CLIO PRESS
OXFORD, ENGLAND · SANTA BARBARA, CALIFORNIA
DENVER, COLORADO

British Library Cataloguing in Publication Data

Quilliam, Neil
Syria. – Rev. Ed. – (World bibliographical series; v. 73)
1. Syria – Bibliography
I. Title
016.9'5691

ISBN 1–85109–317–6

ABC-CLIO Ltd.,
Old Clarendon Ironworks,
35A Great Clarendon Street,
Oxford OX2 6AT, England.

ABC-CLIO Inc.,
130 Cremona Drive,
Santa Barbara,
CA 93117, USA.

Designed by Bernard Crossland.
Typeset by Columns Design Ltd., Reading, England.
Printed in Great Britain by print in black, Midsomer Norton.

THE WORLD BIBLIOGRAPHICAL SERIES

This series, which is principally designed for the English speaker, will eventually cover every country (and some of the world's principal regions and cities), each in a separate volume comprising annotated entries on works dealing with its history, geography, economy and politics; and with its people, their culture, customs, religion and social organization. Attention will also be paid to current living conditions – housing, education, newspapers, clothing, etc. – that are all too often ignored in standard bibliographies; and to those particular aspects relevant to individual countries. Each volume seeks to achieve, by use of careful selectivity and critical assessment of the literature, an expression of the country and an appreciation of its nature and national aspirations, to guide the reader towards an understanding of its importance. The keynote of the series is to provide, in a uniform format, an interpretation of each country that will express its culture, its place in the world, and the qualities and background that make it unique. The views expressed in individual volumes, however, are not necessarily those of the publisher.

VOLUMES IN THE SERIES

Contents

Contents

Preface

The information revolution has presented the scholar and the student with both opportunity and difficulty. It offers ready access to a plethora of information through the Internet, CD-ROM and electronically linked libraries and publishers. However, wading through the volume of material takes time, and instead of tracking down articles or valuable books, one is compelled to spend hours discriminating between academic and non-academic works. Thus, one can no longer presume to offer a comprehensive compilation, only a summary of the more weighty studies. In addition, the re-orientation of university life has increased the volume of annual publications, and makes any printed bibliography rapidly outdated. A bibliographical compilation, therefore, can at best offer an introduction to the major texts, contributors and areas of discourse.

The information cited within this bibliography has been collected from the following libraries: University of Durham (England), American University of Cairo (Egypt), King Abdul Aziz University (Saudi Arabia), the Institut Français d'Etudes Arabes de Damas (Syria), and the Asad Library (Syria). The following websites proved essential in acquiring titles and locations: http://www.amazon.com; http://www.cup.-cam.ac.uk; http://www.sunypress.edu; and http://www.routledge. com.

The majority of references in this book are written in English, but I have included a limited number of Arabic and French sources. This is due in part to the remit of the series, which is aimed at an English-speaking readership, and in part to a limited familiarity on my behalf with the Arabic and French canons on Syrian materials.

Note on transliteration

The integration of Arabic sources into this bibliography has added to the normal complications of standardizing references. To minimize these complications, I have used the Library of Congress transliteration system.

To denote long vowels ‾ is placed above the vowel. However, I have injected a slight variation with the use of ' for *hamza*, and ' for *ayn*. With the authors of Arabic sources, only *hamzas* and *ayns* have been taken into consideration, in order to make searching the author index easier. Well-known names like Nasser, Sadat and Asad follow convention.

My academic year in Saudi Arabia (September 1998-July 1999) has not helped in the compilation of this bibliography. I have tried, wherever possible, to acquire a broad range of sources, especially in the fields of literature, history and foreign relations. However, I am aware of thinner chapters in the fields of agriculture and education, despite receiving the assistance and support of two close friends located in Damascus and Cairo.

Acknowledgements

I am sincerely indebted to Maggie Kamel for her unyielding support, editorial assistance and connection to the information world beyond my confines in Jeddah. Indeed, without Maggie's help, I could not have gained access to the materials, sent by attachment, through the auspices of the British Council, Jeddah. As always, she has proved to be a constant in a world of variables.

Nur Laiq has lent this bibliography authenticity. After our brief sojourn in Damascus, she studiously excavated the library of the Institut Français d'Etudes Arabes de Damas (IFEAD) and the Asad Library, sending reams of articles through the matrilineal world of Damascus' main post office. Nur has opened the doors of old Damascus and allowed us to peer in.

I would also like to thank the following: Ray Hinnebusch, for encouraging me to commence this bibliography; Neville McBain, who generously provided a life-line of electronic facilities at the British Council, Jeddah; Cathy Costain, who provided access to the British Council's library and information service, Cairo; and Isis Fahmy, from the General Egyptian Book Organization (GEBO), who kindly donated her invaluable translation skills. I am also very grateful to Michel Niéto, the librarian of IFEAD, who indulged me with his English, and unearthed numerous lists of IFEAD's latest acquisitions.

Since the last edition of this bibliography, the discourse surrounding the archaeology, history, foreign policy and political economy of Syria has deepened. Wherever possible, I have tried to capture the essence of these discourses, and have made my own small contribution.

Neil Quilliam
August 1999

Introduction

In compiling this bibliography, I have endeavoured to build upon Ian Seccombe's foundations, deferring to his inclusion of classic studies, whilst including the most significant books and articles written over the last ten years. In addition, I have sought to convey the essence of contemporary academic discourse taking place within Middle Eastern studies. Academics working in the disciplines of archaeology, history, religion, political economy, political science and international relations have been engaged in rigorous inter-disciplinary struggles. Moreover, some noted academics have participated and pursued their analysis across the disciplines.

Several events, in the past decade, have added fuel to the academic struggle for Syria, namely: new archaeological excavations; the periodic release of official government papers; the collapse of the Soviet Union; the almost universal application of economic liberalization; the Iraqi invasion of Kuwait; the Madrid Peace Conference; and the PLO-Israeli peace accords. These events have stoked the temper of debate, and I have attempted to draw a collection of works together that reflect the principal areas of discussion.

To appreciate the tenor of discourse, one should first reflect upon Syria's place in the Middle Eastern sub-system and in the hierarchy of the world's states. Hinnebusch and Ehteshami's book *Syria and Iran: middle powers in a penetrated regional system*, touches upon the essence of the debate. Is Syria an unreliable rogue state or the key to regional stability? The reasoning that emanates from both sides of the debate, whether ideological or pragmatic, demonstrates the centrality of Syria's geopolitical role in the region, and reminds the researcher of the timeless geopolitical constraints placed upon the rulers of this bridgehead between Orient and Occident.

Geography

Syria has been the keystone of the Middle Eastern region for over 3,500 years. Lying between the Mediterranean and the Euphrates, it has served as a trade route between Orient and Occident. Syria's geographical and strategic position at the eastern end of the Mediterranean Sea and the convergence of three continents established its importance long ago. Damascus and Aleppo were located on the main trade corridors, the control of which, through the Palmyra oasis and the Turkish mountain wall, gave successive administrations power over their neighbours.

However, Syria's geography has forced upon it a long history of occupation and acculturation, and subsequently, the creation of an unstable mosaic society. Syria has been part of the Assyrian, Chaldean, Persian, Greek, Roman, Islamic, Saljuq, Mongolian, Ottoman and French empires, each leaving an imprint upon the structures of society. Syria's current metamorphosis emerged from the political machinations of the British and the French during the First World War and the resulting Mandate era. Carved from the Ottoman *vilayets* of Tripoli, Damascus and Aleppo, the newly sculpted state lacked proportion, form and essence. The weight of history was squeezed into the modern truncated state of Syria; its early contortions, from liberation to coup to dictatorship, express a past of occupation, assimilation and contest.

Accordingly, history is not so precise that we can refer to one Syria. The term conveys different meanings and conceals numerous connotations. Historical Syria makes reference to the region, and includes the Sinai peninsula and the mountains of southern Turkey. The Arabs called historical Syria 'Bilad al-Sham', which included the modern states of Syria, Lebanon, Israel, Jordan and the autonomous areas of Gaza and the West Bank. The Fertile Crescent (Iraq) and Greater Syria (Transjordan) schemes sought to re-unite parts of historical Syria into one state. The Syria of this bibliography is defined by the term modern Syria, which refers to the state of the Syrian Arab Republic, so named in 1961. The republic is co-extensive, except for Alexandretta (Hatay), with the League of Nations Mandate of 1923-46.

The land of Syria amounts to 185,180 square kilometres, and comprises six distinctive regions: the Mediterranean coastal plains along the length of the country's seacoast; the mountain range that characterizes Syria, including Jabal al-Nusayriyah, the anti-Lebanon range and Mount Hermon; an extensive plateau beyond the mountain ranges, which is divided by a south-west and north-east zone of complex folds associated with the Palmyra folds; the steppe land of Aleppo, Hama and Homs; Jabal al-Druze and the cultivated plain of the Hauran; and in the north-east, Dayr al-Zur, where the discovery of oil in the 1970s transformed the region from a desert into the country's main source of income.

Population

The current population of Syria is 16.5 million. The traditional population concentration axis, along the humid steppe belt, Damascus, Homs, Hama and Aleppo, has more recently extended into the Latakia and Tartous areas. Although Syria's population is small in absolute terms, it doubled between 1963 and 1987, and its current birth rate, 3.4 per cent, is one of the highest growth rates in the world. The population is set to rise to 18 million by the year 2000; and the demographic composition of Syria (currently 59 per cent is under the age of 20), is likely to undergo a radical transformation. The population can be divided according to language, religion or ethnic group. Approximately, 82.5 per cent of the population speak Arabic as their first language. The dominant group has, for more than 1,000 years, been Syrian Arabs, who constitute 90 per cent of the population. The great majority of Syrian Arabs are Sunni Muslims. However, other Arab sub-groups, especially religious confessions, form alternative constellation centres. These sub-groups are: the 'Alawis (11.5 per cent), Druzes (3 per cent), Isma'ilis (1.5 per cent), Christians (14.1 per cent of whom 4.7 per cent are Greek Orthodox Christians) and Jews (0.78 per cent). The majority of the population are Sunni Muslims (68.7 per cent). The ethnic minorities include: Armenians (4 per cent), Kurds (8.5 per cent), and Turcomans (3 per cent). The Kurds and the Turcomans, although ethnic minorities, are Sunni Muslims and therefore belong to the majority of the population.

Early history

In the first half of the 3rd millennium BC, Syria experienced the emergence of urban culture. This urbanization flowed from the city culture of Mesopotamia, and spread throughout the Syrian plateau in the form of dynamic cities. For two centuries, the Kingdom of Ebla (Tell Mardikh) appears to have ruled northern Syria and counterbalanced the influence of the great Mesopotamian cities, whilst controlling transit trade and guaranteeing the safe passage of merchants. When Ebla lost its power, possibly to Naram Sin of the Akkadian dynasty, Syria experienced a period of cultural and economic decline.

The Egyptians conquered Syria and Mesopotamia in 1600 BC, and the contest deepened as the Assyrian, Hittite and Babylonian invasions followed. The Babylonian Empire was a short-lived one, and by the middle of the 6th century BC, the star of the Persian kingdom was beginning its ascent. After the Persian conquest of Babylon in 539 BC, Syria's fortunes took a new course. The Persian destruction of the

Babylonian Empire resulted in a new political unity, as the entire region of Syria and Palestine was combined into one Persian satrapy.

After Alexander conquered Egypt in 332 BC, Syrian and Palestinian trade became internationalized. Alexander's Syrian successor, Seleucus, established Greek settlers in Dura-Europhos (Salhiya) and Laodicea (Latakia), tying their fortunes together with the Empire. Palmyra (Tadmor) also began to grow in importance during the reign of Seleucus. Continuing the trend, Palmyra was included in the Roman province of Syria by Pompey. Its role, as an entrêpot, expanded during the reign of Hadrian (AD 117-38) and ended with Queen Zenobia's revolt against Rome (AD 268-72). Under the Emperor Constantine, Syria was sub-divided into two provinces with Antioch as its capital. During the Byzantine period many Christian monuments were built in Syria, which was ruled by the Ghassanids, Christian Arabs loyal to Byzantium.

Islamic Empires

Despite the infusion of so many cultural influences, the most enduring and predominant one has been Islamic. The capitulation of Damascus in AD 635 to the Muslim armies, and the subsequent establishment of the Umayyad Caliphate, under Mu'awiyah, located Syria at the heart of an intellectual and cultural age. The Islamic caliphate was wrested from the Umayyads in AD 750, after the defeat of Marwan II, the last Umayyad caliph, at the Battle of the Great Zab River in Mesopotamia, and transferred to Baghdad under the 'Abbasid dynasty.

In 1055 the 'Abbasids were overpowered by the Saljuqs, who took what temporal power may have been left to the caliph but respected his position as religious leader, restoring the authority of the caliphate, especially during the reigns of al-Mustarshid, al-Muqtafi, and al-Nasir. However, the Saljuqs paved the way for the first Crusade; Antioch was captured in 1098 and Jerusalem followed suit in 1099.

With a new sense of purpose, Nur al-Din re-captured Damascus in 1154 and re-united Syria as a Muslim state. His successor, Salah al-Din al-Ayyubi, seized Jerusalem from the Crusaders at the Battle of Hattin in 1187. After the death of Salah al-Din in 1193, the Ayyubid Empire disintegrated and numerous dynasties inherited local control. Following the distribution of his terrorities among vassal relations, who enjoyed autonomous internal administration of their provinces, the Ayyubid regime became a decentralized, semi-feudal family federation. The Ayyubids introduced into Egypt and Jerusalem the *madrassa*, an academy of religious sciences. Culturally an extension and development of the Fatimids, the Ayyubids were great military engineers, building the citadel of Cairo and the defences of Aleppo. The Ayyubid reign ended with Mamluk accession to power in 1250.

The Mamluks were a warrior caste, who emerged from their enslavement by successive Islamic empires, and ruled from Cairo. The two dynasties, Bahri (1250-1382) and Burjis (1382-1517), were composed of Turks and Mongols, and Circassians respectively. Although Sultan Baybars of Egypt, the most influential ruler of the Mamluk dynasty, defeated the Mongols at 'Ain Jalut in 1260, the victory heralded an extended period of administrative mismanagement and economic decline. As the balance of power started to swing in favour of the neighbouring Ottomans, the two empires engaged in a series of wars throughout the late 15th century. The Ottoman Sultan Selim I sought to prevent the Mamluks from allying themselves with the Safavids of Persia, and brought an end to Mamluk rule in Egypt and Syria.

Ottoman Rule, 1517-1918

The Battle of Marj Dabiq in 1516 ensured that Syria fell under Ottoman rule for the next four centuries. Consequently, Syria was divided into the three *vilayets* of Tripoli, Damascus and Aleppo. Whilst Ottoman rule was administered through the system of 'pashas', the communities living beyond the major cities enjoyed some autonomy from the pasha and the Sublime Porte. The social structure of Syria, a legacy of its past, guaranteed the pre-eminence of the tribal sheikhs, overlords and mountain chiefs, who exercised control over the local population. The 'Alawis and the Druzes, in particular, were able to use their topographical advantages to achieve a considerable degree of autonomy.

The relationship between the centre and the periphery was a constant source of tension; the pashas, co-operating with the local elites, extracted optimum revenue from the local population, emboldening their own positions at the expense of the central Ottoman authorities. The collapsing Ottoman system received a boost of centralization when Ibrahim Pasha, the son of Egypt's Muhammed 'Ali, ventured into Syria in 1831. He imposed conscription and taxation, and limited the authority of the landowners until the restoration of Ottoman control in 1840.

Despite the unpopularity of Ibrahim Pasha's reforms, they influenced the economic and political structure of the Ottoman Empire. The *Tanzimat* reforms, introduced under the rule of Sultan Mahmud II, were designed to reconfigure the administration of the empire. The pashas were replaced by salaried officials, whilst the influence of landowners was curbed. Commensurately, European influence, in the form of trade, education and military organization, unduly influenced the Ottomans in meeting the challenge of neighbouring empires.

During the oppressive reign of Sultan Abdulhamid II (1876-1909), the Young Turks commenced their discussion of secular ideas, and expressions of an Arab consciousness were beginning to awaken. In the first years of the 20th century, the demand for greater administrative autonomy changed into calls for Arab independence from societies such as al-'Ahd and al-Fatat. Their existence, one could argue, was a reaction to the growing secular nationalism of the Young Turks.

Arab Nationalism

The modern history of Syria has its origins in the events of the First World War and the postwar settlements. The Ottoman's decision to enter the war alongside Germany and Austro-Hungary galvanized Great Britain into fanning the flames of Arab insurrection against Ottoman rule.

In their correspondence, Sharif Hussein ibn 'Ali (Grand Mufti of Mecca) and Sir Henry McMahon (British High Commissioner in Egypt) established a loose understanding concerning Britain's support of Arab aspirations in return for an Arab revolt against the Turks. Under the leadership of Faysal, the third son of Sharif Hussein, the Arab Revolt contributed to the defeat of the Turks in the region. Faysal's entry into Damascus in 1918, in spite of the Australian presence, signalled the end of Ottoman rule with the signing of the Mudros Armistice.

In the aftermath of the war, Faysal and the Arab nationalists sought to establish an independent Arab kingdom in Greater Syria. Woodrow Wilson's support of Arab independence, and the report of the King-Crane commission, however, were not enough to give Faysal's ambitions sufficient momentum. Moreover, the vague details comprising the McMahon-Hussein correspondence conflicted with Britain's other commitments, contained in the Sykes-Picot Agreement (May 1916) and the Balfour Declaration (November 1917). Henceforth, Britain's policy objectives conflicted directly with those of the Arab nationalists.

Nevertheless, in March 1920, the General Syrian Congress pro-claimed the independence of Syria (including Palestine and Trans-jordan) under Faysal's rule. France and Britain responded by mobilizing their diplomatic offensives, and in 1920 the Supreme Allied Council, meeting at San Remo, approved the partition of Greater Syria into French and British Mandates. The Mandate over Syria was awarded to France and enforced with troops. Following the Battle of Maysalun on 25 July 1920, the French installed themselves in Damascus.

French Mandate, 1920-46

In order to consolidate their rule, the French implemented a policy designed to weaken the political centre. They divided the country into a number of mini-states; Mount Lebanon was detached from Syria with the surrounding Muslim environs of Sidon, Tripoli and Beq'a. The remaining territory was sub-divided into four mini-states: Aleppo, Damascus, Latakia and Jabal al-Druze.

In 1925, the Druzes, under the leadership of Sultan Pasha al-Attrash, started an open revolt against the French authorities. The revolt spread to the nationalist groups in Aleppo and Damascus, and culminated with the Druzes moving into the Damascus region. The French crushed the Arab Revolt in 1927, with a systematic bombardment of Damascus.

The French permitted the formation of the National Bloc in 1928, which comprised a loose alliance of nationalists and landowners. The National Bloc was elected into power in April 1928 under the leadership of Hashim al-Atasi and Ibrahim Hananu. Hananu drafted a constitution calling for the re-assembly of Syria, which gained support from the constituent assembly, but the High Commissioner imposed his own constitution in 1930.

With the election of Leon Blum's Popular Front government in 1936, French-Syrian relations looked set to improve. A Franco-Syrian Treaty of Alliance was signed, which acknowledged the indispensability of territorial unity to an independent Syria, and envisioned independence within three years. Although the French parliament never ratified the treaty, Jabal al-Druze and Latakia returned to the Syrian state.

In 1936, al-Atasi's nationalist government fell under considerable pressure over the issue of Alexandretta. The League of Nations recommended that after Syria had achieved independence, Alexandretta would become a self-governing state. In July 1938, however, as a prelude to war, the French ceded Alexandretta to Turkey. The nationalist backlash compelled al-Atasi to resign, and parliament was once again suspended. The French re-instated direct rule through a Council of Directors, and re-established the separate units of Jabal al-Druze and Latakia.

The defeat of France in June 1940 led to a significant change in Franco-Syrian relations. Within a year, after the invasion of the Allied forces, the Vichy High Commissioner, General Henri Dentz, was replaced by General Catroux who promised the Syrians independence.

Shukri al-Quwwatli now led the National Bloc, and in 1943 formed a new government, whereby the Syrians incrementally assumed administrative control of the country. As independence beckoned, disturbances broke out over the issue of disbanding the Troupes Spéciales du Levant. A cease-fire was enforced following British

Introduction

military intervention and in February 1946 the United Nations demanded full French withdrawal from Syria. With their final departure on 17 April 1946, Syrian independence was secured.

Independence

The first years of independence were characterized by a succession of coups, coupled with domestic and regional instability. The loss of the Arab-Israeli War, the first of a series of humiliations, rocked the credibility of the government. The patterns of allegiance, once the cement of society, were cracking as more radical parties appealed across vertical ties, and became national, regional and international in character. The military, an institution generally beyond the reach of the notable families, was also preparing itself for domestic intervention.

In March 1949, Colonel Husni Za'im staged the first of three coups that year. Four months later, Za'im was deposed by Brigadier-General Sami al-Hinnawi. In December 1949, the leadership changed once again with the seizure of power by Colonel Adib Shishakli. A further coup removed Shishakli from power in February 1954.

During the mid-1950s, the political leaders of Syria were caught in a number of regional contests for power, with Syria as the prize. The Saudis, Egyptians and Iraqis struggled to pull Syria into their respective orbits. As Britain and the United States competed with the Soviet Union for regional influence, Syria and Egypt established a joint military command. The Cold War setting exacerbated international and regional tensions and propelled Syria and Egypt into the Soviet camp. Furthermore, the tripartite collusion amongst Britain, France and Israel, during the Suez crisis of 1956, reinforced Syria's alliance with the Soviet Union, and by the end of 1957, the Ba'thists, together with the communists, had assumed control of the country.

Nevertheless, communism was not only perceived as a threat to Western interests, but it also posed a challenge to the influence of the Ba'th Party. In February 1958, the Ba'thists sought protection through a merger with Egypt, in the form of the United Arab Republic (UAR). However, the structure of the union, which included dissolving all Syrian parties including the Ba'th, harmed the interests of too many Syrians. An increasing number of administrative posts held in Syria were transferred to Egyptian control, whilst leading Syrian politicians were called to Egypt. The inequity of the union was symbolized by the appointment of Abdul Hakim 'Amer as supervisor of the nationalization and land reform programmes. The UAR was terminated in 1961, when a military coup was staged in Damascus and Syria seceded from the union.

Elections, held in December 1961, returned an assembly dominated by moderates and conservatives, and Nazim al-Qudsi was elected as president. The new government amended many of the nationalization programmes; however, domestic tensions led to yet another coup in March 1962.

The Ba'th Party seized power in March 1963. As part of its rhetorical foundation, the party called for the destruction of Israel and the break-up of the Arab state sub-system. Damascus became the revolutionary centre of the region for social and political change. The Ba'th Party sought to mobilize the support of the rural population with the creation of a Leninist party state. Salah al-Bitar, one of the founders of the Ba'th Party, was appointed prime minister. However, the next three years saw repeated changes in government and continuing unrest, which was vigorously repressed. Conflict between the moderate and radical elements in the Ba'th culminated in the coup of 23 February 1966, led by two Ba'thist generals, Salah al-Jadid and Hafiz al-Asad.

Rising tension along the Syrian-Israeli frontier in late 1966 led Syria into a new defence pact with Egypt. Armed clashes broke out near lake Tiberias in April 1967, and Syria, fearing an imminent Israeli invasion, called on Egypt to honour the pact. During the course of the ensuing Six-Day War, Israeli forces overran the Golan Heights.

As a consequence of the Six-Day War, Arab nationalism lost much of its resonance. The repercussions were manifest in the internal challenges set by the military wing of the Ba'th Party against the civilian wing of the party. Asad's military wing started to mobilize its support and in November 1970 Asad ousted the civilian Ba'thists and took over the premiership. The military coup of 1970 saw Asad assume office as the leader of the Ba'th Party and the state. The new regime implemented a set of domestic and foreign policies based upon realpolitik, rather than the ideological imperatives of its predecessors.

Syria under Asad

The new Syrian leader started to forge the state from the issues of state security and state interest. The resulting quasi-corporatist state was built upon three pillars: the armed forces and the security services; the Ba'th Party; and the political system. Owing to the nature of state-society relations, the state was governed by two systems, namely, neo-patrimonialism and institutionalism.

The struggle with Israel has formed the basis of Syria's national interest, and has invested it with a historical mission. The responsibility assumed by the Syrian state towards the loss of Palestine has also helped to legitimize the authoritarian nature of the state. Furthermore, it has granted the state a chance to rise above the competition amongst domestic forces, and to preserve exclusive rights to the areas of high politics.

The decisions of high politics are formulated within the Regional Command of the Ba'th Party, and amongst Asad's closest advisers. Policies are then justified downstream through the party apparatus. Relative autonomy from domestic forces, enforced through repression, has allowed the Syrian state to exercise a foreign policy based upon rational considerations, rather than on class or sectarian interests.

The Syrian state, however, still lacks sufficient legitimacy, and remains dependent upon the gel of neo-patrimonialism and the security services to sustain its longevity. Its extensive patronage networks have supported the state's autonomy. Moreover, neo-patrimonialism has prevented the political process from being adequately institutionalized. It could be argued that the state's long-term vulnerability lies in its dependence upon patronage and its reluctance to empower the existing political institutions.

The armed forces and the security services have constituted the backbone of the Ba'th state. They have guaranteed the longevity of the regime, in particular when the state was threatened by civil war between 1979 and 1982. The uprising in Hama posed a serious threat to the security of the state, and the state's resilience to this challenge was possible only through coercion. The reliance upon the armed forces and the security services illustrated the failure of the state's political institutions to pre-empt or contain the grievances of the Muslim Brotherhood.

By balancing interests, Asad has provided the state with a degree of autonomy that has enabled it to make decisions based on a rational set of principles. The decision to join the US-led coalition against Iraq in 1990 represents one incident where the state's action was founded upon a rational criteria, whilst appearing to contradict the common Arab interest. The decision-makers enjoyed enough autonomy to disregard public opinion, and were thus able to follow a policy determined by national interest. Syria's decision was portentous, as it elevated its national interest over the Arab interest, and risked its own legitimacy.

The risk to the domestic legitimacy of the Syrian state, in this case, was subjugated to the demands of the international political system. The change in the distribution of global power compelled Syria to adjust to the New World Order. The Syrian state was insulated enough to adjust to the New World Order, without precipitating domestic unrest and without having to legitimize its decision beforehand.

Economy

The Syrian economy is most accurately described as state capitalist, where the state exercises control over strategic industries, but allows the private sector to operate in a controlled market. Endowed with limited natural resources, a small population and an unstable political heritage, Syria has faced many constraints in the path of its economic development. Economic growth has been constrained by two factors: government policies, and regional instability.

Although the Syrian economy experienced some growth between independence and 1970, mainly in industries controlled by the state, such as textiles, food processing and tobacco, conflicting state policies hindered the pace of that growth. In addition, Syria's recent history has shaped its economic policies, and wherever possible, the economy has remained subordinate to foreign policy. In other words, the Syrian economy has been held hostage to the fortunes of the regime.

The policies of economic liberalization, otherwise known as *infitah*, introduced by Asad in the 1970s, resulted in growth; gross domestic product (GDP) grew by more than 150 per cent between 1973 and 1980. *Infitah* served two purposes. First, it was used to embolden the legitimacy of the regime; by attracting the support of the disaffected bourgeoisie, Asad could strengthen the state. Secondly, the incorporation of the business class into the economy provided an economic boost to Syria's challenge to Israel. Thus, the project of national integration pursued by the Syrian Ba'th Party dictated that the economy served the reconstruction of Syrian society, and helped to sustain the Syrian state in its conflict with Israel.

The role of the public sector has somewhat diminished since the mid-1980s. The state's ability to lead the economy and to determine the course of socio-economic development has receded due to the austerity budgets of the 1980s and the rationalization programme introduced to reduce inefficiency within the bureaucracy.

The private sector experienced new growth between 1986 and 1990. Its share of foreign trade was reduced to 10 per cent in the first part of the 1980s, but reached 20 per cent in 1986, and 45 per cent in 1990. The manufacturing industries benefited from the incorporation of the private sector into the national economy as they contributed 43-46 per cent to net domestic product (NDP) in 1990, compared to 30-35 per cent in the early 1980s. By 1990, the private sector contributed an estimated 55 per cent of Syria's GDP. The private sector had employed 60 per cent of the labour force in the 1970s and the 1980s; this figure had reached a remarkable 75 per cent by 1991.

The introduction of economic liberalization measures in 1972, 1986 and 1991 saw a change in economic policy. Though the changes were precipitated by differing circumstances, they indicated a new flexibility within the Syrian political system. They also illustrated the impending influence of the global economy and the vulnerability of the Syrian state.

The Syrian state has managed, to date, to insulate itself from the determinants of the global economy. Whereas most of the states on the periphery of the global economy have traded part of their autonomy for aid, loans and international investment, Syria has, to a large extent, insulated its economy. This has been achieved through two ways: the subjugation of economics to power politics; and the extraction of geopolitical rent. Despite its structural adjustment programmes, the Syrian economy is still dependent upon the security of the regime and on the success of its foreign policy. Although domestic industry and agriculture form a significant part of its economic base, Syria's ability to extract rent for its military services has served it well.

Unlike most Third World states, prescribed economic policies to cure Syria's economic ailments have been introduced independently of external pressure. The introduction of piecemeal reforms was designed to alleviate immediate economic problems, while maintaining over-staffed public services. The continuation of these inefficient services has offered the state a residual base of legitimacy and support.

Syria's debt to the World Bank, which amounted to $400 million in 1993, has not forced it to concede to World Bank pressures. The withdrawal of credit facilities has affected Syria's ability to borrow, yet Syria's geopolitical position has enabled it to receive rent or loans from the Gulf Arab states.

During the Cold War, the international political system provided Syria with enough leverage over the Soviet Union to avoid encasing itself in internationally administered debt. Ironically, the demise of the Soviet Union and the subsequent Iraqi invasion of Kuwait reduced its debt burden and granted Syria the opportunity to attract more Gulf Arab aid. The recent drop in the price of oil and the onset of another drought, however, demonstrates the economic vulnerability of the Syrian state. Moreover, a shortfall in political rent due to the renewal of relations between Saudi Arabia and Iran does not bode well for Syria's economic future.

Gulf War and the New World Order

Iraq's invasion of Kuwait afforded the US-led coalition the occasion to challenge the actions of an aggressor state (Iraq) in order to guarantee the territorial integrity of a victimized state (Kuwait). The reaction of this coalition codified the New World Order.

Adjusting to the New World Order was an essential part of Syria's foreign policy in the post-Cold War era. US-Syrian relations had reached an all time low during the 1980s, due to the bombing of the US marine base in 1983, the episode of hostage taking, and Syria's association with international terrorism. Libya had paid for its policies in 1986, and Iraq was on the verge of war; there was little choice, therefore, but to accept the dominant role of the United States in the world order.

In order to occupy a place in the postwar regional order and to achieve its regional ambitions, Syria joined the US-led coalition. This move appeared to contradict Syria's foreign policy goals of the 1970s and 1980s. But the revival of an international peace conference attracted Syria, and encouraged Asad to ally Syria to the conservative Gulf Arab states and their international guardians.

The consequent reduction in Iraq's military capacity and the elimination of its political threat to Syrian interests in the region, and especially in Lebanon, were benefits enjoyed by Syria, but they did not constitute a major factor in the decision-making process. Moreover, the destruction of Iraq weakened the Arab balance of power with Israel, and invited more external actors to the region. The lifting of sanctions was incidental to the decision, especially as the United States failed to remove Syria from its list of terrorist states.

The end of the Cold War and Iraq's invasion of Kuwait offered Syria the chance to place itself at the centre of the Arab-Israeli conflict. The Madrid Peace Conference provided the forum for an international resolution to the Arab-Israeli conflict; participation at this conference represented Syria's principal benefit from joining the Gulf War coalition. The reconvening of an international conference, a follow-up to the Geneva conference, had been a long-term goal of Syria; its conditions to attend were set in place, namely, a framework based on UN Resolutions 242, 338 and 425.

The Peace Process

Syria's foreign policy has been consistent since 1974: in its quest to secure influence in the Levant, Syria has sought to contain Israeli hegemony. A comprehensive solution to the Arab-Israeli conflict, based upon UN Resolutions 242, 338, and 425, held the potential to satisfy Syria's goals.

During the conference, Syria tried to co-ordinate the policies of Jordan, Lebanon and the Palestine Liberation Organization (PLO). Diplomatic unity offered the Arab states a chance to resist Israeli pressure in the negotiating process. The bilateral talks, however, sent the Palestinians and the Jordanians down a different track. The PLO and Jordanian assignation to the Oslo accords and the Jordan-Israel peace treaty, respectively, represented a serious set-back for the Syrians, as their influence in the Levant was undermined. Geopolitically isolated, Syria has remained an observer. However, the limited nature of the treaties has left Syria some leverage in the peace process. It has two possible options: to conclude a separate peace deal with Israel, in which Israel withdraws from the Golan Heights in exchange for peace and normalization; or to wait for the peace deals to unravel, and then search for a comprehensive solution. Syria may hold some Palestinian cards, in the form of the rejectionist Palestinian groups, but these groups do not constitute a bridge to peace. At most, Syria can try to spoil the PLO-Israel peace agreement, but the policies of the Likud government and the corruption of 'Arafat's regime are already pursuing this option.

Peace, sponsored by the United States, has presented itself as the best strategic choice for Syria. Comprehensive peace held the prospect of checking Israel's hegemonic ambitions and placing Syria at the centre of the region's affairs. The Wye plantation talks, a series of bilateral talks sponsored by the United States, revealed Syria's pragmatic acceptance of a separate peace, based solely upon the Golan Heights. Peace therefore offers the prospect of regional and domestic stability as Syria moves towards the uncertainty of the post-Asad era. The issue of succession has yet to be settled.

Syria's search for hegemony has been driven by a need to stabilize its domestic polity and regional position. Its lengthy engagement in Lebanon has been an expression of its desire to check Israeli expansion as much as to extend its own interests. Since the 1970s, Syria has moved away from the role of victim, in the playground of regional and international powers, towards the role of bully. Its weakness, however, has remained its unstable home environment. Without an accountable political system and rule of law, Syria will continue to lack a durable economic base and will remain dependent upon external sources of revenue. The exchange of security for pocket-money, however, is a short-lived policy.

Once again, Syria's fortunes look precarious. The consolidation of military ties between Israel and Turkey, the warming of relations between Saudi Arabia and Iran, and the peace treaties of the early 1990s serve to undermine Syria's role as front-line state and arbiter between Iran and the Gulf Arab states. The precipitative drop in the oil price, the subsequent reduction in external rent, the assault of globalization, and the issue of succession look set to challenge Syria's place in the new Middle East order. The perpetual struggle for Syria commences once again.

The Country and Its People

1 **The Middle East.**
Edited by Michael Adams. New York; Oxford: Facts on File, 1988.
865p. maps. (Handbooks to the Modern World).

Basic information on Syria is provided on p. 135-42. The work covers geography, history, economy, population and the constitution, and paints a number of biographical sketches. It is divided into five parts: background; countries of the Middle East; politics; economics; and social affairs.

2 **Syrian Arab Republic.**
M. Graeme Bannerman. In: *The government and politics of the Middle East and North Africa.* Edited by David E. Long, Bernard Reich.
Boulder, Colorado: Westview Press, 1995, 2nd ed., p. 198-219. bibliog.

A useful introductory textbook to the politics of the Middle East. The chapter on Syria describes the socio-economic environment and political systems since independence. Bannerman also provides a section on foreign policy.

3 **Damas: miroir brisé d'un orient arabe.** (Damascus: broken mirror of an Arab Orient.)
Edited by Anne-Marie Bianquis, Elizabeth Picard. Paris: Editions Autrement, 1993. 257p. maps. bibliog. (Série Monde, H.S. no. 65).

This book contains a variety of topics dedicated to Damascus, and constitutes an excellent introduction to the history, religion, politics and society of Syria's capital city. The study is divided into five sections: 'Et le bédouin devint citadin' (And the bedouin becomes a townsman), p. 18-57; 'Histoire de rêves' (History of dreams), p. 59-115; 'Images' (Images), p. 117-63; 'Damas la sainte' (Damascus the holy), p. 165-93; and 'Le quotidien, l'intime' (The daily, the intimate), p. 195-239. In the introduction, Bianquis depicts the significance of Damascus throughout history, to Muslims, Christians and France. A general chronology (p. 242-43) and a political chronology of the French Mandate period (p. 244-47) are provided. Maps of the Near East (p. 240) and Damascus (p. 241) are also included.

1

4   **The Arab world: a personal view.**
    Gerald Butt, foreword by Peter Mansfield.   London: BBC, 1987. 152p.
    maps.

This work was published to accompany a series of programmes prepared in
consultation with the BBC Educational Broadcasting Council. Butt presents a picture of
the modern Arab world, examining the perception of the Arabs in his first chapter (p. 9-
21), and providing a brief outline of Islam in chapter two (p. 22-32). Syria is reviewed
in a separate section (p. 89-96). This is a useful introduction to the Arab world and will
be of particular value to readers unacquainted with Syrian history or politics.

5   **Come, tell me how you live.**
    Agatha Christie Mallowan.   London: Collins, 1946. rev. ed. 1975. 192p.
    map.

An anecdotal account by the famous writer of her life and travels with her husband,
archaeologist Sir Max Mallowan, on his expeditions to Syria during the 1930s. She
provides a commentary on daily life during the excavations at Chaqar Bazar and Tell
Brak.

6   **The Arab Republic of Syria.**
    Richard Hrair Dekmejian.   In: *Politics and government in the Middle
    East and North Africa.*   Edited by Tareq Y. Ismael, Jacqueline S.
    Ismael, foreword by Timothy Niblock.   Miami, Florida: Florida
    International University Press, 1991, p. 188-208.

A basic article about Syrian history and politics. It provides a brief account of the
country's history and its significance within the Arab world, from the Umayyad era to
the Asad period. Dekmejian addresses issues such as the struggle for independence,
the advocacy for Arab unity, the union with Egypt, rule under the Ba'th Party, and the
internal and external challenges to Asad's regime. It amounts to a chronological
account with little analysis. However, it is a useful introduction to Syrian history for
students of Middle Eastern studies.

7   **Syria: modern state in an ancient land.**
    John F. Devlin.   London: Croom Helm; Boulder, Colorado: Westview
    Press, 1983. 140p. maps. bibliog. (Profiles/Nations of the Contemporary
    Middle East).

The introductory chapters outline Syria's early history, including Ottoman rule, and
describe the physical environment, the pattern of settlement and the division into
sectarian communities, emphasizing the importance of sectarian differences in modern
politics. The work also provides an account of the formation of modern Syria,
describing the brief rule of King Faysal after the Arab Revolt, the imposition and
administration of the French Mandate and the rise of the nationalist movement. The
political instability of the early independence years, the formation and ideals of the
Ba'th Party, the eventual union with Egypt, and the collapse of the United Arab
Republic (UAR) and subsequent in-fighting among the Ba'th are also examined.
Devlin discusses the political dynamics in contemporary Syria, emphasizing the role
of the military and the centralized government structure, and examines in detail
President Hafiz al-Asad's rise to power, the 'corrective' movement of 1970, the
subsequent growth in opposition to 'Alawi minority rule, and Syria's changing

economic philosophy, development planning, trade and external aid, together with a sectoral review of the economy. The final chapters examine external affairs, particularly Syria's role in the Arab-Israeli conflict, and in the Lebanese civil war, its fluctuating relations with Iraq and Jordan, and its support for Iran in the Iran-Iraq War.

8   Syria, Lebanon, Jordan.
John B. Glubb.   London: Thames & Hudson; New York: Walker, 1967. 236p. maps.

A general history of geographical Syria from prehistoric times to 1966. The author discusses the physical and social environment, forms of social organization, differing forms of governance, manners and social customs.

9   Arabs in tent and town.
A. Goodrich-Freer (H. H. Mrs Spoer).   Edinburgh: Dunedin Press, 1924. 325p.

A first-hand account of life in Palestine. It covers many aspects of daily life in the southern part of Greater Syria, such as the role of women, childhood, village life, desert life, pilgrimage, hospitality, bread, olives, coffee, weather and animals.

10   An a to z of the Middle East.
Alain Gresh, Dominique Vidal, translated by Bob Cumming.   London; New Jersey: Zed, 1990. 261p. maps.

The book was first published in French under the title *Les cent portes du proche-orient* (The hundred gates of the Near East), Paris: Editions Autrement, 1987. A chronology of the period 1947-90 is provided on p. xiii-xx. This is useful as a reference guide, but offers only limited analysis.

11   Inside the Middle East.
Dilip Hiro.   London: Routledge & Kegan Paul, 1982. 471p. maps. bibliog.

A political and economic survey of the 'core' countries of the Middle East, including Syria. It includes an outline of Faysal's brief rule, the imposition of instability, the union with Egypt (1958-61) and the rise of the Ba'th Party. Hiro also examines the assumption of power by Asad, the rise of opposition groups, such as the Muslim Brotherhood, and Syria's relations with Israel and the superpowers.

12   'Abqariyāt wa-a'lām. (Geniuses and famous figures.)
'Abd al-Ghani al-'Itri.   Damascus: Dār al-Bashā'ir, 1996. 479p. bibliog.

A collection of biographies describing fifty Syrian figures (living and dead) who have contributed to politics, academia, journalism and literature. This is a somewhat subjective but useful reference book for libraries.

13   Syria: the land of Lebanon.
Lewis Gaston Leary.   New York: McBride, Nast, 1913. 225p.

An intimate and personal account of Syria. Leary's book, a companion volume to his previous book, *Real Palestine of to-day*, was designed to compensate for the literary

3

shadow cast by Israel, obscuring Syria. The result is a rather quaint and affectionate look at the lands of the Bible.

14 Nomads and settlers in Syria and Jordan, 1800-1980.
Norman N. Lewis. Cambridge, England: Cambridge University Press, 1987. 249p. maps. bibliog.

This book looks at the life of the people of the *'badiyah'*, the bedouin region which comprises the desert and steppe areas of Syria. It is here that the nomads live, except in the summer months when they migrate, with their flocks, into the 'transitional zone'. Farmers and nomads have intermittently contended for control of the transitional zone. The author focuses upon the relationship between the nomads and the land since the 19th century, revealing how the process of sedentarization has changed this relationship. Lewis bases his research on years of interaction with the people of the *'badiyah'*, and on 19th-century consular records.

15 Syria.
Ivor Lucas. In: *The Middle East.* Edited by Michael Adams.
New York; Oxford: Facts on File, 1988, p. 497-510. maps.
(Handbooks to the Modern World).

This article, written by a former British Ambassador to Syria (1982-84), serves as an introduction to Syria. It offers insights into the following subjects: the early history of Syria; Ottoman rule; the French Mandate; independence; the ascent of Asad; the Arab-Israeli conflict; relations with Lebanon; and Syrian-Iranian relations.

16 The Arabs.
Peter Mansfield. London: Penguin, 1992. 3rd ed. 557p. map.

An introduction to the history, politics and economy of the modern Arab world. The summary of recent Arab history includes a discussion of the Arab Revolt, the imposition of the Mandate system and the disaster in Palestine. Part two surveys the Arab world in gazetteer fashion. Chapter twenty (p. 410-16) provides an outline of Syria's chaotic political history since its independence in 1946, with mention of the rise of the Ba'thists and the dominance of the 'Alawi minority. Since Asad's ousting of Salah Jadid in September 1970, Syria has enjoyed relative political stability. The moderate liberalization of economic policy under Asad, and Syria's intervention in Lebanon are commented upon. The work was first published as *The Arab World: a comprehensive history* (Harmondsworth, England: Penguin, 1976).

17 Syria and Jordan: the desert and the sown.
Peter Mansfield. *Asian Affairs*, vol. 16, part I (Old Series, vol. 72), (February 1985), p. 20-28.

The article is based on a lecture given to the Royal Society for Asian Affairs on 22 February 1984. Mansfield provides an historical overview of Syria and Jordan. The author explains that they were once part of one country; however, due to the artificial borders created by the British, territorial nationalism grew in both countries. Mansfield concludes that, at the time of the lecture, there were 'no prospects of (Jordan) being swallowed up, and becoming part of Syria', but that the future of the two countries were inextricably linked (p. 28).

18 **Syria.**
Tabitha Petran. London: Ernest Benn; New York: Praeger, 1972.
284p. maps. bibliog.

A comprehensive and detailed introduction to the geography, history, economy and politics of the Syrian Arab Republic. It provides a useful summary of Syria's early history, and a detailed account of the rise of the nationalist movement, the Arab Revolt, Faysal's Arab government, and the establishment of the French Mandate. It examines French policy, the 1925-27 revolt, and the constitutional negotiations of the 1930s. The achievements of independence are also described, and the author goes on to discuss the rise of the Ba'th Party, the February 1966 coup, the emergence of the neo-Ba'th, and their economic and social development programme. It concludes with a consideration of the Syrian defeat in the Six-Day War in June 1967, the rift between the political and military leadership, and the rise of Asad.

19 **The biographical dictionary of the Middle East.**
Yaacov Shimoni. New York; Oxford; Sydney: Facts on File, 1991.
255p. maps. bibliog.

Provides the reader with approximately 500 biographies of personalities who have played a role in the Middle East. Kings and rulers, heads of governments, party leaders, religious figures, revolutionaries, and military leaders are all portrayed according to the author's assessment of their influence within the region.

20 **Encyclopedia of the modern Middle East.**
Reeva S. Simon, Philip Mattar, Richard W. Bulliet. New York: Simon & Schuster Macmillan, 1996. 4 vols. bibliog.

A useful reference guide, suitable for schools and public libraries. It integrates the issue of the Arab-Israeli conflict into the fabric of Middle Eastern politics and culture.

21 **Syria.**
Great Britain: Naval Intelligence Division, prepared by Oxford Sub-centre, 1943. 485p. maps. bibliog.

Covers a wide range of subjects on Syria, including: geology; climate; vegetation; industry; agriculture; population; communication; and history from the Graeco-Roman period to the Second World War.

22 **Damas, Beyrouth, regards croisés.** (Damascus, Beirut, opposite views.)
Jade Tablet. In: *Damas: miroir brisé d'un orient arabe* (Damascus: broken mirror of an Arab Orient). Edited by Anne-Marie Bianquis, Elizabeth Picard. Paris: Editions Autrement, 1993, p. 136-45.
(Série Monde, H.S. no. 65).

Tablet explains how Damascus and Beirut were culturally close during the Ottoman era, but stand in sharp contrast in contemporary times, as they have followed divergent paths. Tablet examines these differences in terms of politics, economics, culture and architecture. Beirut is well planned and has been modernized, whereas Damascus embodies the contradictions of an Arab city torn between tradition and modernity.

23 **Mirror to Damascus.**
Colin Thubron.   London: Heinemann, 1967. 226p.

Thubron calls his exegesis on Damascus a work of love; his book is not designed to fill a bibliographical breach, nor to record the vanishing headlands of old custom, but to pay homage to a much-neglected city. This work is essentially a personal and descriptive account of Damascus' place in history and constitutes an enchanting and indulgent read.

24 **The Syrian coastal town of Jabala: its history and present situation.**
Sato Tsugitaka.   Tokyo: Institute for the Study of Languages and Cultures of Asia and Africa, 1988. 89, 121p. maps. bibliog.
(Studia Culturae Islamicae, no. 35).

Tsugitaka provides a history of Jabala, a small town thirty kilometres south of Latakia, and the surrounding countryside. It is divided into three parts, covering: town and villages in Jabala (p. 13-36); the history of Jabala (p. 37-81); and Arabic information on the history of Jabala (p. 1-113). The first and second parts are written in English while the third part is written in Arabic. Photographs of sites from Jabala are provided.

Geography

25 The rural geographic environment of the Syrian coastal region and the Shizuoka region: a comparative study of Syria and Japan.
Adel Abdulsalam.   Tokyo: Institute for the Study of Languages and Cultures of Asia and Africa, Tokyo University of Foreign Studies, 1985. 174p. (Studia Culturae Islamicae, no. 24).

A comparative study of the Syrian coastal region and Shizuoka region of Japan. It is divided into three sections. The first two parts offer comprehensive reviews of the regions, which cover geography, history, demography, and rural settlements. The third part provides a comparative analysis, and concludes that problems of the future should be solved with mutual solutions.

26 The Middle East: a geographical study.
Peter Beaumont, Gerald H. Blake, J. Malcolm Wagstaff.   New York: Halsted Press, 1988. 2nd ed. 623p. maps. bibliog.

The authors observe that the Middle East region was as vital to world affairs in the late 1980s as it had ever been. Blake and Wagstaff provide a broad description of the physical and political environment of the Middle East. As well as economic and industrial development, issues associated with population growth and the central role of petroleum in the region are addressed. Syrian agriculture receives particular attention in chapter thirteen (p. 370-86).

27 La Ghouta, un paradis entre montagne et steppe. (Ghouta, a paradise between mountain and steppe.)
Anne-Marie Bianquis.   In: *Damas: miroir brisé d'un orient arabe* (Damascus: broken mirror of an Arab Orient).   Edited by Anne-Marie Bianquis, Elizabeth Picard.   Paris: Editions Autrement, 1993, p. 18-33. (Série Monde, H.S. no. 65).

The author describes the Ghouta oasis, discussing the agricultural conditions of the oasis since Ottoman rule, the reforms of 1958, and the impact of urbanization. The work constitutes an excellent introduction to the agricultural base of Ghouta.

Geography

28 The Cambridge atlas of the Middle East and North Africa.
Gerald H. Blake, John Dewdney, Jonathan Mitchell. Cambridge, England; New York; Melbourne: Cambridge University Press, 1987. 124p. maps. bibliog.

This atlas covers a variety of topics, such as physical environment, culture, demography and economics. Maps are accompanied by an informative text. This is a useful tool for seminars, as it includes reliable data and economic statistics.

29 The atlas of the Arab world: geopolitics and society.
Rafic Boustani, Philippe Fargues, preface by Maxime Rodinson. New York; Oxford: Facts on File, 1990. 144p. maps.

According to Boustani and Fargues, 'statistics capture the current situations of nations'. They eschew lesser scientific and empirical studies through their statistical approach. They argue that when one is able to extract social phenomena from cold numbers, statistics provide a battery of instruments to help understand the logic of the population; these instruments are so much more accurate than the 1,000 year-old texts, so dear to orientalism. The aim of their geopolitical atlas of the Arab world is to challenge the complacent discourse of the 'softer' social sciences, emphasizing the great variety of forces at work in the Arab world. The fact that nations in the area have benefitted in differing degrees from the discovery of oil and the inconsistent adoption of openness have created a dominant rift in the Arab world, and the authors conclude that their approach is the most apposite to understanding this rift. The result is a challenging and engaging work.

30 Atlas of the Middle East.
Edited by Moshe Brawer. London: Collier Macmillan; New York: Macmillan; Jerusalem: Carta, the Israel Map, 1988. 140p. maps. bibliog.

This atlas is divided into two parts: the region, which includes geology, climate, fauna and flora, population, oil and political history; and country surveys. The section on Syria (p. 105-10) covers topography, population, economy, history, government and politics.

31 Iraq-Syria boundary.
Bureau of Intelligence and Research, USA. Washington, DC: Department of State, 1970. 8p. map. (International Boundary Studies, no. 100).

Describes the alignment of the 376-mile boundary between Iraq and Syria. This artificial boundary resulted from the division of British and French spheres of influence following the Allied defeat of Ottoman Turkey in 1918. Demarcation of the boundary was provided for by the Franco-British Convention of December 1920 and its delimitation was subsequently confirmed by a League of Nations commission in September 1932.

8

32 Jordan-Syria boundary.
Bureau of Intelligence and Research, USA. Washington, DC:
Department of State, 1969. 10p. map. (International Boundary Studies,
no. 94).

Describes the alignment and relief of the 233-mile Jordan-Syria boundary, and briefly reviews the historical background to this boundary, the McMahon-Hussein letter, the Sykes-Picot Agreement and the Arab Revolt. Demarcation of the boundary was provided for by the Franco-British Convention of December 1920, and its current alignment is based on the Anglo-French Protocol signed in Paris in October 1931.

33 Syria-Turkey boundary.
Bureau of Intelligence and Research, USA. Washington, DC:
Department of State, 1978. 15p. map. (International Boundary Studies,
no. 163).

Describes in detail the alignment of the 511-mile Syria-Turkey boundary, which was initially delimited by Article 27 of the 1920 Treaty of Sèvres and subsequently demarcated by Franco-Turkish agreements of October 1921, May 1926 and June 1929. The Hatay-Syria boundary was demarcated by a Franco-Turkish commission during 1938 prior to the transfer of the sanjaq of Alexandretta to Turkey in July 1939.

34 A dictionary of Arabic topography and placenames.
Nigel Groom. London, Beirut: Librairie du Liban & Longman, 1983.
369p.

A transliterated Arabic-English dictionary with an Arabic glossary of topographical words and place-names.

35 L'urbanisation contemporaine de la Syrie du nord. (The contemporary urbanization of north Syria.)
Marc Lavergne. In: *Alep et la Syrie du nord* (Aleppo and northern Syria). Edited by Viviane Fuglestad-Aumeunier. Aix-en-Provence, France: EDISUD, 1991-94, p. 193-208. maps. bibliog. (La Revue du Monde Musulman et de la Méditerranée, no. 62).

Lavergne avers that north Syria was created in the 20th century as a result of an artificial boundary, which affirmed Damascene superiority in the new national Syrian space. This study focuses on the major changes that have taken place, between the Mediterranean coast and the Euphrates, from the 1970s to the 1990s. Lavergne examines the changes in demography, patterns of home ownership, and the infrastructure in three *muhafazas* (provinces) of Latakia, Aleppo and Idlib, and the region of Ghab, which belongs to the *muhafaza* of Hama.

36 The Middle East: a social geography.
Stephen Hemsley Longrigg, revised by James Jankowski. London:
Gerald Duckworth, 1970. rev. ed. 291p. maps. bibliog.

Examines various aspects of social geography in the Middle East. An historical introduction is followed by a discussion of the social geography of the region in modern times and by country-specific chapters. The section on Syria (p. 130-34) offers an overview of its physical geography, religious groups, natural resources and economic development.

9

37 **Cambridge encyclopedia of the Middle East and North Africa.**
Trevor Mostyn, Albert Hourani.   Cambridge, England; New York;
Melbourne: Cambridge University Press, 1988. 504p. maps. bibliog.

This work is divided into six parts: lands and peoples; history; society and economy;
culture; individual countries, including coverage of Syria on p. 422-27; and inter-state
relations. Further readings are suggested at the completion of each section. This is a
very useful source for students of Middle Eastern studies.

38 **Notes on the soils of Syria.**
Alexander Muir.   *Journal of Soil Science*, vol. 2, no. 2 (1951),
p. 163-82.

Describes the physical and chemical characteristics of ten major soil groups in Syria
and their occurrence in the desert, steppe and Mediterranean zones.

39 **Daīr al-Zūr: dirāsah tabī'īyah, tarīkhīyah, basharīyah, iqtisādīyah.**
(Dayr al-Zur: a physical, historical, population and economic study.)
'Ali Hasan Musa.   Damascus: Wizarat al-Thaqāfah, 1993. 430p. maps.
bibliog. (Silsilat Bilāduna, no. 3).

A broad study outlining the province of Dayr al-Zur, which is located in the north-east
of Syria. It covers many subjects related to the province, such as history, geology,
climate, geography, resources, flora and fauna, archaeology, animal husbandry, culture
and infrastructure.

40 **Mawsū'at al-mudun al-'arabīyah wa-al-islāmiyah.** (The encyclopaedia
of Arab and Islamic cities.)
Yahya Shami.   Beirut: Dār al-Fikr al-'Arabī, 1993. 452p. bibliog.

This book is divided into two parts: Arab cities (p. 3-226); and Islamic cities (p. 227-
431). Both parts are further subdivided into two sections dealing with Asian and
African cities. Syria is covered on p. 48-67. The book offers information on the
following areas of interest: location of cities; population; economic activity;
archaeology; and historical significance.

41 **Al-mu'jam al-jughrāffī lil qutr al-'arabī al-surrī.** (The geographical
dictionary of the Syrian territory.)
Al-'Imad Mustafa Talas.   Damascus: Centre for Military Studies,
1990-92. 4 vols. maps.

An illustrated geographical dictionary of Syria. The first volume is divided into two
parts: the first outlines the state of Syria as whole, while the second describes the main
regions in Syria, including climate, population, geology, plant and animal life, and
resources. The other three volumes deal with population centres in Syria, examining
their history, administrative divisions and monuments.

42   **Soil taxonomy and the soil map of Syria and Lebanon.**
R. Tavernier, A. Osman, M. Ilawi.   In: *Proceedings of the 3rd
international soil classification workshop.*   Edited by F. H. Beinroth,
A. Osman.   Damascus: Arab Centre for the Study of Arid Zones and
Dry Lands, 1981, p. 83-93.
Discusses the classification of soils in Syria and Lebanon, outlining the problems of
using the US Department of Agriculture's soil taxonomy as the basis for the soil map
of the country.

43   **Erosion and sedimentation along the Euphrates Valley in northern
Syria.**
T. J. Wilkinson.   In: *The environmental history of the Near and Middle
East since the last Ice Age.*   Edited by W. C. Brice.   London:
Academic Press, 1978, p. 215-26.
Examines current fluvial activity in the Euphrates Valley and its effects on the
landscape around the site of Dibsi Faraj. Particular attention is paid to the processes of
erosion and sedimentation, and the various stages in the evolution of this landscape
during the late Quaternary period are reconstructed.

Syria, Lebanon, Jordan.
See item no. 8.

**Historical geography of Palestine, Transjordan and southern Syria in
the late 16th century.**
See item no. 242.

The formation of the Transjordan-Syria boundary, 1915-32.
See item no. 333.

NIV atlas of the Bible.
See item no. 425.

Atlas of the Arab-Israeli conflict.
See item no. 659.

Geology

44   **The karst groundwater of Syria.**
David J. Burdon, Chafic Safadi.   *Journal of Hydrology*, vol. 2, no. 4
(1964), p. 324-47.

Describes the extent of karst in Syria and its importance as a groundwater resource.
The stratigraphy and structure of limestone and evaporite formations are reviewed,
and the processes of karstification described. The volume and geochemistry of spring
discharge is examined for four major karst aquifers (Barada, Figeh, Sinn and Ras-al-
'Ain).

45   **Ras-al-Ain: the great karst spring of Mesopotamia, an**
      hydrogeological study.
David J. Burdon, Chafic Safadi.   *Journal of Hydrology*, vol. 1, no. 1
(1963), p. 58-93.

Lying just south of the Syrian-Turkish frontier, Ras-al-'Ain is one of world's largest
karst springs, with an average annual discharge of 1,219 million cubic metres. This
article describes the geology, hydrology and hydrochemistry of the springs, presenting
discharge-gauging data for the period 1942-59. The study concludes by examining
options for more efficient use of the spring-water for irrigation.

46   **Mineral resources of the Arab countries.**
F. Habashi, F. A. Bassyouni.   Québec, Canada: Groupe de Recherche
en Economie de l'Energie et des Ressources Naturelles, Université
Laval, dossier no. 1, 1979. 128p.

Details the occurrence of metallic and non-metallic minerals in each of the Arab
countries, including Syria.

47 **Hydrogeology of the Syrian steppe and adjoining arid areas.**
J. Khouri. *Quarterly Journal of Engineering Geology*, vol. 15, no. 2
(1982), p. 35-54.
A useful review of Syrian hydrogeology. Three groundwater flow regions are defined, and their structure, flow, recharge and hydrochemistry are described.

48 **Petroleum-bearing formations in northeastern Syria and northern Iraq.**
M. Hamed Metwalli, G. Philip, M. M. Moussly. *Association of American Petroleum Geologists Bulletin*, vol. 58, no. 9 (September 1974), p. 1781-96.
Deals with the subsurface geology of the Jebissa area in north-eastern Syria, in an attempt to clarify the stratigraphical, tectonic and palaeographical setting of the petroleum-bearing formations.

49 **Ophiolites du nord-ouest syrien et évolution de croûte océanique tethysienne au cours du Mésozoïque.** (North-west Syrian ophiolites and the evolution of the Tethyan oceanic crust during the Mesozoic.)
Jean-François Parrot. *Tectonophysics*, vol. 41, no. 4 (1977), p. 251-68.
The Baer-Bassit area of north-west Syria is composed of an ophiolite suite and a Triassiac to Lower Cretaceous volcano-sediment formation. This study suggests that the area is the southern margin of the northern part of the Tethyan oceanic crust.

50 **Large historical earthquakes and seismic risk in northwest Syria.**
J. P. Poirier, B. A. Romanowicz, M. A. Taher. *Nature*, vol. 285, no. 5763 (May 1980), p. 217-20.
Arabic documents containing descriptions of material damage and ground deformation caused by earthquakes in north-west Syria are used to establish a catalogue of local seismic activity from the 7th-8th century and to assign epicentral intensities to these earthquakes. The authors show that large earthquakes affecting the area have a recurrence interval of ca. 340 years. Using this data the maximum seismic moment and magnitude of the largest earthquakes in north-west Syria are predicted.

51 **Geologie von Syrien und dem Libanon.** (Geology of Syria and the Lebanon.)
Reinhard Wolfart. Berlin: Gebrüder Borntraeger, 1967. 326p. maps. bibliog. (Beiträge zur Reigonalen Geologie der Erde, Band 6).
This is a comprehensive study of the geology of Syria and Lebanon. The introductory chapter distinguishes six major physio-graphical units (Mediterranean, central Syrian mountains, the Hauran, north-west Syria, south-east Syria, and Jazira), describing each in turn. Detailed discussion of Syria's geological history, stratigraphy and structure follow, together with an examination of tectonic features in this unstable edge of the Arabian Shield. The concluding chapters are devoted to a review of groundwater resources, oil, asphalt, and other mineral deposits. The development and distribution of regional soil associations are described, and their significance for agricultural production is assessed. An important feature of the work is its extensive bibliography, which contains more than 650 items published over the period 1832-1966. The book also includes an English summary (p. 281-85).

Geology

Report of the reconnaissance survey of Paleolithic sites in Lebanon and Syria.
See item no. 152.

Bibliography of Levant geology.
See item no. 849.

Tourism and Travel Guides

52 Islamic Bosra: a brief guide.
Fleming Aalund, Michael Meinecke, Riyadh Sulaiman al-Muqdad.
Damascus: German Archaeological Institute, 1990. 56p. maps. bibliog.
This booklet formed part of a photographic exhibition of Islamic Bosra. It presents a
comprehensive documentation of the ancient city's Islamic monuments and serves as a
helpful historical and architectural guide, especially for the general traveller.

53 Halabiyah and Zalabiyah.
Wafa Ayash.   Damascus: Salhani, 1995. 35p.
A very brief introduction to the cities of Halabiyah and Zalabiyah, which constitutes a
cheap accessible roadside guide for weary travellers.

54 Aleppo: tourist guide.
A. Bahnassi.   Syria: Publications of Art and Architecture. 56p. maps.
A basic guide to the historical and architectural sites of Aleppo, produced locally. It
offers some basic Arabic phrases, but lacks the depth of Burns (see item no. 56).

55 Syria.
Andrew Beattie, Timothy Pepper.   London: The Rough Guides, 1998.
281p. maps. bibliog. (The Rough Guide).
Beattie and Pepper offer a comprehensive guide to Syria. Particularly suited for
travellers or backpackers, the book offers practical information on the following
subjects: accommodation; cuisine; transport; monuments; museums; religious sites;
and cultural attitudes. One is able to visit the main centres of Syria equipped with
useful information, and essential tips on behaviour and expectation. The authors cover
Damascus, the Hauran and the Golan Heights, the Orontes Valley, the Coast and the
Mountains, Aleppo, the Euphrates, and Palmyra (Tadmor). Whilst some guides
contain small inaccuracies, for instance, telephone numbers, the Rough Guide is a
reliable ally under most circumstances and the advice on restaurants is particularly
welcome.

56 Monuments of Syria: an historical guide.

Ross Burns.   London; New York: I. B. Tauris, 1992. 297p. maps.
bibliog.

This book is a useful historical and architectural guide to Syria and has become a
recent classic. It divides Syria into its natural geographic regions, and then suggests
appropriate travel itineraries. Burns offers an extensive survey of Syria's monuments,
providing maps for each site. This is an excellent companion for travel and
exploration, although its size makes it somewhat cumbersome.

57 Damascus: ash-Sham.

Photographs by Jean Paul Garcin, Robert Azzi, Olivier Martel, Anouar
Ghafour.   Tunis: Librairie Universille, 1982. 157p. bibliog.

This is a timeless book that introduces the reader to Damascus through photographs. It
covers a wide range of topics including the city's history, climate, archaeology and
way of life.

58 Syria today.

Jean Hureau, translated by Philip Parks.   Paris: Editions JA, 1977.
255p. maps.

A general guidebook for travellers and tourists. The preliminary chapters provide an
overview of the country and its people, the economy, culture and history. Subsequently,
the guide is divided into a town-by-town and site-by-site gazetteer with detailed
descriptions of major sites. Street maps of Aleppo and Damascus are provided, as well
as plans of Palmyra and the Crac des Chevaliers. There are suggested touring routes of
eight, fifteen and thirty days' duration. Essential information on customs, health, travel,
festivals and holidays, accommodation, food, currency and exchange is provided, and
the guide is illustrated with ninety-two pages of colour photographs.

59 Syria in view.

Michael Jenner.   Harlow, England: Longman, 1986. 142p. map.
bibliog.

Jenner studies historical Syria as the cradle of numerous civilizations. He reviews
ancient Syria through the archaeological excavations at Ugarit, Mari and Ebla, and
also considers the presence of Aramaean, Phoenician, Greek and Roman civilizations
in Syria. Christianity in Syria is then examined through the presence of its churches
and places of worship. Plates of Syria's monuments are provided (p. 47-78). The
Islamic era and the distinct architectural contribution of the Umayyads are examined
along with the monuments left by the Crusaders. Finally, Jenner visits Damascus and
Aleppo and considers the continuous dimension of their histories, drawing upon both
ancient and modern architecture. This is an excellent book for tourists; one is left with
the impression of visiting a museum with a truly competent guide.

60 Syria: land of contrasts.

Peter Lewis.   London: Namara, 1980. 160p. map.

A guide to Syria comprising a collection of photographs (by Robin Constable) and a
brief text covering the following: history and contemporary society; Damascus; Syria
before Christ (Ebla and Ugarit); Christian and Muslims; Crusades; Aleppo; Palmyra;
Bosra; the Druze; and Syria today.

61   **The Azm Palace of Hama, a historical, architectural, artistic
     illustrated study.**
     Complied in Arabic by al-Masri, Abdul-Rahim, Shihade, translated by
     Muhammad Sa'id Irabi.   Hama, Syria: Islah Press. 32p.
This work describes the history of the 'Azm Palace in Hama, as well as providing a
biographical account of its commissioners – three pashas of the 'Azm family. It also
accounts for the blend of architectural styles; however, it does use quite obscure
terminology, thus making it a rather laborious read. In addition, the quality of the
palace plans and the accompanying photographic illustrations are poor.

62   **Damascus: its history, development and artistic heritage.**
     Abdulqader Rihawi, translated by Paul E. Cheveded.   Damascus:
     Rihawi, 1977. 188p. maps. bibliog.
A useful guide to the historical monuments and other features of Damascus. It includes a
concise history of the city, describing its growth and characteristics in each historical
period. Detailed descriptions of major features are provided, covering: the city walls
and gates; *suqs* and *khans*; streets and houses; the distribution of water and public
baths; the Umayyad mosque; the citadel; the cemeteries and mausoleums; the 16th-
century Takkiya Sulaimaniyya (the asylum of Sulaimaniyya); and the 'Azm Palace.

63   **Jordan and Syria: a lonely travel survival kit.**
     Damien Simonis, Hugh Finlay.   Hawthorn, Australia; Berkeley,
     California; Chiswick, England: Lonely Planet, 1997. 3rd ed. 376p.
     maps. bibliog.
A guidebook for travellers on a shoe-string budget. Lonely Planet Guides are less
comprehensive than Rough Guides, but they are pocket-sized, making them easier
to carry. The nature of the essential information provided – telephone numbers,
accommodation, transport and prices – is prone to perpetual change, and therefore
figures occasionally prove to be unreliable. Where the Lonely Planet authors have
established patron-clientele relationships, such as the Traditional Palmyra Restaurant,
Palmyra, travellers are guaranteed a warm welcome if their copy of the guide is made
visible. This guide is a must for travellers who wish to avoid the over-priced tourist
traps of the (self-appointed) five-star hotels.

From the Holy Mountain: a journey in the shadow of Byzantium.
See item no. 468.

Syria: a historical and architectural guide.
See item no. 818.

Travellers' Accounts

64 Travels of Ali Bey in Morocco, Tripoli, Cyprus, Egypt, Arabia, Syria and Turkey, between the years 1803 and 1807.
Ali Bey el-Abassi (Domingo Badia y Leblich).   London: Longman, Hurst, Rees, Orme and Browne, 1816. Reprinted, Farnborough, England: Gregg International, 1970. 2 vols.

The *Travels of Ali Bey* describes the journey of the Spanish traveller Domingo Badia y Leblich, as a Muslim pilgrim from Tangiers to Mecca. On his return journey in 1807, he passed through Syria. This account includes descriptions of Damascus with comments on population, commerce and industry, health and education. Leblich then travelled north to Antioch via Palmyra, Homs, Hama, and Aleppo.

65 Damascus and Palmyra: a journey to the East, with a sketch of the state and prospects of Syria under Ibrahim Pasha.
Charles G. Addison.   London: Richard Bentley, 1838. 2 vols. Reprinted, New York: Arno Press, 1973. 263p.

An account of Addison's journey from Malta, around the Mediterranean coast to Damascus, and then to Palmyra in 1835. Many details of the customs and society of Damascus are vividly recorded, although from a highly personal point of view. The account includes details of the flora, fauna, scenery and the life of the bedouin. The work also includes an extended commentary on Turkish rule in Syria, the causes of economic decline and Muhammad 'Ali's conquest.

66 A study of ibn Battutah's account of his 726/1326 journey through Syria and Arabia.
Adel Allouche.   *Journal of Semitic Studies*, vol. xxxv, no. 2 (autumn 1990), p. 283-99.

This article re-examines the chronology of ibn Battutah's first visit to Damascus and Aleppo on his journey to Mecca. The author examines the composition of ibn Battutah's *rihlah*, primarily focusing on his encounter with ibn Taymiyah in Aleppo.

By examining the *rihlah*, Allouche accounts for the findings of Hrbeh and Gibb, whilst offering his own suggestions.

67 Syria, the Holy Land, Asia Minor etc., illustrated in a series of views drawn from nature.
W. H. Barlett, W. Pruser, J. Carne.   London: Fisher & Sons, 1836-38.
3 vols.

Reproduces three volumes of etchings made in the early 1830s by the travelling artists William Barlett and William Purser. The etchings form the basis for descriptive vignettes of life in Ottoman Syria by John Carne. The subjects of these descriptions and illustrations include views of Antioch, Damascus and the Orontes Valley.

68 Amurath to Amurath.
Gertrude L. Bell.   London: Macmillan, 1924. 2nd ed. 370p. map.

A personal account of Gertrude Bell's five-month expedition from Aleppo down the Euphrates to Hit, and through northern Iraq to Konia in Turkey. The narrative concentrates on the description of historical sites and monuments, but also includes a discussion of politics and religion in Aleppo.

69 Syria, the desert and the sown.
Gertrude L. Bell.   London: Heinemann, 1907. Reprinted, London:
Darf, 1985. 347p. map.

Bell's personal account of her pre-war journey from Jerusalem to Alexandretta via the Hauran, Jabal al-Druze, Damascus, Homs, Hama, Aleppo and Antioch. The book describes the people she met and the places she visited, and comments on political conditions.

70 Unexplored Syria, visits to the Libanus, the Tulül el-Safá, the Anti-Libanus, the northern Libanus, and the 'Alah.
Richard F. Burton, Charles F. Tyrwhitt-Drake.   London: Tinsley, 1872.
2 vols.

A descriptive account of explorations in Syria undertaken by Burton during his sojourn as British Consul in Damascus from 1869 to 1871. Burton's travels took him to the Jabal al-Druze, the Hauran, and to the region east of Damascus.

71 Syrians: a travelogue 1992-1994.
Laurence Deonna.   Pueblo, Colorado: Passeggiata Press, 1996. 110p.

The author paints a picture of Syria's social and cultural life during the first part of the 1990s. In spite of its brevity, and self-confessed subjectivity, it is an engaging travelogue, and reveals an Occidental perspective on Syrian life.

72   **A 17th century travel account on the Yazidis: implications for a socio-religious study.**
Nelida Fuccaro.   *Istituto Universitario Orientale Annali*, vol. 53, no. 3 (1993), p. 241-53.

This article provides a study of the travel memoirs of Michele Febvre, *Teatro della Turchia*, from the 1670s. The memoirs are thought to be the oldest account of the Syrian Kurdish community of the Yazidis.

73   **Ibn Battuta travels in Asia and Africa 1325-1354.**
Translated and selected by H. A. R. Gibb.   London: Routledge, 1929. 398p. maps.

An account of the travels of ibn Battuta (Sheikh Muhammad Abu 'Abdallah), the famous 14th-century Moroccan traveller and writer. In 1325 ibn Battuta left Tangiers for Syria. Although primarily interested in theological matters, the narrative of his journey includes descriptions of Aleppo, Antioch, Latakia and Damascus, where, in 1326, he joined the *hajj* caravan. On a later journey (1348), ibn Battuta travelled from Baghdad to Damascus via Palmyra and the Syrian desert.

74   **Syria and the Holy Land, their scenery and their people.**
Walter Keating Kelly.   London: Chapman & Hall, 1984. 451p.

A classic mid-Victorian travel guide which includes an account of a journey from Beirut to Damascus, with detailed descriptions of Damascus and its environs. Kelly also discusses the history and customs of the Druzes, and describes an excursion to Palmyra.

75   **The modern Syrians; or, native society in Damascus, Aleppo, and the mountains of the Druses, from notes made in those parts during the years 1841-2-3.**
A. A. Paton.   London: Longman, Brown, Green & Longman, 1844. 309p.

An account of travels in Syria during the early 1840s. It includes descriptions of Aleppo, Damascus and Ghouta, with comments on trade, manufacturing, government and the position of the Jewish and Christian minorities. Paton also describes conditions in the Jabal al-Druze. The book includes appendices on the origins and doctrines of the Druze religion.

76   **Oriental encounters: Palestine & Syria 1894-1896.**
Marmaduke Pickthall.   New York: Knopf, 1929. 277p.

Pickthall's embellished account of his time in Palestine, much of which he spent with a Syrian friend, 'sojourning among the *fellahin* [peasants], and sitting in the coffee shops of Ramleh, Lydda, [and] Gaza'. After failing to join the FCO, Pickthall, dreaming of an eastern paradise, arrived in the Levant at the age of eighteen. Twenty years later he composed his tales of oriental life. They are a sumptuous read for those who share Pickthall's dream of 'Eastern sunshine, palm trees, camels [and of] desert sand, as of a Paradise'.

77 **An Arabian princess between two worlds: memoirs, letters home, sequels to the memoirs: Syrian customs and usages.**
Sayyida Salme/Emily Ruete, edited with an introduction by E. Van Donzel. Leiden, the Netherlands: Brill, 1993. 549p. bibliog. (Arabic History and Civilization Studies and Texts, vol. 3).
Sayyida Salme, later baptised as Emily, was the princess of Oman and Zanzibar. She was born in 1844 and lived till 1924. She wrote her memoirs during the period 1875 to 1886, when they were published. Between 1889 and 1914 she lived in Jaffa and Beirut. It is from this period that she provides this reflection of her thoughts on life in the Levant.

78 **Desert traveller: the life of Jean Louis Burckhardt.**
Katherine Sim. London: Gollancz, 1969. 447p. maps. bibliog.
A biography of Burckhardt based on his journals and correspondence. It describes his Swiss childhood and his engagement by the African Association to search for the source of the River Niger. Burckhardt's travels in Syria and Arabia Petraea were seen as an essential preparation for the work which he was to undertake in the guise of a returning Muslim pilgrim. The work describes his two-and-a-half year stay in Aleppo (1809-12), where he studied Arabic and began to explore the region, visiting Palmyra, Damascus and the Hauran. The book also describes his rediscovery, in 1812, of the 'lost' Nabatean city of Petra, his crossing of the Sinai, his discovery of the Great Temple of Rameses II at Abu Simbel, and his pilgrimage to Mecca as Sheikh Ibrahim.

79 **The memoirs of a French gentleman in Syria: Chevalier Laurent D'Arvieux (1635-1702).**
Elizabeth Sirriyeh. *British Society for Middle Eastern Studies Bulletin*, vol. 11, no. 2 (1984), p. 125-39.
Sirriyeh's essay contextualizes Chevalier Laurent D'Arvieux's experience in the Levant, and seeks to contrast his accounts with other influential travellers, such as Constantin-François Chassebeuf. D'Arvieux's memoirs, amounting to six volumes, contain contemporary prejudice, and yet, deconstruct many myths about the Arabs, Moors and Islam. Sirriyeh argues that D'Arvieux's engagement with the inhabitants of the region, which included learning Arabic, Persian and Turkish, enabled this merchant, traveller and consul to appreciate many features of Middle Eastern society missed by casual observers. D'Arvieux's impressions of the *bedu* went beyond the savage, and his understanding of town, language and religion was more constructive than that of his predecessors. Whilst acknowledging that D'Arvieux's memoirs do contain many negative images of the region, and in particular deplorable depictions of the Turks, Sirriyeh laments the fact that his work was not more influential in shaping the Western psyche towards the Middle East.

80 **Letters from Syria.**
Freya Stark. London: Murray, 1942. 194p. map.
Contains personal reflections and observations made while travelling through Syria and Lebanon between November 1927 and October 1929. The author visited Damascus and Jabal al-Druze.

81 **Palestine under the Moslems: a description of Syria and the Holy Land from AD 650 to 1500.**
Translated from the works of the medieval Arab geographers by Guy Le Strange, with a new introduction by Walid Khalidy.   Beirut: Khayats, 1890. Reprinted, 1965. 604p. (Khayats Oriental Reprints no. 14).
The aim of this book was to translate work that lies 'buried' in the Arabic texts of Muslim geographers and travellers of the Middle Ages. The book is divided into two parts. Part one is primarily an anthology of geographical, historical, architectural and devotional Islamic writings on Palestine and Syria. The anthologies date from 650-1500 and have been translated from Arabic and Persian. Part two comprises a geographical dictionary of places in Palestine and Syria. Each item is followed by short references to the relevant Muslim authorities. The list of Islamic sources used by Le Strange attests to the quality of scholarship employed.

82 **Western travellers to Southern Syria and the Hawran in the nineteenth century: a changing perspective.**
Andrew Vincent.   *Asian Affairs*, vol. XXIV, Part II (June 1993), p. 164-69.
Vincent examines the accounts of Europeans travelling to Syria, especially to southern Syria, and the Hauran, or Bashan as it is called in the Bible, during the 19th century. Due to the changes taking place in Europe during the latter half of the 19th century, travel accounts assumed an 'imperial consciousness'. Vincent observes, therefore, that the writings of the early 19th century tend to be more 'reliable and better sources'.

83 **Travels through Syria and Egypt in the years 1783, 1784 and 1785.**
Constantin-François Comte de Volney.   London: Robinson, 1787. Reprinted, Farnborough, England: Gregg International, 1972. 2 vols.
De Volney's observations constitute one of the most detailed descriptions of late 18th-century Syria. The narrative covers the geography, climate and natural history of Syria, describing the manners and customs of its inhabitants, the ruined cities, its economy, and the administration of the Ottoman government. The geography and economy of the provinces of Aleppo and Damascus are also examined.

84 **Travels in Araby of Lady Hester Stanhope.**
John Watney.   London: Cremonesi, 1975. 294p.
A biography of Lady Hester Stanhope (1776-1839), the adventurous and eccentric niece of former British Prime Minister, William Pitt. She travelled extensively in the Arab world and was the first European woman to visit Palmyra. This biography includes an account of her stay in Damascus in 1812 and her expedition to Palmyra in 1813 with Dr Charles Meryon.

85 **Travels in Turkey, Asia-Minor, Syria, and across the desert into Egypt during the years 1799, 1800 and 1801 in company with the Turkish Army, and the British Military Mission.**
William Wittman. London: Gillet, 1803. Reprinted, New York: Arno Press, and The New York Times, 1971. 595p. map.

Wittman, a surgeon belonging to the Royal College of Surgeons, was attached to the British Military Mission, acting alongside the Army of the Grand Vizier against a common enemy, the French. This book provides an account of Wittman's experience during the three-year campaign. The traveller depicts military life and articulately points out the cultural differences between the British, Turks and Arabs.

86 **The ruins of Palmyra, otherwise Tadmor in the desert.**
Robert Wood. Farnborough, England: Gregg International, 1753. Reprinted, 1971. 107p.

Robert Wood and James Dawkins visited Palmyra for two weeks in 1751. During their stay they made detailed plans and architectural drawings of all major monuments. The fifty-seven plates included in this volume were made by Giovanni Battista Borra, an Italian architect who accompanied them. The work is introduced by an account of Palmyra's ancient history, based primarily on Pliny. The ruins of Palmyra enjoyed remarkable success in 18th-century Europe and were the stimulus for many subsequent visits.

From the Holy Mountain: a journey in the shadow of Byzantium.
See item no. 468.

Flora and Fauna

87 **Birds of Lebanon and the Jordan area.**
  S. Vere Benson.   London: International Council for Bird Preservation,
  1970. 218p. map. bibliog.
A comprehensive, illustrated field guide for ornithologists, covering Lebanon, Syria
and Jordan, with notes on species identification, range and habitat.

88 **Modern pollen precipitation in Syria and Lebanon and its relation
  to vegetation.**
  S. Bottema, Y. Barkoudah.   *Pollen et Spores*, vol. 21, no. 4 (1979),
  p. 427-80.
Examines the relationship between pollen, rain and vegetation patterns. The limited
vegetation of the Syrian desert makes it ideal for an assessment of long-distance
pollen transportation. The composition of seven vegetation zones is described, and the
characteristics of the pollen assemblage (from eighty-five surface samples in six areas)
are ascribed to the various vegetation zones. Distribution maps are produced for ten
important pollen types.

89 **Flore du Liban et de la Syrie.** (Flora of Lebanon and Syria.)
  Louis Bouloumoy.   Paris: Vigot Frères, 1930. 430p.
A description and classification of the flora of Syria and Lebanon, which includes 512
illustrative plates.

90 **The faunal remains of four prehistoric and early historic sites in Syria as indicators of environmental conditions.**
Anneke T. Clason.   In: *Beiträge zur umweltgeschichte des Voderen Orients* (Contributions to the environmental history of Southwest Asia). Edited by Wolfgang Frey, Hans-Peter Verpmann.   Wiesbaden, FRG: Ludwig Reichart Verlag, 1981, p. 191-96. (Beihefte zum Tübinger Atlas des Vorderen Orients).

Describes some of the remains of animal and bird species from four sites (Nahr al-Humur, Hadidi, Ta'as and Buqrus) on the steppe and flood plains of the Euphrates in the 1970s. The remains, dating from 7800 BC to AD 1400, are used to reconstruct the vegetation patterns of the Euphrates Valley prior to its extensive reclamation and agricultural use.

91 **Handbook of the birds of Europe, the Middle East and North Africa: the birds of the western Palearctic.**
Edited by Stanley Cramp.   Oxford; London; New York: Oxford University Press, 1977-85. 4 vols.

A comprehensive reference work, providing extensive and fully-illustrated accounts of species, arranged in the following sections: field characteristics; habitat; distribution; population; movements; food and feeding habits; social patterns and behaviour; voice; breeding; egg markings; plumage; and flight patterns. It includes Syria and neighbouring states in its geographical coverage, and comprises four volumes dealing with: ostriches to ducks; hawks to bustards; waders to gulls; and terns to woodpeckers.

92 **The mammals of Arabia.**
David L. Harrison.   London: Ernest Benn, 1964-72. 3 vols. bibliog.

A comprehensive reference work which describes the distinctive characteristics and distribution of the mammals of Arabia arranged by family and genus. Syria is included in the geographical coverage. The three volumes are entitled: Volume one – Insectivora. Chiroptera. Primates (1964); Volume two – Carnivora. Hyracoidea. Artiodactyla (1968); and Volume three – Lagomorpha. Rodentia (1972).

93 **Herb drugs and herbalists in Syria and North Yemen.**
Gisho Honda, Wataru Miki, Mitsuko Saito.   Tokyo: Institute for the Study of Languages and Cultures of Asia and Africa (ILCAA), Tokyo University of Foreign Studies, 1990. 156p. bibliog. (Studia Culturae Islamicae, no. 39).

A study of traditional medicine, defined by the authors as 'pre-modern scientific medicine'. The authors study the practice of traditional medicine by herbalists throughout the Middle East. This book is based on the authors' field research conducted in North Yemen in 1980 and Syria in 1984-85. The book is divided into four parts: names of herbalists' materials (p. 3-20); illustrations (p. 23-64); references and index (p. 67-72); and samples and prescriptions by herbalists, written in Arabic (p. 76-156).

94 **The venomous snakes of the Near and Middle East.**
Ulrich Joger.   Wiesbaden, FRG: Ludwig Reichart Verlag, 1984. 115p.
(Beihefte zum Tübinger Atlas des Vorderen Orients: Reihe A,
Naturwissenschaften, Nr. 12).

A summary description of the taxonomy and distribution of venomous snakes in the
Near and Middle East, including three species (Vipera lebetina obtusa, Vipera
palaestinae and Vipera bornmuelleri) found in Syria.

95 **Nouvelle flore du Liban et de la Syrie.** (New flora of Lebanon and
Syria.)
Paul S. Mouterde.   Beirut: Dar el-Machreq, 1966-79. 6 vols.

A comprehensive reference work which describes and illustrates the flora of vascular
plants occurring in Lebanon and Syria. The work is arranged by class and sub-class,
and includes notes on range, habitat and taxonomy. Each of the three text volumes is
accompanied by an atlas with full-page plates of nearly all species. The volumes
published so far cover all families up to and including the Campanulaceae. Since the
author's death in 1972 the *Nouvelle flore* has been edited by A. Charpin and W.
Greuter.

96 **A late Quaternary pollen diagram from north-western Syria.**
J. Niklewski, W. Van Zeist.   *Acta Botanica Neerlandica*, vol. 19, no. 5
(1970), p. 737-54.

Presents a pollen analysis of a core from the western side of the Ghab Valley. The pollen
diagram reveals the extreme conditions experienced at the end of the Wurm Glacial, and
shows the increasing proportion of arboreal pollen from ca. 11,400 years ago.

97 **Flowers of the Mediterranean.**
Oleg Polunin, Anthony Huxley.   London: Chatto & Windus, 1965.
257p. map. bibliog.

An illustrated guide to the flora of the Mediterranean basin, including Syria. Over 700
species are described, with details on habitat, distribution, time of flowering and uses.
The work is arranged by family, genera and species. An introductory chapter discusses
the vegetation of the Mediterranean in more general terms. Over 300 plants are
illustrated with colour photographs.

98 **Flora of Syria, Palestine and Sinai: a handbook of the flowering
plants and ferns, native and naturalized, from the Tauras to Ras
Muhammad and from the Mediterranean Sea to the Syrian desert.**
George E. Post, revised by John E. Dinsmore.   Beirut: American
University of Beirut, 1932-33. 2 vols. maps. bibliog.

First published in 1896, this comprehensive handbook provides a descriptive flora of
the vascular plants of the region arranged by family, genera and species. It describes
each species, with details of internal range by district, habitat, life-forms, phenology
and Arabic vernacular names.

99   **Euphrates and Tigris, Mesopotamian ecology and destiny.**
      Edited by Julian Rzóska.   The Hague, the Netherlands: Dr W. Junk,
      1980. 122p. maps. bibliog. (Monographiae Biologicae, vol. 38).
A brief natural history of the Euphrates and Tigris river basins, describing the
hydrological regime and hydrobiology of the two rivers. The study includes chapters
on water characters, phytoplankton and on the ichthyofauna.

100   **Contribution à l'étude de la matière médicale traditionnelle chez
      les herboristes d'Alep.** (A contribution to the study of traditional
      medical preparations used by the herbalists of Aleppo.)
      Floréal Sanagustin.   *Bulletin d'Etudes Orientales*, vol. 35 (1983),
      p. 65-112.
Describes Aleppo's thriving herbal pharmacy sector. The author distinguishes three
categories of herbalist and notes that many of the materials used follow traditions
known since the 10th century. The bulk of the article comprises a glossary of over 310
traditional herbal medicines found in Aleppo. The glossary includes: Arabic and Latin
names; origins; characteristics; and medical uses. The work also contains a substantial
bibliography and over 300 black-and-white illustrative plates.

101   **Flore libano-syrienne.** (The Lebanese-Syrian flora.)
      J. Thiébaut.   Cairo: Institut d'Egypte, 1936, 1940; Paris: Centre
      National de la Recherche Scientifique, 1953. 3 vols.
Comprises a classification of the vascular plants of Lebanon and Syria with notes on
habitat and local range. It is extensively illustrated with line drawings and plates.

102   **Holocene vegetation and climate of northwestern Syria.**
      W. Van Zeist, H. Woldring.   *Palaeohistoria*, vol. 22 (1980), p. 111-25.
Presents the results of a palynological analysis of three sedimentary cores from the
Ghab Valley. The vegetational and climatic history of the late Glacial and early
Holocene periods are reconstructed. The evidence points to changes in climate,
especially humidity. The beginning of the Holocene epoch was characterized by a
moister climate.

103   **Geobotanical foundations of the Middle East.**
      Michael Zohary.   Stuttgart, Germany: Gustav Fischer Verlag;
      Amsterdam: Swets & Zeitlinger, 1973. 2 vols. maps. bibliog.
A comprehensive survey of the flora, vegetation and biogeography of the Middle East.
The introductory chapters provide an analysis of landforms, climate, soils and plant-
geographical regions, including desert vegetation. Detailed chapters outline
phytogeographical territories, vegetation units and their ecological interrelations. The
role of man as an agent of ecological change is also examined. In each section
material is presented on a regional basis and includes Syria and Lebanon.

Prehistory and Archaeology

104 **The 1988 excavations at Tell Sabi Abyad a Neolithic village in northern Syria.**
Peter Akkermans, Marie le Mière. *American Journal of Archaeology*, vol. 96, no. 1 (January 1992), p. 1-22.

A report on the excavations at Tell Sabi Abyad in the Upper Balikh Valley of northern Syria, which clarifies the organization, ecology and chronology of this Neolithic settlement. These excavations have also provided a detailed picture of the Halaf settlement (latter 6th and early 5th millennium BC), and the character of its construction. Photographs and tables of radiocarbon dating from Tell Sabi Abyad (p. 4) are included.

105 **An image of complexity: the Burnt Village at later Neolithic Sabi Abyad, Syria.**
Peter Akkermans, Marc Verhoeven. *American Journal of Archaeology*, vol. 99, no. 1 (January 1995), p. 5-32. maps.

The excavation of Sabi Abyad, located in the Upper Balikh Valley on the Syro-Turkish border, revealed a settlement from the 6th millenium BC that had been destroyed by fire. The aptly named Burnt Village offers an insight into the socio-economic organization of later Neolithic society.

106 **Secrets of the Qadesh mound.**
Taqui Altounyan. *Geographical Magazine*, vol. 53, no. 10 (October 1980), p. 42-46.

Ancient Qadesh, site of the Egyptian-Hittite struggle in 1300 BC, was identified as Tell Nebi Mend in the Orontes during excavations by Maurice Pezard in 1921. This article describes new excavations conducted since 1975, which have established the stratigraphy of the site up to and during the Hellenistic-Roman period when it was re-founded as Laodicea and Libanum.

107 **Ugarit and the powers.**
Michael C. Astour. In: *Ugarit in retrospect, fifty years of Ugarit and Ugaritic.* Edited by Gordon D. Young. Wiona Lake, Indiana: Eisenbrauns, 1981, p. 3-29.

An important outline of Ugarit's political and commercial connections with major regional powers. It describes Ugarit during the age of the Ebla archives, the beginning of Ugarit's commercial connections with the Egypt of the Middle Kingdom, Ugarit as a peripheral client state of Halab, and changes in the political situation in the mid-16th century BC with the rise of the Hittite Kingdom to the north and the kingdoms of Mitanni, Hurri and Haniqalbat to the east. It concludes with an account of Ugarit under the Hittite Empire.

108 **Apamée et la Syrie du nord aux époques hellénistique et romaine.**
(Apamea and north Syria during the Hellenic and Roman eras.)
Jean-Charles Balty. In: *Alep et la Syrie du nord* (Aleppo and northern Syria). Edited by Viviane Fuglestad-Aumeunier. Aix-en-Provence, France: EDISUD, 1991-94, p. 15-26. bibliog. (La Revue du Monde Musulman et de la Méditerranée, no. 62).

Balty investigates Hellenistic and Roman influences in north Syria. He focuses upon Macedonian Syria with its four major cities: Antioch, which was the county town in the Roman province of Syria; Latakia; Séleucie de Piérie; and Apamea. This valuable article combines useful information on Syria's history and archaeology.

109 **Tell Sheikh Hasan: a settlement of the Roman-Parthian to the Islamic period in the Balikh Valley/northern Syria.**
Karin Bartl. *Archéologie Islamique*, vol. 4 (1994), p. 5-17.

This article documents the architectural finds of Tell Sheikh Hasan, which was first excavated in 1983. Tell Sheikh Hasan is one of the few sites in the Balikh Valley to have been continuously inhabited from the end of the 1st century until the early/middle Islamic period in the 13th century.

110 **Ebla: an archaeological enigma.**
Chaim Bermont, Michael Weitzman. London: Weidenfield & Nicolson, 1979. 244p.

The discovery of the palace at Ebla in 1975 inspired the authors to produce this book. After visiting the archaeologists concerned with the excavations, and then studying the available texts, Bermont and Weitzman describe and assess the discoveries, with particular regard to the Bible. To assist the reader, they include an introduction to cuneiform, and one chapter is dedicated to pointing out the uses and limitations of archaeology as a guide in Bible studies.

111 **Syria.**
Edwyn Robert Bevan. In: *The house of Seleucus, vol. 1.* London: Edward Arnold, 1902, p. 206-37.

In this classic work, Bevan explores the achievements of the Seleucid Empire. He examines the major cities that formed the centres of life in Seleucus and also considers the composition of the population. He also examines Cilicia, which, according to ancient geography, belonged to Syria rather than to Asia Minor.

112 **The standardization hypothesis and ceramic mass production:
    technological, compositional, and metric indexes of craft
    specialization at Tell Leilan, Syria.**
    M. James Blackman, Gil J. Stein, Pamela B. Vandiver. *American
    Antiquity*, vol. 58, no. 1 (January 1993), p. 60-80.

In this paper, the authors examine the indexes most frequently used to infer specialized
craft production in complex societies. There are three parts to the paper: the definition of
craft specialization and the standardization hypothesis; an assessment of technological,
compositional and metric indexes of standardization; and a discussion of the ways in
which ancient cultural and natural processes can combine with modern sampling
problems, and blur the evidence of standardization in specialized mass production.

113 **Palmyra.**
    Iain Browning.   London: Chatto & Windus, 1979. 233p. maps.
    bibliog.

A comprehensive account of Palmyra (Tadmor), 'the bride of the desert', which rose
to fame as a trading centre after the collapse of the Nabatean Empire in AD 106. Its
history as a trading centre is examined through the unique record of the Palmyrene
Tariff and its history during the Hellenistic Seleucid Empire is outlined. Its rise to
importance began when it was included in the Roman Province of Syria by Pompey
(ca. 64 BC), when Palmyra was used as a tributary buffer against the Parthians.
Trajan's annexation of Petra in AD 106 brought greatly increased trade to Palymra.
The major expansion of the city began during the reign of Hadrian (AD 117-38), and
ended with Bat Zabbai (Queen Zenobia's) revolt against Rome (AD 268-72). The site's
rediscovery by the West, through visiting English merchants from Aleppo in 1678 and
1691, is described, and the detailed studies of later travellers, including Robert Woods
and James Dawkins (1751), Comte de Volney (1787), Lady Hester Stanhope (1813)
and Comte Melchoir de Vogüé (1853), are discussed. Systematic archaeological study
began in the early 20th century with the German Archaeological Mission under
Thomas Wiegand. The work includes a detailed discussion of the characteristics and
evolution of Palmyra in the late 1970s, examining the main buildings and monuments,
their design and their history.

114 **Carved ivories from Til Barsib.**
    Guy Bunnens.   *American Journal of Archaeology*, vol. 101, no. 3
    (July 1997), p. 435-50. maps.

Bunnens reports on the twelve carved ivories discovered by the University of
Melbourne at Tell Ahmar (ancient Til Barsib). The report raises questions about the
use of ivory in Syria and its implications. Photographs and drawings of the ivories are
also included.

115 **The American archaeological expedition to Syria, 1899-1901.**
    Edited by Howard Crosby Butler, Robert Garrett, Enno Littman,
    William Prentice.   New York: Century, 1903, 1904, 1908, 1914.
    4 vols.

Inspired by the work of the mid-19th-century explorer, Vogüé, the American
archaeological expedition to Syria undertook a systematic topographical, architectural
and epigraphical survey of north-central (the area east of the Orontes from Aleppo to

Apamea) and southern (the Hauran) Syria between October 1899 and May 1900. Volume one, *Topography and itinerary*, edited by Robert Garrett (1914), presents a detailed itinerary of the expedition and an account of the topography of the two regions. Volume two, *Architecture and other arts*, edited by Howard Butler (1903), deals with the classical architecture, the sculptures, mosaics and wall-paintings of the monuments visited by the expedition. Volume three, *Greek and Latin inscriptions*, edited by William Prentice (1908), and volume four, *Semitic inscriptions*, edited by Enno Littmann (1904), present the material collected during the journey.

116 **New horizons in the study of ancient Syria.**
Edited by Mark W. Chavalás, John L. Hayes.   Malibu, California: Undena, 1992. 232p. map. bibliog. (Bibliotheca Mesopotamia, vol. 25).
A volume of papers, delivered to the American Historical Association meeting in Chicago in 1991, focusing on ancient Syria. The topics covered include: an historical sketch of Syria from 3000 to 1000 BC; and the archaeology, literature and culture of this period.

117 **The art of Palmyra.**
Malcolm A. R. Colledge.   London: Thames & Hudson, 1976. 320p. maps. bibliog.
Describes Palmyrene art-forms in detail. Palmyrene art is classified by function, context and period. The functions and art-forms discussed include: funerary sculptures; funerary paintings and stucco; honorific and monumental sculpture; iconography; and art in private houses. The book also has sections on artists' techniques (including painting, mosaic, metalwork, textiles, pottery and glass), style, foreign influences and the role of the patrons.

118 **Excavations at Tell-al-Raqā'i: a small rural site of early urban northern Mesopotamia.**
Hans H. Curvers, Glenn M. Schwartz.   *American Journal of Archaeology*, vol. 94, no. 1 (January 1990), p. 3-23. map.
A report on the excavation of Tell-al-Raqqa in the Middle Habur Valley, which records the social and economic organization of a small rural community in the 3rd millennium BC. The report offers evidence of centres of collection, storage, processing and distribution in the Middle Habur Valley. The excavators suggest that a close integration of rural and urban economies existed. A number of photographs of the site and finds, as well as drawings of ceramics, are provided.

119 **Umm el-Marra, a Bronze Age urban centre in Jabul plain, western Syria.**
Hans H. Curvers, Glenn M. Schwartz.   *American Journal of Archaeology*, vol. 101, no. 2 (April 1997), p. 201-27.
A report from the excavations at Tell-Umm al-Marra, 1994-95. The Jabul plain is located between Aleppo and the Euphrates Valley, and the reporters suggest that it could serve as an 'archaeological linchpin' between the East and the West. The meeting point between the eastern excavations of southern Mesopotamia, and the western excavations in the vicinity of Aleppo, could help to integrate the results of both archaeological finds. The report contains photographs and drawings of ceramics.

120 Mari and Karana, two old Babylonian cities.
Stephanie Dalley. London; New York: Longman, 1984. 218p. maps. bibliog.

A popular account of the two city-states of north-west Mesopotamia which flourished during the 2nd and 3rd millenium BC. Mari (Tell Hariri) in Syria was discovered in August 1933. André Parrot's subsequent excavations at the Palace of Zimri-Lim uncovered more than 20,000 clay tablets written in the cuneiform Akkadian language, which have provided the basis for a detailed socio-economic and political history of Mari in the Middle Bronze Age under Yahdun-Lim and his son Zimri-Lim. Based on the correspondence from the royal archives, the study provides details on: the organization and technology of the industrial workshop; the currency and rates of exchange; the division of labour; food and drink; the role and status of women; cults and beliefs; warfare and diplomacy; animals; and transport and communications. The work concludes with a review of Mari in the Late Bronze/Early Iron Age, and its destruction in 1760 BC by Hammurabi, King of Babylon.

121 Remarks on some objects from Umm el-Marra, 1994-1995.
Sally Dunham. *American Journal of Archaeology*, vol. 101, no. 2 (April 1997), p. 228-39.

This article adjoins the report by Johns Hopkins University and the University of Amsterdam on the excavation at Tell-Umm al-Marra, entitled 'Umm el-Marra, a Bronze Age urban centre in Jabul plain, western Syria', by Hans H. Curvers and Glenn M. Schwartz (see item no. 119). Dunham refers to the three finds that illustrate glyptic art: an alabaster amphoriskos with a duck-head handle; a bronze ladle with a bird-head handle; and three Persian terracotta figurines. She attributes their characteristics to the environmental influences of the Bronze Age (the glyptic art and amphoriskos), and the Hellenistic period (ladle and figurines).

122 The Chalcolithic culture of Golan.
Claire Epstein. *Biblical Archaeologist*, vol. 40, no. 5 (May 1977), p. 57-62.

Reports on the discovery of a previously unknown Chalcolithic (4th millenium BC) site in the central Golan. Sites with architectural, ceramic and lithic features, similar to those found at Teleilat Ghassul in the Jordan Valley, are identified.

123 Historical atlas of the Middle East.
G. S. P. Freeman-Grenville. New York; London; Toronto; Sydney; Tokyo, Singapore: Simon & Schuster, 1993. 144p. maps, bibliog.

A general reader which contains 113 maps with commentaries covering the period from ca. 2050 BC to 1993.

124 **Research on Roman temples in Syria; the Tychaion at es-Sanamain, a preliminary report.**
Klaus Stefan Freyberger. In: *The Near East in antiquity; German contributions to the archaeology of Jordan, Palestine, Syria, Lebanon and Egypt, volume 1: lectures held under the patronage of H.E. the Minister of Culture and H.E. the Ambassador of the Federal Republic of Germany.* Edited by Susanne Kerner. Amman: Goethe Institut, and al-Kutba, 1990, p. 29-37.

This is a study of a Roman temple dating from AD 191, which lies in the village of al-Sanamain near Damascus. The author reports on its inscriptions and architectural style, whilst also comparing it to other Roman temples in Syria.

125 **City in the desert, Qasr al-Hayr east.**
Oleg Garbar, Renata Holod, James Knustad, William Trousdale. Cambridge, Massachusetts: Harvard University Press, 1978. 2 vols. (Harvard Middle East Monographs, nos. 23 and 24).

These two monographs chronicle the six seasons of excavation (starting in 1964), by the University of Michigan, at the desert-city of Qasr al-Hayr. The reports describe the physical and historical setting of the site, its structures, artefacts and culture. The town depended on a sophisticated water-gathering system for its survival. Originally created in the 8th century, Qasr al-Hayr thrived under the Umayyad caliphate. Its creation is explained in terms of the need to develop the hinterland of the middle Euphrates Valley, to strengthen and control communications between Syria and Iraq, and to solve internal political problems. Appendices include a catalogue of finds, covering decorated stoneware, mosaics, paintings, metalwork, coins and inscriptions.

126 **Dura-Europos, a fortress of Syro-Mesopotamian art.**
Marie-Henriette Gates. *Biblical Archaeologist*, vol. 47, no. 3 (September 1984), p. 166-81.

Concentrating on the synagogue, mithraeum and Christian chapel of this ancient Syrian city (founded in the 4th century BC), the author illustrates how the art and architecture of different religious faiths share a common heritage. An analysis of wall-paintings in these monuments reveals the basic conservatism of the city. New cults were made to conform to pre-existing architectural and artistic norms.

127 **Arabs in sixth-century Syria: some archaeological observations.**
Heinze Gaube. *British Society for Middle Eastern Studies Bulletin*, vol. 8, no. 2 (1981), p. 93-98.

Gaube highlights the lack of archaeological data used to verify historical records. His critique of historians is well-argued and serves to underscore the conflicting, and often contradictory, socio-economic histories of heterogeneous Syria. The ruin of Khirbat al-Bayda, situated thirty kilometres north of Namara, is used as an illustrative model to put his observations in context. In response, Gaube appeals to the student of Bilad al-Sham (Greater Syria) to search for further evidence pertaining to the fields of physical geography, soil fertility, hydrography and archaeology.

Prehistory and Archaeology

128   The Assyrian Empire: renewed rise of Assyria, the reign of
      Ashur-nasir-pal.
      H. R. Hall.   In: *The ancient history of the Near East: from the earliest
      times to the battle of Salamis*.   London: Methuen, 1952, 11th ed.,
      p. 444-517.
The division of the Jewish kingdom, and the resulting internecine war in Palestine,
coincided with a renewal of Assyrian power. Between Ashur-rabi, in whose reign the
Syrian cities Pethor and Mutkini were lost to the Aramaen invaders, and Ashur-nasir-
pal, who recovered north Syria, nearly two centuries elapsed. For over a century after
the reign of Ashur-rabi, knowledge of Assyrian history remains blank. Hall attempts
to fill this void with a descriptive account of Assyrian history.

129   Paleolithic site of the Douara cave and the paleogeography of
      Palmyra Basin in Syria. Part I: stratigraphy and paleogeography
      in the late Quaternary.
      Edited by Kazuro Hanihara, Yutaka Sakaguchi.   Tokyo: University of
      Tokyo Press, 1978. 121p. maps. bibliog. (University of Tokyo Museum
      Bulletin, no. 14).
First discovered in 1967 and subsequently excavated by the Tokyo University
scientific expeditions in the 1970s, the Douara cave lies eighteen kilometres north-east
of Palmyra on the southern slopes of Jabal al-Douara. The cave provided the location
for a flint factory during the Middle and Epi-Palaeolithic periods. This first volume
describes the Pleistocene stratigraphy, the palaeoenvironment and palaeogeography of
the Douara region. Evidence of the presence of a Palmyrene pluvial lake is discussed,
and palynological evidence of climatic change is presented.

130   Paleolithic site of the Douara cave and the paleogeography of
      Palmyra Basin in Syria. Part II: prehistoric occurrences and
      chronology in Palmyra Basin.
      Edited by Kazuro Hanihara, Takeru Akazawa.   Tokyo: University of
      Tokyo Press, 1979. 238p. maps. bibliog. (University of Tokyo Museum
      Bulletin, no. 16).
Discusses the Middle Palaeolithic and Epi-Palaeolithic assemblages from the Douara
cave site, together with upper Palaeolithic and Epi-Palaeolithic assemblages from the
Palmyra Basin. Flint factory sites in the Palmyra Basin are identified and a prehistoric
chronology of the area is presented.

131   Paleolithic site of the Douara cave and the paleogeography of
      Palmyra Basin in Syria. Part III: animal bones and further
      analysis of archaeological materials.
      Edited by Kazuro Hanihara, Takeru Akazawa.   Tokyo: University of
      Tokyo Press, 1983. 167p. bibliog. (University of Tokyo Museum
      Bulletin, no. 21).
A detailed analysis of the animal bone remains from the Palaeolithic Douara cave site,
together with a micro-wear analysis of flint microliths from the upper and Epi-
Palaeolithic assemblages.

132 **Goods, prices and the organization of trade in Ugarit.**
Michael Heltzer. Wiesbaden, FRG: Dr Ludwig Reichart Verlag,
1978. 163p. map. bibliog.
Analyses available texts from the 14th and 13th centuries BC from Ugarit concerning
commercial goods, and explains Akkadian and Ugaritic measurements and terms for
various goods and prices, comparing prices of basic commodities with those of other
contemporary societies. The role of merchants and the problems of maritime and
overland transport are also examined.

133 **The internal organization of the Kingdom of Ugarit.**
Michael Heltzer. Wiesbaden, FRG: Dr Ludwig Reichart Verlag,
1982. 212p. bibliog.
A detailed description and analysis of various elements of internal organization in the
Kingdom of Ugarit. In particular, it examines military organization, temple organization
and personnel, and royal administration and palace personnel. The roles of different
members of the royal hierarchy are also discussed. The work, which is based on the
royal archives of the 14th and 13th centuries BC, also discusses the royal economy,
including crafts and agriculture.

134 **The rural community in ancient Ugarit.**
Michael Heltzer. Wiesbaden, FRG: Dr Ludwig Reichart Verlag,
1976. 120p. map. bibliog.
Based on a study of administrative, legal and commercial documents in the Akkadian
and Ugaritic languages, this monograph deals with the communal organization of the
villages of the Kingdom of Ugarit in the 14th to 13th centuries BC. It examines tax
collection and the tithe, conscription and the labour services imposed on the villagers,
and discusses the administration of local government in the villages. The study also
provides a series of demographic estimations.

135 **The discovery of Dura-Europos.**
Clarke Hopkins, edited by Bernard Goldman. London; New Haven,
Connecticut: Yale University Press, 1979. 309p. map. bibliog.
A popular account of the excavations at Dura-Europos, the Hellenistic and later
Roman fortified city on the Euphrates. The city was rediscovered in 1920 and early
excavations were conducted by Franz Cumont in 1922-23. A series of ten Franco-
American campaigns were undertaken between 1928 and 1937. The author describes
each of these ten campaigns, and provides an extended discussion of the spectacular
wall-paintings of the Christian chapel and the Jewish synagogue. It includes an outline
history of Dura-Europos from its foundation ca. 300 BC to its destruction by the
invading Persian Sassanids in AD 256.

136 **Gazelle killing in Stone Age Syria.**
Anthony J. Legge, Peter A. Rowley-Conwy. *Scientific American*,
vol. 257, no. 2 (August 1987), p. 88-95. map.
The authors investigate how agriculture came to replace hunting as mode of
subsistence. The site of Tell Abu Hureyra, on the banks of the Euphrates in northern
Syria, was occupied by hunter-gatherers from the Mesolithic to the Neolithic periods.
For nearly 1,000 years after agriculture started, hunting remained the principal mode

of subsistence. It was the rapid decrease in the gazelle population that probably initiated the move to animal husbandry instead. From their evidence, the authors conclude that agriculture gradually replaced hunting over a long period of time.

137 **Trends in the local pottery development of the Late Iron Age and Persian period in Syria and Lebanon, ca. 700 to 300 B.C.**
Gunnar Lehmann. *Bulletin of the American Schools of Oriental Research*, no. 311 (August 1998), p. 7-33.

Lehmann has written an engaging article about the production and distribution of pottery in Syria and Lebanon. As part of his analysis, he contentiously suggests that archaeological studies should be conducted without reference to history. In other words, archaeology should remain an independent discipline, free from the constraints of the historical record.

138 **The history of ancient Syria and Palestine: an overview.**
Niels Peter Lemche. In: *Civilizations of the ancient Near East.* Jack M. Sasson (editor-in-chief). New York: Scribner, 1995, p. 1,195-218. maps. bibliog.

Lemche offers a broad overview of Syria and Palestine's ancient history. Whilst this article lacks depth, it does cover two millennia, introduce the reader to methodological issues, and offer material from Mari and Amarna archives. In comparison to the ancient civilizations of Mesopotamia and Egypt, few written sources are available on Syro-Palestinian ancient history. However, modern archaeological studies, turning away from major cities, have led to the accidental discovery of archives. After reviewing the Early Bronze Age, Middle Bronze Age, Hittites and Hurrians, Hyksos, Aramaens, Israel and Judah, and Assyrians, Lemche concludes that Syria and Palestine were never politically autonomous for any significant length of time. The power structures, as well as the distribution of the population, always encouraged major political powers to meddle in the affairs of Syria and Palestine.

139 **Syria: publications of the Princeton University archaeological expeditions to Syria in 1904-05 and 1909, division IV, Semitic inscriptions.**
Enno Littman. Leiden, the Netherlands: Brill, 1949. 105p.

The Arabic inscriptions published in this book were copied in 1904-05, mostly by Littman, but no. 19 is a copy of one of Gertrude Bell's inscriptions. The sequence of inscriptions is as follows: building; mosques; funerary; and graffiti. The dated inscriptions are given first, in chronological order, followed by the undated inscriptions.

140 **Ebla: an empire rediscovered.**
Paolo Matthiae, translated by Christopher Holme. London: Hodder & Stoughton, 1980. 237p. maps. bibliog.

A detailed account of the Tell Mardikh expedition and the identification of the site as the 3rd millennium BC Ebla. The architecture and artefacts from the first great urban expansion of Ebla, which occurred during the Mature and Late Protosyrian periods (ca. 2400-2000 BC), are described. Around 2000 BC the city was destroyed by fire; Matthiae describes the new city plan, architecture and pottery of Ebla in the subsequent Archaic and Mature Old Syrian periods (ca. 2000-1600 BC), when Ebla was at the height of its cultural and economic prestige. The second half of the book focuses on the history and culture of Ebla during the period described in the royal archives of the Early Bronze Age (2400-2250 BC). The structure of the Eblaite language is described, and the archives and documents of the central administration are used to outline elements of Ebla's political history, economic structure, administration and religion. The final chapters consider Eblaite culture and the foundation of an artistic and architectural civilization in pre-Hellenistic Syria.

141 **A survey in northeastern Syria.**
Diederik J. W. Meijer.   Leiden, the Netherlands: Nederland Institut Voor het Nabije Oosten, 1986. 58p. maps. bibliog.

This book provides an archaeological survey of the north-east region of Syria. It consists of two catalogues: one containing sites; and the other referring to the pottery discovered.

142 **The Oxford encyclopedia of archaeology in the Near East.**
Eric M. Meyers (editor-in-chief).   New York; Oxford: Oxford University Press, prepared under the auspices of American Schools of Oriental Research, 1997. 5 vols. maps. bibliog.

Provides archaeological information on the region, from the Early Bronze Age to the Crusades. Its aim is to make the results of archaeological studies accessible to readers interested in the ancient Near East. Syro-Palestine is at the core of the work. Site entries constitute 450 of the 1,100 entries. This is a good reference for libraries and students of archaeology.

143 **Ebla: a third-millennium city-state in ancient Syria.**
Lucio Milano.   In: *Civilizations of the ancient Near East.*   Jack M. Sasson (editor-in-chief).   New York: Scribner, 1995, p. 1,219-30. bibliog.

Referring to the cuneiform tablets discovered at Ebla, Milano examines some mechanisms of cultural interaction, including the use of writing, the organization of labour, cultic practices and the management of power. The relationship between king and society, the efficacy of the palace economy and the role of the temples are all considered from a domestic perspective. Although Ebla was destroyed by fire between 2400 and 2350 BC, Milano asserts that diverse facets of Syrian society, emanating from the legacy of the 3rd millennium, have left Syria with a distinct cultural tradition.

144 **The art of Dura-Europos.**
Ann Perkins.   London: Oxford University Press, 1973. 130p. map.

The large number of works of art from Dura-Europos permits an unusually detailed examination of the nature of provincial art and provides a picture of the city during its various phases and under differing influences. This study examines three art forms: architecture, wall-paintings and sculpture. The author notes that from its origins Dura-Europos was a planned city, and describes its architectural evolution through the Hellenistic, Parthian and Roman periods. The wall-paintings of major religious buildings such as the Temple of Bel, the Christian baptistery and the synagogue, together with those of private houses, are discussed. The stylistic elements of the main sculptural forms – cult reliefs, architectural reliefs and figurines – are also described.

145 **The archives of Ebla, an empire inscribed in clay.**
Giovanni Pettinato.   New York: Doubleday, 1981. 374p. maps. bibliog.

A popular account of the excavations at Tell Mardikh (Ebla), focusing on the discovery in 1974-76 of more than 15,000 clay tablets from the Early Bronze Age royal archives. The book describes the typology and structure of Eblaite, the oldest Semitic language of western Syria, which was current around 2300 BC. Interpretation of the archives has permitted a reconstruction of the civilization of Ebla. This account describes the social structure, administration and organization of Ebla. It also illustrates its domestic politics and international relations, economic resources, agriculture, industry and commerce, culture and religion.

146 **Tell Bderi: the development of a Bronze Age town.**
Peter Pfalzner.   In: *The Near East in antiquity; German contributions to the archaeology of Jordan, Palestine, Syria, Lebanon and Egypt, volume 1: lectures held under the patronage of H.E. the Minister of Culture and H.E. the Ambassador of the Federal Republic of Germany.*
Edited by Susanne Kerner.   Amman: Goethe Institut, and al-Kutba, 1990, p. 63-79.

Pfalzner provides a report of the excavation at Tell Bderi, which is situated in the north-east of Syria and which dates back to the 5th millennium BC. This paper includes a brief history of this Bronze Age town, together with an inventory of the houses and their contents, such as written documents, found at the site.

147 **Ancient Damascus: a historical study of the Syria city-state from the earliest times until its fall to the Assyrians in 732 B.C.E.**
Wayne T. Pitard.   Winona Lake, Indiana: Eisenbrauns, 1987. 230p. maps. bibliog.

The author provides an historical study of early Damascus in the Middle Bronze Age and Late Bronze Age, and its relations with the monarchs of united Israel. A biblical reference index is provided on p. 228-30. This work will be useful to students of ancient history.

148 **Tell Minus wares.**
Venetia Porter, Oliver Watson.   In: *Syria and Iran: three studies in medieval ceramics.*   Edited by James Allan, Caroline Roberts.
Oxford: Oxford University Press, 1987, p. 175-248. bibliog. (Oxford Studies in Islamic Art IV).

A study of the 12th-century ceramics found at the site of Tell Minus, located between Aleppo and Hama, in central Syria. The study focuses on the lustre wares and records their form, style and characteristics. An illustrated catalogue is also included. The work concludes with a discussion on the similarities of Tell Minus ware with Fatimid and Raqqa wares, and with other types which do not fit into any of these categories, but appear to be developments from Tell Minus.

149 **Sukas: the N.E. sanctuary and the first settling of Greeks in Syria and Palestine.**
P. J. Riis. Copenhagen: Munksgaard, 1970. 179p. maps.

Details the five campaigns at Tell Sukas, near Jablah on the Syrian coast, between 1958 and 1963. This report describes the excavations of the north-east part of the site in chronological sequence from the Bronze and Early Iron Ages through the three Greek building phases to the new Phoenician and late Hellenistic period. The first Greek temple on the site was built in the Late Iron Age. Evidence of Greek settlement as early as 850 BC is presented. The period of Greek domination was to last until 498 BC.

150 **Tell-al-Raqā', 1989 and 1990: further investigations at a small rural site of early urban northern Mesopotamia.**
Glenn M. Schwartz, Hans H. Curvers. *American Journal of Archaeology*, vol. 96, no. 3 (July 1992), p. 397-419.

This report from an excavation at Tell-al-Raqqa in north-eastern Syria analyses the urbanization and socio-political complexity of a rural community from 1000 BC. This report accounts for the significance of Tell-al-Raqqa as a processor of grains and a rural store.

151 **Life in the ancient Near East, 3100-332 B.C.E.**
Daniel C. Snell. New Haven, Connecticut; London: Yale University Press, 1997. 270p. map. bibliog.

Snell's ancient Near East is commensurate with the contemporary Middle East; he includes Iran, Iraq, Turkey, Syria, Lebanon, Israel and Egypt. Snell observes that Mesopotamia should be central to the study of ancient economies and societies. Accordingly, the appendix assesses theories of ancient economies and societies, and offers a suitable working model for future studies (p. 145-58). In his social and economic history, Snell examines areas that include: the role of the family; the role of women; agriculture; crafts; trade; and government. A series of chronological tables depict the dynasties and kingdoms of Mesopotamia, Egypt, Israel-Palestine and Anatolia. The book contains illustrations of drawings and a number of photographs. The Assyrian Empire is discussed in chapter five (p. 78-98), and the Babylon and Persian Empires are covered in chapter six (p. 99-118). An extensive bibliography can be found on p. 219-59.

152 **Report of the reconnaissance survey of Paleolithic sites in Lebanon and Syria.**
Edited by H. Suzuki, I. Kobari. Tokyo: University of Tokyo Press, 1970. 135p. maps. bibliog. (University of Tokyo Museum Bulletin, no. 1).

Includes an outline of the topography and geology of Syria, together with a description of some 124 Palaeolithic sites, and associated flint implements examined by this expedition to Syria in 1967-68, which centred on the Palmyra basin, the Damascus-Yabroud area and Jabal Ansariyah.

153 **The silver treasures of Resafa/Sergiupolis.**
Thilo Ulbert.   In: *The Near East in antiquity; German contributions to the archaeology of Jordan, Palestine, Syria, Lebanon and Egypt, volume 1: lectures held under the patronage of H.E. the Minister of Culture and H.E. the Ambassador of the Federal Republic of Germany.* Edited by Susanne Kerner.   Amman: Goethe Institut, and al-Kutba, 1990, p. 105-10.

Resafa lies in the north of Syria, where in ca. AD 300 a Roman army officer, Sergius, was executed, becoming a martyr for Christianity. During an excavation in 1982, a church treasure of silver was found, comprising a hanging lamp, an Eucharistic chalice, the single foot of a chalice, a paten and a profane drinking vessel. Ulbert provides a report with illustrations of this treasure.

154 **New evidence for north Syrian chronology from Hammam el-Turkman.**
Maurtis Van Loon.   *American Journal of Archaeology*, vol. 92, no. 4 (October 1988), p. 582-87.

Van Loon examines the finds from an excavation at Hammam al-Turkman, a large multi-period site on the Balikh River in northern Syria. Photographs and figures from the site are provided, in addition to chronological tables and radiocarbon dates from Hammam al-Turkman (p. 587).

155 **1985 excavations at Tell Leilan, Syria.**
Harvey Weiss, Peter Akkermans, Gil J. Stein, Dominique Parayre, Robert Whiting.   *American Journal of Archaeology*, vol. 94, no. 4 (October 1990), p. 529-81. maps.

The article comprises several reports from the 1985 excavation at four Tell Leilan locations: two reports focus on the Acropolis (Weiss, p. 529-42); one on the Lower Town (Akkermans, p. 542-47); and one on the city wall (Stein, p. 547-55). Two reports provide analysis of glyptic assemblages (Parayre, p. 556-67), and cuneiform archives retrieved from buildings excavated in the Acropolis and the Lower Town (Whiting, p. 568-79). A map of Habur Plain (p. 530), and a topographic map of Tell Leilan (p. 531) are provided, and photographs of the site are also supplied.

156 **Archaeology in Syria.**
Harvey Weiss.   *American Journal of Archaeology*, vol. 98, no. 1 (January 1994), p. 101-58. map.

Weiss presents thirty-three archaeological reports supervised by the Directorate General of Antiquities and Museums, Damascus. The reports contain information referring to the location of sites, their finds and their relevance. A comprehensive map of Syria's archaeological sites is also included (p. 102).

157 **After the revolution: post-Neolithic subsistence in northern Mesopotamia.**
Melinda A. Zeder. *American Anthropologist*, vol. 96, no. 1 (March 1994), p. 97-126.
This examination of subsistence at Umm Qseir highlights the remarkable degree of flexibility and individualized response of post-Neolithic economies in the Near East, especially in marginal areas. In order to shed more light on the continuing evolution of food-producing economies in post-Neolithic times, this article focuses on animal-based subsistence strategies in the Khabur drainage of northern Mesopotamia.

Archives royales de Mari: textes, transcrits et traduits. (The royal archives of Mari: texts, transcriptions and translations.)
See item no. 407.

La lingua di Ebla: atti del convegno internazionale. (The language of Ebla: proceedings of an international congress.)
See item no. 408.

Syrie centrale: inscriptions sémitiques. (Central Syria: Semitic inscriptions.)
See item no. 415.

NIV atlas of the Bible.
See item no. 425.

Towards an archaeology of architecture: clues from a modern Syrian village.
See item no. 828.

History

Classical and Islamic (to 1517)

158   **The appointment and dismissal of Khālid B. al-Walīd from the
       supreme command, a study of the political strategy of the early
       Muslim Caliphs in Syria.**
       Khalil 'Athamina.   *Arabica*, vol. XLI, no. 2 (July 1994), p. 253-72.
       bibliog.

This article analyses the circumstances surrounding the appointment and dismissal of
Khalid ibn al-Walid from the post of supreme commander of the Arab armies between
AD 640-43. 'Athamina attempts to redress the imbalance and sins of omission within
the existing body of literature.

159   **The end of the Mamluk sultanate.**
       David Ayalon.   In: *Islam and the abode of war: military slaves and
       Islamic adversaries*.   Aldershot, England; Brookfield, Vermont:
       Variorum, 1994, p. IX 125-48. (Collected Studies, CS 456).

Ayalon's study is based on the two chronicles of ibn Iyas and ibn Tulun which analyse
the fate of the Mamluk military aristocracy during the Ottoman occupation. The
author has divided the study into two separate, but closely connected and
interdependent, articles. In the first, he addresses the question of why the Ottomans
spared the Mamluks of Egypt but not those of Syria. In the second, he studies the
Mamluk military aristocracy during the first years of Ottoman occupation of Egypt.

160 **Mamluk: military slavery in Egypt and Syria.**
David Ayalon. In: *Islam and the abode of war: military slaves and Islamic adversaries*. Aldershot, England; Brookfield, Vermont: Variorum, 1994, p. II 1-21. (Collected Studies, CS 456).
First published in an abridged form in *The encyclopedia of Islam*, VI fasc. 103-104, 1987, 2nd ed. This completed version gives a more comprehensive picture of Mamluk military slavery in Egypt and Syria under the Mamluk sultanate.

161 **Bilad al-Sham during the Abbasid period (132 AH/75 AD – 451 AH/ AD 1059): proceedings of the Fifth International Conference on the History of Bilad al-Sham, 7-11 Sha'ban 1410/4-8 March 1990.**
Edited by Muhammad Adnan Bakhit, Robert Schick. Amman: University of Jordan Press, 1991. 280p.
A collection of papers presented at the conference on 'Bilad al-Sham during the 'Abbasid period'. The topics covered include society, theology and archaeology.

162 **The origins of the Islamic state, vol. i.**
Al-Imam Abu-al 'Abbas Ahmad ibn-Jabir al-Baladhuri, translated by Philip Khuri Hitti. New York: Columbia University Press, 1968. 518p.
Since the publication of *The origins of the Islamic state*, 1866, in Arabic, its author has been recognized as one of the chief authorities on the formation of the Arab state. Hitti's translation has made al-Baladhuri's valuable accounts available to students of history and Middle Eastern studies. Part two is of particular interest to Syria watchers, as it is dedicated to the conquest of Syria.

163 **Damas et l'espace syrien à travers l'histoire.** (Damascus and Syria's space throughout history.)
Thierry Bianquis. In: *Damas: miroir brisé d'un orient arabe* (Damascus: broken mirror of an Arab Orient). Edited by Anne-Marie Bianquis, Elizabeth Picard. Paris: Editions Autrement, 1993, p. 60-69. (Série Monde, H.S. no. 65).
Bianquis presents a concise history of Damascus. Damascus has been rewarded for its geopolitical status; it became the first Islamic capital beyond the Arabian peninsula in AD 660. Bianquis discusses Syria's relations with its neighbours, including the Egyptians, Turks, Mongols and Andalusians. The author then turns his focus towards Damascene-European relations. This is a clear and well-presented introduction to Syrian history.

164 **Pouvoirs arabs à Alep aux xᵉ et xiᵉ siècles.** (The Arab powers in
   Aleppo in the 10th and 11th centuries.)
   Thierry Bianquis. In: *Alep et la Syrie du nord* (Aleppo and northern
   Syria). Edited by Viviane Fuglestad-Aumeunier. Aix-en-Provence,
   France: EDISUD, 1991-94, p. 49-59. bibliog. (La Revue du Monde
   Musulman et de la Méditerranée, no. 62).

As the political power of the 'Abbasids began to wane, competition amongst the
empires' military chiefs arose. With the caliphate in Baghdad no longer the supreme
authority, some notable military officers turned their dynastic ambitions towards Syria
and Egypt. Bianquis examines two of the resulting Arab dynasties in Aleppo, the
Hamdanids and Mirdasids respectively.

165 **The Crusades: a documentary survey.**
   James A. Brundage. Milwaukee, Wisconsin: Marquette University
   Press, 1962. 318p. maps. bibliog.

Assembles a group of readings that serve as an introduction to the history of the
Crusading movement, to the major chronicles and to other contemporary Western
historians, whose narratives underlie most knowledge about the Crusades.

166 **Knowledge and social practice in medieval Damascus, 1190-1350.**
   Michael Chamberlain. Cambridge, England: Cambridge University
   Press, 1994. 199p. maps. bibliog. (Cambridge Studies in Islamic
   Civilisation).

Using Damascus as the focal point, Chamberlain analyses Middle Eastern society and
culture through the study of social practice within a medieval context.

167 **Mamlakat Halab, une vice-royauté des confins de l'empire mamluk
   (648-784/1250-1302).** (Royal Aleppo, a vice-royalty within the
   confines of the Mamluk Empire [648-784/1250-1302].)
   Mounira Chapoutot-Remadi. In: *Alep et la Syrie du nord* (Aleppo and
   northern Syria). Edited by Viviane Fuglestad-Aumeunier. Aix-en-
   Provence, France: EDISUD, 1991-94, p. 81-91. (La Revue du Monde
   Musulman et de la Méditerranée, no. 62).

The author examines the history of Aleppo, with regard to its geopolitics and its
significance to the Mamluks. Chapoutot-Remadi explores the rivalry between Cairo
and Aleppo, from the Ayyubid (Aleppo) and Mamluk (Cairo) perspective. The author
argues that the significance of Aleppo's location, from the Euphrates to the
Mediterranean, served as an invitation to the Mongol invasions, as well as to Mamluk
expansion. A chronology of Mamluk-Mongol relations is provided on p. 88, and of
Mamluk-Armenian relations on p. 89.

168 **East and West in the Crusader states: context, contacts, and confrontations.**
Edited by Krijnie Ciggaar, Adelbert Davids, Herman Teule. Leuven, Belgium: Uitgeverij Peeters, 1996. 203p. maps.
This collection of essays covers a variety of topics from the 11th to the 13th centuries. They are primarily concerned with the interaction between the Crusaders and the East, and cover the areas of history, religion, literature and language.

169 **Venetian merchant activity within Mamluk Syria (886-893/1481-1487).**
Eleanor A. Congdon. *The Medieval Mediterranean: Cultures in Contact*, vol. 7 (1994), p. 1-33.
Congdon builds on Eliyahu Ashtor's work in exploring the role of Venetian leaders in Mamluk Syria of the 1480s. Her study is based on a group of Venetian merchants' letters; the correspondence, written in Italian, is included.

170 **The origin and development of the local histories of Syria.**
Sami Dahan. In: *Historians of the Middle East*. Edited by Bernard Lewis, P. M. Holt. London: Oxford University Press, 1962, p. 108-17.
Describes the origins and development of local history writing, a branch of Islamic historiography, in the form of biographical, historical and topographical works. Important works from the 9th and 10th centuries, and their authors, are briefly discussed. The focus of the essay is 12th- and 13th-century local Syrian historians. The local histories of three regions, Aleppo, Damascus and Jazira, are discussed in detail. These include Kamal al-Din al-Adim's vast history of Aleppo in the form of a biographical dictionary (*Bughyat al-talab fi ta'rikh Halab*), ibn Shaddad's *al-A'laq*, ibn al-Qalanisi's history of Damascus from 444-555 AH, and ibn 'Asakir's eighty-volume history of Damascus. Other writers discussed include ibn Kathir al-Qurashi, ibn Rajab al-Dimashqi and ibn al-Azraq.

171 **A history of Antioch in Syria from Seleucus to the Arab conquest.**
Glanville Downey. Princeton, New Jersey: Princeton University Press, 1961. 752p. maps. bibliog.
A comprehensive, chronological history of the city of Antioch from its foundation by Seleucus Nicator through the Seleucid dynasty and subsequent Roman rule, to the Persian invasion in AD 540 and the Arab conquest of AD 641. The work is based primarily on literary sources including those of Libanius and St John Chrysostom, and the ecclesiastical history of Evagrius Scholasticus. The author discusses these and other sources in the introductory chapters. A separate chapter is devoted to the Christian community of Antioch.

172 **Une grande famille de shafiites alépins: les Banū l-'Agamī aux xiie-xiiie siècles.** (A great family of Aleppine Shaf'is: the Banu al-'Agami in the 12th and 13th centuries.)
Anne-Marie Eddé. In: *Alep et la Syrie du nord* (Aleppo and northern Syria). Edited by Viviane Fuglestad-Aumeunier. Aix-en-Provence, France: EDISUD, 1991-94, p. 61-71. (La Revue du Monde Musulman et de la Méditerranée, no. 62).

A genealogy of seven generations that summarizes two centuries of Aleppine history. The Banu al-'Agami are representative of the Aleppine political elite, and this article studies their specific role within Syrian society. The personal biographies reflect the political, religious and social practices of the day. Tables of the family's genealogy are provided on p. 62 and p. 65.

173 **Damas et le djihad contre les croisés.** (Damascus and the jihad against the Crusades.)
Nikita Elisséeff. In: *Damas: miroir brisé d'un orient arabe* (Damascus: broken mirror of an Arab Orient). Edited by Anne-Marie Bianquis, Elizabeth Picard. Paris: Editions Autrement, 1993, p. 40-44. (Série Monde, H.S. no. 65).

An account of Nur al-Din's achievements during his Damascene reign from 1154 until 1174. He succeeded his father, Zenkki, in ruling Aleppo in 1146 and conquered Damascus in 1154. The article briefly depicts his encounters with the Crusaders, and the monuments he left behind.

174 **Fihris al-makhtūtāt al-'arabīyah al-mahfūzah fī maktabat al-asad al-watanīyah.** (Index of the Arabic manuscripts preserved in the National Asad Library.)
Damascus: Maktabat al-Asad, 1993. 259p.

An index of the Asad Library's collection of 19,114 Arabic manuscripts.

175 **Alep et la Syrie du nord.** (Aleppo and northern Syria.)
Edited by Viviane Fuglestad-Aumeunier. Aix-en-Provence, France: EDISUD, 1991-94. 208p. maps. (La Revue du Monde Musulman et de la Méditerranée, no. 62).

A collection of articles on Aleppo, covering a variety of topics, such as architecture, economics and history.

176 **Arab historians of the Crusades.**
Selected and translated from the Arabic sources by Francessco Gabrieli, translated from the Italian by E. J. Costello. London: Routledge & Kegan Paul, 1969. 362p.

A chronological account of the Frankish invasions as seen by Arab chroniclers. Excerpts from seventeen original Arabic texts are presented in four sections: from Godfery to Saladin; Saladin and the third Crusade; the Ayyubids and the invasion of Egypt; and the Mamluks and the expulsion of the Crusaders. Preceding the excerpts are brief notes on the authors (such as ibn al-Qalanisi, Kamal ad-Din, Abu Shama, Manaqib Ramid al-Din and ibn Wasil) and their works.

177 The Arabic historiography of the Crusades.
Francesco Gabrieli. In: *Historians of the Middle East.* Edited by Bernard Lewis, P. M. Holt. London: Oxford University Press, 1962, p. 98-107.

Gabrieli examines the leading Arab historians of the Crusades and their writings. These include ibn al-Qalanisi's history of the first two Crusades (*Dhayl*), regarded as the most informed and reliable Arabic source on the early Crusades, and his first-hand account of the siege of Damascus in 1148. Other pieces examined include ibn al-Kathir's *Kamil*, covering the middle Crusader period, and ibn Shaddad's biography of Saladin.

178 The Damascus chronicle of the Crusades: extracted and translated from the chronicle of ibn al-Qalanisi.
H. A. R. Gibb. London: Luzac, 1932. 368p.

Historians have marked the absence of Arabic records of the First Crusade. The *Continuation of the chronicle of Damascus* of ibn al-Qalanisi was frequently quoted by later writers, but was thought to deal with the period posterior to the Second Crusade. This manuscript was one of the Arabic manuscripts preserved in the Bodleian Library, until it was discovered by H. F. Amedroz, who edited and published the text in 1908 together with a summary of contents, notes and extracts from other unpublished sources. Owing to the lack of translation, the recovery of this chronicle seems to have passed unnoticed by European historians. The extracts in this volume constitute the first attempt to make it accessible to Western scholarship.

179 The life of Saladin: from the works of 'Imād ad-Din and Baha' ad-Din.
Hamilton Gibb. Oxford: Oxford University Press, 1973. 76p.

This narrative of Saladin, based on the works of 'Imad al-Din and Baha' al-Din, offers a short account of his life. It traces the important stages of Saladin's life, but excludes all fiscal and administrative policies. It follows the main theme of the *History of the Crusades*, edited by K. Setton (Philadelphia: University of Pennsylvania Press, 1969. 2nd ed.), in the chapter entitled 'Saladin'.

180 The cities of Seleukid Syria.
John D. Grainger. Oxford: Clarendon Press, 1990. 253p. maps.

The Syrian land which Seleucus annexed in 301 BC is the setting for this study. In the years 300 to 298 BC, Seleucus ensured that Syria became the centre of the Seleucid dynasty. The author delineates the term Syria, according to the acquisitions of the Seleucid dynasty, and then investigates Seleucus' criteria for founding new cities. The Syrian city is central to this study, and the author assesses the applicability of central place theory to the Syrian experience. Grainger confines his sources to those within Syria, refuting the comparative approach with Greece, and focuses upon urban development within a specifically Syrian context.

181 **The Vizier and the Ra'is in Saljuk Syria: the struggle for urban self-representation.**
Axel Havemann. *International Journal of Middle East Studies*, vol. 21, no. 2 (May 1989), p. 233-42.

This paper analyses to what extent foreign officials and indigenous leaders of Damascus and Aleppo were willing to, or compelled to, share power with each other under Saljuq suzerainty. Havemann explains how the Saljuq dynasty initiated an institutional arrangement incorporating both Ra'is (leaders) and Vizier into political co-operation. Although the system was not foolproof, it did regulate indigenous resistance to Saljuq authority.

182 **Capital cities of Arab Islam.**
Philip Khuri Hitti. Minneapolis, Minnesota: University of Minnesota Press, 1973. 176p. maps. bibliog.

Reviews Arab history through the fortunes of leading cities. Chapter three (p. 61-84) is entitled 'Damascus: the imperial capital'. The author begins by outlining the early history of Damascus, which was the capital of the Aramean Kingdom in the 2nd millennium BC. From AD 661 to 750 Damascus was the leading city of the Muslim world under Mu'awiyah and the Umayyad dynasty. Damascus' period of great building came under the fifth caliph 'Abd al-Malik (685-705) and his son al-Walid (705-15). The rise of the 'Abbasids saw a long period of decline for Damascus which continued under the Syrian Hamdanid state, when Aleppo became the capital. However, under Nur al-Din and Salah al-Din (Saladin), Damascus enjoyed a brief renaissance, becoming the base for attacks on the Crusader Kingdom of Jerusalem.

183 **History of Syria including Lebanon and Palestine.**
Philip Khuri Hitti. London: Macmillan, 1951. 749p. maps.

A comprehensive chronological history of geographical Syria beginning from the prehistoric (Neolithic and Chalcolithic) period. The political and economic history of the ancient Semitic (Amorites, Canaanites, Arameans, Hebrews and Persians) and the subsequent Hellenistic period is described. Roman rule in Syria is also outlined, and the author discusses intellectual activity and the rise of Christianity, paying particular attention to the Arab era. He also deals with political and social conditions under the Umayyad and 'Abbasid caliphates, Syria's contribution to the Arab renaissance, the Ayyubid and Mamluk sultanates, and the impact of the Crusades. The final two chapters consider Syria under Ottoman Turkish rule, the Arab Revolt and the establishment of the French Mandate.

184 **The age of the Crusaders in the Near East from the eleventh century to 1517.**
P. M. Holt. London; New York: Longman, 1986. 250p. maps. bibliog.

Provides an important account of the political history of the eastern Mediterranean, including geographical Syria, from the eve of the first Crusade to the Ottoman conquest of 1516-17. The work focuses in particular on the progressive consolidation of the lands under the administration of a single Muslim government, the Mamluk sultanate, a movement that was stimulated by the presence of the Christian Frankish states on its periphery. The work is arranged chronologically, and examines the first Crusade (1095-99), the Frankish states and the Muslim response, the reign of Nur al-

Din and the rise of al-Zahir Baybars. Diplomatic and commercial relations and the administration of the Mamluk sultanate are also described.

185   **The memoirs of a Syrian prince Abu'l-Fida', Sultan of Hamah 672-723/1273-1331.**
Translated with introduction by P. M. Holt.   Wiesbaden, FRG: Steiner, 1983. 99p. map. (Freiberger Islamstudien Band IX).
Abu al-Fida' was the ruler of Hama from 1310 to 1331. His memoirs open the door to a contemporary history of the Mamluk sultanate, which he was in an excellent position to write about. He provides an eyewitness account of the last days of the overthrow of the Latin Kingdom of Jerusalem and of the hostilities against the Mongols and the Armenians. The memoirs also reflect his thoughts on other rulers of his period and the relations of the sultanate with its neighbours. Abu al-Fida''s reflections serve as an important primary source for the history of his era.

186   **A history of the Arab peoples.**
Albert Hourani.   London: Faber & Faber, 1991. 551p. bibliog.
Hourani's book is essential reading for all students studying the Middle East. It covers the Arab world from the 7th century until the mid-1980s. Hourani addresses a diverse number of issues, including the life of cities, the culture of the *'ulama*, the culture of courts and people, the Ottoman Empire, European power, the culture of imperialism, the end of empire, the climax of Arabism, and Arab disunity. Whilst the book is an excellent read, students favouring a clinical text book analysis may find it difficult to follow his undulating train of thought.

187   **From Saladin to the Mongols: the Ayyubids of Damascus, 1193-1260.**
R. Stephen Humphreys.   Albany, New York: State University of New York Press, 1977. 504p. maps. bibliog.
A comprehensive and detailed study of political and institutional change in the Ayyubid Empire between the death of Saladin and the arrival of the Mongol armies in Syria. The first chapter reviews the structure of politics during the reign of Saladin, emphasizing the personal nature of Saladin's authority and the lack of institutional machinery. The second chapter examines the origin and evolution of the Ayyubid confederation. Subsequent chapters present a chronological history of the Ayyubid Empire, concentrating on the crucial principality of Damascus. The author discusses the rise of al-'Adil, the reigns of al-Mu'azzam 'Isa and al-Ashraf Musa, the third civil war, and Damascus as an Egyptian province. The final chapter considers the development of centralized government under the last Ayyubid Sultan, al-Nasir Yusuf, and provides a clear account of the Mongol invasion of Syria.

188   **A'lām al-fikr fī Dimashq bayīn al-qarnayīn al-awal wa-al-thanī 'ashr lil-hijrah.** (Famous figures of thought in Damascus between the first and twelfth hijrah centuries.)
Ihsan bint Sa'id Khlusi.   Damascus: Dār Ya'rib, 1994. 451p. bibliog.
A biographical dictionary of historians, physicians, philologists and poets between the 1st and 12th centuries AH.

189   **Antioch: city and imperial administration in the later Roman Empire.**
J. H. G. W. Liebeschuetz.   Oxford: Oxford University Press, 1972.
302p. maps. bibliog.

A detailed history of Antioch, the best-known provincial city of Rome, based largely
upon the letters and speeches of the Antiochene orator Libanius (314-93), and
focusing on the 4th century. The author demonstrates how, following the restoration
of stability in the empire through the reforms of Diocletian and Constantine, the
municipal oligarchy at Antioch lost control of the city's government to the imperial
governors. He describes in detail the relationship between the governors and the civil
council, and the transformation of civic institutions during this period. The history
includes a chapter on the livelihood and class structure of the people of Antioch. The
concluding chapter deals briefly with developments in the 5th century, and in
particular with the reforms of Anastasius and Justinian.

190   **From Diocletian to the Arab conquest.**
J. H. G. W. Liebeschuetz.   Aldershot, England: Variorum, 1990.
499p. maps. bibliog.

A collection of papers presented by Liebeschuetz over the last thirty years. The
articles on Syria address the following issues: the Christianization of Syria and the
accompanying epigraphic evidence; the financial and administrative problems of
Antioch and the villages of northern Syria from the 4th to the 6th centuries; and the
military organization of Syria in the 6th century.

191   **Saladin: the politics of the Holy War.**
Malcolm C. Lyons, D. E. P. Jackson.   London; New York: Cambridge
University Press, 1982. 456p. maps. bibliog.

A comprehensive and detailed biography of Saladin which uses contemporary sources
and in particular extant diplomatic and private correspondence largely attributed to
Saladin's administrator, Qadi al-Fadil.

192   **L'administration d'Alep sous les mamluks circassiens (ixe/xv^e
siècles): le cas des Banū Saffāh.** (The administration of Aleppo under
the Circassine Mamluks [9th/15th centuries]: the case of Banu Saffah.)
Bernadette Martel-Thoumian.   In: *Alep et la Syrie du nord* (Aleppo
and northern Syria).   Edited by Viviane Fuglestad-Aumeunier.
Aix-en-Provence, France: EDISUD, 1991-94, p. 72-80. bibliog.
(La Revue du Monde Musulman et de la Méditerranée, no. 62).

The divisions of Saladin's empire, originally allocated amongst his children, remained
unchanged under Mamluk rule. Syria was divided into seven administrative units or
mamlakat, known also as *niyabat*, whose significance varied over time. These units
were Damascus, Aleppo, Hama, Tripoli, Safad, Gaza and Kerok. The military,
administrative and religious functions of the principal administrators are examined
briefly. The Banu Saffah are an example of a Shaf'i Muslim family of Aleppine origin.
This family was installed in the administration and judiciary. The author uses the
dictionary of al-Tabbakh *Islam an-nubala' bi-tarikh Halab xii/xix* (Islam of the
nobility in the history of Aleppo xii/xix) as a main source for the biographies of this
family. A genealogy of the Banu Saffah is presented on p. 77.

193 **The problem of Hellenistic Syria.**
Fergus Millar. In: *Hellenism in the East: the interaction of Greek and non-Greek civilizations from Syria to Central Asia after Alexander.* Edited by Amélie Kuhrt, Susan Sherwin-White. Berkeley, California; Los Angeles: University of California Press, 1987, p. 110-33.

Millar argues that, as is evident from the first book of Maccabees, Syria was dominated by war and political instability, a possible consequence of Hellenistic rule in Syria. Moreover, it illustrates the possibility of a communal historical consciousness and a national culture in the Syrian region. He raises the question of whether the various Aramaic-speaking areas of the Fertile Crescent should be seen as representing a single culture and, if so, one should not attempt to study one area in isolation. Millar concludes that understanding Hellenistic Syria is problematic, given the relative scarcity of direct and contemporary evidence of any non-Greek culture, either in the Achaemenid or the Hellenistic period itself.

194 **The Roman Near East: 31 BC-AD 337.**
Fergus Millar. London: Harvard University Press, 1993. Reprinted, 1994. 587p. maps. bibliog.

A social history of the region during the period 31 BC-AD 337. It makes use of valuable resources, especially inscriptions, to examine the political structures and languages of the region. The book is based on 'surviving' inscriptions in Greek, Latin, Aramaic and Arabic.

195 **An Ayyubid notable and his world: ibn al-'Adīm and Aleppo as portrayed in his biographical dictionary of people associated with the city.**
David Morray. Leiden, the Netherlands; New York; Cologne, Germany: Brill, 1994. 235p. bibliog. (Islamic History and Civilization, vol. 5).

Morray presents a detailed study of the literary works of ibn al-Adim, who was a writer, teacher, historian and statesman, during the 13th century. Ibn al-Adim's reputation emanated from his classic work, the *Bughyah*, a biographical dictionary of people connected to Aleppo. His work amounts to ten volumes, including 2,500 folios. Morray assesses aspects of the work, the author's world, the compilation and writing of the *Bughyah*, and the author himself.

196 **An Arab-Syrian gentleman and warrior in the period of the Crusades: memoirs of Usāmah ibn-Munqidh.**
Usamah ibn-Munqidh, translated and introduced by Philip Khuri Hitti. Princeton, New Jersey: Princeton University Press; London: I. B. Tauris, 1987. 265p. map.

This book is based on a photostatic reproduction of the original manuscript from the Escurial, held in the American Embassy in Madrid, of ibn-Munqidh's (1095-1188) memoirs (*Kitab al-i'tibar*). Hitti provides an essential commentary, and relays the problems encountered when translating this work and the life of ibn-Munqidh. A map of ibn-Munqidh's journeys is provided on p. 257.

197 **The expansion of the Muslims and mountain folk of Northern Syria, the Jarājima the Umayyad period.**
Keiko Ohta. *Orient* (Tokyo), vol. XXVII (1991), p. 74-93.
Ohta studies the indigenous Jarajima population of the Amanus mountains in northern Syria. Despite the commensurate withdrawal of the Byzantine army and the expansion of the Islamic Empire, the Jarajima population remained in their homeland. In order to investigate the social history of this area, known as Thughur during the early Islamic era, the author analyses the policies of the superpowers, and the role played by Jarajima during the Arab-Byzantine struggle. This article assesses the socio-political changes brought about by the Muslim conquests. A list of sources on Jarajima is provided p. 75-76. This is a commendable article for students of religion, history and anthropology.

198 **The history of Aleppo known as ad-durr al-muntakhab by ibn ash-Shihna.**
Keiko Ohta. Tokyo: Institute for the Study of Languages and Cultures of Asia and Africa (ILCAA), Tokyo University of Foreign Studies, 1990. 420p. bibliog. (Studia Culturae Islamicae, 40).
This history of Aleppo was written as a continuation of volume one of *al-A'laq al-khatira* by ibn Shaddad, which dealt with Aleppo and Jund Qinnasrin. Its central part is based on *al-A'laq al-khatira,* but the author has used other sources, including works by ibn al-Adim, ibn Khatib, Yaqut al-Hammawi, ibn al-Wardi and ibn 'Abd al-Haqq. The text is divided into three parts: quotations from other works; accounts by the author; and commentary.

199 **The harvest of Hellenism: a history of the Near East from Alexander the Great to the triumph of Christianity.**
F. E. Peters. London: Allen & Unwin, 1972. 800p. maps.
A major history of the Near East, including Syria, from the death of Alexander (323 BC) to the Principate of Theodosius (379-AD 95). The study includes a chapter on the Seleucid Empire, of which Syria was the heartland, describing its organization and administration. Major *poleis* (towns) founded during this period were Antioch, Apamea and Laodicea (Latakia). The book also deals with Roman intervention in Syria, the Sassanian invasion and Queen Zenobia's revolt.

200 **The Latin Kingdom of Jerusalem: European colonialism in the Middle Ages.**
Joshua Prawer. London: Weidenfeld & Nicolson, 1972. 587p. maps. bibliog.
In this analysis the early Crusades and the 12th-century Kingdom of Jerusalem, which included the Hauran and other parts of contemporary western Syria, are seen as a European colonial movement. The author examines in detail the establishment, government, economy and culture of the Crusader society.

201 **The ideological significance of the dār al-'adl in the medieval Islamic Orient.**
Nasser O. Rabbat. *International Journal of Middle East Studies*, vol. 27, no. 1 (February 1995), p. 3-28.
The author examines the Islamic institution of *dar al-'adl*, which first emerged in Damascus in ca. 1163. *Dar al-'adl* was a court, convened by the ruler, for reviewing and redressing the grievances of his subjects. After examining *dar al-'adl* in Damascus (p. 6-9), Aleppo (p. 9-10) and Cairo, Rabbat investigates why these institutions appeared only in these three cities. The author provides illustrations of the locations of *dar al-'adl* in the three cities. This article is useful to those interested in Islamic studies.

202 **La siège de Damas dans l'histoire et dans la légende.** (The siege of Damascus between history and legend.)
Jean Richard. In: *Cross cultural convergences in the crusader period: essays presented to Aryeh Grabois on his sixty-fifth birthday.* Edited by Michael Goodich, Sophia Menache, Sylvia Schein. New York: Peter Lang, 1995, p. 225-35.
Richard offers a historical analysis of the siege of Damascus in 1148 as it was portrayed in Syrian poems. More is written in the West about the siege of 1148, which lasted for two years to free André de Chauvigny. To the Syrians, the siege of 1148 remains an episode of exploitation by the Christian knights of their Muslim adversaries.

203 **Caravan cities.**
Michael I. Rostovtzeff, translated by D. Talbot Rice, T. Talbot Rice. Oxford: Oxford University Press, 1932. 232p. bibliog.
The author provides an historical survey of the caravan trade, focusing on the role of selected cities in Syria, Jordan and Palestine, which he visited in 1928. The ruins of two of these cities, Palmyra and Dura-Europos, are described in some detail (chapters four to six). The latter was a combined caravan station and frontier town while the former was the largest caravan centre in the Syrian desert during the Roman period.

204 **Baybars I of Egypt.**
Syedah Fatima Sadeque. Dacca, Pakistan; Oxford: Oxford University Press (Geoffrey Cumberlege), 1956. 379p.
Sadeque chronicles the reign of Baybars I, whom she considers to be the real founder of the Mamluk regime in Egypt. As a part of the Mamluk Empire, Syria receives particular attention throughout the book; the struggle for Damascus and Aleppo between Baybars and Hulagu is recounted on p. 38-54. The author consults three main sources: European chroniclers of the 13th-century Crusades; Persian writings on Mongol history; and Arab historians.

205 **Syria under Islam: empire on trial, 634-1097.**
Kamal S. Salibi.   Dalmar, New York: Caravan, 1977. 193p. maps.
bibliog.

Salibi presents a history of Bilad al-Sham (Greater Syria) during AD 634-1097,
together with genealogical charts. The main contribution of the study lies in its
examination of Syria as the crucible of the Muslim Empire. The development of
administration, demography and ethnicity within the Muslim Empire is also explored.
Clear and accessible coverage of the period under study is provided by the author,
who focuses on the attitude of the Orthodox community towards the French Mandate
in Beirut and Damascus. Whereas the Damascene community openly opposed the
Mandate, the Beirut Orthodox community was divided between resistance and
welcome. Mercantilism had created a new middle class in Beirut, whose immediate
interests were tied to the flourishing of a westward-looking community. The same
process was less intrusive in Damascene life, thus the two Orthodox communities
followed different paths of communal and national development.

206 **Crusaders and Muslims in twelfth-century Syria.**
Edited by Maya Shatzmiller.   Leiden, the Netherlands: Brill, 1993.
235p. bibliog. (The Medieval Mediterranean Peoples, Economies, and
Cultures, 400-1453, vol. 1).

This book comprises a collection of papers on the Crusades presented at a conference
at the University of Western Ontario in 1988. The essays explore a wide range of
issues connected to the Crusades, including historical and theological issues, and the
relationship between the Crusaders and the Muslims.

207 **Crusader warfare, 1097-1193.**
R. C. Smail, bibliographical introduction by Christopher Marshall.
Cambridge, England; New York; Melbourne: Cambridge University
Press, 1995. 2nd ed. 276p. maps. bibliog.

Whereas many historians of the art of war have focused on the battlefield, Smail shifts
the focus towards the political and social institutions of the Crusader states, thus
examining the integral role of warfare in Latin Syria.

208 **Palmyra and its empire: Zenobia's revolt against Rome.**
Richard Stoneman.   Ann Arbor, Michigan: The University of
Michigan Press, 1994. 246p. maps. bibliog.

Stoneman studies the history of Queen Zenobia and her revolt against the Roman
Empire in AD 272. He dismisses the more fictional approach, which has led many
writers to fantasize about Queen Zenobia's qualities, but instead grounds his work in
historical sources. A good bibliography is provided on the subject, with ancient
sources on p. 225-26 and secondary sources on p. 226-38. The author describes the
Syrian scene, covering different aspects of life, such as the taxation system and
religious life, during the 3rd century. Stoneman also examines Zenobia's portrayal in
modern literature (p. 197-200). A chronology is supplied on p. 201-05. Towards the
end of the book, there is a collection of plates of Zenobia and Palmyra.

209 **The conquest of 'Akka (690/1291), a comparative analysis of Christian and Muslim sources.**
Andreas d'Suoza. *The Muslim World*, vol. LXXX, no. 3-4 (July-October 1990), p. 234-50.
The author emphasizes the value of analysis and the use of comparative sources when researching history, using the fall of 'Akka (Acre) as a case-study. He consults two French sources, *Les gestes des Chiprois*, and *Chronique d'Amadi* by Gerard Montreal; and two Arabic sources, *Kitab al-mukhtasar fi akhbar al-bashar* (The abridged book in the news of people) by Abu al-Fida', and *Dhayl mir'at al-zaman* (Tail of the mirror of time) by Qutb al-Din al-Yunani. He also provides a chronological table of events related to the fall of Acre (p. 250). This is a well-written article with clear analysis and an affirmed hypothesis.

210 **Prospérité économique de la Syrie du nord à l'époque byzantine (IVᵉ-VIIᵉ s).** (Economic prosperity of north Syria in the Byzantine era [4th-7th centuries].)
Georges Tate. In: *Alep et la Syrie du nord* (Aleppo and northern Syria). Edited by Viviane Fuglestad-Aumeunier. Aix-en-Provence, France: EDISUD, 1991-94, p. 41-47. bibliog. (La Revue du Monde Musulman et de la Méditerranée, no. 62).
North Syria was one of the most urbanized regions in the Byzantine Empire during the 4th to 7th centuries. Tate investigates the reasons for north Syria's economic prosperity during this time.

211 **State and rural society in medieval Islam: sultans, muqta's and fallahun.**
Sato Tsugitaka. Leiden, the Netherlands: Brill, 1997. 337p. maps. bibliog. (Islamic History and Civilization Studies and Texts, vol. 17).
This book examines the *iqta'* system and its connection with urban and rural society. The *iqta'* system has been compared by scholars to European feudalism of the Middle Ages. It was introduced by Amir Mu'izz al-Dawla in the 10th century to provide revenue from land for his soldiers. This book charts its history, from its beginnings in Iraq to the middle of the Mamluk era in the 16th century in Syria and Egypt. The author uses primary sources in Arabic and Persian.

212 **Economic survey of Syria during the tenth and eleventh centuries.**
Muhsin D. Yusuf. Berlin: Klaus Schwarz Verlag, 1985. 312p. maps. bibliog. (Islamkündliche Untersuchungen, Band 114).
Based on Arabic chronicles and other contemporary writings of the 10th and 11th centuries, this detailed study examines economic change in geographical Syria during this period. The opening chapter sets the political context by demonstrating the diminishing political importance of Syria from the time of the 'Abbasid dynasty. At the end of the 11th century, Syria was divided into several small independent states. Subsequent chapters provide an account of the general economic situation and changes in the standard of living. Agriculture, land tenure, irrigation, crops and yields are discussed in detail. The author examines the considerable influence of political

authorities on agriculture, describes the agricultural revolution which took place during the Hamdanid period, and deals with the characteristics and expansion of the crafts and industrial sectors.

213 **The emirate of Aleppo, 1004-1094.**
Suhayl Zakkar. Beirut: Dar al-Amanah, 1971. 282p. map. bibliog.
A detailed history of 11th-century Aleppo. The author traces the growth and activities of the Mirdasid dynasty, founded by Salih Mirdas, after the fall of the Hamdanid dynasty and the imposition of direct Fatimid rule, which arose to fill the gap between the Byzantine, Fatimid and eastern powers. The Mirdasid dynasty ended with the Turcoman and Saljuq conquest.

214 **Damascus under the Mamluks.**
Nicola A. Ziadeh. Norman, Oklahoma: University of Oklahoma Press, 1964. 140p. maps.
A short, snappy and dynamic history of Damascus during the reign of the Mamluk dynasty. The chapters include an analysis of: the Damascus of Saladin and ibn Jubayr; European travellers in Damascus; Damascus and its suburbs; people and problems; and city administration and intellectual life. This work makes for excellent reading, but readers should not be discouraged by the Bram Stoker-esque title page.

Damas au VIIe/XIIIes: vie et structures religieuses dans une métropole islamique. (Damascus in the 7th/13th centuries: religious life and structures in an Islamic metropole.)
See item no. 424.

Ottoman (1517-1918)

215 **Problems in the Ottoman administration in Syria during the 16th and 17th centuries: the case of the sanjak of Sidon-Beirut.**
Abdul-Rahman Abu-Husayn. *International Journal of Middle East Studies*, vol. 24, no. 4 (November 1992), p. 665-75.
Despite the absorption of the former Mamluk-administered territory of Syria into its realm, the Ottoman Empire was unable to produce administrative stability within the sanjaq of Sidon-Beirut. The interminable struggle between the Druzes, especially under the leadership of the Ma'n chiefs of the Shuf mountains, and the Ottoman authorities is portrayed in an engaging and informative manner. The contradiction between policy and practice, exacerbated by the bureaucratic competition between Tripoli and Damascus, illuminates the complexities of administrating the Ottoman Empire.

216 **The establishment and dismantling of the province of Syria, 1865-1888.**
Butrus Abu-Manneh.   In: *Problems of the modern Middle East in historical perspective, essays in honour of Albert Hourani.*   Edited by John Spagnolo.   Reading, England: Ithaca Press, published for The Middle East Centre, St Antony's College, Oxford, 1992, p. 7-26. (St. Anthony's Middle East Monographs, no. 26).
This article reviews the history of the Ottoman province of Syria, which was created during the early *Tanzimat* years. Spagnolo examines the Ottoman Law of the Provinces, under which the Syrian province was established. He also studies the impact of its creation upon the relationship between Damascus and Lebanon, and between Porte and province in the later *Tanzimat* period.

217 **Nationalism and the Arabs.**
Aziz al-Azmeh.   *Arab Studies Quarterly*, vol. 17, no. 1 & 2 (winter/spring 1995), p. 1-17.
Originally presented as the 19th George Antonius Lecture at St Antony's College, Oxford, this is a highly engaging paper that challenges many of the prevailing characterizations of Arab nationalism. Arab nationalism, it is argued, is not an immediate political tool, nor is it messianic, rather, it is the creation of political organization. Moreover, Arab nationalism developed alongside Turkish nationalism as part of a universal trend of acculturization. Al-Azmeh refutes Antonius' notion that the Ottomans and the Arabs were unnatural allies, and questions the status of Arab-British relations.

218 **Village and city in Egypt and Syria: 1500-1914.**
Gabriel Baer.   In: *The Islamic Middle East 700-1900.*   Edited by A. L. Udovitch.   Princeton, New Jersey: Darwin Press, 1981, p. 595-652.
Describes the principal forms of urban-rural contact (economic, political-administrative, religious-cultural, population movement) in Syria under Ottoman rule, and compares these patterns with those in Egypt. Relations between Aleppo and Damascus and their agricultural hinterlands were stronger than those in Egypt but were spatially more limited. The author demonstrates that a variety of relations existed, which resulted from different socio-political structures.

219 **The Ottoman province of Damascus in the sixteenth century.**
Muhammad Adnan Bakhit, foreword by P. M. Holt.   Beirut: Librairie du Liban, 1982. 309p. bibliog.
The author's sources for this work are impressive and they include both Arabic and Turkish manuscripts. Bakhit has managed to construct a meticulous account of the administration of Damascus in the 16th century. In addition, he has illuminated the relations between the Ottomans and Damascus' notable families.

220 **Ottoman rule in Damascus.**
Karl K. Barbir.   Princeton, New Jersey: Princeton University Press,
1980. 216p. bibliog. (Princeton Studies in the Near East).
Based on Ottoman sources, this book demonstrates the central government's concern
with the problems of governing Syria during the 18th century. The author argues that
the prestigious 'Azm family and other Syrian officials were Ottoman by training and
aspiration, rather than Syrians taking advantage of a failing empire to establish an
independent state. The work describes the characteristics, functions and finances of
the Ottoman governorship of Damascus and its evolution during the 'Azm dynasty of
the 18th century. The author also discusses the efforts of the central government to
contain the growing influence of provincial groups such as the notables, *janissaries*
(Ottoman soldiers) and tribesmen. The operation of the pilgrimage is reviewed in
some detail, as the author believes it was central to Ottoman rule in Damascus.

221 **Wealth, privilege, and family structure: the 'akarīs of 18th century
Damascus according to the qāssm 'askarī inheritance records.**
Karl K. Barbir.   In: *The Syrian land in the 18th and the 19th century:
the common and the specific in the historical experience.*   Edited by
Thomas Philipp.   Stuttgart, Germany: Steiner, 1992, p. 179-95.
(Berliner Islamstudien, Band 5).
Barbir examines the function and structure of the *'askari qassam* court (p. 180-82). In
order to learn about family size, indebtedness, net worth, status and occupation, he
uses a statistical sample from an 18th-century inheritance register. He argues that the
distinction between the privileged, *'askari*, and the non-privileged, *ra'aya*, was not
just wealth but 'political privilege, exemption from extra-*shari'a* taxes, and access to
other sources of wealth and investment such as tax-farming and *waqf* management'.
The appendices include an inventory of movable property values, levels of
indebtedness, occupation and the status of members.

222 **Political factions in Aleppo, 1760-1826.**
Herbert L. Bodman.   Chapel Hill, North Carolina: University of North
Carolina Press, 1963. 160p. map. bibliog. (James Sprunt Studies in
History and Political Science, vol. 45).
An important and detailed study of political structure in the province of Aleppo before
the era of reform and the abolition of the *janissary* corps in 1826. The author identifies
the factors affecting the control of the *wali* (governor) over the province and describes
the composition and function of Ottoman officialdom in Aleppo. Using French and
British consular records, Bodman discusses the struggle for power between the two
main political factions, the *janissaries* and the *ashraf* (descendants of the Prophet).

223 **Report on the commercial statistics of Syria.**
John Bowring.   London: W. Cloves for H. M. Stationery Office, 1840.
Reprinted, New York: Arno Press, 1973. 144p.
An elaborate report by Sir John Bowring addressed to H. M.'s Principal Secretary of
State for Foreign Affairs, Lord Palmerston. It offers a wide range of statistics,
including figures on population, economy, industry, trade and Syria's commercial
relations. The appendices include consul reports from Beirut, Damascus and Aleppo.

224 **Consciences syriennes et representations cartographiques à la fin du XIXe siècle et au debut du XXe siècle.** (Consciousness of Syrians and cartographic representations at the end of the 19th century and the beginning of the 20th century.)
Dominique Chevallier. In: *The Syrian land in the 18th and the 19th century: the common and the specific in the historical experience.* Edited by Thomas Philipp. Stuttgart, Germany: Steiner, 1992, p. 1-10. maps. (Berliner Islamstudien, Band 5).
Chevallier charts the rise of Syrian consciousness towards the end of the 19th century. The author draws two distinct maps of Syria: one conceived by the French (p. 7); and the other perceived by the Syrian nation (p. 8).

225 **Two histories of Syria and the demise of Syrian patriotism.**
Youssef M. Choueiri. *Middle Eastern Studies*, vol. 23, no. 4 (October 1987), p. 496-511.
The histories of Ilyas Matar and Jurji Yanni (an Orthodox Christian of Greek origin) are reviewed by Choueiri, with particular reference to the emergence of Syrian patriotism. The concept of a Syrian national identity gained wide currency during the Turkish revolution of 1908 and the ensuing reforms. Ilyas Matar was one of the first Western-educated Syrians to attempt to write his country's history according to the rudiments of European scholarship. His conception of Syria, as a distinct entity, focused primarily upon a geographical definition stretching from the Euphrates and the Syrian desert in the east to the Mediterranean Sea in the west, and from Asia minor in the north to the Sinai peninsula in the south. Within their histories, both Matar and Yanni paid homage to Queen Zenobia and the resistance of the Palmyrene state to the Romans and the Parthians. It proved to be a critical conjuncture in Syrian history and the cradle of Syrian patriotism. For both authors, the history of Palmyra symbolized the self-assertion of Syria, and subtle overtures contained within Matar's work, clothed in sycophantic terms, were directed towards the Ottoman sultans. Syrian patriotism was weakened by the emergence of Arab nationalism, and has remained on the sidelines with the Syrian Social Nationalist Party (SSNP), whilst the Lebanese Christian population have based their identity on the fortunes of Phoenicia.

226 **Islamic reform, political and social changes in late Ottoman Syria.**
David Dean Commins. New York: Oxford University Press, 1990. 199p. bibliog.
This study approaches religious reform in 19th-century Damascus from the perspective of a social history of intellectuals, the experiences and outlooks of intellectual groups, and their complex interactions with the social, political and economic environment. In establishing a context for Islamic reform, Commins offers a description of the Damascene *'ulama's* place in society, and the stratification within the *'ulama* corps. In addition, he explores the relationship between the *salafis* and other reformist groups in Damascus, the Young Turks and Arabists. The social and political ties between the *salafi 'ulama* and the secularly educated Arabists receives close scrutiny due to the tension between Islam and nationalism, a recurring theme of 20th-century history in the Arab world.

227 **Social criticism and reformist ulema of Damascus.**
David Dean Commins. *Studia Islamica*, vol. LXXVIII (1994),
p. 169-80.

Commins analyses the criticism of social injustices by the reformist *'ulama* in the 19th
century. He examines, in particular, the works and personalities of Muhammad Said
al-Qasimi and his son Jamal al-Din.

228 **Les orthodoxes entre Beyrouth et Damas: une millet chrétienne
dans deux villes ottomanes.** (The orthodox between Beirut and
Damascus: a Christian confession in two Ottoman cities.)
May Davie. In: *State and society in Syria and Lebanon.* Edited by
Youssef M. Choueiri. Exeter, England: Exeter University Press,
1993; New York: St. Martin's Press, 1994, p. 32-45.

The author analyses the impact of economic change upon the Orthodox communities
of Beirut and Damascus at the end of the 19th century. Although both cities shared
similarities, in terms of institutions, culture, society and economy, their political and
economic evolution followed different paths. The opening of Beirut to world trade in
the middle of the 19th century encouraged rapid economic development.
Subsequently, this produced a divergence in the political orientation of the Orthodox
communities in Beirut and Damascus.

229 **Aleppo and Devonshire Square: English traders in the Levant in
the eighteenth century.**
Ralph Davis. London: Macmillan, 1967. 258p. map.

This work is based on the private records of individual merchants and correspondence
between the Levant Company and its merchants in the Levant. Particular attention is
paid to the Aleppo 'factory' (trading station), and a description of the cloth market and
silk trading is included.

230 **Taxation and agriculture in the district of Hama, 1800-1831.**
Dick Douwes, Norman N. Lewis. In: *The Syrian land in the 18th and
the 19th century: the common and the specific in the historical
experience.* Edited by Thomas Philipp. Stuttgart, Germany: Steiner,
1992, p. 261-84. maps. (Berliner Islamstudien, Band 5).

The authors survey the more prominent taxes, levied during the early 19th century, in
the district of Hama. Douwes and Lewis focus on the villagers of the plains, who
suffered from excessive taxation. They describe tax oppression and the ensuing
impoverishment of the peasantry and consider Salih Pasha's reforms of 1818, which
were designed to increase agricultural production.

231 **Damascene probate inventories of the 17th and 18th centuries:
some preliminary approaches and results.**
Colette Establet, Jean-Paul Pascual. *International Journal of Middle
East Studies*, vol. 24, no. 3 (August 1992), p. 373-93. maps.

The authors have produced a study of Damascus, based on probate inventories, which
gives an insight into daily Damascene life in the 17th and 18th centuries. The research

has utilized two registers from the religious courts of Damascus (*qisma 'arabiyya*), and reviews currencies, the price of gold and the rate of exchange.

232   **Censorship and freedom of expression in Ottoman Syria and Egypt.**
Caesar Farah.   In: *Nationalism in a non-national state: the dissolution of the Ottoman Empire.*   Edited by William W. Haddad, William C. Ochsenwald.   Columbus, Ohio: Ohio State University Press, 1977, p. 151-94.

Describes attempts during the later years of Ottoman rule to head off political disintegration by tightening control over the press. The first part of the chapter discusses the evolution of the press in Syria and Egypt during the 19th century. From its origins with Rizq Allah Hassun's short-lived newspaper, *Mi'at al-Ahwad* (1854), and Khalid al-Khuri's *Hadiqat al-Akhbar* (1858), the Syrian press had a strong political orientation. The first press rules were introduced in January 1856 to curb political sedition. The author examines the characteristics and mechanisms of press censorship, demonstrating its influence on the development of the Syrian press.

233   **Pilgrims and sultans: the hajj under the Ottomans, 1517-1683.**
Suraiya Faroqhi.   London; New York: I. B. Tauris, 1994. 244p. map. bibliog.

Faroqhi reviews *hajj* (pilgrimage) as a political and social phenomenon, during early Ottoman rule in the Hijaz (1517-1683). This study examines the caravan routes, the issue of security, and the finances of the holy cities, all within an economic and political context. The book reveals the experience of everyday life for those involved in the *hajj*.

234   **France and the Syrian crisis of 1860-61.**
Leila Tarazi Fawaz.   In: *Franco-Arab encounters: studies in memory of David C. Gordan.*   Edited by L. Carl Brown, Matthew S. Gordon. Beirut: American University of Beirut, 1996, p. 257-69.

This article analyses the French reaction to the Lebanese civil war of 1860. It was during the civil war that the French, for the first time, sent their troops to Ottoman Syria. Fawaz examines the period of their stay and the motives behind the expedition. She argues that the French did not achieve as much as they could have before they withdrew in 1861. Furthermore, she suggests that this was partly due to the inefficiency of the French Commander, General de Beaufort, and partly due to the superiority of the Ottoman diplomat, Fuad Pasha.

235   **An occasion for war: civil conflict in Lebanon and Damascus in 1860.**
Leila Tarazi Fawaz.   New York: I. B. Tauris, 1994. 302p. maps. bibliog.

Fawaz analyses the origins and the course of the civil conflicts in Damascus and Lebanon in 1860. She examines the affect of the political and social structures of the Christian and Druze communities upon the origins of the conflict, and the change in the local balance of power. In this light, the Ottoman and European responses are also considered.

236   **Trade practices in Aleppo in the middle of the eighteenth century: the case of a British merchant.**
Elena Frangakis-Syrett.   In: *Alep et la Syrie du nord* (Aleppo and northern Syria).   Edited by Viviane Fuglestad-Aumeunier.
Aix-en-Provence, France: EDISUD, 1991-94, p. 123-32.
(La Revue du Monde Musulman et de la Méditerranée, no. 62).

This article notes how British businessmen conducted business in Aleppo, during the 18th century, through a case-study of the economic activities of Colville Bridger, a factor (commercial agent) in Aleppo from 1754 to 1765. Bridger's activities were representative of European merchants in the Levant. The author analyses Bridger's correspondence to principals, associates, partners, correspondents and others with whom he shared a business interest, in order to gain insight into a British merchant's trading, informal banking and other monetary exchanges.

237   **The social origins of popular nationalism in Syria: evidence for a new framework.**
James L. Gelvin.   *International Journal of Middle East Studies*, vol. 26, no. 4 (November 1994), p. 645-61.

Gelvin highlights the limitation of the 'politics of notables' model in explaining the political sociability of the inhabitants of Syria in the late Ottoman period. He suggests that evidence from the post-Ottoman period indicates that, from the mid-19th century, a populist political sociability emerged in Syria alongside and/or in place of political sociability described by the 'politics of notables' model.

238   **Changing patterns of economic ties: the Syrian and Iraqi provinces in the 18th and 19th centuries.**
Gad G. Gilbar.   In: *The Syrian land in the 18th and the 19th century: the common and the specific in the historical experience.*   Edited by Thomas Philipp.   Stuttgart, Germany: Steiner, 1992, p. 55-67.
(Berliner Islamstudien, Band 5).

Gilbar examines the change in the pattern of trade between Syria and Iraq during the first centuries of Ottoman rule. The author also investigates the impact of the rail system upon social relations between the two provinces, with reference to the increase in the volume of trade and the role of the merchant class. Gilbar concludes that 'forces operating in favour of the division of the Fertile Crescent were not offset by economic and social factors'.

239   **Modern historiography in the Syrian region.**
Eduard Gombar, Archir Orientalini.   *Quarterly Journal of African and Asian Studies*, vol. 61, no. 4 (1993), p. 363-71.

This article examines the development of historiography from the 19th century to the 1990s in Syria, Lebanon and Jordan. It reviews the way in which historiography has developed from the traditional activity of Muslim and Christian religious scholars to the realm of modern secular universities.

240 **The Russian presence in Syria and Palestine, 1843-1914: church and politics in the Near East.**
Derek Hopwood.   Oxford: Clarendon Press; London: Oxford University Press, 1969. 232p. bibliog.
Hopwood examines the impact of the Russian presence upon the population of Syria and Palestine between 1843 and 1914. He examines Russia's religious interest in the region, and the emotional attachment felt by the population towards Russia. The study stresses the religious affiliation between Orthodox Russians and Orthodox Arabs and provides a valuable bibliography on p. 213-21 which includes Russian, other European and Arabic sources.

241 **The modern Middle East.**
Edited by Albert Hourani, Philip Shukry Khoury, Mary C. Wilson. London; New York: I. B. Tauris, 1993. 691p. maps.
This Middle East reader is designed to complement Parts III-V of Hourani's *A history of the Arab peoples* (London: Faber & Faber, 1991. 551p.). The editors have highlighted a range of themes and topics concerned with the changing politics, economy, society and intellectual climate of the Middle East during the previous two hundred years.

242 **Historical geography of Palestine, Transjordan and southern Syria in the late 16th century.**
Wolf-Dieter Hütteroth, Kamal Abdulfattah.   Erlangen, FRG: Palm & Enke, 1977. 225p. maps. bibliog.
Based on the Ottoman *daftar-i mufassal* (detailed registers) from the last Ottoman census in the Arab provinces (1596-97), this work presents a very detailed study of Ottoman organization, administration, fiscal units, bases of taxation, estimates of population size and settlement pattern in the late 16th century. The area covered includes the Hauran district, south of Damascus.

243 **Settlement desertion in the Gezira between the 16th and 19th century.**
Wolf-Dieter Hütteroth.   In: *The Syrian land in the 18th and the 19th century: the common and the specific in the historical experience.* Edited by Thomas Philipp.   Stuttgart, Germany: Steiner, 1992, p. 284-94. maps. bibliog. (Berliner Islamstudien, Band 5).
Hütteroth contemplates the desertion of upper Mesopotamia and questions whether it emanated from the demise of the Roman-Byzantine Empire or from the Mongol invasions. This article contains the results of research conducted by N. Gyünç and Hütteroth.

244 **Studies in Ottoman history and law.**
Colin Imber.   Istanbul: ISIS Press, 1996. 337p. (Analecta Isisiana XX).
Consists of a collection of Imber's papers from 1971 to 1994. The essays cover various topics concerning Ottoman history and law. Under Ottoman law, Imber addresses issues such as marriage, property and the status of orchards and fruit trees.

Other studies include research on the Dervishes, Shi'as and Christians of the Ottoman Empire, in addition to some essays on the Ottoman navy.

245 **Greater Syria under Ottoman constitutional rule: Ottomanism, Arabism, regionalism.**
Hasan Kayali. In: *The Syrian land in the 18th and the 19th century: the common and the specific in the historical experience.* Edited by Thomas Philipp. Stuttgart, Germany: Steiner, 1992, p. 27-41.
(Berliner Islamstudien, Band 5).
This article is based on a PhD dissertation by the author, entitled 'Arabs and Young Turks: Turkish-Arab relations in the second constitutional period of the Ottoman Empire, 1908-1918' (Harvard University, 1988). In this article Kayali examines Greater Syria during the constitutional period of the Ottoman Empire 'in the context of the region's links with political trends in Istanbul'. The impact of the *Tanzimat* reforms, which commenced in Syria during the 1860s, is explored in terms of a core-periphery issue. The author argues that the Syrian liberal opposition sought reform within a constitutional framework, but did not seek autonomy or independence. He also emphasizes the relevance of this period to the emergence of Arab nationalism.

246 **Arab nationalism in Syria: the formative years, 1908-1914.**
Rashid Khalidi. In: *Nationalism in a non-national state: the dissolution of the Ottoman Empire.* Edited by William W. Haddad, William C. Ochsenwald. Columbus, Ohio: Ohio State University Press, 1977, p. 207-38.
Examines the emergence in pre-war Syria of a movement for local reform, decentralization and resistance to the 'Turkifying' policies of the Committee of Union and Progress (CUP). The chapter discusses the controversy over efforts to impose Turkish as the sole official language in 1910 and the re-organization of Ottoman administration in 1909-10, which involved the dismissal of non-Turks. Khalidi examines in detail the leading role of Shukri al-Asali, the deputy for Damascus, in providing a focus for the growing popular, upper-class and parliamentary discontent against the CUP. Also considered is the growth of secret societies which promoted an Arab national identity.

247 **British policy towards Syria and Palestine, 1906-1914: a study of the antecedents of the Hussein-McMahon correspondence, the Sykes-Picot Agreement, and the Balfour Declaration.**
Rashid Khalidi. London: Ithaca Press, 1980. 412p. map. bibliog.
(St. Antony's Middle East Monographs, no. 11).
Khalidi argues that the decisions previously regarded as having been made under the pressures of wartime had already been anticipated in the years before 1914. The beginnings of partition can be seen in the Anglo-French railway agreements over Syria, 1909-10, which the author views as representing the end of Britain's claims to any determining interest in Syria.

248   **Ottomanism and Arabism in Syria before 1914: a reassessment.**
Rashid Khalidi.   In: *The origins of Arab nationalism.*   Edited by
Rashid Khalidi, Lisa Anderson, Muhammad Muslih, Reeva S. Simon.
New York: Columbia University Press, 1991, p. 50-69. bibliog.

This essay builds upon the argument of Dawn, Hanioglu and Kayali, who opine that a
re-evaluation of the balance between Ottomanism and Arabism prior to 1914 was
required. To address this shortcoming, Khalidi assesses the impact of the Committee
of Union and Progress' policies upon the rise of Arab nationalism. This is essential
reading for those interested in the growing debate over the origins of Arab
nationalism.

249   **Society and ideology in late Ottoman Syria: class, education,
profession and confession.**
Rashid Khalidi.   In: *Problems of the modern Middle East in historical
perspective, essays in honour of Albert Hourani.*   Edited by John
Spagnolo.   Reading, England: Ithaca Press, published for The Middle
East Centre, St Antony's College, Oxford, 1992, p. 119-31.
(St. Anthony's Middle East Monographs, no. 26).

In his study, Khalidi examines the relationship between the social structure of Bilad
al-Sham (Greater Syria) and the rise of Arab nationalism. He focuses upon the impact
of social origin, profession, education and the new trends in religious thought,
especially the *salafi* reformist ideology. Khalidi re-examines these issues in light of
more recent work conducted by C. Ernest Dawn, Philip Shukry Khoury and David
Dean Commins.

250   **Syrian political culture: a historical perspective.**
Philip Shukry Khoury.   In: *Syria: society, culture, and polity.*   Edited
by Richard Antoun, Donald Quataert.   Albany, New York: State
University of New York Press, 1991, p. 13-27. (SUNY Series in
Middle Eastern Studies).

Khoury's historical perspective depicts the role played by the notables of Syrian urban
life during the latter stages of the Ottoman Empire, the French Mandate period and the
early independence era. Although not a 'class for itself' until the end of Second World
War, Syria's notables, a group composed of the religious-mercantile establishment
and the *aghas*, enjoyed the critical role of intermediary between the Ottoman
governors and the local population. They played a similar part during the French
Mandate, attempting to balance the interests of the French and their local client
networks. However, this distinctive political culture lost its efficacy after the Second
World War, as patronage networks collapsed and the new classes, emerging from the
mobilized nationalist movement, seized the political initiative.

251   **Urban notables and Arab nationalism: the politics of Damascus,
1860-1920.**
Philip Shukry Khoury.   London: Cambridge University Press, 1983.
153p. maps. bibliog. (Cambridge Middle East Library).

This detailed study focuses on the social and political life of Ottoman Damascus, and
in particular on the notable families who were to play a disproportionate role in

promoting Arab nationalism before the First World War. The first half of the study describes the political configuration of Damascus in 1860 and explains the ways in which factors such as the development of private land-ownership, the modernization and centralization of the administration, and agrarian commercialization encouraged the emergence of a socially cohesive upper-class urban leadership. Local leaders, who lost office under the impact of the Young Turks' centralizing reforms and Turkification policies, seized upon Arabism as an ideological instrument to re-establish their political position. The final chapter examines political life under King Faysal's short-lived Arab government, emphasizing the continuity of factionalism between rural groups of urban notables.

252   **Ottoman land tenure and taxation in Syria.**
Bernard Lewis.   *Studia Islamica*, vol. 50 (1979), p. 109-24.

Based on Ottoman cadastral records (*defter-i-khaqnai*), the first part of this article describes the three categories of land tenure found in 16th- and 17th-century Syria. These categories were the classical Islamic forms of *'ushri* and *kharaji* and the Ottoman *miri*, state-owned land. The second part describes Ottoman tax classification, assessment and collection.

253   **Change in the position and role of the Syrian 'ulamā' in the 18th and 19th centuries.**
Moshe Ma'oz.   In: *The Syrian land in the 18th and the 19th century: the common and the specific in the historical experience.*   Edited by Thomas Philipp.   Stuttgart, Germany: Steiner, 1992, p. 109-22. (Berliner Islamstudien, Band 5).

Ma'oz examines the changing role of the senior *'ulama* in the Islamic centres of Syria-Palestine, Damascus and Jerusalem, during the 18th and 19th centuries. He notes how their role changed from religious-spiritual leaders, immersed in scholarship and piety, to that of a socio-economic interest group forming part of the political elite. Ma'oz suggests that they abused their religious positions and ignored their traditional roles, through wealth accumulation. However, some traditional *'ulama* did conform to expectations and this group opposed the anti-Islamic actions, especially the *Tanzimat*, and attempted to mobilize the support of the public. Ma'oz concludes that Arab-Islamism which 'possibly emanated from the anti-Ottoman Syrian *'ulama* contributed to the emergence of Islamic Arabism'.

254   **Ottoman reform in Syria and Palestine, 1840-1861: the impact of the Tanzimat on politics and society.**
Moshe Ma'oz.   London: Oxford University Press, 1968. 265p. map. bibliog.

A comprehensive analysis of the *Tanzimat* period of administrative and economic reform in the Ottoman Empire, focusing on its impact in Syria following the re-assertion of control after Egyptian rule. Ma'oz examines the impact of the reforms on the administration, on social and economic change and on the status of non-Muslim subjects. The work concludes with an examination of the causes and events of the 1860 Damascus massacres.

255 **Syrian urban politics in the Tanzimat period between 1840 and 1861.**
Moshe Ma'oz. *Bulletin of the School of Oriental and African Studies*,
vol. 29, no. 2 (1966), p. 277-301.
A major effect of the *Tanzimat* reforms was the transformation in the nature of
government in towns with the establishment of local councils (*majlis*). These were
dominated by the traditional leadership of the *'ulama*, the heads of provincial families
and large landowners. The powers of the *majlis* and its relations with the governor are
described. Although the *majlis* was supposed to assist the governor, in fact it acted as
a check on his authority. The article concludes with a case-study of Aleppo and
Antioch.

256 **The Middle East on the eve of modernity: Aleppo in the eighteenth
century.**
Abraham Marcus. New York; Oxford: Columbia University Press,
1989. 418p. maps. bibliog.
Lamenting the sometimes brief and inaccurate generalities about social and economic
life in the period prior to modernization, the author seeks to redress the balance with
this case-study of Aleppo. He asserts that a detailed historical sketch focusing on one
18th-century society can serve as a useful supplement to the more general texts. In
addition, this book is written to assist students lacking familiarity in the field of
Middle Eastern studies. Marcus has produced a suitable book for both the scholar and
the general reader alike. This is a well-researched work, which provides a
comprehensive study of Aleppine life in the 18th century.

257 **Privacy in eighteenth century Aleppo: the limits of cultural ideals.**
Abraham Marcus. *International Journal of Middle East Studies*,
vol. 18, no. 2 (May 1986), p. 165-84.
Using evidence from the court records of mid-18th-century Aleppo, this article
attempts to reconstruct the practices and attitudes of the townspeople in a variety of
social contexts, focusing in particular on physical privacy and the privacy of
information.

258 **The 1850 events in Aleppo: an aftershock of Syria's incorporation
into the capitalist world system.**
Bruce Masters. *International Journal of Middle East Studies*, vol. 22,
no. 1 (February 1990), p. 3-20.
Departing from earlier models, which dwelled on religious division and the power
play of the *janissaries* and the *ashraf*, Masters uses Wallerstein's world-system model
to explain the underlying causes of the 1850 riots in Aleppo. Moreover, Masters
attributes the underlying causes of the riots to three factors: a change in the
relationship between the state and the individual; economic and social dislocation
emanating from Ottoman-European ties; and the elevation of Christian fortunes due to
their privileged access to Europe. The result is an incisive and convincing hypothesis.

259 **The origins of Western economic dominance in the Middle East: mercantilism and the Islamic economy in Aleppo, 1600-1750.**
Bruce Masters. New York; London: New York University Press, 1988. 240p. maps. bibliog. (New York University Studies in Near Eastern Civilization, no. 12).

An analysis of the Aleppine economy between 1600 and 1750, when the city constituted a salient Middle Eastern trading centre. Based on his doctoral thesis, Masters examines the standard of living in Aleppo, thus providing a useful insight into the livelihoods of those residing in this 'entrepôt where East mingled with West'. Through his focus on Aleppo, Masters addresses the question of why the economies of the West surpassed those of the East. Rather than examining external factors, like the dependency theorists, Masters looks at the internal mechanisms of the Islamic economy. Unlike Western culture, where mercantilism stressed a rise in exports and decline in imports, the culture of the Middle East remained embedded in the Islamic economic tradition. By 1750, the Western conception of the world economy had prevailed. Masters argues that the case of Aleppo is synonymous with the failure of the Middle East to combat the economic challenges of the West. This study utilizes 'indigenous' records of trade in the Levant, and pays attention to the role of Aleppine merchants, their institutions and the complex relations between the West and the Sublime Porte. A good bibliography is provided on p. 227-36.

260 **Ottoman policies toward Syria in the 17th and 18th centuries.**
Bruce Masters. In: *The Syrian land in the 18th and the 19th century: the common and the specific in the historical experience.* Edited by Thomas Philipp. Stuttgart, Germany: Steiner, 1992, p. 11-26. (Berliner Islamstudien, Band 5).

Masters argues that there was no consistent, unified Ottoman policy toward Syria. Although the Porte appreciated the 'strategic location and commercial position' of Syria, most of its policies towards its provinces, such as the capitulations, were not specific to Syria, although Syria was undoubtedly affected by all these policies. Masters identifies Ottoman perceptions of Syria, and the impact of its inconsistent policies upon the Syrian economy.

261 **Power and society in Aleppo in the 18th and 19th centuries.**
Bruce Masters. In: *Alep et la Syrie du nord* (Aleppo and northern Syria). Edited by Viviane Fuglestad-Aumeunier. Aix-en-Provence, France: EDISUD, 1991-94, p. 151-58. bibliog. (La Revue du Monde Musulman et de la Méditerranée, no. 62).

Masters examines the upheavals in the Muslim empires of Asia during the 18th century. World system theorists attribute the upheavals to the change in relationship between these empires and the West. However, revisionist historians argue that Muslim states were beset with internal challenges that made European intervention possible. In this article, Masters assesses both arguments through a case-study of Aleppo.

262 **The sultan's entrepreneurs: the Avrupa Tuecaris and the Hayriye Tuecaris in Syria.**
Bruce Masters. *International Journal of Middle East Studies*, vol. 24, no. 4 (November 1992), p. 579-97.
The response of the Porte, in the first decade of the 19th century, to the proliferation of protégés, who enjoyed the privilege of the European powers, and the weakness of the Muslim commercial sector, was to establish the *Avurpa Tuccaris* and the *Hayriye Tuccaris*. The former incorporated a cadre of non-Muslim Ottoman merchants, whilst the latter sponsored Muslim merchants within the empire. Masters contrasts the impact of this system upon the economies of Aleppo and Damascus, and reveals a critical difference in their application and affect.

263 **The life of Midhat Pasha: a record of his services, political reforms, banishment and judicial murder.**
Ali Haydar Midhat. London: Murray, 1903. Reprinted, New York: Arno Press, 1973. 292p.
An account of the life and work of Turkish politician Midhat Pasha, based on his letters and other documents, written by his son. Midhat Pasha was governor of Bulgaria, but his hostility to Pan-Slavism caused the Russian ambassador at Constantinople to secure his transfer to Baghdad. He later became grand vizier and secured the promulgation of the first Turkish constitution. However, he was exiled by Sultan Abd al-Hamid II, and after being recalled as governor of Syria, Midhat was charged with the murder of Abd al-Aziz, imprisoned and strangled. This work includes two chapters on his period as Governor-General of Syria in 1878-80, outlining his administrative reforms and programme of economic regeneration.

264 **Shareholders and the state: representing the village in the late 19th land registers of the southern Hawrān.**
Martha Mundy. In: *The Syrian land in the 18th and the 19th century: the common and the specific in the historical experience.* Edited by Thomas Philipp. Stuttgart, Germany: Steiner, 1992, p. 217-38. (Berliner Islamstudien, Band 5).
Mundy examines the character of registration found in the late 19th-century land records, *yoklama defteri*, for the town of Irbid, and the centre of the *qada'* 'Ajlun (the court of 'Ajlun) of the sanjaq of the Hauran in the *vilayet* of Syria. The registers date from the late 1870s and 1880s, when *tapu* registration (a system of registering designed as a mediating tool between central administration and local landholders) was introduced to the areas of southern Hauran. The author focuses upon the fiscal relevance, found within the register, and its implications upon the social structures of village life.

265 Regional structure in the Ottoman economy: a sultanic
     memorandum of 1636 A.D. concerning the sources and uses of the
     tax-farm revenues of Anatolia and the coastal and northern
     portions of Syria.
     Rhoads Murphey.   Wiesbaden, FRG: Harrassowitz, 1987. 256p.
     (Near and Middle East Monographs New Series, no. 1).

The book analyses the *maliyeden müdemer* 7075 register (Register MM 7075) which
provides treasury information, such as the projected revenues from tax-farm units,
between June 1636 to April 1637. The author provides a useful statistical analysis
(p. 214-33), and a helpful glossary of technical terms (p. 243-56). A summary of the
register's contents is put into a form suitable for cross-regional (comparative)
analysis. The document is presented in Turkish as it appears in the Ottoman
documents in Istanbul, as well as in English (p. 6-211).

266 The Hijaz railroad.
     William C. Ochsenwald.   Charlottesville, Virginia: University Press
     of Virginia, 1980. 169p. maps. bibliog.

A detailed history of the Hijaz railway, which Ochsenwald regards as a final attempt
by the Ottomans to resist European control and influence. The construction of the
railway (from Damascus to Medina) is seen as a vital part of Sultan Abdulhamid II's
policy of extending Ottoman control over southern Syria and the Hijaz, where control
over the Holy Places would give increased status to the sultan. The work describes the
existing system of railways in Syria and discusses its competition with the French-
controlled Damas, Hama and the Prolongements (DHP) railway. The Franco-Ottoman
Agreement of 1905, to compensate the DHP for possible losses on its Damascus-
Muzeirib line, is also examined. Ochsenwald further details the problems of
construction (1900-08), together with the project's finances, operational history and
administration.

267 The vilayet of Syria, 1901-1914: a re-examination of diplomatic
     documents as sources.
     William C. Ochsenwald.   *The Middle East Journal*, vol. 22, no. 1
     (winter 1968), p. 73-87.

Examines the use of diplomatic correspondence as a basis for research into the
political history of the Middle East in the early 20th century. The work is mainly
concerned with the quarterly reports of the British Consul in Damascus for the years
1901-14, to illustrate types of material available.

268 The Middle East in the world economy 1800-1914.
     Roger Owen.   London: Methuen, 1981. 378p. maps. bibliog.

Following an introductory chapter on the Middle East economies in the period of so-
called 'decline', 1500-1800, the first half of the book focuses on the years 1800-50,
dealing in particular with the economic consequences of Ottoman reform and the
expansion of trade with Europe. The second half includes a discussion of the
economic and social tensions of the 1850s, and their effects on the Syrian provinces.
Owen also considers the Syrian economy in the last years of Ottoman rule, 1880-1914.

269 **Mourir à Alep au xviiie siècle.** (Death in Aleppo in the 18th century.)
Daniel Panzac. In: *Alep et la Syrie du nord* (Aleppo and northern
Syria). Edited by Viviane Fuglestad-Aumeunier. Aix-en-Provence,
France: EDISUD, 1991-94, p. 111-22. bibliog. (La Revue du Monde
Musulman et de la Méditerranée, no. 62).

The city of Aleppo endured a series of natural calamities during the 18th century,
especially between 1756 and 1762: a period of intense cold, 1756; interminable
drought, 1757-58; an earthquake, 1759; and an epidemic plague, 1761-62. The author
studies the impact of the plague upon Aleppo's demography, based upon reports of
local authors, including al-Khoury Boulos, Kanali, Muhammad Ragib al-Tabbakh, and
Kamel al-Gazzi, and on the correspondence of Aleppo's European consuls.

270 **Aspects de la vie matérielle à Damas à la fin du XVIIe siècle
d'après les inventaires après décès.** (Aspects of material life in
Damascus at the end of the 17th century according to death
inventories.)
Jean-Paul Pascual. In: *The Syrian land in the 18th and the 19th
century: the common and the specific in the historical experience.*
Edited by Thomas Philipp. Stuttgart, Germany: Steiner, 1992,
p. 165-78. (Berliner Islamstudien, Band 5).

Pascual studies an inventory from the registers of a Damascene religious court issued
in the latter half of the 17th century. The document reveals information pertaining to
the size, composition and consumption of the civilian population.

271 **Social structures and political power in Acre in the 18th century.**
Thomas Philipp. In: *The Syrian land in the 18th and the 19th
century: the common and the specific in the historical experience.*
Edited by Thomas Philipp. Stuttgart, Germany: Steiner, 1992,
p. 91-108. (Berliner Islamstudien, Band 5).

Philipp tries to understand how Acre's unique development in the 18th century
allowed for its socio-political deviation from tradition. This is a valuable article,
particularly in light of the paucity of information available on Acre. Philipp examines
the rise, prosperity and demise of Acre as a player in the world economy. His research
is based upon the work of local historians, eyewitness accounts, official reports,
French consular correspondence and European travellers' reports.

272 **The Syrian land in the 18th and the 19th century: the common and
the specific in the historical experience.**
Edited by Thomas Philipp. Stuttgart, Germany: Steiner, 1992. 353p.
maps. (Berliner Islamstudien, Band 5).

Offers an extensive academic study of Ottoman Syria in the 18th and 19th centuries.
The book is divided into four parts, covering: identity; elites and political power;
urban life and social structure; and rural life, agricultural production and land-
ownership. The book provides analysis and research based upon findings from
Ottoman registers.

273 **Syria and the Syrian land: the 19th century roots of the 20th century developments.**
Itamar Rabinovich. In: *The Syrian land in the 18th and the 19th century: the common and the specific in the historical experience.*
Edited by Thomas Philipp. Stuttgart, Germany: Steiner, 1992, p. 43-54. (Berliner Islamstudien, Band 5).

Rabinovich traces the differing evolutions of the conceptualization of Syria throughout the first half of the 20th century. The author argues that the evolution did not take place from the 19th to the 20th century, but from 'the Ottoman to the post-Ottoman period'. Rabinovich investigates the conflict over Syrian state identity and its relationship with Jordanian, Lebanese and Palestinian identity.

274 **Changes in the relationship between the Ottoman central administration and the Syrian provinces from the sixteenth to the eighteenth centuries.**
Abdul-Karim Rafeq. In: *Studies in eighteenth century Islamic history.* Edited by Thomas Naff, Roger Owen. Carbondale, Illinois: Southern Illinois University Press; London: Feffer & Simons, 1977, p. 53-73.

Discusses the important transition in the relationship between central government and the Syrian provinces in the 17th and 18th centuries. As the control of Ottoman central authority receded, autonomous tendencies increased, giving rise to local centres of power. Rafeq focuses in particular on the changing role of the *janissaries* and the 'Azm family in Damascus, who used their prestige to serve both provincial and central interests.

275 **City and countryside in a traditional setting: the case of Damascus in the first quarter of the eighteenth century.**
Abdul-Karim Rafeq. In: *The Syrian land in the 18th and the 19th century: the common and the specific in the historical experience.*
Edited by Thomas Philipp. Stuttgart, Germany: Steiner, 1992, p. 295-332. (Berliner Islamstudien, Band 5).

Rafeq examines the prevailing patterns relating to sales deeds, lease contracts, credit and money-lending in the Damascene countryside during the first quarter of the 18th century. The dominant social groups, who presided over the rural economy, are examined through a detailed study of Damascene court records. These include, in addition to the registers of the regular Damascene tribunals, the *qassam 'askari'* registers. Rafeq concludes from his research that the interplay of political, economic and social factors often affected the application of *shari'a* in the courts. Tables on property sales, prices, leases and rents are provided.

276 **The law-court registers of Damascus, with special reference to craft corporations during the first half of the 19th century.**
Abdul-Karim Rafeq.   In: *Les Arabes par leurs archives (XVIᵉ-XXᵉ siècles).* (The Arabs according to their archives [16th-20th centuries]). Edited by Jacques Berque, Dominique Chevallier.   Paris: Editions du CNRS, 1976, p. 141-62.
This survey of the law court registers of Damascus, which cover the period 1583 to 1886-87, describes the type of registers and materials available. Particular attention is paid to the early 19th-century registers as a source of material on the Damascus craft corporations.

277 **Le mahmal en route pour La Mecque.** (The mahmal on the way to Mecca.)
Abdul-Karim Rafeq, translated by Anne Déchanet.   In: *Damas: miroir brisé d'un orient arabe* (Damascus: broken mirror of an Arab Orient). Edited by Anne-Marie Bianquis, Elizabeth Picard.   Paris: Editions Autrement, 1993, p. 49-57. (Série Monde, H.S. no. 65).
After the conquest of Syria, the Ottoman sultan assumed the title of guardian of the holy places of Mecca and Medina. Two caravans were organized to travel to the Hijaz every year, one from Damascus and one from Egypt. In this informative and well-written chapter, Rafeq describes the Damascene pilgrimage caravan, its composition, transportation and military security en route to Mecca. He also describes the commercial activities associated with the pilgrimage.

278 **Ottoman historical research in Syria since 1946.**
Abdul-Karim Rafeq.   *Asian Research Trends: a Humanities and Social Science Review*, no. 2 (1992), p. 45-78. bibliog.
This article examines the writing of Ottoman history in post-independence Syria. Rafeq provides brief reviews of the main sources available, which include biographical dictionaries, chronicles, travel accounts, Islamic legal-treaties and judicial accounts.

279 **The social and economic structure of Bāb-al-Musallā (al-Midān), Damascus, 1825-1875.**
Abdul-Karim Rafeq.   In: *Arab civilization challenges and responses: studies in honor of Constantine K. Zurayk.* Edited by George N. Atiyeh, Ibrahim M. Oweiss.   Albany, New York: University Press of New York, 1988, p. 272-311. map.
This paper portrays one of the most famous neighbourhoods in Damascus, Bab al-Musalla, part of Midan al-Hasa. Due to its strategic location, Bab al-Musalla facilitated the Syrian pilgrimage to the Hijaz, and provisions and camels were sold from here to the pilgrims. The socio-economic structure of Bab al-Musalla and its degree of social integration are examined. Rafeq explains why the period 1825-75 was so significant and how the developments within the Arab world and the Ottoman Empire irrevocably affected the socio-economics of Bab al-Musalla.

280 **Social groups, identity and loyalty, and historical writing in Ottoman and post-Ottoman Syria.**
Abdul-Karim Rafeq. In: *Les arabes et l'histoire créatrice* (The Arabs and creative history). Edited by Abdul-Karim Rafeq, Dominique Chevallier. Paris: Press de l'Université de Paris, Sorbonne, 1995, p. 79-93.
Rafeq explores the relationship between the Syrians and the Ottomans through the recording of history during Ottoman times and the post-independence period. He divides his study into three parts: Arab identity and Ottoman rule; the impact of Europe since the 19th century; and Arab historiography during independence.

281 **Syrian historical studies on Syria.**
Abdul-Karim Rafeq. *Middle East Studies Association Bulletin*, vol. 9, no. 3 (October 1975), p. 1-16.
A useful review of the style and content of historical writing by Syrians. Before the mid-20th century, this followed the traditional pattern of annals, biographical notes and general histories. Typical of this period are the biographical dictionaries of Muhammad Jamil al-Shatti and 'Abd al-Razziq al-Bitar, and the histories of Muhammad Adib al-Hisnni and Muhammad Raghib al-Tabbakh. The 20th century has seen an increase in the writing of memoirs, for example by Ahmad Qaddri, 'Adil Arsalan, 'Abd al-Rahman Shahbandar, Hasan al-Halim, Khalid al-'Azm and Sati al-Husri. Since independence there has been a flood of works on the Syrian revolt against French rule, for example in the writing of Jamil al-'Alwani, Zafir al-Qasim, 'Abd al-Latif al-Yunus, 'Abd al-Rahman al-Kayali and others.

282 **Alep à l'époque Ottomane (xvie-xixe siècles).** (Aleppo in the Ottoman era [16th-19th centuries].)
André Raymond. In: *Alep et la Syrie du nord* (Aleppo and northern Syria). Edited by Viviane Fuglestad-Aumeunier. Aix-en-Provence, France: EDISUD, 1991-94, p. 93-109. maps. bibliog. (La Revue du Monde Musulman et de la Méditerranée, no. 62).
The Ottoman conquest of Syria is believed to have contributed to Aleppo's rise in importance. In this article, the author examines Aleppine architecture under Ottoman rule during the 16th century. In accounting for the decline of Aleppo in the 17th century, Raymond considers it to be a consequence of external and internal challenges to the Ottoman Empire. However, Aleppo was prosperous again in the 18th century, and its architecture reflects this change in fortune.

283 **Groupes sociaux et geographie urbaine à Alep au XVIIIe siècle.** (Social groups and urban geography in Aleppo during the 18th century.)
André Raymond. In: *The Syrian land in the 18th and the 19th century: the common and the specific in the historical experience.* Edited by Thomas Philipp. Stuttgart, Germany: Steiner, 1992, p. 147-63. maps. (Berliner Islamstudien, Band 5).
Raymond studies the composition of Aleppo's ethnic and social groups in the 18th century. He argues that understanding the social structure of the city during the

Ottoman period requires an intimate knowledge of the socio-ethnic distribution of its residents. Maronite Christians are examined on p. 153-56, and *janissaries* and *ashrafs* on p. 156-60. Raymond draws upon the works of J. Sauvaget, J. C. David, Heinz Gaube and Eugen Wirth, A. Abdel Nour and A. Marcus.

284 **Damascus merchants and trade in the transition to capitalism.**
James A. Reilly. *Annales Canadiennes d'Histoire* (Canadian Journal of History), vol. XXVII (April 1992), p. 1-27.

This article charts Syria's incorporation into the world economy during the 19th and 20th centuries. The author assesses its impact upon Damascus' merchant class and on regional trade. Amongst his sources, Reilly consults consular documents and travellers' reports, which add value to this study.

285 **From workshops to sweatshops: Damascus textiles and the world economy in the last Ottoman century.**
James A. Reilly. *Review Fernand Brandel Centre*, vol. XVI, no. 2 (spring 1993), p. 199-213.

Reilly assesses the way in which the integration of the Damascus textiles industry into the world economy, during the 19th century, affected the local economy. The author concludes that Damascene merchants were able to adapt to the demands of the capitalist system instead of being swallowed by it.

286 **Past and present in local histories of the Ottoman period from Syria and Lebanon.**
James A. Reilly. *Middle Eastern Studies*, vol. 35, no. 1 (January 1999), p. 45-65.

Whereas an Arab historiography of the Ottoman Empire reflects the values and concerns of the present, the nationalist paradigm of earlier generations saw little value or interest in the Ottoman Empire, except as a 'seed bed' for the development of nationalism. Reilly considers an Arab historiography of the Ottoman period through seven local histories.

287 **Properties around Damascus in the nineteenth century.**
James A. Reilly. *Arabica*, vol. XXXVII, no. 1 (March 1990), p. 91-114.

Using a sample from *shari'a* court registers, Reilly examines Damascene interest in rural properties during the 19th century. He divides rural property into three categories: landed, residential and commercial. He shows how the rural economy was sophisticated and developed institutions in order to meet the needs of urban centres.

288 **Property, status, and class in Ottoman Damascus: case studies from the nineteenth century.**
James A. Reilly. *Journal of the American Oriental Society*, vol. 112, no. 1 (January-March 1992), p. 9-21.

Using information from *shari'a* law court registers, Reilly examines the relationship between status group affiliation and property ownership in the four branches of Damascus' economy in the second half of the 19th century. These branches were:

grain wholesaling; primary food processing; spinning and weaving of textiles; and other services. Reilly asserts that the data suggests only a tenuous relationship between status group affiliation and economic activities. In other words, the social order of Damascus was in transition, moving from one based upon traditional prestige to one based on property ownership.

289 **Status groups and propertyholding in the Damascus hinterland, 1828-1880.**
James A. Reilly. *International Journal of Middle East Studies*, vol. 21, no. 4 (November 1989), p. 517-39.

Reilly assesses the impact of Ottoman integration into the world economy upon rural property-holding around the city of Damascus. Using *shari'a* court archives, he concludes that the economy of the Syrian interior was markedly less transformed than that of the coastal areas, and that the agricultural sector of the economy witnessed less disruption than the trade and craft sectors.

290 **Women in the economic life of late-Ottoman Damascus.**
James A. Reilly. *Arabica*, vol. XLII, no. 1 (March 1995), p. 79-106.

Reilly examines the conditions of women in Ottoman Damascus in the late 19th and early 20th centuries. In particular, he looks at their contribution to the economy, and assesses the challenges they faced. Reilly analyses women's relations to property, production and services, discussing property under three categories: residential, agricultural and commercial. The capitalist transformation of Damascus led to a decline in the general economic status of women, but it helped to consolidate the position of aristocratic women, who were able to challenge segregation.

291 **Moneylending and capital flows from Nablus, Damascus and Jerusalem to qadā' al-salt in the last decades of Ottoman rule.**
Eugene L. Rogan. In: *The Syrian land in the 18th and the 19th century: the common and the specific in the historical experience.* Edited by Thomas Philipp. Stuttgart, Germany: Steiner, 1992, p. 239-60. (Berliner Islamstudien, Band 5).

Rogan examines money-lending practices, which appear in the local Islamic court and Ottoman land registers, in order to gain a better understanding of the capital market and the effect of credit upon the local economy. He concludes that on the whole the practices engendered positive change, and encouraged trade, thus reviving the regional economy.

292 **Review of recent studies on the nomads (Yuruks) in the Ottoman Empire.**
Ilham Sahin. *Asian Research Trends: a Humanities and Social Science Review*, no. 7 (1997), p. 139-52. bibliog.

The Yuruks, or Turkmen, meaning nomads, were part of the Turks who migrated from Central Asia to Anatolia between the 11th and 13th centuries. Within Anatolia, they migrated according to the seasons. When Anatolia fell under Ottoman rule in the early 16th century, the Yuruks migrated to the Balkans. This article provides a useful review and bibliography of previous studies on the Yuruks. The author has divided the works into three categories: publications of archival documents; anthropological, sociological and folkloric studies; and historical studies. The bibliography lists historical studies conducted in the 20th century.

293 **The achievement of Midhat Pasha as governor of the province of Syria, 1878-1880.**
Najib E. Saliba. *International Journal of Middle East Studies*, vol. 9, no. 3 (August 1978), p. 307-23.

Midhat Pasha was appointed as governor of Syria in November 1878 at a time when the province had been suffering from years of neglect and was badly in need of administrative reform. Saliba describes in detail the elaborate reform programme drawn up by Midhat Pasha, which covered the civil service, finance, gendarmerie and police, and the tribunal system. His proposals were considerably diluted by the sultan, who remained suspicious of Midhat's role in the deposition of two previous sultans. Midhat was also handicapped by Ottoman over-centralization, his constant need to refer to Istanbul for approval, and his lack of control over the military. His failure to stem the Druze insurrection led to his first resignation, which was rejected in October 1879. He resigned again in May 1880 over the sultan's plan to reduce civil service salaries, which he believed would lead to more corruption.

294 **The Missionary Herald: reports from Ottoman Syria, 1819-1870.**
Edited by Kamal Salih, Yusuf K. Khoury. London: NABU, published for the Royal Institute for Inter-Faith Studies, Amman, Jordan, 1995.
5 vols. maps.

Scholars have long recognized the importance of Syria Mission Station reports as a prime source for 19th-century Ottoman Syria. These reports were sent from different cities, towns and villages of a land whose territory was ultimately to be divided between Lebanon, Syria, Jordan and Palestine. These reports were originally published in the *Missionaries Herald*, a journal first issued in 1805 as the official organ of the American Board of Commissioners for Foreign Missions (Boston). The authors of the reports were Protestant missionaries, mostly Presbyterians or Congregationalists, from the Near East. The volumes are supplemented with a chronology and a missionary list.

295 **Families in politics: Damascene factions and estates of the 18th and 19th centuries.**
Linda Schatkowski Schilcher, foreword by Albert Hourani.
Weisbaden, Germany; Stuttgart, Germany: Steiner, 1985. 248p. maps.

Schatkowski Schilcher offers a broad survey of Damascus during the last two centuries. Building on the systematic urban histories of Sauvaget, Lapidus and Abu Lughod, the author brings the following themes together: the relationships amongst the notables; and the relationship between the notables and the population. Schatkowski Schilcher shows how the domination of the 'Azm family led to the creation of a powerful and long-lived faction, closely linked to the Ottoman government. However, the impact of European economic expansion upon the local economy, and the ensuing Ottoman reforms, changed the local balance of power and produced a shift in family alliances and the rise of new factions. This work contributes to our knowledge of Syria's political, social and economic history.

296 **The famine of 1915-1918 in Greater Syria.**
Linda Schatkowski Schilcher. In: *Problems of the modern Middle East in historical perspective, essays in honour of Albert Hourani.* Edited by John Spagnolo. London: Ithaca Press, published for The Middle East Centre, St Antony's College, Oxford, 1992, p. 229-58. (St Anthony's Middle East Monographs, no. 26).

In this article the author provides a brief survey of the famine in Greater Syria during the First World War. She examines the causes and consequences of this famine, which took the lives of more than 500,000 people in Syria, and looks at the issue of culpability. She also considers the socio-economic effects of the famine and argues that the new forms of political allegiance in Greater Syria were rooted in this period.

297 **Violence in rural Syria in the 1880s and 1890s: state centralization, rural integration, and the world market.**
Linda Schatkowski Schilcher. In: *Peasants and politics in the modern Middle East.* Edited by Farhad Kazemi, John Waterbury. Miami, Florida: Florida International Press, 1991, p. 50-84.

Contemporary historians continue to 'unearth' rural histories in an attempt to understand the relationship between peasants and politics. The author investigates twenty years of events in the Hauran towards the end of the 19th century. She observes the geography and economy of the region, and argues that the region was irrevocably influenced by Syria's entry into the world economy.

298 **A'yān Dimashq fī al-qarn al-thālith 'ashr wa-nisf al-qarn al-rabi' 'ashr min 1201-1350 H.** (Notables of Damascus in the 13th century and first half of the 14th century from 1201-1350 AH.)
Muhammad Jamil al-Shatti, Muhammad Bahgat al-Bitar, introduced by 'Izz al-Din al-Badrawi al-Naggar. Damascus: Dār al-Bashā'ir, 1994. 3rd ed. 465p.

A biography of notables in Damascus. The author claims to shed light on the social, cultural, economic and political life in Syria and Damascus, but some of the biographies are very short and lacking in depth.

299 **French influence in Syria prior to World War One: the functional weakness of imperialism.**
John P. Spagnolo. *The Middle East Journal*, vol. 23, no. 1 (winter 1969), p. 45-62.

Traces French influence in geographical Syria prior to 1914. The study begins by outlining France's claims to the roles it had played in Syria from the period of the Crusades, and Ottoman capitulations (1535), to the establishment of its protectorate over the Catholics of the Ottoman Empire. It examines France's commercial links, such as its investment in the development of transport routes linking the coast with the interior in the 19th century (for example, Comte de Perthius' investment in Beirut's port and the Damascus-Aleppo railway). Spagnolo shows how French interests were subject to internal conflicts, not least the conflict over defending the territorial integrity of the Ottoman Empire and the need to prepare for Ottoman disintegration.

300   **Some Arabic manuscript sources on the Syrian crisis of 1860.**
Fritz Steppart.   In: *Les Arabes par leurs archives (XVIe-XXe siècles)*
(The Arabs according to their archives [16th-20th centuries]).   Edited
by Jacques Berque, Dominique Chevallier.   Paris: Editions du CNRS,
1976, p. 183-92.
Discusses the value of unpublished accounts by contemporary Arab observers of the
1860 Damascus massacres. Steppart reviews manuscripts by several Christians as well
as by two Sunni Muslims and a Druze. The accounts contain important factual and
graphic information.

301   **The press and the journalist as a vehicle in spreading national**
       ideas in Syria in the late Ottoman period.
Eliezer Tauber.   In: *Die welt des Islams, NS Band XXX.*   Leiden, the
Netherlands: Brill, 1990, p. 163-77.
This article examines the role of the press in promoting anti-Ottoman ideas. Tauber
provides a detailed coverage of Syrian newspapers, with an analytical reference to the
political orientation of each newspaper and their increasing role in promoting the
nationalist movement in Syria.

302   **Syrian and Iraqi nationalist attitudes to the Kemalist and**
       Bolshevik movements.
Eliezer Tauber.   *Middle Eastern Studies*, vol. 30, no. 4 (October
1994), p. 896-915.
Using British and French archival materials, memoirs and contemporary chronicles,
Tauber assesses the rumours attributed to Syrian-Iraqi-Kemalist and Bolshevik
collusion and unequivocally dismisses the idea of collusion. He notes that certain links
did exist between the Arab nationalist organizations and the Kemalists, but claims that
this owed its origins to the intersection of their common histories rather than
sympathies for postwar Turkey. The incompatibility of Bolshevism, Turkism and pan-
Arabism prevented any assimilation of interest being translated into action; however,
the prospect of such collusion fuelled the paranoia of some British officials in the War
Office and India Office.

303   **Ottoman political reform in the provinces: the Damascus Advisory**
       Council in 1844-45.
Elizabeth Thompson.   *International Journal of Middle East Studies*,
vol. 25, no. 3 (August 1993), p. 457-75.
Thompson has produced a useful paper that re-examines the early *Tanzimat* period,
and in so doing, uses the Damascus Advisory Council as an example to refute the
conventional views of centre-periphery relations. In addition, Hourani's emphasis on
the rivalry amongst personal networks, a feature of notable politics, is dismissed with
reference to the institutionalization of the local political process through the Council.
As the Council gained autonomy (see the Harfush affair, in which the historical duty
of the Damascus Council to oversee tax assessment and collection was expanded),
consensus and local interest replaced personal politics. Thompson lends her
hypothesis weight with a dynamic and engaging style.

304   **A modern history of Syria including Lebanon and Palestine.**
Abdul Latif Tibawi.   London: Macmillan, 1969. 441p. maps. bibliog.
The first part of this history discusses geographical Syria (modern-day Lebanon,
Palestine and Syria) under Ottoman rule, from the time of Ahmad Pasha's defence of
Acre against Napoleon in 1799 to the despotic rule of Abdulhamid and the rise of
Arab nationalism in the late 19th century. The anarchy which prevailed after the
French campaign and the death of Ahmad Pasha in 1804 is illustrated, together with
the military occupation of Syria by Muhammad 'Ali and the subsequent Egyptian rule
(1832-41). Part one concludes with a description of the *Tanzimat* reforms, the civil
disturbances of the late 1850s, and the 1860 massacres. Part two examines the
emergence of the modern Syrian Arab Republic from the Anglo-French pre-war
agreement, to the Arab Revolt and the brief period of independence under Faysal. The
struggle for independence from the French Mandate is covered in some detail,
including the 1925 insurrection, the 1936 Franco-Syrian Treaty and the French cession
of Alexandretta to Turkey. The work concludes with an examination of the political
instability of the 1950s and 1960s, the brief union with Egypt (1958-61) and the rise
of the Ba'th Party to power.

305   **In the house of the law: gender and Islamic law in Ottoman Syria
and Palestine.**
Judith E. Tucker.   Berkeley, California; Los Angeles; London:
University of California Press, 1998. 221p. bibliog.
Explores the ways in which the intellectuals and the general population of a particular
society and culture – in this case the urban milieu of Syria and Palestine in the 17th
and 18th centuries – posed questions about gender and devised answers that suited
their sense of tradition and need. Tucker seeks to understand how these particular
Muslim communities constructed a legal discourse on gender during a 'normal'
period. The author chooses to focus upon the legal process, partly due to practicality,
as it offers a rich body of sources. She reflects upon the status of contemporary
debates on gender and Islam.

306   **Mashāhid wa-ahdāth dimashqīyah fī muntasaf al-qarn al-tāsi'
'ashar, 1256-1277 H, 1840-1861 M.** (Damascene scenes and events in
the mid-19th century, 1256-1277 AH, AD 1840-1861.)
Muhammad Sa'id al-'Ustwani, edited by As'ad al-'Ustwani.
Damascus: As'ad al-'Ustwani, 1994. 272p. map.
The editor is the great-grandson of Sa'id al-'Ustwani, who was a judge in Damascus
during the mid-19th century. The book is based on a manuscript written by Sa'id al-
'Ustwani. The first part outlines the economic conditions and religious orientations of
the Ottoman Empire, and in particular Damascus, in the mid-1860s. It charts the
reforms implemented by the Ottomans and the significance of the Syrian province to
the empire. The events of the revolt of 1860 are also examined. In the second part, the
diaries of Sa'id al-'Ustwani, from 1840 to 1862 (1256-77 AH), are presented.

307 **Alep dans la première moitié du xixe siècle – un exemple de stabilité et de dynamique dans l'économie.** (Aleppo in the first half of the 19th century – an example of stability and dynamism in the economy.)
Eugen Wirth. In: *Alep et la Syrie du nord* (Aleppo and northern Syria). Edited by Viviane Fuglestad-Aumeunier. Aix-en-Provence, France: EDISUD, 1991-94, p. 133-49. maps. bibliog. (La Revue du Monde Musulman et de la Méditerranée, no. 62).
Wirth examines the economic history of Aleppo during the first half of the 19th century. The article is based upon the reports of European consuls.

308 **A history of the Levant Company.**
Alfred C. Wood. London: Cass, 1964. 2nd ed. 267p. bibliog.
A history of the Levant Company, which had a monopoly of trade between England and the Ottoman Empire, from its establishment in 1581 to its demise in 1825. The book includes a survey of the company's trading stations (or 'factories') in the Mediterranean, including the Aleppo factory which dealt primarily in cotton and which was by 1586 a regular seat of trade for the company. The book gives an account of life in the Levant factories, much of it dealing with Aleppo.

309 **Jamāl pāsha al-Safāh: dirāsah fī al-shakhsīyah wa-al-tārīkh.**
(Jamal Pasha al-Safah: a study of personality and history.)
Na'im al-Yafi. Latakia, Syria: Dār al-Hiwār, 1993. 175p. bibliog.
The author provides a portrait of Jamal Pasha al-Safah, one of the prominent leaders of the Committee of Union and Progress. Al-Safah is described as a tyrant and this tyranny is attributed to three factors: his character; the environment; and the support provided by his coterie. Al-Yafi examines al-Safah's collaboration with the Jews in establishing their national home in Palestine, and his role in the massacre of Armenians. Regrettably, the use of emotive and inflammatory language detracts from the gravity of this study.

310 **The making of the modern Near East: 1792-1923.**
Malcolm Yapp. London; New York: Longman, 1987. 404p. maps. bibliog.
Yapp provides a general outline of the Near East in terms of society, economy and politics in the 19th century. Each country of the Near East is treated separately, and the review of Syria falls into three sections: reform in the Near East, 1792-1880, p. 128-37; nationalism and revolution in the Near East, 1880-1914, p. 201-11; and the remaking of the Near East, 1918-23, p. 322-27. Yapp provides a bibliography on Syria on p. 364-65. This is a good introduction to the Near East and Syria.

A'lām al-fikr fī Dimashq bayīn al-qarnayīn al-awal wa-al-thanī 'ashr lil-hijrah. (Famous figures of thought in Damascus between the first and twelfth hijrah centuries.)
See item no. 188.

From Ottomanism to Arabism: essays on the origins of Arab nationalism.
See item no. 314.

The rise of Arabism in Syria.
See item no. 315.

Mudhakkirātī 'an al-thawrah al-'arabīyah al-kubrā: 1357 H, 1956 M.
(My memoirs about the great Arab revolution: 1357 AH, AD 1956.)
See item no. 326.

Ottoman populations 1830-1914, demographic and social characteristics.
See item no. 399.

The population of Ottoman Syria and Iraq, 1878-1914.
See item no. 400.

The population of Aleppo in the sixteenth and seventeenth centuries according to Ottoman census documents.
See item no. 402.

Emigration from Syria.
See item no. 403.

Religious reformers and Arabists in Damascus, 1885-1914.
See item no. 418.

The Druzes and the Maronites under the Turkish rule, from 1840 to 1860.
See item no. 457.

The Armenians: from genocide to resistance.
See item no. 462.

Armenians in the service of the Ottoman Empire, 1860-1908.
See item no. 464.

The Armenian communities in Syria under Ottoman dominion.
See item no. 466.

The Christian population of the province of Damascus in the 16th century.
See item no. 467.

Jewish-Christian relations in Aleppo as a background for the Jewish response to the events of October 1850.
See item no. 469.

The Orthodox-Catholic clash in Aleppo in 1818.
See item no. 471.

Communal conflicts in Ottoman Syria during the reform era: the role of political and economic factors.
See item no. 473.

La verité sur la Syrie. (The truth over Syria.)
See item no. 475.

The Damascene Jewish community in the latter decades of the eighteenth century: aspects of socio-economic life based on the register of the shari'ā courts.
See item no. 476.

Jews in late Ottoman Syria: external relations.
See item no. 479.

Jews in late Ottoman Syria: community, family and religion.
See item no. 480.

The Arab Revolt and the Arab Kingdom (1916-20)

311 **French overseas: the Great War and the climax of French imperial expansion.**
Christopher M. Andrew, A. S. Kanya-Forstner.   London: Thames & Hudson, 1981. 302p. maps. bibliog.

Examines the first phases of French overseas expansion (1914-24) which accompanied the First World War, the subsequent peace settlements, and France's pre-war and wartime imperial aims. The authors argue that French concern that its rivals were staking out spheres of influence in Syria began in around 1911 when Africa was being replaced by the Middle East as its central focus. Particularly important are chapters seven and eight, which provide a detailed analysis of France's postwar aims and the constraints of the Paris Peace Conference. The authors discuss the confrontation between Georges Clemenceau and David Lloyd George over the future of Syria, the King-Crane Commission and Faysal's role at the conference. They then argue that the resolution of the Syrian problem had less to do with the agitation of French colonialists than with Britain's increasing fear of over-stretching its imperial defences.

312 **French policy toward the Levant 1914-1918.**
F. W. Brecher.   *Middle Eastern Studies*, vol. 29, no. 4 (October 1993), p. 641-64.

This article closely examines the negotiations between Britain and France between 1914 and 1918. It charts the development of French policy towards the Levant, and pays particular attention to France's reserved approach to the Zionist programme. Brecher addresses a number of critical questions, such as what France knew of England's parallel negotiations with Sharif Hussein of Mecca, and how France responded to Britain's issuance of the Balfour Declaration. A short biography of Georges Picot is also offered as an addendum.

313 **Documents on British foreign policy, 1919-1939. First series, vol. XIII.**
Edited by Rohan Butler, J. P. Bury.   London: Her Majesty's Stationery Office, 1963. 747p.

Covers documents and correspondence on British policy in the Middle East between January 1920 and March 1921. Chapter two (p. 215-428) relates to British policy towards Saudi Arabia, Syria and Palestine in 1920, covering the policy issues which arose for Britain and France following the establishment of an independent Arab state in Syria under Faysal in March 1920. It also deals with events after Faysal's fall, and with the delimitation of the border between the French and British Mandate areas.

314 **From Ottomanism to Arabism: essays on the origins of Arab nationalism.**
C. Ernest Dawn.   Chicago; London: University of Illinois Press, 1973. 212p.

A collection of Dawn's essays that elaborate on the origins and progress of Arabism in Syria and discuss the pre-war nationalist movement. Dawn examines in particular the social and economic differences between the anti-Ottoman and the pro-Ottoman groups, casting light on the social determinants of the spread of Arabism. He concludes that neither the growth of Arabism, the Arab Revolt, nor the Turkish collapse brought about a major change in the Arab elite who ruled Syria. The work also contains a reprint of the author's article, 'The rise of Arabism in Syria' (see item no. 315).

315 **The rise of Arabism in Syria.**
C. Ernest Dawn.   *The Middle East Journal*, vol. 16, no. 2 (spring 1962), p. 145-68.

Discusses the formation and composition of the early secret societies that campaigned for decentralization within the Ottoman Empire, and examines the part played by the Syrian Arabists before and during the First World War. The development of the nationalist movement after the war is described with particular reference to the participants and their background. Dawn argues that the Arabists in Syria were those members of the elite who had no vested interest in the Ottoman state, and that following the collapse of the Ottoman Empire they were joined by the Ottomanist Arabs who were left with no alternative to Arabism. Appendices provide details of age, education, family, status and occupation for membership of the pre-1914 Arab movement and of the nationalist movement of 1919-20.

316 **Syria and Mesopotamia in British Middle Eastern policy in 1919.**
John Fisher.   *Middle Eastern Studies*, vol. 34, no. 2 (April 1998), p. 129-79. map.

Fisher provides a very detailed account of British policy formulation amongst the Foreign Office, War Office, and Prime Minister towards Syria and Mesopotamia in 1919. The main contention amongst policy advisers emanated from the Sykes-Picot Agreement of 1916. In the aftermath of the First World War, Britain was faced with irreconcilable promises and the rise of Arab nationalism. Syrian Arab resistance to the prospect of French tutelage held the potential of challenging British interests in Mesopotamia. British policy, therefore, revolved around the efficacy of the Sykes-Picot Agreement as a point of reference between Britain and France at the Paris Peace

Conference. Fisher identifies the main actors and describes the course of events that led to the granting of the Mandate system.

317   An American inquiry in the Middle East: the King-Crane Commission.
Harry N. Howard.   Beirut: Khayats, 1963. 369p. maps. bibliog.

An extremely detailed account of the origins, organization, investigations and recommendations of the American section of the Inter-allied Commission on Mandates. The so-called King-Crane Commission was appointed by President Woodrow Wilson to investigate the conflicting aspirations of the Allies and the Arabs at the Paris Peace Conference. The commission visited Syria and Palestine from 10 June to 21 July 1919, considered the political aspirations laid out by the Syrian Congress, and concluded that a French Mandate in Syria would be unacceptable. The commission also found that the majority of Arabs in Palestine wanted to be part of a united and independent Syria. The appendix reproduces the commission's recommendations.

318   The day of Maysalun: a page from the modern history of the Arabs.
Abu Khaldun Sati al-Husari, translated by Sidney Glazer.
Washington, DC: Middle East Institute, 1966. 187p.

A personal account, by a leading Arab participant, of the events which led to the defeat of the Syrians by General Henri Gouraud's French forces at Maysalun on 24 July 1920 and the occupation of Damascus. It was first published in Arabic in 1945. Al-Husari was a minister in the government, which remained in power until the Day of Maysalun. He was responsible for negotiating with Gouraud and accompanied King Faysal to Europe after the defeat. Appendices reproduce the main documents relating to the events of 1920.

319   An evaluation of the Arab government in Damascus, 1918-1920.
Khairia Kasmieh.   In: *State and society in Syria and Lebanon.*
Edited by Youssef M. Choueiri.   Exeter, England: Exeter University Press, 1993; New York: St. Martin's Press, 1994, p. 27-31.

The author examines the Arab government of 1918-20, which was established after the liberation of Damascus from the Ottoman Empire in 1918. Kasmieh explores the strengths and weaknesses of the government, and suggests that a combination of factors, external and domestic, contributed to its failure.

320   The capture of Damascus, 1 October 1918.
Elie Kedourie.   *Middle Eastern Studies*, vol. 1, no. 1 (October 1964), p. 66-83.

A criticism of T. E. Lawrence's account of the capture of Damascus in October 1918. Using the war diaries of the General Staff of the Australian Mounted Division, Kedouri argues that Damascus could not have been captured by the Sharifians, but that they were allowed to occupy it and claim its capture. This claim is seen as being instrumental in eroding the British position in Mesopotamia and in creating the complex postwar situation in Syria. The essay was reprinted in Kedouri's book, *The Chatham House version and other Middle Eastern studies* (p. 33-51).

321   **An awakening: the Arab campaign, 1917-18.**
      Sir Alec Seath Kirkbride.   London: University Press of Arabia, 1971.
      134p. map.

Kirkbride, who was attached to the Arab army and was actively involved in intelligence and sabotage work during the Arab campaign, provides a personal account of the Arab rebellion against the Turks during the First World War. The fall of Damascus and the subsequent problems faced by Amir Faysal in establishing an independent Arab administration are discussed.

322   **Lutfī al-Haffār (1885-1968): mudhakkarātuh, hayātuh wa-'sruh.**
      (Lutfi al-Haffar [1885-1968]: his memoirs, life, and time.)
      Salma al-Haffar al-Kuzbari.   London, Beirut: Riad el-Rayyes, 1997.
      455p. bibliog.

A personal account of the life of Lutfi al-Haffar, who succeeded Mardam Bey as Prime Minister, by his daughter. It covers the French Mandate, the response of the national resistance, and the Arab-Israeli wars of 1948 and 1967. Al-Kuzbari offers an insight into her father's attitude towards the Syrian-Egyptian union between 1958-61. Reproductions of handwritten memoirs and a collection of photographs are included.

323   **Seven pillars of wisdom.**
      Thomas Edward Lawrence.   London: Cape, 1935. Reprinted,
      Harmondsworth, England: Penguin, 1962. 700p. maps.

Lawrence's personal and controversial account of the Arab Revolt against Turkish rule has been highly criticized, but nevertheless its vivid descriptions ensure that it remains a classic of English prose. It narrates the Arab Revolt from its origins in the Hijaz through Faysal's campaigns in Transjordan to the fall of Damascus in 1918.

324   **Un roi arabe: Faysal, un espoir déçu.** (An Arab king: Faysal, a
      disappointed hope.)
      Nadime Méouchy.   In: *Damas: miroir brisé d'un orient arabe*
      (Damascus: broken mirror of an Arab Orient).   Edited by Anne-Marie
      Bianquis, Elizabeth Picard.   Paris: Editions Autrement, 1993,
      p. 70-79. (Série Monde, H.S. no. 65).

Recounts Faysal's brief rule of Damascus. Méouchy shows how Arab hopes were raised with the Arab Revolt and Faysal's capture of Damascus, and then crushed as Faysal's government collapsed. She concludes that the experience served to nourish the already mounting Arab resentment towards the French.

325   **T. E. Lawrence: an Arab view.**
      Sulayman Musa, translated by Albert Butros.   London; New York:
      Oxford University Press, 1966. 301p. bibliog.

An important study of the Lawrence legend from an Arab point of view. It examines the claims and contradictions of Lawrence's own account of the Arab Revolt against the Turks and his part in it. It also discusses events after the fall of Damascus, including the King-Crane Commission and the Paris Peace Conference. Musa concludes with an account of Lawrence's role and personality.

326 **Mudhakkirātī 'an al-thawrah al-'arabīyah al-kubrā: 1357 H,
1956 M.** (My memoirs about the great Arab revolution: 1357 AH,
AD 1956.)
Ahmad Qadri. Damascus: Wizārat al-Thaqāfah, 1993. 2nd ed. 289p.
(Qadāyā wa-Dawarāt al-Nahdah al-'Arabīyah).
A personal account of the Ottoman presence in Syria during the early 20th century.
The author examines Turkey's reasons for entering the First World War, Gamal
Pasha's rule in Syria and Faysal's government.

327 **Arabism, society, and economy in Syria, 1918-1920.**
Abdul-Karim Rafeq. In: *State and society in Syria and Lebanon.*
Edited by Youssef M. Choueiri. Exeter, England: Exeter University
Press, 1993; New York: St. Martin's Press, 1994, p. 1-26.
Rafeq explores the history of Arabism, and then assesses the origins of the Arab
nationalist movement in the 19th century. In doing so, he analyses Turkish-Arab
relations after four hundred years of occupation, and investigates the issue of Arab
loyalty under Ottoman rule. From an analysis of Syrian society, institutions and
economy during the first Arab government, he then scrutinizes the ensuing political
chaos that culminated in two major revolts under Faysal's governance. The conclusion
asserts that the political troubles under Faysal's rule owed their origins to the legacy
of the Ottoman era and the Anglo-French conspiracies against the 'dream' of an
independent Arab state.

328 **Syria from the Paris Peace Conference to the fall of Damascus.**
Abdul Latif Tibawi. *Islamic Quarterly*, vol. 1, no. 2 (June 1967),
p. 77-122.
An account of the political history of Syria during Faysal's brief rule in the two years
following the armistice. It outlines the resolutions of the Syrian Congress and
discusses the confrontation between Arab national aspirations and foreign ambitions.
The San Remo Peace Conference (1920) ignored the resolutions of the Syrian
Congress by imposing a French Mandate. Tibawi describes events from the arrival of
French troops under Gouraud until Faysal's departure from Syria.

329 **Ahmad Mrāywid: qā'id thawrat al-Jūlān wa-janūb Lūbnān
wa-sharq al-Urdun.** (Ahmad Mraywed [1886-1926]: leader of Golan,
South Lebanon and Transjordan revolution.)
Mahmud 'Ubaydat. Beirut, London: Riad el-Rayyes, 1997. 441p.
bibliog.
A subjective account of the life of Syrian nationalist Ahmad Mraywed and his struggle
against the Ottoman Empire and the Anglo-French occupation. The work includes: a
letter from Mraywed to Qay'id 'Ubaydat (p. 416); a document of the possessions of
the Mrayweds (p. 417); an invitation to one of the national committee meetings in
Damascus (p. 418); a page from the organization of the Supreme Committee (p. 419);
Faysal's objection to Gouraud's intervention in religious affairs in Lebanon (p. 420);
and a letter from Mraywed to Sheikh Kasib (p. 421).

330 **The Arab Bureau, British Policy in the Middle East 1916-1920.**
Bruce Westrate. Pennsylvania: The Pennsylvania State University
Press, University Park, 1992. 240p. bibliog.
The Arab Bureau, created in 1916, constituted the British intelligence office in Cairo,
and its staff included the legendary Lawrence of Arabia. Westrate examines the role
played by the Bureau in the formulation of Middle East policies, and assesses its
efficacy in serving imperial interests.

331 **The struggle for Arab independence: Western diplomacy and the
rise and fall of Faisal's Kingdom in Syria.**
Zeine N. Zeine. Beirut: Khayat, 1966. 2nd ed. 297p. bibliog.
Deals with the rise of Arab nationalism in Syria from the Arab Revolt to the
establishment of the French Mandate in 1920. Zeine considers the Sykes-Picot
Agreement, the 1919 Paris Peace Conference and the resulting postwar settlement in
the former Ottoman territories. Anglo-French rivalry at the Paris Peace Conference is
examined in detail, as is Faysal's rule in Syria and the French military campaign to
enforce the Mandate.

The Arabs.
See item no. 16.

Syria.
See item no. 18.

**Urban notables and Arab nationalism: the politics of Damascus, 1860-
1920.**
See item no. 251.

A modern history of Syria including Lebanon and Palestine.
See item no. 304.

The making of the modern Near East: 1792-1923.
See item no. 310.

Arab dissident movements, 1905-1955.
See item no. 342.

**France in Syria: the abolition of the Sharifian Government, April-July
1920.**
See item no. 348.

Rashid Rida.
See item no. 420.

Rashīd Ridā and Faysal's kingdom in Syria.
See item no. 430.

Rashīýd Ridā as pan-Arabist before World War I.
See item no. 431.

Rashīd Ridā's political attitudes during World War I.
See item no. 432.

French Mandate (1920-46)

332 **Safhah min al-ayām al-hamrā': mudhakarāt al-qā'id Sa'īd al-'ās 1889-1936.** (A page from the red days: memoirs of the leader Sa'id al-'Aas 1889-1936.)
Sa'id al-'Aas. Beirut: al-Mou'sasah al-'Arabīyah, 1988. 240p.

Contains the author's memoirs of the 1925 revolt. He highlights the roles played by notable figures during the uprising, noting their personal battles with the French. The book also includes the following articles: 'Thawrat Hama' (The revolt of Hama) by Fawzi al-Qaqujy (p. 9-17); 'Al-ijtimā' al-sirī al-awal li-'i'lan al-thawrah' (The first secret meeting for the declaration of the revolt) by Shahbandar (p. 27-30); and 'Gawāb sultan 'il ā Andrea' (The sultan's letter to Andrea) (p. 57-58).

333 **The formation of the Transjordan-Syria boundary, 1915-32.**
V. M. Amadouny. *Middle Eastern Studies*, vol. 31, no. 3 (July 1995), p. 533-49. maps.

As Amadouny discloses the negotiating positions of the British and the French over the delimitation and demarcation of the Transjordan-Syrian boundary, he gently asserts that the boundary itself contributed to the modernization of the cartographical knowledge of the region. The allocation of the boundary in 1920, and its demarcation in the summer of 1932, institutionalized the separate state system imposed by the mandate powers, led to the contraction of *bedu* mobility, and increased the pace of sedentarization.

334 **Thawrat al-hurrīyah fī al-mintakah al-sādisah bī-Dimashq 1925-1926, wādī Barādah wa-al-Muhajirīn wa-al-Sālhīyah bīqiyadat Sā'īd ibn 'Ukāsh.** (The freedom revolt in the sixth area in Damascus 1925-26, Barada Valley and the Muhajirin and Salhiya under the leadership of Sa'id ibn 'Ukash.)
'Adnan al-'Attar. Damascus: Dār Sa'd al-Dīn, 1991. 214p. map.

This work is based upon information from Sa'id ibn 'Ukash's son, Hassan, and participants in the revolt. In addition, evidence has been collected from 'Abd al-Mu'ti al-Madani, who had access to material from Arabs serving in the French army and who later joined the National Arab Syrian army in 1945. It addresses the underlying causes of the revolt and the origins of *awlad* 'Ukash (sons of 'Ukash). A list of participants in the revolt, including their city of origin and place of martyrdom, is provided (p. 19-22). In the appendix more documents are supplied, such as the birth certificate of Sa'id ibn 'Ukash's son, articles from Arabic periodicals, British documents registering the activities of the insurgents on their route from Damascus to Beirut, and the French suppression of news relaying their defeat.

335 **The Mandate system.**
Norman Bentwich. London; New York: Longmans, Green, 1930. 200p.

A general survey of the legal and administrative aspects of the postwar Mandate system. Bentwich discusses the origins, history and organization of each of the League of Nation's Mandates, including the French Mandate in Syria.

336 **L'insurrection syrienne contre le mandat.** (The Syrian insurrection against the Mandate.)
Lenka Bokova. In: *Damas: miroir brisé d'un orient arabe* (Damascus: broken mirror of an Arab Orient). Edited by Anne-Marie Bianquis, Elizabeth Picard. Paris: Editions Autrement, 1993, p. 80-86. (Série Monde, H.S. no. 65).

A review of the 1925 insurrection and its climax in Jabal al-Druze during the spring of 1927. The conflict between the guerrillas of Ghouta and the French forces produced a dynamic of its own. Bokova examines the conflict and the French response, and notes that whereas the Syrians referred to this episode as the 'great Syrian revolt' or the 'revolt of Sultan Al-Attrash', the French glossed over this era of armed conflict.

337 **The 1941 invasion of Syria and Lebanon: the role of the local paramilitary.**
N. E. Bou-Nacklie. *Middle Eastern Studies*, vol. 30, no. 3 (July 1994), p. 512-29. maps.

Bou-Nacklie provides an account of the Troupes Spéciales (Lebanese and Syrian soldiers who were recruited and commanded by French officers), during the invasion of Syria and Lebanon in 1941, and their response to the arrival of the allied forces. The ethnic tensions between the Druzes and the Tcherkess divisions of the Troupes, a consequence of colonial policy, further complicated the invasion. Desertions from the Vichy authorities to the Free French reinforced the socio-political cleavages within Syria and Lebanon. The author also provides a detailed description of the ensuing battle.

338 **The Avenantaires: Syrian mercenaries in French Africa.**
N. E. Bou-Nacklie. *Middle Eastern Studies*, vol. 27, no. 4 (October 1991), p. 654-67.

The author addresses the complicated issue of demobilizing the Avenantaires (who were administered together with the Troupes Spéciales) during the transition from French to Syrian rule. The ethnic composition of the Avenantaires exaggerated the status of minority groups within the Levant. The French used the Avenantaires as a check against Sunni-led nationalism, in order to undermine the security of minority groups in the post-colonial period. Hence, the French government instigated a repatriation programme aimed at settling mercenaries in its East and West colonies.

339 **Les Troupes Spéciales: religious and ethnic recruitment, 1916-46.**
N. E. Bou-Nacklie. *International Journal of Middle East Studies*, vol. 25, no. 4 (November 1993), p. 645-60.

Bou-Nacklie challenges the thesis of Longrigg and Beeri, who, among others, purport that French recruitment in Syria and Lebanon, during the Mandate period, was based on religious and ethnic discrimination. Bou-Nacklie argues that whilst the French employed a policy of 'divide and rule', it was only designed to serve French interests and not to promote discrimination.

340 **Tumult in Syria's Hama in 1925: the failure of a revolt.**
N. E. Bou-Nacklie. *Journal of Contemporary History*, vol. 33, no. 2
(April 1998), p. 273-89.
Bou-Nacklie studies the Hama revolt of 1925 and outlines the strategic and cultural
significance of Hama to Syria. After detailing the events of the revolt, the author
discusses its relevance as a 'prologue to the most important Syrian revolt', namely that
of Damascus. The article offers a clear picture of the revolt, the spontaneous
demonstrations and the struggle amongst the different sects of Hama. The Hama revolt
has received scant attention in English, and this article constitutes a welcome addition
to the subject.

341 **Beirut's role in the political economy of the French Mandate
1919-39.**
Marwan R. Buheiry. Oxford: Centre for Lebanese Studies, 1986. 22p.
(Papers on Lebanon, no. 4).
Buheiry's paper examines the development of Beirut as a regional centre for trade and
culture during the French Mandate. He also deals with the conflicting perceptions of
the city's economic prospects in the wake of the dramatic transformations in the map
of the Levant. Buheiry opines that whilst Beirut prospered on the whole, albeit in the
sectors of trade, real estate, communications and education, the rest of the country
received scant attention. He concludes that the price paid in national terms for the
modernization of Beirut, and its projection as a seductive advertisement for French
administrative achievement, may have been too high.

342 **Arab dissident movements, 1905-1955.**
Edited by A. L. P. Bundett. London: Archive Editions, 1996. 724p.
This work depicts the famous and infamous movements, as well as individuals, who
sought to destabilize the status quo. The material falls into four main chronological
sequences: anti-Ottoman agitation; anti-British, French and Italian movements (1919-
39); the First World War; and postwar agitation for self-determination. The sources
emanate from the Public Records Office in London. Among the sections related to
Syria are: 'Syria: call for self-government by the Syrian Central Committee at Paris,
1908' (p. 65-71); and 'Syria 1914: Revolutionary Arab Committee' (p. 293-301).

343 **A comparative view of French native policy in Morocco and Syria,
1912-25.**
Edmund Burke. *Middle Eastern Studies*, vol. 9, no. 2 (May 1973),
p. 175-86.
Burke traces in detail the origins of French native policy in Syria during the early
Mandate years, 1920-25. He argues that French policy in Syria was strongly marked
by the example of Louis Lyautey's administration of Morocco, 1912-25. Indeed,
General Henri Gouraud sought to model his policies on those of Lyautey, whom he
had served in Morocco, and he was followed in this by his successor, Maxime
Weygand. However, the paternalistic methods characteristic of Lyautey were ill-suited
to the realities of the politically sophisticated and strongly nationalistic Syrian people.

344   **The tariff of Syria 1919-1932.**
Norman Burns.   Beirut: American University of Beirut Press, 1933.
Reprinted, New York: AMS P, 1973. 317p. map. bibliog.
A detailed study of the customs and tariff system imposed in Syria during the French
Mandate. The Mandate declaration required Syria to accord a minimum tariff to all
member countries of the League of Nations but did not require them to extend
reciprocal treatment. The organization and administration of customs and the relations
with Turkey, Palestine, Egypt and Iraq are described. The effects of the tariff on the
growth of Syria's agriculture, industry and foreign trade are also examined. Burns
concludes that overall the tariff wall obstructed Syrian economic development. The
appendices are particularly valuable, providing detailed tabulations of Syria's foreign
trade by value and volume, and origin and destination for the period 1921-32.

345   **The photography of Kamil Chadirji: social life in the Middle East
1920-1940.**
Edited by Rifat Chadirji.   Surrey, England: LAAM, 1991. 83p.
This book consists of a collection of photographs of the Middle East, taken by
Chadirji between the 1920s and the 1940s. Chadirji was a member of the al-Ahali
group and became the Iraqi Minister of Economics and Transport in the 1930s. The
book also provides a biographical account of his life (1897-1968).

346   **Reflections on France, Lebanon, and the Syrian area.**
Dominique Chevallier.   In: *Franco-Arab encounters: studies in
memory of David C. Gordan.*   Edited by L. Carl Brown, Matthew S.
Gordan.   Beirut: American University of Beirut, 1996, p. 179-97.
This article provides a brief study of Syria and Lebanon's struggle for independence
in the early 20th century. Chevallier examines the role played by the French in the
Levant, and questions whether Syria and Lebanon were anything more than France's
creations.

347   **Conditions of work in Syria and Lebanon under the French
Mandate.**
International Labour Review, vol. 39, no. 4 (April 1939), p. 513-26.
Summarizes a French government study, undertaken in 1939, which compares the
level of employment, including hours of work, holiday entitlement and wages, in the
traditional and modern manufacturing industries of Syria. Comparisons are also made
with conditions in 1913, and the article describes the collapse of employment in
traditional industries, which were dominated by cotton and silk weaving, from
309,500 in 1913 to only 170,800 in 1937. The distribution of modern manufacturing
employment is also detailed, and the traditional guild organizations of Aleppo are
described. The work goes on to discuss the establishment of new occupational
associations, and makes recommendations for improvements in labour legislation.

348 **France in Syria: the abolition of the Sharifian Government, April-July 1920.**
Dan Eldar. *Middle Eastern Studies*, vol. 29, no. 3 (July 1993), p. 487-504.
Eldar analyses the difference between Gouraud and Faysal's conception of an independent Syria. Faysal thought of Syria as one nation sharing a common territory, history and aspirations, and not just as an area consisting of 'Arab speaking populations within Syrian territory'. Eldar also examines the circumstances that led to the abolition of the Sharifian government in 1920. The article is based on a thesis written at Tel Aviv University entitled 'French policy in the Levant and its attitude towards Arab nationalism and the Zionist movement, 1914-1920'.

349 **War, water and negotiation in the Middle East: the case of the Palestine-Syria border, 1916-1923.**
Adam Garfinkle. Tel Aviv: Tel Aviv University, The Moshe Dayan Center for Middle Eastern and African Studies, 1993. 156p. maps. bibliog.
A diplomatic account of the lengthy negotiations over the Palestine-Syria boundary. The French and the British commenced talks with the Sykes-Picot Agreement in 1916 and concluded with the signing of the Paulet-Newcombe line in 1923. Garfinkle pays close attention to a triad of interested parties, the French, British and Zionists; his analysis, however, rather obliquely omits any allusion to the Arabs. This rather strange omission detracts from an otherwise well-researched book.

350 **Laissez-faire, outward-orientation, and regional economic disintegration: a case study of the dissolution of the Syro-Lebanese customs union.**
Carolyn Gates. In: *State and society in Syria and Lebanon.* Edited by Youssef M. Choueiri. Exeter, England: Exeter University Press, 1993; New York: St. Martin's Press, 1994, p. 74-83.
Lebanon's laissez-faire trade policy during the 1940s stood in sharp contrast to Syria's protectionist trade policy, which ensured the dissolution of Syro-Lebanese economic integration. Lebanon's engagement with the economies of France, Britain and the United States contradicted Syria's policies of state intervention and Arab unity. The Lebanese commercial elite, seeking their own 'politico-economic' interests, preferred to opt for a divorce with Syria, thereby foregoing long-term economic gains. All efforts between 1945-50 which aimed at fostering economic integration between the two states failed with the collapse of the union in 1950.

351 **The Anglo-French clash in Lebanon and Syria, 1940-45.**
A. B. Gaunson. New York: St. Martin's, 1987. 233p.
In this engaging study, Gaunson assesses de Gaulle's belief that Britain could not resist the temptation to supplant its old rival in the Levant. The author attempts to recreate the events and personalities of the Levant affair, and uses new evidence to explain Britain's wartime presence in Lebanon and Syria.

352   **French policy in Syria and Zionism: proposal for a Zionist settlement.**
Yitzhak Gil-Har.   *Middle Eastern Studies*, vol. 30, no. 1 (January 1994), p. 155-65.

Gil Har's article focuses upon the *volte-face* in French policy towards Zionism in 1925. The competition for territory between Britain and France in the Levant had intensified the search for reliable proxies. According to the French, the Zionists, with their propensity for land acquisition, served British interests and posed a constant threat to the integrity of the French Mandate. French distrust of the Zionists, however, dissipated after the appointment of de Jouvenel as the High Commissioner of Syria in November 1925. Although implementing a policy of 'divide and rule', the French had failed to entice the Armenians, Assyrians and Kurds to settle in the eastern region of Jazira. The region bordered British Iraq and was sparsely populated, hence problematic to administer, and this encouraged the French to adopt a policy of settlement. Despite having the patronage of the British, the Zionists held the potential of extending French influence in Jazira. French policy was geared towards the settlement of Zionists in Syria's eastern provinces. The Zionists agreed in principle to the expansion of their homeland; however, their vision was to annex the territories of southern Syria, and in particular the Hauran region, bordering Palestine. Thus arose an incompatibility between French and Zionist interests.

353   **Comment la France s'est installée en Syrie (1918-1919).** (How France was installed in Syria, 1918-19.)
Comte R. de Gontaut-Biron.   Paris: Plon-Nourrit, 1922. 354p. maps.

By virtue of being close to the High Commissioner, Gontaut-Biron was able to offer an insider's account of French ambition in Syria. He opines that the installation of the French was achieved in two stages: the Anglo-French military occupation of October 1918-November 1919; and the expelling of the British military by the French. The author avers that there was nothing left of the Turkish administration and education systems, and whilst the British were unperturbed, the French sought to maximize their interests. Gontaut-Biron provides a copy of the Anglo-French-Russian accord of 19 February 1916 (in the appendix, p. 342-44), and the letters exchanged between M. Paul Cambon, the French Ambassador in London, and Sir Edward Grey, the British Minister of Foreign Affairs. This accord formed the basis of the French-British accord of 16 May 1916 (appendix, p. 344-48). This is a valuable study for those interested in the postwar negotiations and the Mandate era.

354   **The Hatay (sanjak of Alexandretta).**
Stephen Heald.   In: *Documents on international affairs, 1937.*
Edited by Stephen Heald.   London: Oxford University Press, 1939, p. 465-516.

A selection of documents relating to the status of the sanjaq of Alexandretta (Hatay) and the Franco-Turkish dispute. The documents include: extracts from the proceedings of the League of Nations Council of 1936 and 1937; the Statute of the Sanjak of 29 May 1937; the Fundamental Law of the Sanjak of 29 May 1937; and the Franco-Turkish Agreement of 29 May 1937.

355 **Treaty of Friendship and Alliance between France and Syria, September 9, 1936.**
Stephen Heald. In: *Documents on international affairs, 1937.* Edited by Stephen Heald. London: Oxford University Press, 1939, p. 445-58.
Contains details of the treaty which provided for the termination of the French Mandate after three years, subject to the acceptance of the League of Nations.

356 **Economic organization of Syria.**
Edited by Sa'id B. I. Himadeh. Beirut: American University of Beirut, 1936. Reprinted, New York: AMS, 1973. 466p. map. bibliog.
A valuable collection of essays covering various aspects of economic structure and conditions in Syria (including Lebanon) under the French Mandate. Particularly useful are the extensive statistical tables for the 1920s and early 1930s. Statistical appendices cover: imports and exports by commodity, destination and entry point; and government receipts and expenditures for the period 1927-32. The ten chapters cover the following themes: population; natural resources; land tenure; agriculture; industry; transport and communications; internal trade; foreign trade; the monetary and banking system; and the fiscal system.

357 **Monetary and banking system of Syria.**
Sa'id B. Himadeh. Beirut: American University of Beirut Press, 1935. Reprinted, New York: AMS Press, 1975. 386p. bibliog.
This book surveys the characteristics of the banking and currency system in Syria during the early years of the French Mandate. It begins by describing the local economic conditions and provides a history of the monetary and banking system prior to the Mandate. Himadeh describes the introduction of the franc exchange standard, and discusses the effects of fluctuations on the value of the franc to the Syrian pound. The book includes a discussion on the organization, administration and operations of commercial banks (including The Banque de Syrie et du Grand Liban) and financing institutions.

358 **Syria: a short history.**
Philip Khuri Hitti. London: Macmillan, 1959. 271p. maps.
A condensed version of Hitti's *History of Syria including Lebanon and Palestine* (London: Macmillan, 1951). The final chapter of the volume, dealing with the Arab Revolt and the establishment of the French Mandate, has been expanded into four chapters covering the following topics: the rise of nationalism; war and oppression; the French Mandate; and the independent republic.

359 **Syria and Lebanon: a political essay.**
Albert Hourani. London: Oxford University Press, 1968. 2nd ed. 402p. maps. bibliog.
First published in 1946, this detailed political history of Syria and Lebanon from the Arab Revolt to 1945 is still considered an important analysis of this formative period. The history is divided into three parts, dealing with: the period from the First World War to the peace settlement; the impact of Westernization and the growth of Arab nationalism; and the French Mandate and political history to the early 1940s. The

postscript covers the events of October 1943 to April 1945, examining the position at the time of the Allied occupation. Appendices reproduce the texts of some sixteen key documents including: the 1922 Mandate; the 1936 Treaty of Friendship and Alliance; the decrees relating to the autonomy of Jabal al-Druze, the 'Alawis and Jazira, 1939; the Franco-Turkish agreements on the sanjaq of Alexandretta, 1938, and its cession, 1939; General Henri Dentz's proclamation concerning the Syrian constitution, 1941; and General Catroux's proclamation, 1941.

360 **Le Grand-Liban et le projet de la confédération syrienne d'après des documents français.** (Greater Lebanon and the scheme of the Syrian federation according to French documents.)
Wajih Kawtharani.   In: *State and society in Syria and Lebanon*.
Edited by Youssef M. Choueiri.   Exeter, England: Exeter University Press, 1993; New York: St. Martin's Press, 1994, p. 46-61.

According to this chapter, the French conceived of a scheme to thwart the first Syrian state by considering utilizing the divisions amongst the Syrian population to weaken the appeal of the nationalist movement. The scheme, according to correspondence between General Gouraud and the French Ministry of Foreign Affairs, was designed to establish a government that would preserve the status of French interests in Syria. The article describes how France was awarded the Mandate, and how Syria and Lebanon were subsequently divided. It argues that the Lebanese Christians were reluctant to enter into a federation with Syria, as they believed that Lebanon was more developed than Syria; moreover, they were suspicious of the Sunni majority in Syria. The Lebanese Christians, therefore, agreed to establish Beirut as a strong French centre in the Middle East. This article is based on French documents; Kawtharani observes that these documents were not declarations, but rather expressions of French interest.

361 **Divided loyalties? Syria and the question of Palestine, 1919-39.**
Philip Shukry Khoury.   *Middle Eastern Studies*, vol. 21, no. 3 (July 1985), p. 324-48.

Examines Syria's involvement in the affairs of Palestine and the impact of the 1936-39 Palestinian revolt on Syria. Khoury highlights the contradictions facing the National Bloc government in Syria between its pan-Arab ideology and Syrian self-interest. The National Bloc leaders felt that support for the rebellion would alienate the British and jeopardize Syria's diplomatic efforts with France. They also feared that the revolt could lead to unrest in Syria itself, upsetting the political balance, and that it would pose economic problems for Syria.

362 **Factionalism among Syrian nationalists during the French Mandate.**
Philip Shukry Khoury.   *International Journal of Middle East Studies*, vol. 13, no. 4 (November 1981), p. 441-69.

Describes the origins and growth of factionalism among Syrian nationalist politicians in the early 1920s and demonstrates how this division weakened the Syrian independence movement. The collapse of the 1925 revolt led to the first rupture in the Syrian-Palestinian Congress and the division of the Syrian nationalist leadership into two opposing camps, the Lutfallah-Shahbandar and the Arslan-Istiqlaslist factions. The movement was isolated from parallel groups in Iraq and Palestine, and its leaders became embroiled in personal and ideological disputes, which were subsequently exploited by the French.

363 **A reinterpretation of the origins and aims of the Great Syrian Revolt, 1925-1927.**
Philip Shukry Khoury.   In: *Arab civilization challenges and responses: studies in honor of Constantine K. Zurayk.*   Edited by George N. Atiyeh, Ibrahim M. Oweiss.   Albany, New York: University Press of New York, 1988, p. 241-71.

Khoury argues that after the First World War, the political movements of protest and resistance were more broadly based and better organized, especially with the breakup of the Ottoman Empire and European partition of its Arab provinces into smaller administrative units. In this article, he analyses the origins and evolution of the Great Syrian Revolt, and reappraises the role played by the Druze leadership. Khoury observes that the role of the Druzes, who started the revolt, tends to be underestimated by historians.

364 **Syria and the French Mandate: the politics of Arab nationalism, 1920-1945.**
Philip Shukry Khoury.   London: I. B. Tauris, 1987. 698p. bibliog.

An in-depth history of Syrian politics between the two World Wars. The essence of Khoury's contribution lies in his description and analysis of the Arab nationalist movement in Syria. He focuses on the National Bloc, provides analyses of its major players, and offers a detailed study of the People's Party and the Syro-Palestinian Congress. Khoury has produced an essential work for all students of Middle Eastern studies.

365 **The Syrian independence movement and the growth of economic nationalism in Damascus.**
Philip Shukry Khoury.   *British Society for Middle Eastern Studies Bulletin*, vol. 14, no. 1 (1988), p. 25-36.

The conflict between Syrian nationalism and pan-Arabism is delicately brought out in this article. The National Bloc, founded in 1928, was the party of the comprador elite and commercial class. Under the leadership of al-Burudi, the party adopted a policy of economic nationalism as a means of liberating Syria. This policy comfortably accommodated the pan-Arab call for liberation; however, the conflict of interests between the National Bloc leadership and the population remained a latent force. This ambiguity of Syrian nationalism and pan-Arabism emerged during the Palestinian revolt of 1936-39, when the National Bloc discouraged the Palestinian leadership from endorsing the struggle. Syrian entrepreneurs lost a valuable market through the revolt, and al-Quwwatli (leader of the National Bloc and Syria's president during the 1930s) was reputed to have lost potential Jewish clients. Furthermore, Khoury assesses the contribution of the National Bloc towards eroding French economic power, and succinctly charts the demise of the National Bloc and the emergence of the more pan-Arab People's Party from Aleppo.

366 **Syrian urban politics in transition: the quarters of Damascus**
     during the French Mandate.
     Philip Shukry Khoury. In: *The modern Middle East.* Edited by
     Albert Hourani, Philip Shukry Khoury, Mary C. Wilson. London;
     New York: I. B. Tauris, 1993, p. 429-65. maps.

Khoury examines the impact of the French Mandate, during the inter-war years, upon
the political life of Damascus. In its capacity as the capital and centre of the national
independence struggle against the French, Damascus embodied, shaped and reflected
nearly all the major political trends of the period. However, the integration of the Middle
East into the world economy displaced traditional subsistence living with a national
market-oriented approach. Khoury concludes that the demands of national politics
forced the traditional style and methods of urban politics reluctantly to give way, as
personal support systems broke down. This article first appeared in *International
Journal of Middle East Studies*, vol. 16, no. 4 (November 1984), p. 507-40.

367 **Syria and Lebanon under French Mandate.**
     Stephen Hemsley Longrigg. London: Oxford University Press, 1958.
     404p. maps. bibliog.

A classic account of Syria and Lebanon's political history under the French Mandate.
As an introduction to French rule, the author outlines the history of the later Ottoman
period, the pre-war Anglo-French agreements and the Arab Revolt. Faysal's short-
lived Arab Kingdom and the subsequent occupation of Damascus by French troops in
1920 are also described. Longrigg provides a comprehensive chronological review of
the French administration, including the division of the country into separate states,
the suppression of the Druze rebellion (1925-26) and the constitutional developments
of the period 1928-35. The negotiation of the 1936 Franco-Syrian Treaty, with its
provisions for independence, and the cession of the Alexandretta sanjaq to Turkey in
1939, are also described in detail. The work concludes with an outline of Vichy rule
during the period 1940-41, the Anglo-French 'liberation' campaign and the transfer of
power from France to independent Syria in 1946. In addition to political
developments, the book also contains a chapter on the Syrian economy under French
rule. Appendices include the text of the July 1922 League of Nations Mandate for
Syria and Lebanon.

368 **Syria's quest for independence.**
     Salma Mardam Bey. Reading, England: Ithaca Press, 1994. 242p.
     bibliog. (Geographical Handbook Series).

This book was first published in Arabic in Lebanon. The author presents a narrative
political history of Syria during the Second World War and of its struggle for
independence. A brief history and outline of the country are provided. Although the
text appears to be subjective, it refers to original sources from Jamil Mardam Bey,
including an article entitled 'La Ligue Arabe' (The Arab League).

369 **Syria and the State Department, 1937-47.**
     James Melki. *Middle Eastern Studies*, vol. 33, no. 1 (January 1997),
     p. 92-106.

Melki offers an insight into US State Department policy towards Syria during the
1940s. He argues that the decision not to send a military mission to Syria was ill-

advised as it could have positively altered the course of the Arab-Israeli conflict. Melki further suggests that the first military coup of Za'im in 1949 could have been avoided.

370 **The Syrian revolt of 1925.**
Joyce Laverty Miller. *International Journal of Middle East Studies*, vol. 8, no. 4 (October 1977), p. 545-63.
Miller examines the origins of the 1925 revolt, which began in Jabal al-Druze, and describes the composition, activities and aims of the four main groups involved. These groups were: the Druze; *maouls* (outlaw bands); local notables in Hama and Homs; and loosely-knit nationalists centred in Damascus. Miller suggests that the wide geographical spread of incidents, combined with the claims of nationalist leaders such as 'Adil Arslan and Abdul Rahman Shahbandar, made it appear to be a nationalist revolt, but that in fact its disparate nature was its downfall.

371 **Surrīyah 1916-1946: al-tarīq ilā al-hurrīyah.** (Syria 1916-46: the path to freedom.)
Walid al-Mu'allim. Damascus: Tlasdar, 1987. 637p. bibliog.
Al-Mu'allim provides an historical account of Syria's path to freedom from 1916 to 1946. He deals with the correspondence between Sharif Hussein and the British, the Sykes-Picot Agreement, the French Mandate and Syrian resistance. The problem of Alexandretta is discussed in chapter nine (p. 299-321). The author provides documents, such as the Sykes-Picot Agreement, Faysal's speech in Damascus, and the report of the American commission submitted at the Paris Peace Conference, in the appendix (p. 443-620).

372 **Britain, Turkey and the Levant question during the Second World War.**
Yossi Olmert. *Middle Eastern Studies*, vol. 23, no. 4 (October 1987), p. 437-52.
France's capitulation in June 1940 aroused British concerns in the Levant. Syria, under the Vichy administration of Dentz, represented a threat to British interests in Transjordan, Iraq, Saudi Arabia and Palestine. The role of Turkey was deemed to be critical to the policy decisions being taken in the War Cabinet, as Turkey provided some strategic defence against the advancing German armies, but its territorial aspirations over northern Syria and Mosul complicated negotiations, in particular with regard to Arab sensitivities. Olmert's research is based upon evidence procured from Foreign Office documents that highlight the inter-departmental tensions between Turkish, French and Arab interests.

373 **A false dilemma? Syria and Lebanon's independence during the mandatory period.**
Yossi Olmert. *Middle Eastern Studies*, vol. 32, no. 3 (July 1996), p. 41-73.
This article traces the histories of Syria and Lebanon from the defeat of the French in May-June 1940 until the founding of the League of Arab States in May 1945. Against the backdrop of France's traditional interest in Lebanon and Britain's desire to maintain regional stability, Olmert analyses the inter-communal relationship between

the Syrian and Lebanese leaderships. In pursuit of their independence, both political entities stressed their distinct territorial integrity, and despite earlier demands, Syria's call for the inclusion of Lebanon in a Greater Syria was ultimately dropped as self-interest prevailed over pan-Arabism. The conclusion of the Alexandria Protocol, therefore, enshrined the status quo of the region and the territorial independence of Lebanon.

374 **The Christian Lebanese national movement and formation of Greater Lebanon 1920.**
Walid Phares. *Journal of South Asian and Middle Eastern Studies*, vol. XVI, no. 4 (summer 1993), p. 73-81. map.
This article covers the call of the Christian Lebanese National Movement to form Greater Lebanon after the First World War. The Christians asked the French to annex Akkar (in the north), Beqa' (in the west) and Jabal Amel (in the south), in addition to the city ports of Tripoli, Saida, Tyre and Beirut to Mount Lebanon. Running contrary to this was a demand for a smaller Lebanon; a Lebanon created away from the Syrian and the Muslim environment. Phares provides an account of both groups, including their arguments and philosophies.

375 **In search of Arab unity: 1930-1945.**
Yehoshua Porath. London; Totawa, New Jersey: Frank Cass, 1986. 376p. bibliog.
Porath has produced a coherent account of the search for Arab unity between 1930 and 1945. His research essentially relies upon British and Jewish archival material; he readily acknowledges the absence of Arabic sources and his dependence upon the memoirs of Arab statesmen. Porath's analysis draws upon the interaction of three factors: Arab attempts at unity; an Arab solution to the Palestine problem; and British policy towards these two factors. The description and analysis begins with Iraq, when it obtained formal independence in 1930, until the creation of the Arab League in 1945. Britain's policy towards Arab unity is closely scrutinized. Students of Middle Eastern history and politics will find this book to be factual, manageable and well-documented.

376 **Between nationalists and moderates: France and Syria in the 1930s.**
Itamar Rabinovich. In: *The Islamic world from classical to modern times: essays in honour of Bernard Lewis.* Edited by C. E. Bosworth, Charles Issawi, Roger Savory, A. L. Udovitch. Princeton, New Jersey: The Darwin Press, 1989, p. 801-19.
This article traces the tempestuous relationship between France and Syria during the period prior to independence. The parliamentary elections of 1931-32 and the issue of the Syrian presidency receive special attention.

377 **Syrie 1929, itinéraire d'un officier.** (Syria 1929, itinerary of an officer.)
Pierre Rondot. In: *Damas: miroir brisé d'un orient arabe* (Damascus: broken mirror of an Arab Orient). Edited by Anne-Marie Bianquis, Elizabeth Picard. Paris: Editions Autrement, 1993, p. 95-104. (Série Monde, H.S. no. 65).
This work is based on notes, written at the time, pertaining to the confrontation between the French and the nationalist Syrians. The author uses his experience and personal viewpoint to depict the political situation.

378 **Rasā'il.** (Letters.)
Antun Sa'adah. Beirut: Dār al-Fikr, 1989. 153p.
A collection of seventy-seven letters by Sa'adah written between 1934 and 1946. Sa'adah was a Syrian nationalist who was the founder and leader of the Syrian Nationalist Socialist Party.

379 **Europe leaves the Middle East, 1936-54.**
Howard M. Sachar. New York: Knopf, 1972. 687p.
Sachar discusses the growth of the Arab nationalist movement and describes the negotiations for a Franco-Syrian treaty (1936), in which a freely-negotiated contractual partnership between independent states would replace the Mandate. The cession of Alexandretta to Turkey is also examined. The Franco-British campaign against the Vichy French regime in Syria is described, together with Catroux's proclamation for Lebanese and Syrian independence (1941) and the subsequent political developments, including the Anglo-French crisis of 1945, which led to independence in 1946.

380 **Prelude to conflict: communal interdependence in the sanjak of Alexandretta, 1920-1936.**
Robert B. Satloff. *Middle Eastern Studies*, vol. 22, no. 2 (April 1986), p. 147-80.
In this robust piece of research, Satloff challenges the orthodoxy of existing historical studies that primarily focus upon the ethnic tensions within the sanjaq of Alexandretta and ignore the peaceful years between 1921 and 1936. The article explores two issues, one historical and the other historiographical. The historical section emphasizes the communal interdependence of the various Alexandrettan communities and the centripetal administrative framework that produced affluence across ethnic lines. Moreover, Satloff argues that it was a combination of foreign interference and the disruption of local elite power by an insurgent youth that broke the status quo, and not the ethnic divisions of the sanjaq. Historiographically, this article surveys the available sources, and criticizes the prevailing analyses as grounded in convention rather than inquiry.

381 **Coming to terms with failed revolutions: historiography in Syria, Germany and France.**
Birgit Schaebler. *Middle Eastern Studies*, vol. 35, no. 1 (January 1999), p. 17-44.
The author argues that the writing of history in Syria and Lebanon is problematic and that Syrian and Lebanese historians face the same problems as those recording German and French history. A comparative analysis of national histories, which pays particular attention to revolution, illustrates the degree of passion and controversy that often detracts from clarity, methodology and objectivity.

382 **French imperialism in the Middle East: the failure of policy in Syria and Lebanon, 1900-1914.**
William I. Shorrock. Madison, Wisconsin: University of Wisconsin Press, 1976. 214p. map. bibliog.
Discusses the origins of French involvement in Syria and Lebanon, and argues that the period 1901-14, rather than the war itself, was the crucial era for the establishment of the French claim to a special position in Syria and Lebanon, a claim later recognized by the Mandates Commission. French negotiations with Turkey and Germany, in 1913 and 1914, over the Ottoman loan and the Baghdad railway set aside the area as a French economic sphere of influence, consolidating its traditional role as protector of the Christian population. However, these negotiations also contributed to the Syrian population's growing suspicion of the French.

383 **Fulfillment of a mission: the Spears mission to Syria and Lebanon, 1941-1944.**
Edward Spears. London: Seeley; Hamden, Connecticut: Archon, 1977. 311p.
An account of Spears' mission to Syria and Lebanon between 1941 and 1944. Spears acted as Churchill's personal envoy to the French government. The book reveals the depth of Spears' disillusionment with France, and in particular with de Gaulle.

384 **The formation of modern Syria and Iraq.**
Eliezer Tauber. London, England; Portland, Oregon: Frank Cass, 1995. 417p. bibliog.
The complexities of Arab unity are addressed by Tauber who considers the formation of modern Syria and Iraq. Tauber's thesis rests upon the assumption that although political activists spoke of Arab unity, Syrianism and Lebanonism had deep roots originating in the second half of the 19th century. Furthermore, Tauber challenges the view that places the blame for the emergence of local movements on the shoulders of European imperialism. However, the mandatory regulations of Syria, Lebanon and Iraq ended the dream of establishing a greater Arab state, as separate national identities prevailed over the general Arab idea.

385 **The struggle for Dayr al-Zur: the determination of borders between Syria and Iraq.**
Eliezer Tauber. *International Journal of Middle East Studies*, vol. 23, no. 3 (August 1991), p. 361-85.
The paradox of the sanjaq Dayr al-Zur becoming an integral part of Syria, as a result of al-'Ahd al-Iraqi's policies, is examined in this piece of research. Whilst the border dispute between Syria and Iraq was under scrutiny at the Paris Peace Conference of 1919, the sanjaq of Dayr al-Zur, accordingly, was being fought over by the local tribes and supporters of Ramadan al-Shallash, a member of al-'Ahd al-Iraqi, and the British forces. Ironically, as al-Shallash captured Dayr al-Zur, it was awarded to Syria at the Paris Peace Conference, although inadequate communications between the British Civil Commissioner, Wilson, and the War Office, prolonged the battle. Despite the terms of the Anglo-French agreement, the struggle for securing the Syrian-Iraqi borders continued until the French conquered Syria in July 1920.

386 **The definitive settlement of the frontier between Iraq and Syria.**
Arnold J. Toynbee. In: *Survey of international affairs, 1934*. Edited by Arnold J. Toynbee. London: Oxford University Press, 1935, p. 301-04.
Describes the appointment of an independent commission in 1932 to report to the Permanent Mandate Commission on the problems of the Iraqi-Syrian frontier.

387 **The question of a constitution for Syria.**
Arnold J. Toynbee. In: *Survey of international affairs, 1930*. Edited by Arnold J. Toynbee. London: Oxford University Press, 1931, p. 304-13.
This work deals with the draft constitution drawn up by Syrian nationalists in the Constituent Assembly. The text put the French High Commissioner (Henri Ponsot) in a difficult position since five of the articles were irreconcilable with French obligations under the Mandate. The Assembly refused to revise the text and Ponsot dissolved the Assembly. In May 1930 Ponsot signed an *arrêt* which imposed a constitution on Syria.

388 **Le mandat français.** (The French Mandate.)
Christian Velud. In: *Damas: miroir brisé d'un orient arabe* (Damascus: broken mirror of an Arab Orient). Edited by Anne-Marie Bianquis, Elizabeth Picard. Paris: Editions Autrement, 1993, p. 87-94. (Série Monde, H.S. no. 65).
Velud examines the French administration of Syria during the Mandate. At first, the Syrians welcomed the arrival of Faysal, the British and the French as liberators. The author examines the resulting division of the country into the 'statelets' of Greater Lebanon, Aleppo and Damascus, the two autonomous territories, and its impact upon the Syrian population. The Syrian revolt of 1925 is examined, alongside Syrian disaffection with the French ruling over the issues of the Treaty of 1936, the sanjaq of Alexandretta, and the promises of independence.

389 'Creating phantoms': Zaki al-Arsuzi, the Alexandretta crisis, and
the formation of modern Arab nationalism in Syria.
Keith D. Watenpaugh. *International Journal of Middle East Studies*,
vol. 28, no. 3 (August 1996), p. 363-89.

According to the author, the contribution of al-Arsuzi, the ideological father of the
Ba'th Party, to the formation of modern Arab nationalism has been somewhat neglected
by Western academics. This piece of research, conducted in Damascus and Aleppo
between 1992 and 1993, attempts to compensate for this errant omission of scholarly
work. Watenpaugh asserts that al-Arsuzi's experience during the Alexandretta crisis of
1936-39 was fundamental to the formation of Syrian Arab nationalism. During this
period, al-Arsuzi recognized the significance of modern education, the media, and the
role of social clubs in cultivating a national self-consciousness. This experience was
translated into action in Alexandretta, culminating with the formation of the Ba'th Party
in 1940. Despite breaking his alliance with the other founders of the Ba'th Party,
Michel 'Aflaq and Salah al-Din Bitar, in 1943, al-Arsuzi continued to be a source of
ideological inspiration, and was coaxed out of retirement by the current Syrian
leadership in the 1960s.

The Arabs.
See item no. 16.

Syria.
See item no. 18.

A modern history of Syria including Lebanon and Palestine.
See item no. 304.

The making of the modern Near East: 1792-1923.
See item no. 310.

French policy toward the Levant 1914-1918.
See item no. 312.

Syria: development and monetary policy.
See item no. 390.

**Drūz Surrīyah wa-Lubnan fī 'ahd al-intidab al-firinsī, 1920-1943:
dirāsah fī tarīkhahum al-sīyasī.** (The Druzes of Syria and Lebanon in the
time of the French Mandate, 1920-43: a study in their political history.)
See item no. 455.

Failure of collaboration: Armenian refugees in Syria.
See item no. 465.

The Near East since the First World War: a history to 1995.
See item no. 563.

Independent Syria (1946-61)

390 Syria: development and monetary policy.
Edmund Y. Asfour. Cambridge, Massachusetts: Harvard University
Press, 1959. 158p. (Middle East Monographs, no. 1).
A monograph on Syria's monetary policy and its role in economic development. Part
one considers the structure of the Syrian economy in the 1950s and outlines the basic
economic problems. Part two presents a useful description of Syria's monetary and
banking system. Newly established institutions in the 1950s, such as the Currency and
Credit Board and the Central Bank, are described, and the monetary policy of the
French Mandate period is discussed. The final part of the monograph examines the
aims and characteristics of monetary policy in Syria since independence.

391 In search of 'historical correctiveness': the Ba'th party in Syria.
Ulrike Freitage. *Middle Eastern Studies*, vol. 35, no. 1 (January
1999), p. 1-16.
Freitage examines the attempts to revise and re-define Arab history, with particular
reference to the Ba'th Party. The author argues that these attempts highlight the
tension between an ideological and a scholarly approach to history. Research in
history, as in the other humanities, will always be deeply influenced by the
contemporary concerns of scholars, therefore the subject matter remains susceptible to
historical change.

392 The economic development of Syria.
International Bank for Reconstruction and Development. Baltimore,
Maryland: Johns Hopkins Press, 1955. 486p. maps.
The report of a mission organized by the International Bank for Reconstruction and
Development (IBRD), at the request of the government of Syria, to review Syria's
economic potential, and to submit recommendations for the formulation of a long-term
development programme. The report comprises a detailed sectoral review of the
economy and the outline of a five-year programme for social and economic
development. The mission recognized that the execution of the recommendations
would depend largely on the availability of foreign finance and the overcoming of
administrative difficulties.

**393 Economic integration in the United Arab Republic: a study in
resource development.**
Ragaei el-Mallakh. *Land Economics*, vol. 36, no. 3 (1960), p. 252-65.
El-Mallakh examines the economic aspects of the merger in 1958 between Syria and
Egypt, and looks at the economic developments in the two countries prior to the
union. The complementary and competitive elements of the two economies are
outlined. The study also assesses the prospects for economic development in the
United Arab Republic.

394 **Watan wa-'askar: qabla an tudfan al-haqīqah fī al-turāb: mudhakkirāt 28 aylūl 1961 – 8 ādhār 1963.** (A nation and soldiers: before the truth is buried in the dust, memoirs 28 April 1961-8 March 1963.)
Muti' al-Samman, introduced by Shakir Mustafa. Beirut: Baysān, 1995. 445p.

The author gives a personal account of the events that followed the failure of the Syrian-Egyptian union of 1958-61. As an officer in the army, he gained access to information relating to Syria's inner military zone. However, the memoirs lack chronological development, and this often distracts the reader from appreciating the value of the author's insights.

395 **The break-up of the United Arab Republic.**
Patrick Seale. *The World Today*, vol. 16, no. 7 (July 1960), p. 471-79.

Seale describes the army coup in Damascus of September 1961 and Syria's secession from the UAR. The motives for the coup are examined and the wider causes of the union's failure are explored. Particular emphasis is paid to the repressive rule of 'Abd al-Hamid Sarraj (Minister of the Interior, and Vice President of the UAR), and Nasser's reaction to the secession is also discussed.

396 **Syrian politics and the military, 1945-1958.**
Gordon H. Torrey. Columbus, Ohio: Ohio State University Press, 1964. 438p. maps. bibliog.

An informative, chronological study of Syrian political history in the period 1945-58 which emphasizes the role of the military. After an introduction covering Syria's political parties (Nationalist Bloc, Communist and Syrian Social Nationalist) prior to independence, Torrey discusses the era of parliamentary democracy (1945-49) and the successive coups of 1949 by Husni Za'im, Sami Hinnawi and Adib Shishakli. The increasing role of the military during the Shishakli regime and his eventual overthrow in March 1954 by Hisham Atasi are described. Torrey goes on to discuss post-Shishakli politics and the ascendancy of the left, placing particular emphasis on the Melki affair of April 1955. The work concludes with a discussion of Syria's reaction to the 1956 Suez crisis and the union with Egypt in 1958. Appendices include a list of cabinet office-holders between 1946 and 1955.

Lutfī al-Haffār (1885-1968): mudhakkarātuh, hayātuh wa 'sruh. (Lutfi al-Haffar [1885-1968]: his memoirs, life, and time.)
See item no. 322.

Laissez-faire, outward-orientation, and regional economic disintegration: a case study of the dissolution of the Syro-Lebanese customs union.
See item no. 350.

The Near East since the First World War: a history to 1995.
See item no. 563.

Secret war in the Middle East: the covert struggle for Syria, 1949-61.
See item no. 636.

The struggle for Syria: a study of post-war Arab politics, 1945-1958.
See item no. 637.

Population

397 **International migration and development in the Arab region.**
John S. Birks, Clive A. Sinclair. Geneva: International Labour
Office, 1980. 175p. map. bibliog.

Examines international migration in the Arab world, describing patterns and trends of
labour flow in the mid-1970s. In 1975 Syria, which is discussed on p. 50-57, had
around 70,000 people working in other Arab countries, excluding Lebanon.

398 **The Syrians in America.**
Philip Khuri Hitti. New York: Doran, 1924. 139p. map.

An early classic study tracing the history of 'Syrian' emigration to the United States
from the arrival of Antonius al-Bishallany at Boston in 1854 to the imposition of
immigration restriction in the early 1920s. Hitti estimated that some 200,000
'Syrians', the majority being Lebanese Christians, were residents in the United States
by 1924. Depressed economic conditions, together with religious and political
upheavals, are identified as the principal causes for this wave of Syrian emigration.
Hitti describes the characteristics of the Syrian population in America, including their
geographical distribution, occupations, housing conditions, family life and relations
with their homeland. A list of 'Syrian' newspapers and magazines published in the
United States during the 1920s is provided in the appendices, together with the names
of 'Syrian' priests.

399 **Ottoman populations 1830-1914, demographic and social
characteristics.**
Kemal H. Karpat. Madison, Wisconsin: University of Wisconsin
Press, 1985. 242p. (Turkish and Ottoman Studies).

This book comprises statistical tables drawn from censuses, registers and yearbooks
covering the demographic, social and economic characteristics of the population in the
Ottoman Empire from 1830 to 1914. Population figures are given by administrative
district, including the Syrian provinces, for each census conducted during this period.
Other tables cover population by ethnic and religious origin, livestock holdings, cereal

production, agricultural land area, education expenditure, distribution of schools and number of pupils.

400 The population of Ottoman Syria and Iraq, 1878-1914.
Justin A. McCarthy. *Asian and African Studies*, vol. 15 (March 1981), p. 3-44.

A broad analysis of the populations of Syria and Iraq during the later Ottoman era. Tables comparing the populations of *vilayets* in Syria and Iraq are examined, and the causes of population change are discussed. The data is drawn from Ottoman censuses, registers and yearbooks.

401 The Syrians in Egypt 1725-1975.
Thomas Philipp. Stuttgart, FRG: Steiner, 1985. 188p. bibliog. (Berliner Islamstudien, Band 3).

A history of Syrian migration to Egypt and of the Syrian community in Egypt. The first wave came in the period 1730-80, and was dominated by Greek Catholics; the author examines the role they played in the struggle for local autonomy. The motivation and composition of the second wave, from the mid-19th century to 1914, is also considered. The author analyses the occupational and educational background of the migrants, and goes on to compare and contrast the development of the Syrian intelligentsia and the Syrian commercial bourgeoisie in Egypt. Finally, Philipp discusses the exodus of Syrians from Egypt in the 1960s.

402 The population of Aleppo in the sixteenth and seventeenth centuries according to Ottoman census documents.
André Raymond. *International Journal of Middle East Studies*, vol. 16, no. 4 (November 1984), p. 447-60.

Using Ottoman census documents (*tapu defteri*) for 1537-38 and 1584, together with a similar count for 1683 reproduced by the French traveller d'Ariveux, Raymond estimates the population of Aleppo and the distribution of its inhabitants.

403 Emigration from Syria.
Najib E. Saliba. *Arab Studies Quarterly*, vol. 3, no. 1 (1981), p. 56-67.

Saliba considers the background, causes and scale of emigration to the United States from the Ottoman province of Syria during the period 1878-1920. Between 1899 and 1919 almost 90,000 'Syrians' entered the United States, a large majority of whom were Christians. Saliba suggests that religious persecution was a minor, rather than a primary, factor in emigration, and argues that the outflow was stimulated by economic depression, political insecurity and reports of economic opportunity in the West. The article was reprinted in *Arabs in the new world: studies on Arab-American communities*, edited by Sameer Y. Abraham and Nabeel Abraham (Detroit: Wayne State University, 1983, p. 30-43).

404 **Dimension de la famille et attitude des femmes syriennes à l'égard de la contraception.** (Family size and the attitude of Syrian women towards contraception.)
Mouna L. Samman. *Population* (Paris), vol. 32, no. 6 (1977), p. 1267-76.

Based on a survey of some 5,770 women conducted in 1973, this article discusses age-specific fertility, family size by duration of marriage, as well as attitudes towards, and practice of, contraception and abortion.

405 **Syrian Arab Republic: report of mission on needs assessment for population assistance.**
United Nations Fund for Population Activities. New York: UNFPA, 1980. 138p. map. (Report no. 24).

Although Syria does not have a comprehensive population policy, the government has established a number of institutions, such as the National Committee for the Development of Population Awareness and the Syrian Family Planning Association, as part of its efforts to integrate human resources, planning and development. This report presents the salient demographic, social and economic characteristics of the Syrian population and reviews the availability and reliability of demographic data. Population dynamics and policy considerations are outlined, with particular emphasis on maternal and child health facilities, health services, health education and family planning. Recommendations for external assistance in implementing policies appropriate to both population problems and development objectives are presented.

406 **Population and migration.**
J. Williams. Madison, Wisconsin: University of Wisconsin, 1980. 51p. bibliog. (Working Papers, Human Resources for Rural Development in the SAR, no. 1).

This report examines demographic trends, including rural-urban fertility differentials, migration flows and patterns, within the Syrian rural population. The author describes efforts to provide more rural non-farm employment alternatives to rural out-migrants.

Demographic Yearbook.
See item no. 747.

Quarterly Statistical Bulletin.
See item no. 752.

UNESCO Statistical Yearbook.
See item no. 754.

Language

407 **Archives royales de Mari: textes, transcrits et traduits.** (The royal
archives of Mari: texts, transcriptions and translations.)
Paris: Librairie Orientaliste Paul Geuthner, 1950- . 19 vols.

An important reference work, the ARMT (Archives Royales de Mari Textes) Series
makes available transliterations and translations of texts from the 2nd and 3rd
millennium BC city-state of Mari (Tell Hariri). Each volume is from a particular part
of the archives, or reflects a specific theme.

408 **La lingua di Ebla: atti del convegno internazionale.** (The language
of Ebla: proceedings of an international congress.)
Edited by Luigi Cagni.   Naples, Italy: Instituto Universitario
Orientale, Seminario di Studi Asiatica, 1981. 406p.

The proceedings of this conference, held at Naples in April 1980, contain some
twenty-two papers on various aspects of the Eblaite language. Particularly important
papers include: a descriptive presentation of the Eblaite language and writing during
the Kish civilization by I. J. Gelb; the linguistic classification of Eblaite by M.
Dahood; the terminology of metals by H. Waetzoldt; the verbal system and personal
names by H. Muller; and the relationship between Eblaite and Akkadian by R. E.
Caplae.

409 **Sur le système verbal du neo-Arméen de Ma'lula.** (On the verb
system of neo-Aramaic at Ma'lula.)
David Cohen.   *Journal of Semitic Studies*, vol. 24, no. 3 (autumn
1979), p. 219-39.

This article presents an analysis of the neo-Aramaic dialect, and in particular its verb
system, which is still used in the Syrian villages of Ma'lula, Djub'adin and Bakh'a
near Damascus.

Language

410   **Ugaritic textbook.**
Cyrus H. Gordon.   Rome: Pontifical Biblical Institute, 1965. 547p.
bibliog. (Analecta Orientalia 38).

Provides a complete linguistic tool for the study of the Ugaritic tablets discovered in 1929 by Claude Schaeffer, dating from the first half of the 14th century BC. This comprehensive textbook covers the following areas: alphabet; orthography; phonetics; grammatical structure; syntax; and poetic structure. In addition, the author discusses linguistic affinities and paradigms. The volume includes a selection of Ugaritic texts in transliteration and a classification. This is an update of Gordon's *Ugaritic grammar* (1940), *Ugaritic handbook* (1947) and *Ugaritic manual* (1955), also published by the Pontifical Biblical Institute.

411   **Levantine Arabic for non-natives: a proficiency-oriented approach.**
Lutfi Hussein.   New Haven, Connecticut: Yale University Press, 1993. Student book 128p., teacher's manual 366p.

A textbook for beginners who are seeking to develop oral skills in colloquial Levantine Arabic, the dialect used in Jerusalem and in contemporary Syria, Lebanon, Jordan and Palestine/Israel. It is the first textbook of colloquial Arabic to be developed according to the principles of the proficiency movement in foreign language teaching, where emphasis is placed on the use of meaningful drills, context and a balance between linguistic accuracy and active use of the language. The textbook is accompanied by ten audiocassettes.

412   **A basic grammar of the Ugaritic language with selected texts and glossary.**
Stanislav Segert.   Berkeley, California; London: University of California Press, 1984. 213p. bibliog.

The first part of the book provides a basic grammar in which the author describes the stages and styles of the Ugaritic language, writing and phonology, word formation, morphology and sentence structure. The second part offers a selection of alphabetic and syllabic texts, and a glossary of Ugaritic.

413   **Grammatical analysis and glossary of the northwest Semitic vocables in Akkadian texts of the 15th-13th centuries BC from Canaan and Syria.**
Daniel Sivan.   Neukirchen-Vluyn, Germany: Verlag Butzon & Bercker Kevelaer, 1984. 306p. bibliog. (Alter Orient and Alter Testament, Band 214).

Examines the north-west Semitic languages of the 15th to the 13th century BC as reflected in the Akkadian texts from Palestine and Syria. The study is divided into two parts: the first is a detailed grammar which describes the phonology, morphology and verb structure of Akkadian; the second comprises a glossary, listing all the words in syllabic documentation with references and definitions.

414   **A dictionary of Syrian Arabic: dialect of Damascus,
      English-Arabic.**
      Karl Stowasser, Moukhtar Ani.   Washington, DC: Georgetown
      University Press, 1964. 269p. (Arabic Series, no. 5).
A useful and accessible dictionary for students of Arabic specializing in the Syrian
dialect.

415   **Syrie centrale: inscriptions sémitiques.** (Central Syria: Semitic
      inscriptions.)
      Le Comte Melchoir de Vogüé.   Paris: J. Baudry, 1868. 148p.
This volume reproduces over 400 Safaitic inscriptions collected in central Syria
(Palmyra and the Hauran) by de Vogüé and M. W. H. Waddington in 1861 and 1862.

A dictionary of Arabic topography and placenames.
See item no. 34.

Walid Ikhlassy: a postmodern Syrian fictionalist.
See item no. 789.

Mijalat Majma' al-Llughat al-'Arabīyah bī-Dimashq. (Review of the Arab
Academy in Damascus.)
See item no. 847.

Religion

416 A tenth-century Nusayri treatise on the duty to know the mystery of divinity.

Meir M. Bar-Asher, Aryeh Kofsky. *Bulletin of the School of Oriental and African Studies*, vol. LVIII, Part 2 (1995), p. 243-50.

This article consists of a reproduction of the Nusayri treatise accompanied by an annotated English translation. The text is a report of sessions held in 952 by the Nusayri sage, Abu Muhammad 'Ali ibn 'Isa al-Jisri. The main focus of the text is on the 'correct knowledge of the mystery of divinity'. An account of some of the basic doctrines of early Nusayri theology is also provided.

417 'Abd al'Qādir al-Jazā'irī and Islamic reform.

David Dean Commins. *The Muslim World*, vol. LXXVIII, no. 2 (April 1988), p. 121-31.

Commins focuses on the contribution of 'Abd al'Qadir al-Jaza'iri (an Algerian military and religious leader) to the intellectual life of Damascus, where he lived from 1855 until his death in 1883. Commins provides evidence of al-Jaza'iri's 'reformist tendencies', and suggests that a re-evaluation of his life, integrating the various stages of his career, would help to explain his reformist tendencies.

418 Religious reformers and Arabists in Damascus, 1885-1914.

David Dean Commins. *International Journal for Middle East Studies*, vol. 18, no. 4 (November 1986), p. 405-25.

Examines the positive response of the religious reformers (*salafis*) to the *Tanzimat* reforms of the Ottoman Empire, between 1839 and 1876, and their impact on the newly emerging Arabists. The *salafi* called for the invocation of *ijtihad* (the use of reason to arrive at a knowledge of truth in religious matters) and the harmonization of Islam with reason, progress and modernity. This appealed to the youth studying in the secular schools, and in particular Maktab Anbar. As a result, an alliance was formed between the religious reformers and the founding members of the Arab Renaissance Society in opposition to the traditional political and religious elite. Commins argues

114

that this convergence of ethnic and new class interests provided the foundation for Arab nationalism.

419 **State and Islamism in Syria.**
    Raymond A. Hinnebusch. In: *Islamic fundamentalism.* Edited by
    Abdel Salam Sidahmed, Anoushiravan Ehteshami. Boulder,
    Colorado: Westview Press, 1996, p. 199-214.
Hinnebusch offers the reader a succinct account of the relationship between the Syrian state and political Islam. He examines the potency of Islam through political context, social composition and ideology. In contrast to the popular base of Khomeini's movement, Hinnebusch argues that the Muslim Brotherhood in Syria has lacked populist appeal, due to its confinement to the cities and its capitalist ideology. The policies of economic liberalization and political decompression, adopted by the Syrian regime since 1991, have sought to co-opt and utilize the moderate wing of political Islam to embolden legitimacy and assist in economic development.

420 **Rashid Rida.**
    Albert Hourani. In: *Arabic thought in the liberal age, 1798-1939.*
    London; New York: Oxford University Press, 1962. Reprinted with
    new preface, New York: Cambridge University Press, 1983, p. 222-44.
Hourani has written an interesting biography of Rashid Rida, one of the founders of the *salafi* reform movement. He pays particular attention to Rida's thoughts over Islamic and secular states. Hourani suggests that Rida believed the Islamic state to be superior to the secular, even for minorities (Jews and Christians).

421 **The lion encyclopedia of the bible: life and times, meaning and message, a comprehensive guide.**
    Tring, England; Batavia, Illinois: Lion; Sutherland, Australia:
    Albatross, 1986. rev. ed. 352p. maps.
Provides essential reference and background information to help readers understand the Bible. Accurate information is presented in a simple, straightforward way, with illustrations.

422 **The social bases and discursive context of the rise of Islamic fundamentalism: the cases of Iran and Syria.**
    Mansoor Moaddel. *Sociological Inquiry*, vol. 66 (summer 1996),
    p. 330-55. bibliog.
Moaddel traces the rise of Islamic fundamentalism in Iran and Syria up to the socio-economic and political developments of the 1950s and 1960s. The antagonism between the state and the 'property owning class', it is argued, produced a dynamism that combined the interests of the propertied and the dispossessed. Rather than treating ideology as an abstract idea, Moaddel proposes that it serves as a discourse, an 'autonomous process', that has an 'objective presence' in society. Thus, he concludes that Islamic fundamentalism is a product of the interaction between state and society. The Syrian case receives specific attention on p. 344-50. This work offers a useful combination of theory and empiricism.

423 **Muhammad Rashīd Ridā: fatāwā al-imām Muhammad Rashīd Ridā.** (Muhammad Rashid Rida: fatwas of the imam Muhammad Rashid Rida.)
Edited by Salah al-Din al-Munjid, Yusuf Khuri. Beirut: Dār al-Kitāb al-Jadīd, 1970. 6 vols.

A collection of Rashid Rida's *fatwas*, originally published in his newspaper *al-Manar* in answer to readers' questions on religious matters. A personal biography of Rida is included in the first volume (p. 9-23). This is an excellent source for students of Islamic studies.

424 **Damas au VIIe/XIIIes: vie et structures religieuses dans une métropole islamique.** (Damascus in the 7th/13th century: religious life and structures in an Islamic metropolis.)
Louis Pouzet. Beirut: Dar el-Machreq, 1988. 527p. maps. bibliog.
(Langue Arabe et Pensée Islamique, tome XV).

Pouzet provides a detailed study of religious life in Damascus during the 7th century AH. He examines the Damascene origins of the four Sunni *madhabs* (schools of thought) – Hanbali, Hanifi, Malki and Shaf'i. He also focuses upon the religious institutions of Damascus and their approaches to teaching Islam in accordance with the Koran and the *hadith* (collection of sayings of the Prophet). The interaction between politics and religion is addressed through the issue of Muslim and non-Muslim (*ahl al-dhimmah*) relations, and the confrontation between Islam and the Christian West. The appendices include: a chronology of important *'ulama* in the Great Mosque and the *Muhtasibs* of the 7th century AH (p. 411-24); the number of *madrassas* and content of religious pronouncements (p. 425-28); the transmission of the *hadith* to Damascus (p. 429-42); the *zawiyas* in Damascus (p. 245-48); a detailed chronology of 658/1260 and the occupation by the Mongols (p. 449-53); and the union of women *muhadditat* (p. 455-56). Pouzet has composed an invaluable bibliography in French, English (p. 455-56), German and Arabic (p. 457-73).

425 **NIV atlas of the Bible.**
Carl G. Rasmussen, maps by Carta, Jerusalem. Grand Rapids, Michigan: Regency Reference Library, Zondervan, 1989. 256p. maps. bibliog.

The book is divided into two sections. In the first, the physical geography of the biblical lands, from Egypt to Mesopotamia, is examined, with coverage of Syria and Lebanon on p. 62-64. The second section is historical, and focuses on events from the 3rd millennium BC until the fall of Jerusalem in AD 70. The maps, prepared by Carta, allow the reader to enter into the world of the Bible. An interesting bibliography on the archaeology, history and geography of the Holy Land is provided. The timeline of biblical history (p. 216-17) gives the reader a quick overview of the history of the ancient Near East from 3200 BC to AD 400. The gazetteer and index assist the reader in locating places both in this atlas and on contemporary maps.

426 **Damascene intellectual life in the opening years of the 20th
     century: Muhammad Kurd 'Ali and al-Muqtabas.**
     Samir Seikaly. In: *Intellectual life in the Arab East, 1890-1939.*
     Edited by Marwan R. Buheiry. Beirut: Center for Arab and Middle
     East Studies, American University of Beirut, 1986, p. 125-53.

Challenging Cairo's position as the intellectual capital of the Arab world, Seikaly
seeks to account for Damascus' contribution to intellectual life at the turn of the 19th
century. The author recounts the intellectual impact of Muhammad Kurd 'Ali and his
journal *al-Muqtabas.* Kurd 'Ali's insistence upon the need to maintain the historic link
between the Arabs and Turks was reflected in the content of the *al-Muqtabas.*
However, references were frequently made to the distinct Arab *umma*, which Seikaly
connotes as a fully crystallized nationalist idea. This point alone illustrates the
ambiguities within both Kurd 'Ali and Seikaly's work.

427 **Imperial Germany: a view from Damascus.**
     Samir M. Seikaly. In: *Arab civilization challenges and responses:
     studies in honor of Constantine K. Zurayk.* Edited by George N.
     Atiyeh, Ibrahim M. Oweiss. Albany, New York: University Press of
     New York, 1988, p. 312-25.

The author analyses Muhammad Kurd 'Ali's appreciation of Germany's unique
cultural ethos. Early Arab thinkers looked to England and France for a 'mental
rediscovery', as they represented two poles of intellectual attraction. Seikaly suggests
that whilst Kurd 'Ali understood the need to borrow from the West in order to initiate
the process of regeneration and reform, the task of discriminating between good and
bad was difficult. Seikaly avers that the case of Germany offered Kurd 'Ali a
satisfactory solution.

428 **Muhammad Rashīd Ridā's perspectives on the West as reflected in
     al-Manār.**
     Emad Eldin Shahin. *The Muslim World*, vol. LXXIX, no. 2 (April
     1989), p. 113-32.

Shahin considers Rida's views of the West. Although Rida was critical of Western
civilization, he did not reject it outright. Neither did he imitate the West; his aim was
to separate Islam from the West, whilst borrowing those aspects which could 'reaffirm
[the] strengths of Islamic traditions'. Shahin explains that the development of Rida's
attitude towards the British and the French shifted from revolution, to moderation, and
finally to violence. Shahin provides a good analysis of Rida's philosophical
background.

429 **The Islamic alternative: cause or effect?**
     Tamara Sonn. *International Journal*, vol. XLVI, no. 2 (spring 1991),
     p. 291-325.

Sonn analyses the link between Islamic fundamentalism, radicalism and terrorism,
arguing that failing to understand one's 'self-image' often leads to an inability to
understand Western misconceptions. She examines the self-perception of the region in
terms of the Islamic world, Arab world and the Middle/Near East, and focuses on the
challenges of history and modernity. Syria is covered in this analysis. This is a

particularly useful article for undergraduate students grappling with conflicting labels, images and concepts.

430 **Rashīd Ridā and Faysal's kingdom in Syria.**
Eliezer Tauber. *The Muslim World*, vol. LXXXV, no. 3-4 (July-October 1995), p. 235-45.

Tauber examines the animosity between Rida and Faysal. Their antagonism towards each other arose from their differing perceptions of the relationship between subject and ruler in an Islamic regime, with Rida declaring that the nation retained the right to depose and replace a bad ruler. The article contains too much narrative, and its analysis is weak; however, it offers an interesting perspective on Arab nationalism.

431 **Rashīýd Ridā as pan-Arabist before World War I.**
Eliezer Tauber. *The Muslim World*, vol. LXXIX, no. 2 (April 1989), p. 102-12.

Tauber suggests that Rida's secret Arab society, the Society of the Arab Association, was the first, prior to the First World War, to call for the establishment of an independent and decentralized Arab state. He examines the ideology of the Society; Rida's methodology included the removal of the *amirs* from the Arabian peninsula before developing a framework for the protection of the Arab state and its inhabitants.

432 **Rashīd Ridā's political attitudes during World War I.**
Eliezer Tauber. *The Muslim World*, vol. LXXXV, no. 1-2 (January-April 1995), p. 107-21.

In this useful historical analysis, Tauber follows the activities of Rashid Rida during the First World War. Rida's efforts focused on establishing a united Arab state from the Ottoman Empire. His plans, however, were frustrated by the Sykes-Picot Agreement. In addition, the Hussein-McMahon correspondence ran counter to Rida's ideas, and caused tension between the two leaders of nascent Arab nationalism. Rida started an anti-Hashemite campaign against the Sharif of Mecca and called upon Muslims to 'save Hijaz from heresy and oppression of Husayn' (p. 120).

433 **Three approaches, one idea: religion and state in the thought of 'abd al-Rahman al Kawakibi, Najib 'Azuri and Rashid Rida.**
Eliezer Tauber. *British Journal of Middle Eastern Studies*, vol. 21, no. 2 (1994), p. 191-200.

Tauber attempts to plug the gap in the historiography of the Arab movement. Whilst most attention has focused on the ideas behind Arab nationalism, scant attention has been paid to the proposed character of the Arab regime. The author contends that despite their different approaches, 'Abd al-Rahman al-Kawakibi, Najib Azuri and Rashid Rida shared a common conception of statehood and all believed in the separation of religion and state. To support his hypothesis, Tauber discusses each thinker's ideas in turn and then draws the relevant parallels.

434 **Sa'id Hawwa: the making of a radical Muslim in modern Syria.**
Itzchak Weismann. *Middle Eastern Studies*, vol. 29, no. 4 (October 1993), p. 601-24.

Weismann paints a portrait of Hawwa (the foremost ideologue of the Muslim Brotherhood in Syria), and his rise to prominence in the Muslim Brotherhood, based on his childhood and adolescent influences. Hawwa's attachment to the city of Hama, and his engagement with Sufism, Muhammad al-Hamid (a Hanafi scholar) and Hassan al-Banna (the first leader of the Muslim Brotherhood), are factors that shaped his commitment to moderation in seeking an Islamic Syrian state.

435 **Islamic revival and national development in the Arab world.**
Ayman al-Yassini. *Journal of Asian and African Studies*, vol. XXI, no. 1-2 (January & April 1986), p. 104-21. bibliog.

Al-Yassini examines the connection between religion and society in the Arab world, and suggests that where states suffer a crisis of legitimacy they revert to a religious rationalization of policies. The author focuses on Saudi Arabia, Egypt and Syria. Saudi Arabia is portrayed as dependent upon religion, Egypt shares a limited dependency, and Syria has attempted to separate religion from politics. The case of Syria is discussed on p. 113-17. Al-Yassini argues that the Syrian state has offended both Muslims and Christians by its determination to 'eliminate [the] religious establishment', and therefore Christians and Muslims have co-operated to resist the government's secular programme. The philosophy of 'Aflaq, the founder of the Ba'th Party, is also briefly outlined on p. 113-14.

Syria: publications of the Princeton University archaeological expeditions to Syria in 1904-05 and 1909, division IV, Semitic inscriptions.
See item no. 139.

Ebla: an empire rediscovered.
See item no. 140.

The silver treasures of Resafa / Sergiupolis.
See item no. 153.

Society and ideology in late Ottoman Syria: class, education, profession and confession.
See item no. 249.

Un zikr chez les soufis. (A zikr at the Sufis.)
See item no. 813.

Minorities

'Alawis

436 Some observations on the social roots of Syria's ruling military group and the causes of its dominance.
Hanna Batatu. *The Middle East Journal*, vol. 35, no. 3 (summer 1981), p. 331-44.

Batatu highlights the close kinship group of military officers connected by tribal (al-Matawirah), sect-class ('Alawi), and ecological-cultural affinity (peasant/small town origin) who dominate Syria's ruling elite. The political dominance of the minority 'Alawi element is explained in part as a consequence of the minority-orientated policy of the French Mandate period, but also as a result of the depressed economic conditions of the 'Alawis. Their rise to dominance in the military was facilitated by the division of the Sunni officers along political, regional and class lines.

437 The Alawis of Syria.
Alasdair D. Drysdale. In: *World minorities, a second volume.* Edited by Georgina Ashworth. London: Quartermaine House/Minority Rights Group, 1978, p. 1-5.

An overview of the 'Alawi sect and its recent history in Syria. During the French Mandate a quasi-autonomous 'Alawi state was set up, but the French administration did little to reverse the cumulative effects of years of social and economic discrimination against the 'Alawis since the late 1940s. However, there has since been a reversal in 'Alawi fortunes, with 'Alawis playing a prominent role in the army and Ba'th Party, especially after the 1963 revolution.

438 **The Syrian armed forces in national politics: the role of the geographic and ethnic periphery.**
Alasdair D. Drysdale. In: *Soldiers, peasants and bureaucrats.*
Edited by Roman Kolkowicz, Andrzej Korbonski. London: Allen &
Unwin, 1982, p. 52-76.

This essay examines the changing role of the periphery in the armed forces and the ways in which civil-military relations have been affected by ethnic factors. The disproportionate representation of minorities in the armed forces began with the French preference for recruits from non-Sunni communities and their reliance on minority troops to suppress the nationalist uprising. In the early years of independence, minority officers played a leading role in several *coups d'état.* The role of the periphery has been especially evident since a military coup installed the Ba'th in power in 1963. Minority, and especially 'Alawi, officers emerged in strength after 1963 because of their strong links with the secularist and socialist Ba'th, and their manipulation of ethnic ties.

439 **The Alawi community of Syria: a new dominant political force.**
Mahmud A. Faksh. *Middle Eastern Studies*, vol. 20, no. 2 (April
1984), p. 133-53.

Examines the radical transformation in the socio-economic and political status of the 'Alawi community from its poverty of the 1950s to 1971 when Asad became President. Faksh describes the distribution and communal structure of the 'Alawis, the largest Muslim minority in Syria. The community is subdivided into four loose tribal associations: Khayyatun, Haddahun, al-Matawirah and Kalbiyyah. The 'Alawi religion, a blend of various Islamic and non-Islamic beliefs and practices, is also described. The author examines 'Alawi relations with other religious groups and the factors which contributed to the development of 'Alawi communal identity prior to independence, in particular the creation of a semi-autonomous 'Alawi state during the French Mandate. The 'Alawi's rise to power since independence, through their role in the military and the Ba'th Party, is examined, and proposals for an independent 'Alawi state are considered and dismissed. Their domination since the mid-1960s has strengthened 'Alawi cohesion but has also led to increasing Sunni opposition.

440 **Minorities in power: the Alawites of Syria.**
Peter Gubser. In: *The political role of minority groups in the Middle
East.*   Edited by R. D. McLaurin.   New York: Praeger, 1979,
p. 17-48.

A useful chapter describing the 'Alawis, their region and their religion. Gubser considers traditional, social and tribal stratification within the 'Alawi community, and notes the competition between traditional tribal chiefs and leaders of clientele groups. The growth and political participation of the 'Alawi new educated middle stratum are discussed. Finally, the chapter reviews the rise of the 'Alawis to national power in the mid-1960s, and the effect of this on the rest of the Syrian population, particularly the urban Sunni majority.

441 **The Alawis of Syria: religious ideology and organization.**
Fuad Khuri. In: *Syria: society, culture, and polity.* Edited by
Richard Antoun, Donald Quataert. Albany, New York: State
University of New York Press, 1991, p. 49-61. (SUNY Series in
Middle Eastern Studies).

In this highly charged area of research, Khuri examines three areas of interest: the
synthetic view of religion; the stratified view of religion; and religious organization.
The article is written without the familiar bias of authorship so common to this area of
study and is therefore a useful introduction for students of Middle Eastern studies.

442 **Syria: accumulation of errors.**
Haytham Manna. *Middle Eastern Studies*, vol. 23, no. 2 (April 1987),
p. 211-14.

In this brief article, Manna highlights the reification of error, which is where
researchers err and this in turn becomes a reality and 'a point of reference'. Manna
gives an example of this: it is claimed by Faksh and Batatu that Asad comes from the
al-Matawirah tribe, whereas, according to the records, he originates from the
Kalbiyyah tribe.

443 **The Alawi capture of power in Syria.**
Daniel Pipes. *Middle Eastern Studies*, vol. 25, no. 4 (October 1989),
p. 429-50.

Yet another lamentable article emerges from Pipes' orientalist catalogue.
Complementing his previous works, Pipes is overly dependent upon spurious evidence
and hearsay to support his hypothesis. The capture of power by the 'Alawis, portrayed
as negating the natural order, is shown to be an abnormal and temporary state of
affairs owing to the sectarian nature of Syrian politics. In an interesting twist, Pipes
uses Sunni Islam, often the target of his ire, as a stick to beat the 'Alawis with, and in
addition, to support his favoured confessional model of domestic politics. His
prophetic vision of Syria – the collapse of the 'Alawi order – exists beyond the ambit
of the academic and belongs more to the realm of the soothsayer.

444 **The compact minorities and the Syrian state, 1918-45.**
Itamar Rabinovich. *Journal of Contemporary History*, vol. 14, no. 4
(1979), p. 693-712.

Rabinovich outlines the relationship between the 'Alawi and Druze minorities and the
Ottoman state and subsequent French administrations.

445 **Middle Eastern political clichés: 'Takriti' and 'Sunni' rule in Iraq;
'Alawi' rule in Syria, a critical appraisal.**
Nikolaos Van Dam. *Orient* (Oplanden), vol. 21, no. 1 (January 1980),
p. 42-57.

Van Dam examines the reasons behind the strong representation of 'Alawis in the
Syrian Ba'thist regime and of Sunnis (particularly Takritis) in Iraq. The author
questions whether labels such as ''Alawi rule'' are justified. In practice so-called
'Alawi rule appears to be limited to a restricted, tribally and regionally related, section
of the 'Alawi community from which many other 'Alawis have been able to profit on

sectarian grounds. The Syrian case demonstrates how regionalism and tribalism within the elite has given rise to a destructive kind of sectarianism.

446 **Suleiman al-Murshid: beginnings of an Alawi leader.**
Gitta Yaffe. *Middle Eastern Studies*, vol. 29, no. 4 (October 1993), p. 624-40. map.
This article charts the religious, mystical and political life of Suleiman al-Murshid. He started life as a tribal chief in the 'Alawi hinterland. Belonging to the Haidari (a kinship group), he formed a leadership based upon its teachings and gained widespread support within the 'Alawi community. He consolidated his social and financial standing through methods adopted by traditional Syrian leaders, eventually becoming a deputy in the Syrian National Assembly.

Isma'ilis and Shi'as

447 **Authority and political culture in Shiism.**
Edited by Said Amin Arjomand.   Albany, New York: State University of New York Press, 1988. 393p.
This book addresses the concept of authority within Shi'ism. Divided into two parts, the first part contains a selection of essays, which deal with: religious authority in Iran between the 16th and 19th centuries; the culture of medieval Shi'ism; and the ideology of Shi'ism during the 1970s and 1980s. The second part contains a selection of documents, previously unavailable in English, that trace the history of Shi'ism.

448 **The Assassins legends: myths of the Ismailis.**
Farhad Daftary.   London; New York: I. B. Tauris, 1994. 213p. bibliog.
Legends of the Assassins have existed since the 12th century, when European Crusaders first encountered the Syrian sect of the Nizari Isma'ilis. Ever since, the Assassin legends have prevailed throughout history and influenced much of the scholarship dedicated to the Nizaris. Daftary departs from this approach, and uses authentic Isma'ili sources to examine the origins of the medieval Assassin legends. Daftary has produced a well-researched book, which also includes the first English translation of Silvestre de Sacy's 19th-century *Memoire on the Assassins*, and a section dedicated to the etymology of their name.

449 **The Isma'ilis: their history and doctrines.**
Farhad Daftary.   Cambridge, England: Cambridge University Press, 1990. 804p. map. bibliog.
This book provides a comprehensive study of the Isma'ili community, who comprise the second largest Shi'a community after the Twelver Shi'as. Daftary explores their origins, history and theology over the last twelve centuries. This is a useful introduction for students or researchers of Islam, religion and anthropology.

450 The trials of Syrian Isma'ilis in the first decade of the 20th century.

Dick Douwes, Norman N. Lewis. *International Journal of Middle East Studies*, vol. 21, no. 2 (May 1989), p. 215-32.

Although the Suwaydani faction of the Syrian Isma'ili community took the lead in discovering the infallible Imam, it was the Hajjawi faction that accepted Sultan Muhammad Shah as Ahga Khan in 1796. Sultan Muhammad Shah reconciled the Hajjawi faction of the Syrian Isma'ilis with the Iranian Isma'ilis, after a split of four centuries. This development served to exacerbate the tensions between the two Syrian factions and further antagonized the Ottoman authorities. The authors highlight the sensitive relationship between the Ottoman and the British Empires with an analysis of Hajjawi relations and the Bombay based Agha Khan. The Hajjawis' belief that the Ottoman caliph was a mere terrestrial monarch and the Agha Khan was the divine impalpable essence pervading the universe hastened their journey to court. Faced with accusations of sedition, treason and paying taxes to a foreign prince, prominent members of the Hajjawi community faced a series of trials both in Damascus and Istanbul. Douwes and Lewis trace the course of these trials, and persuasively argue against any collusion of interest amongst the Hajjawis, the Agha Khan and the British Empire.

451 Belief and law in Imami Shi'ism.

Etan Kohlberg. Aldershot, England; Brookfield, Vermont: Variorum, 1994. 362p.

This book contains a compilation of Kholberg's essays on Shi'ism, which address subjects such as history, doctrine, thought and literature.

452 The Isma'ilis of Syria today.

Norman N. Lewis. *Royal Central Asian Society Journal*, vol. 39, no. 1 (January 1952), p. 69-77.

A brief history, starting from the second half of the 9th century, of the Isma'ili sect, focusing on the Salamiyya group. Since the mid-19th century there have been two groups of Isma'ilis in Syria: one in the Qadmous-Masyaf area, west of Hama; and the other in Salamiyah. The article describes the economy and social organization of the Isma'ili sect in contemporary Syria, and outlines the strained and complex relations of the sect with official Sunni Islam.

453 The Shi'ites: ritual and popular piety in a Muslim community.

David Pinault. London: I. B. Tauris, 1992. 210p. bibliog.

This book is divided into two parts. The first provides an introduction to Shi'ism with a study of its history and theology, and the second explores the relevance of Shi'ism, as a religious ideology, to its adherents. The Shi'a community of Hyderabad receives special attention.

The Druzes

454 **The Druze: a new study of their history, faith, and society; second impression with corrections.**
Nejla M. Abu Izzedin. Leiden, the Netherlands: Brill, 1993. rev. ed. 259p. map. bibliog.
Within the preface, the author highlights the two objectives of this book. The first is to examine the belief system of the Druzes, set within the context of Fatimid Shi'ism. The second is to review the social composition of the Druze community until the 1840s, and to provide a commentary on the role and contribution of the Druzes to the history of Syria and Lebanon. Included in this analysis is an assessment of faith, ethics, the role of women and Druze society.

455 **Drūz Surrīyah wa-Lubnan fī 'ahd al-intidāb al-firinsī, 1920-1943: dirāsah fī tārīkhahum al-sīyāsī.** (The Druzes of Syria and Lebanon in the time of the French Mandate, 1920-43: a study of their political history.)
Hasan Amin al-Ba'ini, introduced by Munir Isma'il. Beirut: al-Markaz al-'Arabī lil-Abhāth wa-al-Tawthīq, 1993. 459p. bibliog.
A political history of the Druzes in Syria and Lebanon, based on a PhD dissertation, University of Lebanon, Beirut, 1991. The author describes the role of the Druzes during the national struggle against the French, and mostly relies upon documents translated from English, French and Spanish.

456 **The Druze.**
Robert Brenton Betts. New Haven, Connecticut: Yale University Press, 1988. 161p. maps. bibliog.
The Druzes are a religious confession concentrated in the mountains of Syria, Lebanon and Israel. This book, as the author states, attempts to provide an overall guide to the Druzes. He gives an overview of their history, from their origins to the late 1980s, and examines their beliefs, customs, social structure and demographics. The result is a useful and accessible history of the Druzes.

457 **The Druzes and the Maronites under the Turkish rule, from 1840 to 1860.**
Colonel Charles Henry Churchill. London: Quaritch, 1862. Reprinted, Reading, England: Garnet Publishing, 1994. 300p.
Churchill arrived in Beirut in 1840, as part of the British forces sent by Palmerston to expel the Egyptians from Syria. He later settled in Lebanon. This book acts as a forum for the expression of Churchill's feelings towards Turkey. He attributes the Druze-Maronite civil war of 1860 to Turkish policy, and opines that the British needed to cultivate relations with the Druzes in order to counter French influence through the Maronite community. Although clearly a subjective account, Churchill's book reveals the objectives of France and Britain in Lebanon, and is also a partisan account of the war.

458   **A history of the Druzes.**
Kais M. Firras.   Leiden, the Netherlands: Brill, 1992. 373p. maps.
bibliog.
The author examines the history of the Druzes using an interdisciplinary approach to
describe, analyse and explain this history. Part one provides an introduction to early
Druze history, whereas parts two and three address the decline of the Druzes in
Lebanon, and the emergence of the Hauran as their new centre. The author focuses in
particular on the rise of the Attrash family. Part four assesses the repercussions of the
Mandate system on the socio-political structures of the Druze community. The book
concludes with a short survey of the Druze communities in Syria, Lebanon and Israel.
The author uses a wide range of primary and secondary sources in Arabic, Hebrew
and French.

459   **Minorities in isolation: the Druzes of Lebanon and Syria.**
Peter Gubser.   In: *The political role of minority groups in the Middle
East.*   Edited by R. D. McLaurin.   New York: Praeger, 1979,
p. 109-34.
Gubser describes the Druzes, their region, religion, socio-political structure and
leadership. In 1970 Syria had a predominantly rural Druze population of c. 150,000,
concentrated in the province of Suweida and in the Hauran. After reviewing the
composition of the Druze leadership, the author outlines its political orientation since
independence. Early Syrian efforts to suppress centrifugal tendencies led some Druzes
to invite King 'Abdullah (of Jordan) to annex Jabal al-Druze. Other Syrian presidents,
notably al-Quwwatli, tried to exploit differences between the al-Attrash and Abu Asali
factions. Following the repression of the 1954 revolt, the Druzes were increasingly
incorporated into the Syrian nation, and by the 1960s had secured a significant role in
the military.

460   **Marriage, divorce, and succession in the Druze family: a study
based on decisions of Druze arbitration and religious courts in
Israel and the Golan Heights.**
Aharon Layish.   Leiden, the Netherlands: Brill, 1982. 474p. bibliog.
(Social, Economic, and Political Studies of the Middle East, vol. xxxi).
This book provides an extensive study of Druze family law; the rulings of Israeli
courts, using adapted Lebanese Druze law, comprise the main sources of
documentation. The author looks at the legal, social and religious aspects of the
subject, and sheds new light on the status of Druze women. This work is most suited
for those interested in legal and sociological aspects of the Druze community in Israel.

461   **Survival and leadership at an interface periphery: the Druzes in
Lebanon.**
Thomas Scheffler.   Beirut: Orient-Institut der Deutschen
Morgenlandischen Gessellschaft, 1997. 32p.
This booklet is based on a lecture given by Thomas Scheffler on 26 February 1997. It
examines the survival and success of the Druze community living within hostile
territory. Scheffler attributes their success to four factors: religion; class system;
political structure; and geography. He argues that whilst each of these have played an
important role towards guaranteeing their survival, the centralization of their political

leadership has been the prime factor for longevity. He concludes that political unity has allowed the Druzes to meet the crises of the 19th and 20th centuries.

Problems in the Ottoman administration in Syria during the 16th and 17th centuries: the case of the sanjak of Sidon-Beirut.
See item no. 215.

An occasion for war: civil conflict in Lebanon and Damascus in 1860.
See item no. 235.

The compact minorities and the Syrian state, 1918-45.
See item no. 444.

Armenians

462 **The Armenians: from genocide to resistance.**
Gerard Chaliand, Yves Ternon, translated by Tony Berret. London: Zed, 1983. 125p. maps. bibliog.
A selection of documents that testify to the deportation and massacre of the Armenian community in the Ottoman Empire between 1915 and 1917. The documents cover the deportations, which centred on Aleppo, the Euphrates camps, and the massacres at Ras al-'Ain and Dayr al-Zur in 1916. The documents include reports on the concentration camps for deportees from the German Consul, Rossler, at Aleppo, the British Government's *Blue Book* (1916), and eye-witness accounts.

463 **The settlement of Armenian refugees in Syria and Lebanon, 1915-39.**
Thomas H. Greenshields. In: *Change and development in the Middle East.* Edited by John I. Clarke, Howard Jones. London; New York: Methuen, 1981, p. 233-41.
Between 1920 and 1929 some 80,000 Armenians arrived in Syria, primarily in Alexandretta, Aleppo and Damascus. Despite subsequent attempts by the League of Nations to resettle Armenians, the pattern already established, with its strong focus on urban arrival points, continued to prevail. Greenshields examines the social, economic and political forces that led to the recreation of former Armenian communities.

464 **Armenians in the service of the Ottoman Empire, 1860-1908.**
Mesrob K. Krikorian. London; Henley, England; Boston, Massachusetts: Routledge, 1977. 149p. maps. bibliog.
This study investigates the contribution made by Armenians to Ottoman public life, especially in eastern Anatolia and Syria, from 1860 until 1908, when the Young Turks assumed power. This study is based on the Ottoman provincial yearbooks, which recorded the names, ranks and functions of paid officials and unpaid community representatives. Aleppo and Damascus receive attention in chapters nine and ten respectively.

465 **Failure of collaboration: Armenian refugees in Syria.**
Ellen Marie Lust-Okar. *Middle Eastern Studies*, vol. 32, no. 1
(January 1996), p. 53- 68.

This article examines how the dynamic between France and the Armenians during the
French Mandate ultimately led to the failure of their relationship. In addition, the
impact of the Armenian migration on Syria, an area often neglected, is addressed. The
congruence of interests between the French and the Armenians arose from the Turkish
expulsion of Armenians from Turkey, and France's colonial policy of supporting
minorities. However, the expediency of the relationship was short-lived, as the Syrian
Muslim population punished the Armenians for their collusion, and the French found
more pliable allies from the natural cleavages of Syrian society.

466 **The Armenian communities in Syria under Ottoman dominion.**
Avedis K. Sanjian.   Cambridge, Massachusetts: Harvard University
Press, 1965. 390p. map. bibliog. (Harvard Middle East Studies,
no. 10).

A detailed study of the evolution and internal organization of Armenian communities
and their social institutions in geographical Syria during the Ottoman era. The study
concentrates on the dominant ecclesiastical institutions of the Armenian community,
with particular emphasis on the Patriarchate of Jerusalem and the Bishopric of Aleppo.
Sanjian also describes the cultural and economic status of the Armenian communities
in Syria, including those in Aleppo, Alexandretta and Antioch. The Turkish pogroms
against the Armenians during the First World War, and their impact on the Armenians
in Syria, are discussed. In Latakia the entire Armenian community was deported.

Jews and Syrian Christians

467 **The Christian population of the province of Damascus in the 16th
century.**
Muhammad Adnan Bakhit.   In: *Christians and Jews in the Ottoman
Empire: the functioning of a plural society*.   Edited by Benjamin
Braude, Bernard Lewis.   New York: Holmes & Meir, 1982, p. 19-66.

Using data from the *tapu defteris* (cadastral registers), this chapter aims to locate and
identify areas in the *vilayet* of Damascus where a Christian presence was registered, to
determine demographic trends and to outline the local history of the Christian minority
in the 16th century. Demographic information is presented on a *liwa* (district) and *nahia*
(sub-district) basis.

468 **From the Holy Mountain: a journey in the shadow of Byzantium.**
William Dalrymple.   London: Flamingo, 1998. 483p. bibliog.

Dalrymple has earned a reputation as a witty travel writer. In his third book, he travels
the Silk Route of ancient Byzantium through the present-day Middle East tracing the
AD 578 journey of John Moschos, the great Byzantine monk, traveller and oral
historian *avant la lettre*. Dalrymple's journey compels him to reassess his earlier

assumptions about the region's religions, and the reasons for the demise of Eastern Christianity. *From the Holy Mountain* is an excellent read, a trusty travel guide, informative on the history and theology of the region, and sensitive to the politics of the day.

469   **Jewish-Christian relations in Aleppo as a background for the Jewish response to the events of October 1850.**
Yaron Harel. *International Journal of Middle East Studies*, vol. 30, no. 1 (February 1998), p. 77-96.
The author analyses the events of Aleppo in October 1850, based on a document discovered in the British Library, depicting the breakdown of Christian-Muslim relations from a Jewish perspective, which, Harel contentiously suggests, makes it more reliable. He outlines the hostility and competition between the Jewish and Christian communities in Aleppo, thus accounting for the unlikely Jewish response. He further challenges Masters' thesis that the events resulted from the incorporation of Syria into the world capitalist system. Harel contends that they were due to a 'breakdown in the older order in the socio-religious domain' (p. 79). The document itself is reproduced on p. 95-96.

470   **Muslim-Christian relations and inter-Christian rivalries in the Middle East: the case of the Jacobites in an age of transition.**
John Joseph.   Albany, New York: State University of New York Press, 1983. 240p. map. bibliog.
A useful modern history of the Syrian Orthodox (Jacobites) and Syrian Catholic Christians, concentrating on social and political developments since the early 19th century, when the Eastern Christian Churches emerged from several centuries of isolation. Jacobites and Syrian Catholics were victims in the repression of the Kurds in 1925 and many, like the Armenians before them, fled to French-ruled Syria, settling mainly in Jazira as well as in Aleppo, Hama and Homs. When tensions rose in Jazira following the signing of the Franco-Syrian Treaty of 1936, the Christians feared for their future in an independent Syria, and demanded autonomy. The Christians supported the Kurdish revolt in Jazira in 1937. Tension between Muslims and Christians in the area subsided from the 1950s onwards with the development of the region's agricultural economy. Joseph outlines the development of the Christian community in Syria up to the 1970s.

471   **The Orthodox-Catholic clash in Aleppo in 1818.**
Hidemitsn Kuroki.   *Orient* (Tokyo), vol. XXIX (1993), p. 1-18.
Kuroki offers a detailed account of the clash between Orthodox and Catholic Christians in Aleppo in April 1818. A background of missionary and Syrian Christians' relations (including Melchites, Armenians, Syrian Jacobites and Catholic Maronites) is provided, which sets the historical and social context. In addition, the author accounts for the response of Aleppo's Muslim community, who sided with the Catholics during the clash. Kuroki provides a number of useful insights into inter-Christian and Christian-Muslim relations. This article will be especially useful for students of history and religious studies.

472 **Conversion to Islam in Syria and Palestine and the survival of Christian communities.**
Nehemia Levtzion. In: *Conversion and continuity – indigenous Christian communities in Islamic lands, eight to eighteenth centuries.* Edited by Michael Gervers, Ramzi Jibean Bikhazi. Toronto: Pontifical Institute of Medieval Studies, 1990, p. 289-311. maps. bibliog.

This article examines the Jacobite and the Greek Orthodox communities within Syria and Lebanon. The author provides a useful survey, noting the internal dynamics of both communities, and the various religious, cultural and demographic changes that took place between the 7th and 16th centuries. Moreover, the relationship between conversion and Islamic rule is carefully scrutinized.

473 **Communal conflicts in Ottoman Syria during the reform era: the role of political and economic factors.**
Moshe Ma'oz. In: *Christians and Jews in the Ottoman Empire: the functioning of a plural society.* Edited by Benjamin Braude, Bernard Lewis. London; New York: Holmes & Meier, 1982, p. 91-103.

Inter-communal relations in the Syrian *vilayets* (provinces) of the Ottoman Empire underwent a substantial transformation during the reform era, which began under Egyptian rule in the 1830s and continued through the *Tanzimat* period to the reign of Sultan Abdulhamid II (1876-1906). The regime's policies served to aggravate and polarize Muslim-Christian and Christian-Jewish relations. This chapter examines the relative weight and impact of religious, political and socio-economic factors. Interestingly, Ma'oz notes that the traditional pattern of Muslim-Jewish relations remained undisturbed. A shorter version of this chapter appeared under the title 'Inter-communal relations in Ottoman Syria during Tanzimat era: social and economic factor', in *Social and economic history of Turkey (1071-1920)*, edited by Hali Inalcik and Osman Okyar (Ankara: Meteksan, 1980, p. 205-10).

474 **Des églises dans la ville.** (Churches in the city.)
Marie-Louise Noujaïm, Claude Therbault. In: *Damas: miroir brisé d'un orient arabe* (Damascus: broken mirror of an Arab Orient). Edited by Anne-Marie Bianquis, Elizabeth Picard. Paris: Editions Autrement, 1993, p. 183-93. (Série Monde, H.S. no. 65).

Damascus is an important city for Christians, as it is the location of Paul's conversion. The authors examine the status of the Christian community in Damascus, discuss their quarters, and argue that religious institutions are showing signs of decline (monasticism and marriage between confessions). The history of Christians (*ahl al dhimmah*) under Islamic rule is briefly outlined. The authors also look at their diminishing public representation, and argue that their feeling of insecurity (reflecting upon the situation of Egyptian Copts) has led many to the path of emigration.

475 **La verité sur la Syrie.** (The truth over Syria.)
Baptistin Poujoulat, introduced by Camille Boustany. Beirut:
Editions Dar Lahad Khater, 1986. 2 vols. (Voyageurs d'Orient, VI).
This book was first published in 1861 under the title *La verité sur la Syrie et
l'expédition Française* (The truth over Syria and the French expedition). It consists of
forty-five letters composed between 6 August and 16 December 1861 by Poujoulat,
who was assigned by the journal *L'Union Franc-Comtoise* to write a report on
Muslim-Christian relations after the events of 1860. The letters are most engaging as
they combine description and narrative set within an unusual context.

476 **The Damascene Jewish community in the latter decades of the
eighteenth century: aspects of socio-economic life based on the
register of the shari'ā courts.**
Najwa al-Qattan. In: *The Syrian land in the 18th and the 19th
century: the common and the specific in the historical experience.*
Edited by Thomas Philipp. Stuttgart, Germany: Steiner, 1992,
p. 197-216. (Berliner Islamstudien, Band 5).
Al-Qattan investigates the socio-economic life of the Jewish community in Damascus
during the last decades of the 18th century. The study is based on fourteen *sijills*
(registers) of Muslim *shari'a* courts, including 104 documents related to the Jewish
community. The article is divided into four main sections: Jews and real estate
(p. 197-202); Jewish residency (p. 202-03); money-lending and credit (p. 203-04); and
Jews and the course of justice (p. 204-07). The author concludes that the *sijills* are a
good source for the socio-economic study of *ahl al-dhimmah* (non-Muslims), due to
their attention to detail and cross-sectarian nature.

477 **Heralds of that good realm: Syro-Mesopotamian Gnosis and
Jewish traditions.**
John C. Reeves. Leiden, the Netherlands; New York; Cologne,
Germany: Brill, 1996. 251p. bibliog.
Reeves offers a systematic examination, from a comparative perspective, of the extant
Manichaean (as well as non-Manichaean) rosters of authentic predecessors (Adam,
Sethel, Enosh, Shem and Enoch). They purportedly proclaimed the Religion of Light
prior to the advent of Mani, who claimed to be the 'seal of prophets'. Reeves
examines the implications of this particular doctrine for the origins of Manichaesm.

478 **The Odyssey of Farah Antun: a Syrian Christian's quest for
secularism.**
Donald M. Reid. Minneapolis; Chicago: Bibliotheca Islamica, 1975.
160p. bibliog.
Farah Antun was one of the first Syrian Christians to promote the idea of secularism.
He started the secularist magazine *al-Jami'ah* and rose to fame with the publication of
his controversial article on ibn Rushd. His ideas were refuted by Muhammad 'Abduh,
and their public debates were conveyed in *al-Jami'ah* and in Rida's magazine *al-
Manar*. This book provides a detailed study and analysis of Antun's life and ideas.

479   **Jews in late Ottoman Syria: external relations.**
Walter P. Zenner.   In: *Jewish societies in the Middle East:
community, culture and authority.*   Edited by Shlomo Deshen, Walter
P. Zenner.   Washington, DC: University Press of America, 1982,
p. 155-86.

Using a variety of historical sources, such as rabbinic court records and the
testimonies of Syrian Jews, this chapter tries to reconstruct the social and economic
life of the Jewish community in late Ottoman Syria. The first part examines Jewish
relations with the Ottoman state, in particular their role in tax collection. Jewish
relations with other *dhimmis* (protected non-Muslim communities), in particular the
Christians, and with their Muslim neighbours are also discussed. The second part
describes the economic life of the Jewish communities in Aleppo and Damascus.

480   **Jews in late Ottoman Syria: community, family and religion.**
Walter P. Zenner.   In: *Jewish societies in the Middle East:
community, culture and authority.*   Edited by Shlomo Deshen, Walter
P. Zenner.   Washington, DC: University Press of America, 1982,
p. 187-209.

Illustrates internal aspects of Jewish communal life in Ottoman Syria. The organization
of Jewish communities is described, and particular attention is given to educational
institutions and the role of rabbinic authority. The work discusses aspects of family and
household life, including customs, marriage, divorce, religious and leisure activities,
and outlines the manifestation of creeping Westernization in the 19th century.

Oriental encounters: Palestine & Syria 1894 – 1896.
See item no. 76.

Syria under Islam: empire on trial, 634-1097.
See item no. 205.

**Les orthodoxes entre Beyrouth et Damas: une millet chretienne dans
deux villes Ottomans.** (The orthodox between Beirut and Damascus: a
Christian confession in two Ottoman cities.)
See item no. 228.

Some Arabic manuscript sources on the Syrian crisis of 1860.
See item no. 300.

Kurds

481 **Ankara, Damascus, Baghdad and the regionalization of Turkey's Kurdish secessionism.**
Suha Bolukbasi. *Journal of South Asian and Middle Eastern Studies*, vol. XIV, no. 4 (summer 1991), p. 15-36.
Bolukbasi contemplates the regionalization of the Kurdish problem, and whether this state of affairs is transitory or permanent. She argues that whilst the regionalization of the problem served the Partia Karkaren Kurdistan (PKK) in the 1980s, the regional prominence of Turkey in the post-Gulf War era will work against Kurdish interests. The roles played by Damascus, Baghdad, the PKK and the KDP (Kurdistan Democratic Party) are assessed. From the Turkish-Syrian perspective, the author concludes that Syria's support of the PKK will continue as long as their mutual animosity towards Turkey continues.

482 **Kurdish material culture in Syria.**
Karin Kren. In: *Kurdish culture and identity.* Edited by Philip G. Kreyenbroek, Christine Allison. London; Atlantic Highlands, New Jersey: Zed in association with the Centre of Near and Middle Eastern Studies, SOAS, 1996, p. 162-73.
A study that draws attention to the importance of ethnographic specimens in the documentation of culture, with specific reference to the Kurds. The author opines, however, that it has not been possible to define Kurdish culture as a single phenomenon due to the depth of variation in regional patterns. The author's study is based on fieldwork, obtained whilst living with a Kurdish tribe in Syria, and is supplemented with material from a Viennese collection, found in the Museum für Völkerkunde. It concentrates on the role of Kurdish women and their contribution to the subsistence economy of their community.

483 **The Kurds, a contemporary overview.**
Edited by Philip G. Kreyenbroek, Stefan Sperl. London: Routledge, 1992. 200p. bibliog.
A comprehensive and accessible book, which provides a foundation for studying the history of the Kurdish people. The topics covered include: a brief history; social and political issues; the legal status of the Kurds; religion; language; and a contemporary assessment of their status in Turkey, Iran, Iraq, Syria and the former Soviet Union. This is an ideal handbook for students of the Middle East.

484 **The Kurds: a nation denied.**
David McDowall, foreword by John Simpson. London: Minority Rights, 1992. 148p. maps.
According to McDowall, the purpose of his book is to explore the identity of the Kurds, their bonds of loyalty, and their historical and recent experience since the demise of the Ottoman Empire. Chapter fourteen, entitled 'Kurds on the periphery: Syria, Lebanon and the USSR' (p. 121-26), conveys the Kurdish experience in Syria, from the Mandate era until the early 1990s. The relationship of the Kurds to the Syrian state has never been institutionalized, as changes in the domestic and regional climate affect the

fortunes of Syria's minorities. As McDowall writes, 'it is difficult in a totalitarian state to measure the rights and freedoms for one particular minority community as distinct from the general restriction on freedoms for the country as a whole'.

485 **The creation of a Kurdish state in the 1990's?**
Robert Olson. *Journal of South Asian and Middle Eastern Studies*, vol. XV, no. 4 (summer 1992), p. 1-25.

Olson assesses the viability of an independent Kurdish state by comparing the regional and international geopolitical environment of the 1920s to that of the late 1980s and early 1990s. The article briefly touches upon Syria's relations with the Kurds.

486 **The Kurdish question and geopolitic and geostrategic changes in the Middle East after the Gulf War.**
Robert Olson. *Journal of South Asian and Middle Eastern Studies*, vol. XVII, no. 4 (summer 1994), p. 44-67.

This article explores the challenges faced by Turkey and Iran over the Kurdish question since the Second Gulf War. Olson also examines Syrian and Iraqi attitudes towards the Kurds. As Syria was already facing economic and political (Lebanon and Israel) problems, Oslon thinks it unlikely that it would encourage an independent Kurdish state along its northern border.

487 **The Kurdish question and Turkey's foreign policy, 1991-1995: from the Gulf War to the incursion into Iraq.**
Robert Olson. *Journal of South Asian and Middle Eastern Studies*, vol. XIX, no. 1 (fall 1995), p. 1-30.

From his analysis of Turkey's Kurdish problems, Olson examines Turkey's relations with its neighbours, Iran, Iraq, Syria and Russia. Faced with the challenge of an autonomous Kurdish zone in northern Iraq and the activities of the PKK, Turkey has sought to conclude regional agreements guaranteeing the territorial integrity of Iraq. The author analyses Turkish-Syrian relations (p. 4-8), and in particular Syria's evolving policy towards the PKK.

488 **The Kurdish question four years on: the policies of Turkey, Syria, Iran and Iraq.**
Robert Olson. *Middle East Policy*, vol. III, no. 3 (September 1994), p. 136-44.

The author gauges the policies of Turkey, Syria, Iran and Iraq towards the Kurdish question in the aftermath of the Gulf War. He assesses the possibility of *rapprochement* amongst the four states, with the issue of water drawing Turkey and Syria closer to one another (p. 136-38). Thus Syria's support of the PKK is re-examined in light of the changing regional environment.

489 **Turkey-Syria relations: Kurds and water.**
Robert Olson. *Middle East Policy*, vol. V, no. 2 (May 1997), p. 168-93.

The author examines relations between Turkey and Syria with respect to water distribution from the Euphrates, Tigris and 'Asi rivers, and the historical dispute over

Hatay (Alexandretta). Olson further addresses the centrality of the Kurdish question to Turkish-Syrian relations. He suggests that Syria's change in policy towards the Kurdish issue, between 1993 and 1996, was motivated by its concern to participate in the Middle East peace process, and the threatening military alignment of Turkey and Israel. In conclusion, Olson intimates that Turkish-Syrian relations are moving in the direction of conflict rather than *rapprochement*.

A 17th century travel account on the Yazidis: implications for a socio-religious study.
See item no. 72.

Turkey challenges Iraq and Syria: the Euphrates dispute.
See item no. 606.

Society and Social Conditions

490 **Ethnicity, clientship, and class: their changing meaning.**
Richard Antoun.   In: *Syria: society, culture, and polity.*   Edited by
Richard Antoun, Donald Quataert.   Albany, New York: State
University of New York Press, 1991, p. 1-12. (SUNY Series in Middle
Eastern Studies).
As an introduction to this multidisciplinary book, Antoun provides a succinct account
of the prevailing theoretical approaches utilized by its authors. Ethnicity,
patrimonialism and class are introduced through the works of Battatu, Drysdale,
Hinnebusch and Sadowski, whilst a religious and cultural approach is taken by Khuri.
This short article offers the student an excellent introduction to the current debates
surrounding Syria.

491 **Syria: society, culture, and polity.**
Edited by Richard Antoun, Donald Quataert.   Albany, New York:
State University of New York Press, 1991. 165p. maps. bibliog.
(SUNY Series in Middle Eastern Studies).
Covers a wide range of topics on Syrian society, such as politics, economics, religion,
foreign policy and women. It is a multidisciplinary study that deals with macro
(politics) as well as micro (women) issues. It is a good source and will be suitable for
all readers interested in Syria.

492 **'Our Moslem sisters': women of Greater Syria in the eyes of
Protestant missionary women.**
Ellen L. Fleischmann.   *Islam and Christian-Muslim Relations*, vol. 9,
no. 3 (1998), p. 307-23.
The influence of Protestant missionaries on Syrian women is addressed by
Fleischmann. In particular, she studies the work of women missionaries from the US
Presbyterian Church, during the period 1850-1940, and uses missionary journals,
pamphlets, magazines, personal letters and memoirs. The sources reveal missionary

women's perceptions of their Syrian counterparts. The missionary women attempted to transport American ideals of home-life to Syria in order to combat the 'citadels of heathenism'; however, such values were alien and ill-fitting to Syrian society. Fleischmann calls for further research on this subject, and recommends a shift in focus away from the missionary and towards the indigenous perspective. The article is particularly suitable for students of women's studies.

493 **Arab unity schemes revisited: interest, identity, and policy in Syria and Egypt.**
Eberhard Kienle. *International Journal of Middle East Studies*, vol. 27, no. 1 (February 1995), p. 53-71.

'In Syria the growing insistence on a community wider than that of the people of the Syrian state correlated with increasing external threats in the 1950s.' This statement succinctly summarizes Kienle's analysis of the differential between Syrian and Egyptian approaches to unity schemes. Whereas Egyptian identity has remained synonymous with the Egyptian nation, Syrian identity has been, until more recently, ambiguous and anchored to a broader Arab identity. This differential contributed to Egypt's independent and diffident approach to unity schemes, and conversely, to Syria's dependence upon the extended community to counter external threats. Recent trends in Syria, nevertheless, indicate the strengthening of a Syrian identity, as the state building strategies of the 1970s have fostered and served regime and state interests. Kienle concludes, however, that the construction of a Syrian community will have a long way to go before it can create a sense of collective identity similar to that of the Egyptians.

494 **Social structure and political stability: comparative evidence from the Algerian, Syrian, and Iraqi cases.**
Jean Leca. In: *Beyond coercion: the durability of the Arab state.* Edited by Adeed I. Dawisha, I. William Zartman. London; New York: Croom Helm, 1988, p. 164-202. (Nation, State and Integration in the Arab World, vol. 3).

Leca comments that the Arab regimes have been stable since the early 1970s. He investigates the evolution of social structure as a factor in explaining this stability by looking at three cases: Algeria, Syria (p. 183-92) and Iraq. He looks in particular at the politico-economic formula in Syria, and describes it as embedded in a regional and internal social context.

495 **Lycéennes en treillis et fonctionnaires voilées.** (Fatigued female high-school students and veiled civil servants.)
Elisabeth Longuenesse. In: *Damas: miroir brisé d'un orient arabe* (Damascus: broken mirror of an Arab Orient). Edited by Anne-Marie Bianquis, Elizabeth Picard. Paris: Editions Autrement, 1993, p. 207-18. (Série Monde, H.S. no. 65).

Longuenesse discusses the conditions of women in Damascus. She argues that the conditions of women have improved in terms of education and work, encouraged by the Ba'th regime, but that these improvements have been undermined by religious practices.

496 **'Mukhalafat' entre montagne et jardins.** ('Mukhalafat' between
mountain and gardens.)
Abdul-Karim Muhallamy.   In: *Damas: miroir brisé d'un orient arabe*
(Damascus: broken mirror of an Arab Orient).   Edited by Anne-Marie
Bianquis, Elizabeth Picard.   Paris: Editions Autrement, 1993,
p. 128-35. (Série Monde, H.S. no. 65).

A description of the poor quarters of Syria, which the authorities refer to as
mukhalafat. The author describes the living conditions of such a district in the
Qassioun Mountain (p. 129-32) and another from the plains al-Dahadil (p. 132-33).
Using as examples two families from the former quarter and one from the latter,
Muhallamy draws a lively picture of typical living conditions in these areas.

497 **Change on the Euphrates: villagers, townsmen and employees in
northeast Syria.**
Annika Rabo.   Stockholm: Studies in Social Anthropology, 1986.
222p. maps. bibliog. (Studies in Social Anthropology, no. 15).

The subjects of this study live in the Raqqa region of north-east Syria. They include
townsmen, newly-arrived employees, and the villagers of Sabgha. The setting is one
of the least developed regions in Syria, now subject to considerable government
attention. This study analyses the political economy of the region's inhabitants against
the backdrop of the Euphrates scheme, which was to revolutionize Syria's irrigation
system and electricity generation. It includes a preface in Arabic and an Arabic-
English glossary.

498 **The rise and fall of secularism in the Arab world.**
Paul Salem.   *Middle East Policy*, vol. IV, no. 3 (March 1996),
p. 147-60.

The author associates the rise of secularism in the Arab world with Napoleon's
invasion of Egypt in 1798, and Muhammad 'Ali's attempt to modernize Egypt. Salem
follows the development of secular and national thinkers in the Arab world, such as
Michel 'Aflaq and Saddah, until the rise of fundamentalism in the 1990s. He argues
that if conflicts in the Middle East fail to be expressed in secular and national terms,
they are in danger of being translated into 'religious and confessional' movements.
Therefore he advises against substituting the 'threat of Islam' for the 'threat of the
Soviet Union'. Such a move would widen the gap between the West and the Arab
world. Instead, Salem calls for a review of European and American foreign policies
towards the Arab world.

The atlas of the Arab world: geopolitics and society.
See item no. 29.

**The social bases and discursive context of the rise of Islamic
fundamentalism: the cases of Iran and Syria.**
See item no. 422.

Over-stating the Arab state: politics and society in the Middle East.
See item no. 504.

Palestinians in Syria: the politics of integration.
See item no. 508.

State and society in Syria and Lebanon.
See item no. 509.

Military elites, military led social movements and the social structures in developing countries: a comparative study of Egypt and Syria.
See item no. 510.

Class and state in Ba'thist Syria.
See item no. 518.

Syria 1945-1986: politics and society.
See item no. 526.

Syria unmasked: the suppression of human rights by the Asad regime.
See item no. 548.

Acting 'as if': symbolic politics and social control.
See item no. 562.

The Golan Heights: twenty years after.
See item no. 660.

Life under occupation in the Golan Heights.
See item no. 666.

Economic policy and class structure in Syria: 1958-1980.
See item no. 702.

Land reform and class structuring rural Syria.
See item no. 740.

The regional equalization of health care and education in Syria since the Ba'thi revolution.
See item no. 763.

Ba'thist ideology, economic development and educational strategy.
See item no. 765.

A quarter of Aleppo in the 19th and 20th centuries: some socio-economical and architectural aspects.
See item no. 825.

Politics

499 **Fī sabīl al-ba'th.** (For the sake of the Ba'th.)
Michel 'Aflaq, introduced by Sa'dun Hamadi.　Beirut: al-Talī'ah,
1959. 252p.
A collection of 'Aflaq's essays on nationalism, socialism, unity and freedom,
composed between 1935 and 1959. It includes speeches and lectures given by 'Aflaq.

500 **Fī sabīl al-ba'th: al-kitābāt al-sīyāsīyah al-kāmilah.** (For the sake of
the Ba'th: the complete writings.)
Michel 'Aflaq.　Beirut: Dār al-Hurrīyah, 1986. 307p.
A collection of 'Aflaq's writings on nationalism, the Ba'th, revolution, Arab struggle
and socialism. A biography of 'Aflaq is also provided.

501 **Nidāl al-ba'th fī sabīl al-wihdah, al-hurrīyah, al-ishtrākīyah:
wathā'q hizb al-ba'th al-'arabī al-ishtrākī.** (The struggle of the
Ba'th for the sake of unity, freedom and socialism: documents of the
Arab Socialist Ba'th Party.)
The Arab Socialist Ba'th Party.　Beirut: al-Talī'ah, 1943-63. 7 vols.
A collection of official documents, including a series of short articles written between
1946 and 1963. This multi-volume work will be very useful to researchers charting the
history and ideology of the Ba'th Party.

502 **The party program.**
The Arab Socialist Ba'th Party.　Damascus: Ministry of Information,
1965. 48p.
An outline of the Ba'th Party, including its role, its relationship with the masses and
its duty to the Arabs.

503 **Syria after two years of the March revolution.**
The Arab Socialist Ba'th Party. Damascus: Ministry of Information,
1965. 175p.
An account of the revolution's achievements after two years. It covers the following
areas: socialism; democracy; industrialization; agriculture and agrarian reform; trade
unionism; and social, cultural and health welfare.

504 **Over-stating the Arab state: politics and society in the Middle East.**
Nazih N. Ayubi. London; New York: I. B. Tauris, 1995. 514p.
bibliog.
Covers a wide range of topics relating to the formation of the Arab state. Using a
political economy approach, the author examines Egypt, Syria, Iraq, Tunisia, Jordan,
Saudi Arabia, Kuwait, the United Arab Emirates (UAE), Algeria, Yemen, Lebanon
and Morocco. He argues that Arab states are 'hard' states, and some of them can be
described as 'fierce', in terms of possessing large bureaucracies, strong armies, and a
willingness to use coercion against their populations. Nonetheless, they cannot be
considered 'strong' states in the 'moral and intellectual sphere'. Ayubi looks at the
disintegration of the Ottoman Empire and its impact upon the Syrian state. Focusing
on the borders, and the composition of the population, he argues that Syria in 1995
was a 'residual entity'. Its objective after independence was to 'preserve' what was
left of Syria rather than to attain unity. The author considers liberalization in Syria
(p. 421-24), showing how it has been regulated and managed in order to extend
patronage within society. The work contains an extensive bibliography on the Middle
East (p. 460-95).

505 **Withered socialism or whether socialism? The radical Arab states
as populist-corporatist regimes.**
Nazih N. Ayubi. *Third World Quarterly*, vol. 13, no. 1 (1992),
p. 89-105.
Ayubi offers a definition of socialism and then assesses its applicability to the Arab
world. He argues that the self-confessed radical states were not socialist, as they did
not embrace the ideology, rather it was the 'political and institutional pursuits that
eventually led them to a semblance of socialism' (p. 92). Socialism in Syria is briefly
analysed on p. 95-96. The following tables are included: government expenditure as
percentage of GDP in Arab states in 1975-82 (p. 91); and the structure of public
expenditure in Arab states in 1981 (p. 93).

506 **Linkage politics in the Middle East: Syria between domestic and
external conflict, 1961-1970.**
Yaacov Bar-Siman-Tov. Boulder, Colorado: Westview, 1983. 176p.
Using Syria as a case-study, the author evaluates two approaches to linkage politics:
the traditional and the quantitative. Syria was selected due to the potential connection
between its internal political instability, the Arab Cold War, and the Arab-Israeli
conflict. From his study, the author identifies three dominant variables underlying the
link between Syria's internal and external conflicts from 1961 to 1966. These were:
the presence of Nasserist linkage groups; the narrow base of legitimization of the
Syrian regime; and the existence of the Syrian-Israeli conflict. The author concludes
that the combination of qualitative and quantitative analysis was particularly effective
in the examination of Syrian conflict linkage.

507   **The Egyptian, Syrian, and Iraqi revolutions: some observations on their underlying causes and social character.**
Hanna Batatu.   Washington, DC: Center for Contemporary Arab Studies, School of Foreign Services, Georgetown University, 1984. 27p.
This was an inaugural lecture given on 25 January 1983. The lecture appears in this volume in both English and Arabic. The author observes that in-depth studies concerning the social origins of officers responsible for the revolutions in the Arab world are sadly lacking. Batatu examines the causative factors underlying the insurrections and focuses on three cases: Egypt, Syria and Iraq. He scrutinizes the social origins of the officers who were responsible for the revolutions, as well as the significance of family units as loci of political and economic interaction. Although the lecture provides an insightful analysis, it is disappointingly brief.

508   **Palestinians in Syria: the politics of integration.**
Laurie A. Brand.   *Middle Eastern Studies*, vol. 42, no. 4 (autumn 1988), p. 621-37.
Brand examines the welfare and legal status of the Palestinian community living in Syria. She argues that the socio-economic and political conditions have facilitated Palestinian integration into Syrian society, thus discouraging the emergence of institutional expressions of a separate identity. However, Brand argues that the recent economic downturn may lead to more exclusionary policies, and that Palestinian organizations, such as the General Union of Palestinian Workers (GUPW) and the General Union of Palestinian Women (GUPWom), may adopt a different political role. A table of UNRWA (United Nations Relief and Works Agency)-registered Palestinians in Syria is provided (p. 625).

509   **State and society in Syria and Lebanon.**
Edited by Youssef M. Choueiri.   Exeter, England: Exeter University Press, 1993; New York: St. Martin's Press, 1994. 158p.
This book covers a wide range of topics relating to Syria and Lebanon from 1919 to 1991. It highlights the similarities and differences between the two communities in terms of their economy, politics and society. It deals with the experiment of the first Arab state (1918-20), as well as contemporary issues such as the Ta'if Accord (which restored a legitimate government in Lebanon following its civil war) and the Gulf War. It shows how the two communities, in spite of sharing a common past, diverged in development during the French Mandate, and how this led to the significant differences of the 1980s. In the introduction, Choueiri presents a very short history of Syria from the 18th to the 20th century. This is a useful source, but one finds that the objective is too ambitious for such a short book.

510   **Military elites, military led social movements and the social structures in developing countries: a comparative study of Egypt and Syria.**
Adnan B. Daoud-Agha.   PhD thesis, University of California, Berkerley, California, 1970. 454p. bibliog. (Available from University Microfilms, Ann Arbor, Michigan).
This study accounts for the different experiences of Syria and Egypt's military elites. Whereas Egypt has endured only one *coup d'état*, and the military have managed to

consolidate power and legitimize the state, the Syrians had endured eight coups before Asad seized power. The author concludes that given the cultural similarity between the two states, their different experiences must emanate from their divergent social structures. Henceforth, the author offers comparative analysis of Syria and Egypt's social structures.

511 **Syria under Asad, 1970-7: the centres of power.**
Adeed I. Dawisha. *Government and Opposition*, vol. 13, no. 3 (1978), p. 341-54.
According to Dawisha, three major institutions dominate the domestic political scene in Syria: the presidency; the Ba'th Party; and the military. Asad's control and authoritative position emanates from his leadership of all three institutions, although he is constrained, to a certain degree, by the armed forces and the Ba'th Party.

512 **The Ba'th party: a history from its origins to 1966.**
John F. Devlin. Stanford, California: Hoover Institution Press, 1976. 372p. bibliog.
A detailed study that traces the rise, spread and ideology of the Ba'th Party from its origins in the 1930s to the schism of 1966 when its founders, Michel 'Aflaq and Salah al-Bitar, were expelled from Syria and the party split into two antagonistic organizations. The author describes the origins and ideology of Ba'thism; the foundation and growth of the party in Syria; and its merger with Akram Hawrani's Arab Socialist party in 1953. The growth of the party outside Syria, its role in the formation of the United Arab Republic, and its incompatibility with the Nasserist system are discussed in the context of the party's tendency towards factionalism. Devlin also examines the emergence of the neo-Ba'th Party following the collapse of the union with Egypt, and the ascendancy of the military in the party. The final chapters examine the February 1966 coup, which established the primacy of the military and their regional supporters. An epilogue deals with the period from February 1966 until the mid-1970s, covering the rise of Asad and the 'corrective' movement. Appendices include: the membership of the national congresses and commands of 1947-66; the regional congresses and commands; and the 1947 party constitution.

513 **Political parties of Africa and the Middle East: a reference guide.**
Edited by Roger East, Tanya Joseph. Harlow, England: Longman, 1993. 354p. maps. (Longman Current Affairs).
Provides information on the political parties of 'sovereign' states in Africa and the Middle East. Syria is covered on p. 283-85. Information given includes details of the constitution, the electoral system and past elections. All known political parties, legal or otherwise, receive attention.

514 **Hafez el-Assad – Syria.**
James Haskins, foreword by Richard W. Bulliet. In: *Leaders of the Middle East*. Hillside, New Jersey; Aldershot, England: Enslow, 1985, p. 47-60.
A slightly bizarre portrait of the Syrian president. Haskins has written a very short biography, using terminology which is more fitting for an undergraduate, and yet he manages to touch upon the ambiguities often ascribed to Asad. The chapter is

chronological in nature and lacks analytical depth. It serves as a snapshot of both Asad and Syria in the post-1970 era.

515 **The political logic of economic rationality: selective stabilization in Syria.**
Steven Heydemann. In: *The politics of economic reform in the Middle East.* Edited by Henri Barkey. New York: St. Martin's Press, 1992, p. 11-39.

Heydemann offers an excellent analysis of Syria's move towards economic reform. In attempting to understand how authoritarian regimes manage economic development and economic crisis, Heydemann focuses upon the Syrian experience. He opines that despite the nature of Syria's weakly institutionalized and patronage-based regime, it has shown a reasonable capacity to implement a set of rationalizing economic reforms. After 1991, through a process of selective stabilization the regime enhanced the incentives for the private sector without significantly disrupting patronage networks. These reforms, now deemed irreversible, contain the potential to push the regime towards further economic adjustment and liberalization.

516 **Authoritarian power and state formation in Ba'thist Syria: army, party, and peasant.**
Raymond A. Hinnebusch. Boulder, Colorado: Westview Press, 1990. 350p. maps. bibliog.

An in-depth study of Syria from the rise of the Syrian Ba'th Party and the formation of Ba'thist state, supported by facts, figures, tables, diagrams and interviews. The narrative deals in exhaustive detail with all the events of Syria's recent history and its agricultural reform. The author argues that the principal concept that lends insight into the rise, durability and nature of the Ba'th is 'authoritarian populism'. The work will be especially useful for students of Middle Eastern and Third World politics.

517 **Bureaucracy and development in Syria: the case of agriculture.**
Raymond A. Hinnebusch. *Journal of Asian and African Studies,* vol. XXIV, no. 1-2 (January & April 1989), p. 79-93. bibliog.

As a case-study, Hinnebusch examines the role of the agricultural bureaucracy within Syria. He identifies the motor of bureaucratic policy as being the president and the ideology of the Ba'th ruling party, rather than the ministerial bureaucracy *per se.* As the state managed to penetrate village life, through a system of patronage, peasant interests were incorporated into the regime. Hinnebusch suggests that private capital accumulation in the village, as well as in the city, has the potential to create an environment conducive to capitalist transformation in the economy.

518 **Class and state in Ba'thist Syria.**
Raymond A. Hinnebusch. In: *Syria: society, culture, and polity.* Edited by Richard Antoun, Donald Quataert. Albany, New York: State University of New York Press, 1991, p. 29-47. (SUNY Series in Middle Eastern Studies).

Hinnebusch explores the impact of state policy, under the Ba'th, on class structure. He argues that it is impossible to make sense of modern Syrian political development

Politics

without resorting to the class variable. After a century of capitalist penetration and modernization, Syria is no longer a simple segmental society, but a complex one in which patronage networks coexist with classes.

519 **Peasant and bureaucracy in Ba'thist Syria: the political economy of rural development.**
Raymond A. Hinnebusch.   Boulder, Colorado: Westview Press, 1989. 325p. bibliog.

The author argues that the role of peasants and the nature of rural society are instrumental to the formation of the state. He presents an empirical study of Syria's rural development policies under the Ba'th Party, and analyses their impact upon the state. The book focuses on the process of policy-making within the agrarian bureaucracy, placing an emphasis on factors such as technocratic considerations, elite orientation, conflicts over ideology and the politics of patronage. The second part of the book reviews the consequences of policy implementation in the areas of economic performance, the provision of services and the incorporation of political allegiances.

520 **Political parties in the Arab state: Libya, Syria, Egypt.**
Raymond A. Hinnebusch.   In: *Beyond coercion: the durability of the Arab state.*   Edited by Adeed I. Dawisha, I. William Zartman. London; New York; Sydney: Croom Helm, 1988, p. 35-60. (Nation, State and Integration in the Arab World, vol. 3).

Hinnebusch looks at the place of political parties in the Arab world and the conditions under which they develop their functions, using Egypt, Syria and Libya as case-studies. He argues that the environment of the Arab world is hostile to the development of a free-functioning party system. Syria is covered on p. 43-50. Hinnebusch opines that Syria provides an instance where a single party has attempted to overcome the fragmentation of communal, class and urban-rural conflicts. Accordingly, the Ba'th Party has offered a solution to the crisis of society through a mixture of pan-Arabism, the creation of a strong popular-based state, and radical social reform.

521 **Political recruitment and socialization in Syria: the case of the Revolutionary Youth Federation.**
Raymond A. Hinnebusch.   *International Journal of Middle East Studies,* vol. 11, no. 2 (1980), p. 143-74.

Discusses party recruitment and socialization practices in explaining the Ba'th Party's success in establishing a strong system of single party rule, and instituting its extensive programme of political and social change. The author looks in particular at the Revolutionary Youth Federation (Ittihad al-shabab al-thawrri) and presents a statistical analysis of its recruitment programme and membership.

522 **State and civil society in Syria.**
Raymond A. Hinnebusch.   *The Middle East Journal,* vol. 47, no. 2 (spring 1993), p. 243-57.

In this article, Hinnebusch addresses the broader debate linking democracy to civil society. Tracing the weakness of Syrian civil society to the military-fiscal apparatus of the Ottoman state, he charts its history from the late Ottoman period to the early

145

Politics

1990s. Whereas the pre-modern Ottoman state tolerated an autonomous civil society, it was fragmented and poorly integrated into the political structure. On the other hand, the Ba'thist state has created a more open social structure and a more inclusive form of authoritarian-corporatist policy that has embraced a more mobilized peasantry, a large educated middle class, and a reviving private bourgeoisie. The more recent shift in balance between state and civil society, in the post-Soviet era, is believed to have initiated an incremental process towards greater political liberalization.

523   **Syria: the politics of peace and regime survival.**
Raymond A. Hinnebusch.   *Middle East Policy*, vol. 3, no. 4 (April 1995), p. 74-87.

This article addresses the issue of whether the current Syrian regime can survive peace with Israel. Hinnebusch is responding to critics who question Syria's sincerity towards peace and who suggest that Asad's regime requires conflict in order to perpetuate its legitimacy. Hinnebusch asserts that through a process of regime adaptation, economic reform and calculated political decompression (or 'controlled' political reform), the Syrian regime has been altering the composition of its legitimacy, thus imbuing it with the ability to deliver peace.

524   **Syria: the role of ideology and party organization in local development.**
Raymond A. Hinnebusch.   In: *Local politics and development in the Middle East.*   Edited by Louis J. Cantori, Iliya Harik.   London; Boulder, Colorado: Westview Press, 1984, p. 99-124.

This essay explores the links between particular types of national regime and local development in Syria under the Ba'th. It begins by outlining changes in national level ideology and development strategies since 1943, focusing on the Ba'th radicals (1965-70) and realists (post-1970). The importance of the essay lies in its detailed portrayal of local level politics and party organization in Syria. Local branches of the party, and of ancillary institutions, are dominated by local political elites. Development appears to proceed within these locally adapted governmental structures rather than around them. Although the outcome of Ba'th development strategies has diverged from its original revolutionary blueprint, the social structure and institutional configuration of the Syrian countryside has changed in three important ways: the traditional 'feudal' structure has been destroyed; the numerically small peasantry have become an important social force; and the role of the state has greatly expanded.

525   **Syria under the Ba'th: state formation in a fragmented society.**
Raymond A. Hinnebusch.   *Arab Studies Quarterly*, vol. 4, no. 3 (1982), p. 177-99.

This article describes various aspects of Ba'th Party rule in Syria from 1963 to 1981, including its organization, policies and authoritarian populist nature. The author outlines the party's rise to power, the emergence of the new elite and the structural bases of the regime. He also notes a persistent gap between objectives and achievements in the Ba'th Party's modernization strategy and in its defence and foreign policies.

Politics

526 **Syria 1945-1986: politics and society.**
Derek Hopwood. London; Winchester, Massachusetts; Sydney;
Wellington: Unwin Hyman, 1988. 193p. bibliog.
A basic introduction to Syria, which will be most suitable for undergraduates and
general readers. It provides information on climate, religious minorities, politics and
history. It also discusses Syria under Asad, the Ba'th Party in power, the economy,
education, culture and literature. A chronology of the period 1918-86 is provided on
p. 185-86.

527 **'Aflaq wa-al-ba'th: nisf qarn min al-nidāl.** (Aflaq and the Ba'th: half
a century of struggle.)
Joseph Ilias. Beirut: Dār al-Nidāl, 1991. 420p. bibliog.
A collection of articles about 'Aflaq, most of which were published in the newspaper
al-Nahar (Beirut). Chapter four (p. 295-361) focuses on 'Aflaq's philosophy. The
appendix includes samples of 'Aflaq's work which were written during the 1930s.

528 **Non-democratic states and political liberalization in the Middle
East: a structural analysis.**
Mehran Kamrava. *Third World Quarterly*, vol. 19, no. 1 (March
1998), p. 63-85.
Kamrava examines how Middle Eastern states resist the popular demand for political
liberalization. He argues that in spite of their diversity, Middle Eastern states are
resilient to domestic demands. Accordingly, states are classified as exclusionary and
inclusionary. Exclusionary states are further divided into *mukhabarat* (secret service)
states (Egypt and Syria); and military states (Algeria and Sudan). Inclusionary states
include Iran, Iraq and Libya, and another division delineates sultanistic regimes, such
as the oil monarchies of the Arabian Peninsula, and the mythical monarchies of Jordan
and Morocco (mythical in that they trace their links to the prophet Muhammad).

529 **Ba'th v Ba'th: the conflict between Syria and Iraq, 1969-1989.**
Eberhard Kienle. London: I. B. Tauris, 1990. 238p. bibliog.
This book examines the issues that have determined Syrian-Iraqi relations since 1968,
with an emphasis on their shared historical/ideological background, and their domestic
and foreign policies. The governments of Syria and Iraq both claim to represent the
Ba'th Party, and one of the constitutional goals of the party is to create an all-
encompassing Arab state. In spite of this ambitious goal, Syria and Iraq have remained
bitter rivals, and, apart from a brief *rapprochement* during 1978-79, have endured a
struggle of propaganda, subversion and conspiracy. Kienle examines the conflict over
resources (oil pipelines, Euphrates water), and the difference between state and society.
An extensive bibliography of English, German, French and Arabic sources is provided.

530 **The return of politics? Scenarios for Syria's second infitah.**
Eberhard Kienle. In: *Contemporary Syria: liberalization between
Cold War and cold peace.* Edited by Eberhard Kienle, preface by
Patrick Seale. London: British Academic Press; New York: St
Martin's Press, 1994, p. 114-31.
Kienle analyses the economic and political reforms of the early 1990s. He argues that
liberalization has resulted in the dominant force within Syria becoming 'less

147

interventionist'; it does not imply a turn towards democracy, only that a council of new players will be considered. Kienle compares the liberalization programme of the 1970s to the programme adopted in the early 1990s. In terms of the political programme, he concludes that the second *infitah* will share the same fate as the first, wherein power continues to reside in the hands of the elite.

531 The political dictionary of modern Middle East.
Agnes Korbani. Lanham, Maryland; New York; London: University Press of America, 1995. 258p. bibliog.

A handy political dictionary of the modern Middle East which offers short definitions with little analysis. It is a useful reference for general readers, and public and school libraries.

532 Class politics and state power in Ba'thi Syria.
Fred H. Lawson. In: *Power and stability in the Middle East.* Edited by Berch Beberoglu. Atlantic Highlands, New Jersey; London: Zed, 1989, p. 15-30.

Using class analysis, Lawson suggests that the instability of Syria has been closely associated with the fluctuation in class relations. Where class interests have prevailed, through the amalgam of interests between the regime and the traditional bourgeoisie, stability has ensued. The article is divided into three sections: 'Consolidating Ba'thi rule, 1963-65' (p. 16-20); 'Restructuring the regime, 1966-68' (p. 20-23); and 'Re-orientating the Ba'th, 1970-83' (p. 24-28). Lawson argues that successive regimes, since 1963, have adopted exclusionary policies and developed 'sectarian affiliations' as the primary foci for political loyalty. Moreover, the regime in Syria has become more 'personalist' under Asad, as he presides over country affairs and is closely tied to special units of Syrian armed forces.

533 Domestic pressures and the peace process: fillip or hindrance?
Fred H. Lawson. In: *Contemporary Syria: liberalization between Cold War and cold peace.* Edited by Eberhard Kienle, preface by Patrick Seale. London: British Academic Press; New York: St Martin's Press, 1994, p. 139-54.

Lawson offers the reader a domestic politics analysis of Syrian foreign policy. In an attempt to satiate the competing demands of his domestic constituency, Asad has prevaricated between overtures of peace and hard-line anti-Israeli rhetoric. The author refers to specific occasions between 1991 and 1993, when Asad offered contradictory public addresses to different audiences, ranging from the Ba'th Party to the Damascus Chamber of Commerce. Lawson's argument is in keeping with his previous work, which suggests that domestic politics plays an over-riding role in the formulation of foreign policy.

534 Domestic transformation and foreign steadfastness in contemporary Syria.
Fred H. Lawson. *The Middle East Journal,* vol. 48, no. 1 (winter 1994), p. 47-64.

Using class analysis, Lawson accounts for Syria's domestic and foreign policies since the late 1980s. Policies, it is argued, are not governed by the international political environment, but rather the need to satisfy the state's dominant social forces. Four powerful social forces are identified: the commanders of the state's military and security apparatuses; the cadre of state-affiliated managers; the large-scale commercial elite; and wealthy agriculturists. The decision-making processes must balance the interests of these competitive groups in order to serve the interests of the state. This is manifest in Syria's relations with Russia, China and North Korea, which satisfy the first two interest groups, and its relations with the Gulf states, which satisfy the commercial and agricultural elite.

535 External versus internal pressure for liberalization in Syria and Iraq.
Fred H. Lawson. *Journal of Arab Affairs*, vol. 11, no. 1 (spring 1992), p. 1-33.

Lawson discusses the change in Ba'thi policies from socialism to capitalism in Syria and Iraq. Using the Egyptian model as a bench-mark, he seeks to identify the predominant factor that has led to the reformulation of policies. Egypt's economic liberalization of the 1970s has been attributed to the following factors: a global shift towards the deregulation of economies; emerging patterns of trade and investment between Arab and Western economies; and the zero-sum character of exports and imports from the Eastern and Western blocs. Lawson concludes that these factors did not play a significant role in Syria and Iraq, and that domestic factors elicited the move towards capitalism.

536 From neo-Ba'th nouveau: Hafiz al-Asad's second decade.
Fred H. Lawson. *Journal of South Asian and Middle Eastern Studies*, vol. XIV, no. 2 (winter 1990), p. 1-21.

With the advent of his second decade in power, Asad's position looked more secure. The Islamist challenge to the regime had been curtailed, and a new coalition of support was emerging in accordance with the demands of the economy. The previous coalition had been composed of a 'coterie' of military officers, Ba'thi officials, rich merchants, small-scale agriculturalists and agrarian workers in the public sector. In the new coalition, the transfer of responsibilities from the public sector to the private sector reintegrated the propertied classes into the national economy and the decision-making process. The article includes tables of gross fixed capital formation by sectors, 1970-86 (p. 4), and of agricultural co-operative bank loans, 1982-86 (p. 15).

537 Why Syria goes to war? Thirty years of confrontation.
Fred H. Lawson. London: Cornell University Press, 1996. 277p. bibliog. (Cornell Studies in Political Economy).

Lawson attempts to understand why Syria goes to war. He argues that the decisions of war and peace are made in accordance with the interests of the dominant 'ruling social coalition'. Moreover, the Syrian leadership tends to respond to domestic crises by provoking a foreign crisis. He uses five scenarios to test his theory: the Six Day War in 1967; the de-escalation of the conflict with Jordan in 1970; the intervention in Lebanon in 1976; the back-down from confrontation with Iraq in 1982; and the *rapprochement* with Turkey in 1994. The result is an unconvincing argument based on superficial evidence.

538 **Al-dimuqratiyya hiyya al-hall? The Syrian opposition at the end of the Asad era.**
Hans Günter Lobmeyer.   In: *Contemporary Syria: liberalization between Cold War and cold peace.*   Edited by Eberhard Kienle, preface by Patrick Seale.   London: British Academic Press; New York: St Martin's Press, 1994, p. 81-96.

Lobmeyer provides a synopsis of the Syrian political scene in the 1980s and the early 1990s. He criticizes the authoritarian political system of Syria; although it possesses all the institutions of a democracy, he points out that even the constitution is authoritarian in nature. Opposition, whether secular or Islamic, is illegal, and Asad ruthlessly curbed the opposition in the 1980s. The opposition, according to Lobmeyer, believes that any sign of political change will be an unlikely by-product of economic liberalization. However, he argues that economic liberalization has meant more rather than less repression.

539 **The paradox of Syria.**
Ivor Lucas.   *Asian Affairs*, vol. XXV, Part I (February 1994), p. 3-12.

Lucas, who was the British Ambassador to Syria from 1982 until 1984, attempts to explain the domestic and foreign policies of Syria. He discusses the circumstances that led to the Ba'thist coup of 1963 and the ultimate rise of Asad. The paradox, as perceived by the author, lies in the misery (in the sense of 'lack of prosperity') that Asad has brought upon his population, in contrast to the fascination generated by Syria's claim to lead the Arab world. Despite pursuing policies that have harmed the Arab interest, such as Syria's support for Iran, and despites the country's appalling human rights record, Asad has managed to earn the respect of both his citizens and the broader Arab world.

540 **The Arab state.**
Edited by Giacomo Luciani.   London: Routledge, 1990. 454p. maps. bibliog.

A collection of essays that attempt to explain the stability and persistence of the Arab state, which begins with an analysis of the Arab state. However, the more familiar characterization of the Arab state as illegitimate and authoritarian is circumvented and the essays examine the interplay between state and society, state and the economy, and the states among themselves. This book has proven to be a standard text for students, as its format, theme and contents are accessible, eclectic and challenging. All of the essays were first published in the four-volume series *Nation, state, and integration in the Arab world.*

541 **Assad, the sphinx of Damascus: a political biography.**
Moshe Ma'oz.   London: Weidenfeld & Nicolson, 1988. 226p. bibliog.

Ma'oz's book has received the status of a *must* for students interested in modern Syria. It offers the reader a clear account of Asad's ascent to power, and an analysis of the domestic and foreign policies of the Syrian regime since 1970. Its Achilles' heel, however, stems from a flirtation with the Greater Syria concept in chapter nine, but this is moderated towards the end of the chapter. The work has also been criticized for placing too much emphasis on the role of Asad, thus ignoring the influence of important systemic factors.

542   **The emergence of modern Syria.**
Moshe Ma'oz.   In: *Syria under Assad: domestic constraints and regional risks.*   Edited by Moshe Ma'oz, Avner Yaniv.   London: Croom Helm, 1986, p. 9-35.

Ma'oz reviews the major socio-political developments in Syria since independence and examines in particular those changes which have occurred under Asad. After a brief historical introduction, the author outlines the obstacles to the development of a national community in Syria. The final section discusses the consolidation of 'Alawi-Ba'thi rule under Asad, and the threat posed by the growing Muslim opposition.

543   **The evolution of Syrian power 1948-1984.**
Moshe Ma'oz.   In: *Syria under Assad: domestic constraints and regional risks.*   Edited by Moshe Ma'oz, Avner Yaniv.   London: Croom Helm, 1986, p. 69-82.

This chapter addresses three questions. What are the factors that make up Syria's national power, and how did they account for changes in its power over time? How did this power evolve over time in relative terms, for instance, compared to changes in the power of other states in the Middle East? What is the relationship between the structural evolution of Syria's power and its foreign policy? Ma'oz concludes that on the domestic stage, Syria's military power provides stability for the Ba'th regime, but on the international stage it has had an inconsistent effect on its performance.

544   **Hafez al-Assad.**
Moshe Ma'oz.   In: *Political leaders of the contemporary Middle East and North Africa: a biographical dictionary.*   Edited by Bernard Reich.   New York; Westport, Connecticut; London: Greenwood Press, 1990, p. 51-64. bibliog.

As a synopsis of his own book, Ma'oz provides a familiar picture of Syria's president. The 'Sphinx of Damascus' is portrayed as consistent, shrewd, manipulative and brutal – all qualities befitting an Oriental despot or a Middle Eastern Machiavelli. The author contrasts the successes of Asad, such as turning Syria into a stable regional power, with his failures, which include a severely damaged economy and a society governed by repression.

545   **Syria under Assad: domestic constraints and regional risks.**
Edited by Moshe Ma'oz, Avner Yaniv.   London: Croom Helm, 1986. 288p. maps. bibliog.

This collection of essays by leading Israeli scholars focuses on three themes. Part one considers the elements of Syrian power, with chapters on: the emergence of modern Syria; the economy under Asad; and Syrian politics from 1948 to 1954. Part two examines Syrian relations with neighbouring states, and includes chapters on: the Turkish-Syrian conflict; Ba'thist Syria and Khomeini's Iran; relations with Iraq, Jordan and the PLO; Syria's policy in Lebanon; and relations with Israel. Part three considers Syria's relations with the two superpowers (the United States and the Soviet Union).

546 **The Syrian paradox.**
Moshe Ma'oz. In: *Syria under Assad: domestic constraints and regional risks.* Edited by Moshe Ma'oz, Avner Yaniv. London: Croom Helm, 1986, p. 251-63.
A review of Syria's aims, constraints and strategy in the region, together with its accomplishments. The author also includes a summary of the issues addressed in each of the articles of the book, including Syria's relations with Iran, Iraq, Turkey, Jordan, Israel, the PLO, United States and the Soviet Union.

547 **Al-jabhah al-wataniyah al-taqadumiyah wa-al-ta'adudiyah al-siyasiyah fi al-kutur al-'arabi al-surri.** (The National Progressive Front and the multiparty system in the Syrian nation.)
Yusuf Marish, introduced by Ahmad Durgham. Damascus: Dār al-Ni'mah, 1993. 286p. bibliog.
The national and international role of the National Progressive Front (a coalition of seven political parties) is examined in this work, which includes a number of interviews with figures from the different Syrian parties.

548 **Syria unmasked: the suppression of human rights by the Asad regime.**
Middle East Watch. London: Yale University Press, 1991. 224p.
Since Asad seized power in Syria in 1970, he has continuously employed repressive measures against the Syrian population. Moreover, Syria remains a human rights offender in Lebanon. This book describes the various forms of repression used in Syria, and provides details of the three agencies that secure Asad's rule: the Ba'th Party, the military, and the security forces.

549 **Sovereign creations: pan Arabism and political order in Syria and Iraq.**
Malik Mufti. Ithaca, New York; London: Cornell University Press, 1996. 286p. bibliog.
A study of Arab nationalism and the numerous unity schemes pursued by Iraq and Syria between 1921 and 1990. The study is divided into three periods: the Hashemite era in Iraq (1921-54); the rise of Nasser in 1952 to the Arab-Israeli War of 1967; and 1967-90. According to the author, the rise of nationalism is correlated with weak state structures and weak regimes.

550 **Safahāt min tārīkh al-hizb al-shīyū'ī al-surrī 1924-1954.** (Pages from the history of the Syrian Communist Party 1924-54.)
Ziyad al-Mulla. Damascus: al-Ahālī, 1994. 224p.
The author divides the Syrian Communist Party's history into three periods: 1924-35 (p. 15-97); 1936-46 (p. 99-180); and 1946-54 (p. 181-208). Although the book provides an overview of the party during this period, it lacks depth and critical analysis.

Politics

551 **Une cité en proie aux passions politiques.** (A city prey to political
    passions.)
    Elizabeth Picard.   In: *Damas: miroir brisé d'un orient arabe*
    (Damascus: broken mirror of an Arab Orient).   Edited by Anne-Marie
    Bianquis, Elizabeth Picard.   Paris: Editions Autrement, 1993,
    p. 105-15. (Série Monde, H.S. no. 65).
The author identifies three critical days in Syria's post-mandate history: 27 February
1958 (p. 105-08), Nasser's historic visit to the new union; 23 February 1966 (p. 108-
11), the *coup d'état* of the pro-Marxist faction in the Ba'th Party; and 9 October 1973
(p. 112-15), the Israeli bombing of Damascus. These three days offer insights into the
post-independence era.

552 **Construire un état, dominer une nation.** (Building a state, ruling a
    nation.)
    Elizabeth Picard.   In: *Damas: miroir brisé d'un orient arabe*
    (Damascus: broken mirror of an Arab Orient).   Edited by Anne-Marie
    Bianquis, Elizabeth Picard.   Paris: Editions Autrement, 1993,
    p. 146-53. (Série Monde, H.S. no. 65).
Picard examines Asad's project of state-building in Syria, and notes how he has
maintained his rule since 1970. In this essentially narrative work, Picard also portrays
Asad's personality.

553 **Greater Syria: the history of an ambition.**
    Daniel Pipes.   New York; Oxford: Oxford University Press, 1990.
    240p. maps. bibliog.
According to Pipes, Greater Syria is an ambition and an ideology. With his usual
unacademic tool-kit of quotations, hearsay and myth, the author sets out to convince
the reader of Syria's ideological struggle for hegemony. The reader is warned not to
scoff at pan-Syrianism, despite its failures, as this would amount to ignoring the
failures of Nazism.

554 **Radical politics and the Syrian Social Nationalist party.**
    Daniel Pipes.   *International Journal of Middle East Studies*, vol. 20,
    no. 3 (August 1988), p. 303-24.
Pipes attempts to reassess the contribution made by the SSNP to the Levant. Whereas
many commentators have dismissed the party as bizarre and odd, Pipes warns the
reader against underestimating its appeal. With a barely concealed agenda, Pipes tries
to associate the pan-Syrian ideology of the SSNP with the policies of the Ba'th Party.
The argument lacks depth and is often based on superficial evidence pertaining to
rumour and the clause 'probably'. The article amounts to an interesting fantasy, which
'probably' reveals more about the author than about Syrian foreign policy.

555 **Syria under Ba'th 1963-66, the army-party symbiosis.**
    Itamar Rabinovich.   Jerusalem: Israel Universities Press, 1972. 276p.
    bibliog.
This detailed political history focuses on the short period 1963-66, during which the
Ba'th founded and consolidated its regime. The period also saw important changes in

153

the relationship between the party, the army and the government that led to the coup of 1966. The author discusses the problems confronting an ideological party in power, the relationship between the military and the civilian leaders of the Ba'th, and the rise of army officers and party radicals from minority communities to political prominence. The relations between Syria and other Arab states, notably Egypt and Iraq, are discussed at some length. The events leading to, and consequences of, the March 1963 coup, the Hafiz-Jadid rivalry of 1965 and the February 1966 coup, are described in detail. Appendices cover the composition of Syrian cabinets, and regional and national commands, 1963-66.

556   **The Ba'th and the creation of modern Syria.**
David Roberts.   London; Sydney: Croom Helm, 1987. 182p. bibliog.

Roberts combines diplomatic experience – he served as Head of Chancery (1963-66) and British Ambassador to Syria (1973-76) – with an academic approach in explaining Syria's modern history. His research offers a succinct account of the intellectual ancestry of Ba'thist ideology, the structure of the Ba'th Party, the relationship between the Ba'th Party and the 'Alawis, and the critical role played by Asad. The contradiction between a Syrian and Ba'thist identity receives close attention, and the author concludes that Syria, as the centre of the Levant, is almost obliged, irrespective of ideology, to extend its interests into Lebanon, Jordan and Palestine.

557   **Syrian politics: cohesion, succession, instability.**
Glenn E. Robinson.   *Middle East Policy*, vol. V, no. 4 (January 1998), p. 159-79.

Robinson avers that the Ba'th Party has remained in power, in spite of its minority-based authoritarian structure, due to the cohesion it has enjoyed among the elements of the state elite. The 'Alawi officers control political power through the security apparatus, whilst the Sunni urban bourgeoisie lie at the centre of economic power. With a divergence of interests between the officers and merchants over issues such as economic liberalization, political liberalization and a withdrawal from Lebanon, Robinson suggests that long-term stability is unlikely. Joining the game of speculation, Robinson also examines four potential succession scenarios in the post-Asad era.

558   **Ba'thist ethics and the spirit of state capitalism: patronage in contemporary Syria.**
Yahya M. Sadowski.   In: *Ideology and power in the Middle East: studies in honor of George Lenczowski.*   Edited by Peter J. Chelkowski, Robert Pranger, foreword by David Pierpont Gardner. Durham, North Carolina; London: Duke University Press, 1988, p. 160-84.

Sadowski explores the significance and growing influence of the Ba'th Party in Syrian political life. He claims that it is neither a 'mass party' nor a 'façade' for regime legitimacy. He acknowledges Asad's autonomy from the party yet notes the regime's respect and responsibility to the party. The party makes use of patronage to entrench its support within the population. He examines the centrality of patronage within Syria, noting that patronage is a vehicle for mobilizing support. Asad has successfully balanced the interests of competing patronage networks, and, at times, removed those that have become too powerful or entrenched.

559 **Patronage and the Ba'th: corruption and control in contemporary Syria.**
Yahya M. Sadowski. *Arab Studies Quarterly*, vol. 9, no. 4 (fall 1987), p. 442-61.
A compact article that efficiently characterizes the Ba'thist period between the seizure of power in 1963 and the campaign against corruption in 1987. Sadowksi examines the transition of the Ba'th Party from its oppositional politics of purism to its state politics of patronage. This well structured piece of work informs the reader of Asad's policy of balancing the interests amongst the strategic elite and the population. Caught between patronage and institutional reform, the regime reversed its first anti-corruption campaign in 1978, but deepened its second campaign, after the removal from office of Asad's brother Rif'at, in accordance with public discontent. Sadowski indicates the limits of regime support within Syria, often perceived as confessional, and the pragmatic response of the president through balancing sectoral interests.

560 **Asad: between institutions and autocracy.**
Patrick Seale. In: *Syria: society, culture, and polity.* Edited by Richard Antoun, Donald Quataert. Albany, New York: State University of New York Press, 1991, p. 97-110. (SUNY Series in Middle Eastern Studies).
Seale examines the problems of development within the Syrian state, caught as it is between institutions and autocracy. This article summarizes the political structures of the state, and lends an insight into the decision-making process, which is suspended between the interests of patronage and state. Whereas Asad's rule remains dependent upon the support of his patronage networks, the responsibility of state-building calls for the energizing and upgrading of the institutional framework. Seale captures the essence of Syria's problems as it seeks to adjust and acclimatize to the challenge of globalization.

561 **The struggle for power in Syria: politics and society under Asad and the Ba'th party.**
Nikoloas Van Dam. London: I. B. Tauris, 1996. 2nd ed. 228p. map. bibliog.
An updated version of Van Dam's earlier classic text, published in 1981. Unfortunately, it does not offer anything particularly new, only a review of the missing years. The issue of Asad's succession is tackled, but as with all hypotheses surrounding this subject, it is based on a number of 'what if' scenarios. Nevertheless, it is an essential book for students of modern history, politics and international relations.

562 **Acting 'as if': symbolic politics and social control.**
Lisa Wedeen. *Comparative Studies in Society and History*, vol. 40, no. 3 (July 1998), p. 503-23.
Wedeen uses an anecdote to differentiate between public and private perceptions of President Asad and his regime. She claims that these stories provide data for social scientists trying to understand political experience as it is actually lived (p. 523). The story itself shows 'the regime's demand that people provide external evidence of allegiance to a cult whose rituals of obeisance are often transparently phony' (p. 504). She notes, however, that people have 'private enclaves of publicity where they

criticize the regime and make jokes' (p. 505). Wedeen endorses an interesting approach, and circumvents a familiar problem for social scientists, but the limitation of her approach is her dependence upon one anecdote, which is treated as evidence. She does question its authenticity, but concludes that this is irrelevant and that its very existence indicates discontent with the Asad regime.

563   **The Near East since the First World War: a history to 1995.**
Malcolm Yapp.   London; New York: Longman, 1996. 2nd ed. 597p.
maps. bibliog. (A History of the Near East).

Yapp provides a general outline of the Near East in terms of society, economy and politics from the First World War until 1995. He assesses Syria in three sections: the years of notables, 1920-58 (p. 85-104), offering a concise overview of the French Mandate; the years of revolution (p. 251-65); and the Near East, 1989-95 (p. 460-63). A good bibliography on Syria appears on p. 523-25.

564   **The Middle East: a political dictionary.**
Lawrence Ziring.   Santa Barbara, California; Denver, Colorado;
Oxford: ABC-Clio, 1992. 401p. map. (Clio Dictionaries in Political
Science).

A good reference guide which defines the terms, events, characteristics, movements and institutions that describe the Middle East during the latter half of the 20th century. It could serve as a useful aid in governments, business and journalism. It is divided into the following seven sections: political geography and geopolitics; Islam; ethnicity and political culture; political parties and movements; Israelis and Palestinians; diplomacy; and conflict.

565   **Asad of Syria – the leader and the image.**
Eyal Zisser.   *Orient* (Oplanden), vol. 35, no. 2 (June 1994),
p. 247-60.

Against the backdrop of Seale's *Asad of Syria: the struggle for the Middle East* (see item no. 674), Zisser attempts to paint two pictures of Asad, the international and the domestic leader. There seems to be no middle ground in the Asad debate: in the West, he has been portrayed as a Machiavellian character responsible for international terrorism, and yet his political adversaries have expressed respect for his tough negotiating style. We are informed that he has transformed Syria into a stable regional power, but the cost is easier to dismiss from afar. The personality cult in Syria offers the population a father figure, a virtuous Arab nationalist who resists the corruption of his peers. Zisser's own analysis contains an attractive quality; contrary to common belief, he says, Asad's source of success is not charisma or his greatness as a thinker and leader. Rather, he is a pragmatic, moderate and perhaps even colourless leader – herein lies the secret of his success.

566   **Syria – the renewed struggle over succession.**
Eyal Zisser.   *The World Today*, vol. 50, no. 7 (July 1994), p. 136-39.

With the death of Asad's eldest son, Basil, the issue of succession was revived. It had been thought that Asad was 'grooming' Basil to become his successor, although his intentions had never been made explicit. Zisser argues that Basil's death might lead to a struggle over succession which could not only jeopardize the stability of the regime, but also its very existence. The author discusses the choice of other possible candidates, namely, 'Abd al-Halim Khaddam, Farouq al-Shar'a, Hikmat Shihabi and Rif'at Asad.

Syrian Arab Republic.
See item no. 2.

The Arab Republic of Syria.
See item no. 6.

Syria: modern state in an ancient land.
See item no. 7.

An a to z of the Middle East.
See item no. 10.

Inside the Middle East.
See item no. 11.

The Arabs.
See item no. 16.

State and Islamism in Syria.
See item no. 419.

The Islamic alternative: cause or effect?
See item no. 429.

Islamic revival and national development in the Arab world.
See item no. 435.

Some observations on the social roots of Syria's ruling, military group and the causes for its dominance.
See item no. 436.

The Syrian armed forces in national politics: the role of the geographic and ethnic periphery.
See item no. 438.

The Alawi community of Syria: a new dominant political force.
See item no. 439.

The Alawi capture of power in Syria.
See item no. 443.

Middle Eastern political clichés: 'Takriti' and 'Sunni' rule in Iraq; 'Alawi' rule in Syria, a critical appraisal.
See item no. 445.

Ethnicity, clientship, and class: their changing meaning.
See item no. 490.

Syria: society, culture, and polity.
See item no. 491.

Politics

Arab unity schemes revisited: interest, identity, and policy in Syria and Egypt.
See item no. 493.

Social structure and political stability: comparative evidence from the Algerian, Syrian, and Iraqi cases.
See item no. 494.

The rise and fall of secularism in the Arab world.
See item no. 498.

Asad's westward turn: implications for Syria.
See item no. 583.

Revisionist dreams, realist strategies: the foreign policy of Syria.
See item no. 626.

The struggle for Syria: a study of post-war Arab politics, 1945-1958.
See item no. 637.

Asad of Syria: the struggle for the Middle East.
See item no. 674.

Domestic politics and the prospects for an Arab-Israeli peace.
See item no. 677.

Domestic politics and regional security: Jordan, Syria, and Israel. The end of an era?
See item no. 678.

Is Syria ready for peace?
See item no. 691.

The Syrian business community, its politics and prospects.
See item no. 704.

The Syrian economy under the Asad regime.
See item no. 707.

Liberalization in Syria: the struggle of economic and political rationality.
See item no. 709.

The political economy of economic liberalization in Syria.
See item no. 710.

Syria.
See item no. 711.

Syria: the politics of economic liberalisation.
See item no. 712.

Contemporary Syria: liberalization between Cold War and cold peace.
See item no. 714.

The political economy of Syria under Asad.
See item no. 718.

The private sector, economic liberalization, and the prospects of democratization: the case of Syria and some other Arab countries.
See item no. 719.

Stages of economic and political liberalization.
See item no. 720.

Land reform and class structure in rural Syria.
See item no. 740.

Ba'thist ideology, economic development and educational strategy.
See item no. 765.

Constitution and Legal System

567 The labour movement in Syria.
Abdel Aziz Allouni. *The Middle East Journal*, vol. 13, no. 1 (winter 1959), p. 64-76.

Allouni describes the provisions of the first Syrian Labour Code, which was promulgated as Law no. 279 in June 1964, relating to: the formation, management and organization of the trade unions; the arbitration of disputes; conditions of employment, wages and compensation; and the establishment of a Directorate of Labour and Social Welfare.

568 The Syrian Law of Personal Status.
J. N. D. Anderson. *Bulletin of the School of Oriental and African Studies*, vol. 17, no. 1 (1955), p. 34-49.

Promulgated during the Shishakli regime, September 1953, the Syrian Law of Personal Status was the most complete codification of personal law enacted in the Middle East, and replaced the Ottoman Law of Family Rights of 1917. Anderson highlights major features and innovations of the 108 articles, which cover marriage, divorce, birth, legal representation, bequests and inheritance.

569 Taxes and investment in the Middle East.
Edited by Paul Bater, for the International Bureau of Fiscal Documentation. Amsterdam: IBFD, 1999. 3 vols. maps.

A guide to taxes and investment in the Middle East which provides useful, up-to-date information on the tax treaties of each state. The information given includes business hours, useful addresses, investment laws and the system of taxes.

570 **Citizenship legislation in the Syrian Arab Republic.**
Uri Davis. *Arab Studies Quarterly*, vol. 18, no. 1 (winter 1996),
p. 29-47.

As part of a broader study addressing the question of citizenship and the state in the
Middle East, Davis examines the present status of the Palestinian community in Syria.
With reference to the Syrian constitution, he illuminates the contradictions between
the provision of citizenship and the process of naturalization. This contradiction has
resulted in the prevalence of *jinsiyyah* (nationality) status over *muwatanah*
(citizenship) status for the Palestinian community. In keeping with the political
changes taking place within the region, the signing of the Declaration of Principles
and the Jordanian-Israeli peace treaty, Davis calls for a revision of the existing
concept of citizenship within the Arab world, which would allow for a more inclusive
multiple Arab citizenship.

571 **The electoral law of Syria.**
The Middle East Journal, vol. 4, no. 4 (October 1950), p. 476-81.

A translation of the sixty-one-article text of the electoral law of 10 September 1949.
The decree was first published in the *Official Gazette*, no. 46, 12 September 1949.

572 **The permanent Syrian Constitution of March 13, 1973.**
Peter B. Heller. *The Middle East Journal*, vol. 28, no. 1 (winter
1974), p. 53-66.

A complete translation of the 156-article March 1973 Constitution, with introductory
comments highlighting important changes from the provisional Constitution of May
1969 and its 1971 amendments. One of the few major changes included is the increase
in the length of the terms served by members of the People's Assembly, from two to
four years.

573 **Constitutional development in Syria with emphasis on the
constitution of 1950.**
Majid Khadduri. *The Middle East Journal*, vol. 5, no. 2 (spring
1951), p. 137-60.

Khadduri reviews constitutional vicissitudes in Syria following its separation from the
Ottoman Empire and examines the provisions of the 148-article draft Constitution
prepared by the Syrian Congress in 1920. In August 1928, the French held elections
for a Constituent Assembly, which established a committee under Ibrahim Hananu to
draft the 1930 Constitution. The author discusses the subsequent attempts to formulate
new treaty relations with France, the amendments of the 1930 Constitution following
independence in 1946, and the military *coup d'état* of 1949. In 1950, Hashim al-Atasi
took office as President, and a committee of thirty-three was appointed under Nazim
al-Qudsi to draft a new constitution. The article mainly comprises a description and
appraisal of the 1950 Constitution, which is compared with that of 1930.

574 **The law of inheritance in the republics of Syria and Lebanon.**
Ibrahim A. Khairallah. Beirut: American University of Beirut Press,
1941. 343p. biblog.

A detailed account of the laws of personal status of the various sectarian and religious
communities in Syria and Lebanon. The origins of the laws, including property

161

ownership, transfer and inheritance, are traced and their modification during Ottoman and French rule is described.

575 **The permanent constitution of the Syrian Arab Republic, 31 January 1973.**
Damascus: Office Arabe de Presse et de Documentation, 1973. 28p.
Contains the complete text of the 156-article 1973 Constitution.

576 **Commercial arbitration in the Arab Middle East: a study in shari'a and statute law.**
Samir Saleh. London: Graham & Trotman, 1984. 489p. bibliog.
Aims to inform Western businessmen and lawyers about the submission of a dispute to voluntary arbitration in the Arab Middle East, with particular emphasis on private sector commercial arbitration. The first part of the book describes the general principles of *shari'a* law and its influence on commercial arbitration. Part two offers a country-by-country survey of modern statute law, describing the extent of *shari'a* influence. The chapter on Syria (p. 97-124) notes that commercial arbitration is governed by the 1953 Code of Civil Procedure in which *shari'a* is barely perceptible.

577 **Property law in the Arab world: real rights in Egypt, Iraq, Jordan, Lebanon, Libya, Syria, Saudi Arabia and the Gulf States.**
Farhat J. Ziadeh. London: Graham & Trotman, 1979. 113p.
Describes the development and characteristics of property law in the region, including Syria. The 1930 Property Law and the Syrian Civil Code are outlined and various agrarian reform measures are detailed.

The question of a constitution for Syria.
See item no. 387.

Marriage, divorce, and succession in the Druze family: a study based on decisions of Druze arbitration and religious courts in Israel and the Golan Heights.
See item no. 460.

Foreign Relations

The Superpowers

578 **Summer madness: the crisis in Syria, August-October 1957.**
Philip Anderson. *British Journal of Middle Eastern Studies*, vol. 22,
no. 1 & 2 (1995), p. 21-42.
Using sources from the British Public Records Office and the Foreign Relations
Series, Anderson attempts to unravel the diplomatic intrigues surrounding the Syrian
crisis of 1957, following the Suez crisis. Written from the perspective of the Cold
War, the article traces the fears and subsequent political machinations of the British
and US establishments, in contrast to the confident self-assertion of the Soviet Union.
Anderson reveals how the balance of Anglo-American power shifted in the aftermath
of the Suez crisis, and how the contest for regional hegemony amongst the Arab states
provided the Soviets with an avenue into the Middle East.

579 **The nature of the Soviet-Syrian link under Asad and under
Gorbachev.**
Helena Cobban. In: *Syria: society, culture, and polity.* Edited by
Richard Antoun, Donald Quataert. Albany, New York: State
University of New York Press, 1991, p. 111-29. (SUNY Series in
Middle Eastern Studies).
After reviewing the history of Soviet-Syrian relations, Cobban assesses the impact of
perestroika and glasnost on the alliance. Although often portrayed as an ideological
alliance, the author notes the pragmatism shared by both partners when conducting
their affairs. In fact, Cobban asserts that the Soviet-Syrian relationship was only a
marriage of convenience, and that both parties understood that they were each other's
second or third choice strategic partner.

580   **The superpowers and the Syrian-Israeli conflict: beyond crisis management?**
      Helena Cobban.   Washington, DC: Center for Strategic and
      International Studies; New York: Praeger, 1991. 182p. (The Washington
      Papers, no. 49).

Cobban traces the strategic contest between Syria and Israel during the period 1978-89. In addition, her analysis draws upon the concomitant relationship between Syria and Israel and their superpower patrons. Whereas the strategic alliance between the United States and Israel afforded Israel significant political and military manoeuvrability, the inherent weakness of the Soviet Union highlighted Syria's vulnerability. Syrian recalcitrance, however, held the potential for inciting superpower conflict. Although outdated since the collapse of the Soviet Union, Cobban's patron-client analysis still holds resonance for students of international relations of the Middle East.

581   **The Soviet Union and the military-economic dimension: a realpolitik perspective.**
      Moshe Efrat.   In: *Superpowers and client states in the Middle East: the imbalance of influence.*   Edited by Moshe Efrat, Jacob Bercovitch.
      London; New York: Routledge, 1991, p. 241-59.

Efrat presents a brief account of the military-economic dimension of the Soviet-Syrian relationship. He offers statistics for the period 1970-85 on the following: defence expenditure; Syrian arms imports; main economic indicators; resources and uses of resources; balance of payments; current account deficit; debt-servicing burden; Soviet economic aid; and Syrian-Soviet trade.

582   **Washington, Damascus and the Lebanon crisis.**
      Yair Evron.   In: *Syria under Assad: domestic constraints and regional risks.*   Edited by Moshe Ma'oz, Avner Yaniv.   London: Croom
      Helm, 1986, p. 209-23.

US policy towards Syria has fluctuated since the mid-1970s. Syria's intervention in Lebanon initially helped to smooth relations, but a pronounced change in US-Syrian relations occurred under the strong anti-Soviet Reagan administration, which came into office in 1981. Evron describes changes in the US perception of Syria's role in Lebanon and outlines US and Syrian policy in the 1982 war.

583   **Asad's westward turn: implications for Syria.**
      Mahmud A. Faksh.   *Middle East Policy*, vol. II, no. 3 (1993),
      p. 49-61.

Faksh analyses Syria's actions in joining the bandwagon of opposition to Iraq during the Gulf War of 1990/91. Did this volte-face signal a fundamental change in Syrian policy or was it merely an expedient to improve the regime's image in the West and help it to survive? The article also attempts to understand the linkage between the international political environment and domestic politics. Faksh portrays Asad as a skilful realist and the West as a mere tool that best serves his goals, namely, the security of his country and the survival of his regime. From the domestic context, the reader learns that whilst Asad remains supreme, the prospect of real political reform remains low. Finally, Faksh appeals to the United States to maximize its opportunity to coax Syria towards moderation and away from radicalism.

584   **Moscow, Damascus and the Lebanon crisis.**
Robert O. Freedman.   In: *Syria under Assad: domestic constraints and regional risks.*   Edited by Moshe Ma'oz, Avner Yaniv.   London: Croom Helm, 1986, p. 224-50.
A detailed examination of the impact of the Lebanese crisis on Syrian-Soviet relations under Brezhnev and Andropov. Syria's involvement presented Moscow with several critical dilemmas. The Soviets had to back their Syrian ally in order to defend their credibility, but in doing so were led close to confrontation with the United States.

585   **The Soviet Union and Syria: a case study of Soviet policy.**
Robert O. Freedman.   In: *Superpowers and client states in the Middle East: the imbalance of influence.*   Edited by Moshe Efrat, Jacob Bercovitch.   London; New York: Routledge, 1991, p. 141-208.
Freedman examines the relationship between the Soviet Union and Syria. He highlights the limitations placed on a superpower by a client state when the client becomes the only lever of influence in a critical region. In analysing the Soviet-Syrian relationship, Freedman reviews the goals of both the Soviet Union and Syria, and determines to what degree each state could offer assistance to achieve the other state's goals.

586   **Soviet policies in the Middle East: from World War II to Gorbachev.**
Galia Golan.   Cambridge, England; New York; Melbourne: Cambridge University Press, 1990. 319p. maps, bibliog. (Cambridge Soviet Union Paperbacks, no. 2).
As a Third World region to the south of the Soviet Union, and in part contiguous with it, the Middle East assumed an importance, albeit secondary, to Soviet defence priorities. However, the region assumed critical importance when placed within the context of the East-West competition for global hegemony. Golan's study examines the content of the former Soviet Union's policies towards the Middle East, including an analysis of Gorbachev's policies of perestroika and glasnost. Chapter ten (p. 140-56) is devoted to the Soviet-Syrian relationship.

587   **Asad's Syria and the New World Order: the struggle for regime survival.**
Raymond A. Hinnebusch.   *Middle East Policy*, vol. II, no. 1 (1993), p. 1-14.
Hinnebusch analyses how Syria has managed to survive the New World Order despite remaining on the US State Department's Terrorist List. The author contends that whereas most analyses of Syria stress single factors, such as repression, sectarianism, class or economics, his own approach seeks to convey the complexities that feed into the decision-making process. In doing so, he addresses the following issues: whether a state that is denounced for its human rights record and remains Israel's main opponent can avoid the fate of Iraq; and whether Syria can make peace with Israel without undermining the nationalist legitimacy and patrimonial political cement of which it is constructed.

588 **The Middle East under pax Americana: how new, how orderly?**
Michael C. Hudson. *Third World Quarterly*, vol. 13, no. 2 (1992), p. 301-16.

Hudson offers a review of the Middle East region in light of the Second Gulf War. He presents Syria's reasons for joining the Gulf War coalition on p. 304-05, and goes on to identify four possible post-war scenarios. Using sociological and neo-realist approaches, he examines each scenario in turn and concludes by suggesting that a system with a low prospect for change will emerge, but that instability will prevail.

589 **To play the hegemon: fifty years of US policy toward the Middle East.**
Michael C. Hudson. *The Middle East Journal*, vol. 50, no. 3 (summer 1996), p. 329-43.

Hudson has written a succinct and adroit account of US Middle East policy over the last fifty years. The article traces the origins and life-story of the 'holy trinity' – oil, Israel and anti-communism – which has formed the basis of policy since the Second World War. Hudson asserts that the United States, irrespective of particular failures, has successfully balanced the inimical interests of Israel and the Arab states. After a brief review of the policy-making process, the conceptual framework of the New Middle East is examined. The peace process and Gulf security are identified as two resoundingly successful policy initiatives of the post-Gulf War era, whilst the demonization of Islam and the failure to support human rights are considered as failures. Hudson observes that hegemons must recognize the responsibility which power and influence bestows upon them.

590 **Soviet policy towards Syria since 1970.**
Efraim Karsh. London: MacMillan, 1991. 235p. bibliog.

This book provides an analysis of Soviet policy, along with its successes and failures, towards Syria over the last two decades. It examines the differences between the policies of Gorbachev and those of his predecessors, but concludes that in essence they have been the same, as their predominant aim has always been regional stability. The Soviets have tried to modify Syria's approach towards the Israelis but with little success. However, Karsh notes that tension between superpowers and their client states is not unfamiliar, and that Syria has remained the Soviet Union's most important ally in the region.

591 **The Soviet Union and Syria: the Asad years.**
Efraim Karsh. London; New York: Royal Institute of International Affairs; Routledge, 1988. 125p. bibliog. (Chatham House Papers).

Karsh shows that until Sadat's trip to Jerusalem and the Israeli-Egyptian peace in 1979, Damascus had had the upper hand as Moscow's only ally in a strategically vital region. After 1977, Asad's isolation, his search for strategic parity with Israel, and domestic problems made him more dependent on the Soviet Union. Karsh argues that the Syrian-Soviet relation presents a case of 'strategic independence' favouring each party in accordance with the vicissitudes in regional and global affairs.

592 **Syria, the Kuwait War, and the New World Order.**
Eberhard Kienle. In: *The Gulf War and the New World Order: international relations of the Middle East.* Edited by Tareq Y. Ismael, Jacqueline S. Ismael. Gainsville, Florida: University Press of Florida, 1994, p. 383-98.

Kienle examines how the collapse of the Soviet Union affected Syria's foreign policy and pushed it towards supporting the US-led coalition and then the US-sponsored peace process. The Kuwait crisis provided an opportunity, but not the cause, for Syria to openly support the New World Order. Syria seized this opportunity, but did not make unnecessary concessions, and, in the process sought to reshape the regional order in the Middle East to its advantage.

593 **United States-Syrian diplomatic relations: the downward spiral of mutual political hostility (1970-1994).**
Erik L. Kundsen. *Journal of South Asian and Middle Eastern Studies,* vol. XIX, no. 4 (summer 1996), p. 55-77.

Kundsen traces the history of US-Syrian relations, emphasizing the highs and lows reached between Asad and US administrations from Nixon to Clinton. The Agreement of 17 May 1983 (between Lebanon and Israel) and the role played by Syria are discussed in detail (p. 67-68). Kundsen avers that Clinton's visit to Syria in 1994 finally broke the ice separating the two states. Although the article is essentially a narrative, it is engaging and well written.

594 **Can US assistance alter Syria's posture toward Israel?**
Fred H. Lawson. *Middle East Policy,* vol. IV, no. 4 (October 1996), p. 102-09.

By acknowledging the impact of economics upon policy formulation, Lawson examines the potential of economic assistance upon Syria's participation in the peace process. He identifies four economic inducements: general economic assistance; particular US products; support for loan requests; and access to technology and expertise. He opines that access to technology and expertise would be the most effective method of altering Syria's policy towards Israel. He also examines Syria's disputes with its neighbours (p. 107-08).

595 **Syria and the United States: Eisenhower's Cold War in the Middle East.**
David W. Lesch. Boulder, Colorado: Westview Press, 1992. 260p. bibliog.

This case-study of US-Syrian relations during the 1950s focuses specifically on the crisis of 1957. Lesch contends that US intervention was intended to subvert the Damascus regime; Eisenhower failed to appreciate the dynamics of the Middle East, and believed that Syria was moving into the Soviet sphere of influence. However, the United States bungled the initiative and propelled Syria and Egypt towards the Soviet camp, thus exacerbating Cold War tensions. Lesch has based his account on newspapers and government archives from the United States, United Kingdom and France.

596 **Cold War and covert action: the US and Syria, 1945-1958.**
Douglas Little. *The Middle East Journal*, vol. 44, no. 1 (winter 1990), p. 51-75.
The author examines US-Syrian relations in the post-First World War era, and provides an account of events that led to the crisis of 1957. He argues that Syria's strategic location and chronic instability contained 'ominous implications' for US interests during the late 1940s.

597 **Syria: the Cuba of the Middle East.**
Daniel Pipes. In: *The long shadow: culture and politics in the Middle East*. New Brunswick, New Jersey; Oxford: Transaction Publishers, 1989. Reprinted, 1990, p. 163-84.
Pipes examines the former alliance of Syria and the Soviet Union. He asserts that the alliance was not based on a 'marriage of convenience' but rather a co-operation in the fields of politics, military and terrorism. Both states shared deep-rooted hostility and animosity towards the United States, and this was apparent in both domestic politics and foreign policy.

598 **Syria and the New World Order.**
Neil Quilliam. Reading, England: Ithaca Press, 1999. 284p. maps. bibliog.
The advent of the New World Order has challenged Syria's role in the Middle East. Traditionally viewed as a pariah state and a Soviet satellite, Syria was looking at an uncertain future as the balance of world power tipped in favour of the United States. The author argues, however, that Syria has been able to adapt to the transformation in the world order. He maintains that Syrian foreign policy has been determined primarily by the international political system, but in conjunction with domestic politics. After reviewing the domestic constraints placed upon the regime, the author examines Syria's relationship to the international political system, and accounts for its decision to join the US-led coalition during the Gulf War of 1990/91 and the reasoning behind its participation in the Madrid Peace Conference.

599 **The Soviet-Syrian relationship since 1955: a troubled alliance.**
Pedro Ramet. Boulder, Colorado: Westview Press, 1990. 290p. bibliog.
Provides a clear analysis of the Soviet-Syrian client relationship, which evolved out of mutual military and economic interests. These were further emphasized to counter the US-Israel relationship, especially after the 1973 War. By the late 1980s Syria had been positioned, along with India, as one of the most important Soviet client states in the world. Despite this, Ramet argues that the closeness shared by the Soviets and the Syrians in the late 1950s was never regained, but that, conversely, it cooled during Gorbachev's era. Together with an examination of the Soviet-Syrian relationship, Ramet analyses the impact of superpower intervention in the Middle East.

600 **Disenchantment with the New World Order: Syria's relations with the United States.**
Merdith Reid-Sarkees, Stephen Zunes. *International Journal*, vol. XLIX, no. 2 (spring 1994), p. 355-77.

The uneasy relationship between the United States and Syria is explored in this article. Syria's support of the US-led coalition in 1990/91 did not lead, contrary to Syrian expectations, to a significant improvement in relations. This produced disillusionment and has since soured Syria's co-operation with the West. The traditional US stance towards Syria, a position adopted during the 1950s, prevents a consolidation of ties, especially with the issues of international terrorism and narcotics unresolved. However, with the expansion of US influence in the post-Gulf War Middle East, Syria is forced to walk a fine line between accommodating US demands and maintaining its nationalist credentials.

601 **The USSR in Syria perspective: political design and pragmatic practices.**
David Roberts. In: *Superpowers and client states in the Middle East: the imbalance of influence.* Edited by Moshe Efrat, Jacob Bercovitch. London; New York: Routledge, 1991, p. 210-40.

In an attempt to understand the Syrian view of the Soviet Union, Roberts examines the ideological background of the Ba'th Party. He suggests that Asad's rise to power marked the emergence of the balance of power politics and the demotion of ideological politics. Thus, the Soviet-Syrian relationship was characterized by self-interest; Syria offered the Soviets a foothold in the Levant, and the Soviets offered Syria superpower support in its confrontation with Israel. The limitations of the relationship demonstrated the pragmatic nature of the alliance.

602 **The United States and Arab nationalism: the Syrian case, 1953-1960.**
Bonnie Saunders. London; Westport, Connecticut: Praeger, 1996. 115p. bibliog.

In this brief work, Saunders examines the US-Syrian relationship during Eisenhower's presidency, against the backdrop of the Cold War and the rise of nationalism. She argues that Eisenhower and his Secretary of State, John Dulles, believed that neutralism and Arab nationalism were akin to communism. According to Saunders, Eisenhower focused on Syria for the following reasons: its proximity to US Cold War allies, mainly Turkey and Israel; its strategic location between the Persian Gulf and the Red Sea; its hosting of the trans-Arabia pipeline, which transported oil from the Gulf states; and finally its unstable and neutralist politics. He therefore tried to alter its radical governments.

603 **Syria.**
Patrick Seale. In: *The Cold War and the Middle East.* Edited by Yezid Sayigh, Avi Shlaim. Oxford: Clarendon Press; New York: Oxford University Press, 1997, p. 48-76.

Seale revisits the Syrian-Soviet relationship, and indicates how the alliance was often misinterpreted through the distorting lens of the Cold War prism. It is argued that both the Syrians and the Soviets pursued their national interests, and when these overlapped, the relationship deepened, thus invalidating the idea of an ideological relationship. The Syrian-Soviet relationship is examined according to three distinct periods: a honeymoon period from 1954 to 1958; a roller-coaster marriage marked by numerous ups and downs, from the mid-1960s to the mid-1980s; followed by divorce and disillusion, when the earlier intimacy and the great co-operative ventures, whether political, military or economic, came to be a distant memory.

604 **Syrian foreign policy in the post-Soviet era.**
Tahir I. Shad, Steven Boucher, Jennifer Gray-Reddish. *Arab Studies Quarterly*, vol. 17, no. 1-2 (winter/spring 1995), p. 77-94.
The change in leadership in Moscow which brought Gorbachev and Yeltsin to power deprived Syria of its long-time diplomatic ally and provider of military and economic aid. This article examines how Syria has pursued policies that have sought to compensate for the loss of Soviet Union support. It is asserted that not only has Syria found alternative sources to replace Soviet financial and military assistance, but also that Syria's overall position in Middle Eastern politics has improved.

605 **The United States in the Middle East: a historical dictionary.**
David Shavit. New York; Westport, Connecticut; London: Greenwood Press, 1988. 441p.
This dictionary provides in alphabetical form information about the people, institutions and events that have affected the relationships between the US and the Middle East. The entries include: seventy-three chiefs of diplomatic missions; influential travellers; a few businesses; and governmental agencies. US military personnel who served in North Africa during the Second World War are excluded.

Turkey

606 **Turkey challenges Iraq and Syria: the Euphrates dispute.**
Suha Bolukbasi. *Journal of South Asian and Middle Eastern Studies*, vol. XVI, no. 4 (summer 1993), p. 9-32.
Bolukbasi reviews Turkish-Syrian and Turkish-Iraqi relations through an array of issues, which include: Euphrates water, the Gundeydogu Anadolu Projesi (GAP) project, and the Kurdish question. The article includes a detailed discussion of the GAP problem (p. 12-15); the Asala dispute (p. 17-19); and the Ataturk Dam controversy (p. 23-25).

607 **Turkish-Israeli-Syrian relations and their impact on the Middle East.**
Alain Gresh. *The Middle East Journal*, vol. 52, no. 2 (spring 1998), p. 188-203.
Gresh considers the complexion of the new regional order in the Middle East. First, he examines the prism of Turkish-Israeli-Syrian relations with regard to the regional

balance of power, the roles of the PKK and Hizballah, and the contention over water rights. The Turkish-Israeli military agreements, signed in February and August 1996, have provided both actors with an additional source of leverage over Syria. Moreover, the alliance serves as a check to Islamic fundamentalism, and is therefore particularly attractive to the United States. An additional axis, the Damascus-Riyadh-Cairo relationship, also characterizes a new regional order, particularly in light of the weakening of US influence in the region. This was symbolized with the boycott of the majority of Arab states of the US-sponsored economic conference on the Middle East and North Africa in Doha in November 1997, and the success of the Islamic Summit by the Organization of Islamic Conference (OIC) in Tehran, December 1997.

608 **Conflict and accommodation in Turkish-Syrian relations.**
David Kushner. In: *Syria under Assad: domestic constraints and regional risks.* Edited by Moshe Ma'oz, Avner Yaniv. London: Croom Helm, 1986, p. 85-104.
Kushner examines Turkish-Syrian relations since Syrian independence in 1946. In the early 1950s relations deteriorated following Turkey's recognition of Israel, its prominence in the pro-Western Baghdad Pact and Syria's increasing pan-Arab and pro-Soviet policy. A process of normalization began in the early 1960s after the dissolution of the UAR. Disagreements remain, however, over issues such as the status of Alexandretta, the Syrian-Turkish border and the use of the waters of the Orontes and Euphrates.

609 **Retour du sandjak.** (Return of the sanjaq.)
Elizabeth Picard. *Maghreb-Machrek*, no. 99 (January-March 1983), p. 47-64.
Deals with the controversial cession of the sanjaq of Alexandretta by the French administration to Turkey following the Franco-Turkish Treaty of July 1938. Picard details the demographic and economic change in Hatay since the Turkish annexation, describes the situation of the Arab minority, and considers the role of the 'Hatay question' in Syro-Turkish relations since independence.

610 **Turkey and the Middle East in the 1990s.**
Sabri Sayari. *Journal of Palestine Studies*, vol. XXVI, no. 3, issue 103 (spring 1997), p. 44-55.
This article examines Turkey's role in the Middle Eastern region in the 1990s. Sayari avers that the worsening of relations between Damascus and Ankara was due to Syria's support of the PKK, and Turkey's aim to divert the waters of the Euphrates for its irrigation scheme, GAP (p. 47-50). These two factors contributed to Turkey's decision to sign a military agreement with Israel.

611 **The oldest threat: water in the Middle East.**
Al J. Venter. *Middle East Policy*, vol. VI, no. 1 (June 1998), p. 126-36.
Venter outlines the water problems of the Middle East, beginning with Boutros Ghali's statement that the 'next war in the Near East would not be about politics, but over water' (p. 126). He analyses the reasons behind the disputes between Syria and Turkey, which include the Kurds, the Alexandretta province and the Turkish dams,

especially the GAP scheme (p. 129-32). The construction of the hydro-electric dam along the Syrian and Jordanian border is also covered (p. 134-35).

Ankara, Damascus, Baghdad and the regionalization of Turkey's Kurdish secessionism.
See item no. 481.

The Kurdish question and geopolitic and geostrategic changes in the Middle East after the Gulf War.
See item no. 486.

The Kurdish question and Turkey's foreign policy, 1991-1995: from the Gulf War to the incursion into Iraq.
See item no. 487.

The Kurdish question four years on: the policies of Turkey, Syria, Iran and Iraq.
See item no. 488.

Turkey-Syria relations: Kurds and water.
See item no. 489.

La politique régionale de Hafez al-Asad. (The regional politics of Hafiz al-Asad.)
See item no. 621.

Defence and security policies of Syria in a changing regional environment.
See item no. 624.

Iran

612 **Syria's support of Iran in the Gulf War: the role of structural change and the emergence of a relatively strong state.**
Elie Chalala. *Journal of Arab Affairs*, vol. 7, no. 2 (fall 1988), p. 107-20.

Chalala explains Syria's reasons for supporting Iran in its eight-year war with Iraq. Three explanations are offered: a shared hostility towards Israel and the United States; a convergence of sectarian interest between the 'Alawis and the Shi'as; and the traditional rivalry between Syria and Iraq. Chalala charts the events that led to the alliance, namely: the Iranian revolution; Iraq's decision to start the war; the 1982 Israeli invasion of Lebanon; and the rise of the Shi'a community in Lebanon. Two additional factors, which are not classed as structural, are the emergence of an autonomous Syrian state, and the fluctuation of Saudi-Syrian relations.

613 **Syria and Iran: middle powers in a penetrated regional system.**
Anoushiravan A. Ehteshami, Raymond A. Hinnebusch. London; New
York: Routledge, 1997. 238p. bibliog.

Running counter to the more dominant view of Syria and Iran as rogue states,
Ehteshami and Hinnebusch show how Syrian foreign policy accords with the rational
actor model, and how Iran's government factions are compatible with a pragmatic
foreign policy. The Syrian-Iranian alliance is closely examined, with particular
attention paid to Lebanon and the Arab-Israeli peace process. The authors argue that
the Syrian-Iranian alliance is defensive in nature and that, moreover, it constitutes a
force for regional stability. The work includes a chronology of Syrian-Iranian relations
(p. 207-22).

614 **The odd couple: Ba'athist Syria and Khomeini's Iran.**
Yair Hirschfeld. In: *Syria under Assad: domestic constraints and
regional risks.* Edited by Moshe Ma'oz, Avner Yaniv. London:
Croom Helm, 1986, p. 105-24.

Hirschfeld presents a detailed analysis of Iran and Syria's motives for maintaining
their seemingly incompatible alliance. He shows that the alliance has been of major
strategic importance to Iran in its war with Iraq. Syria has played a major role through
the closure of the Iraqi-Syrian oil pipeline and has also prevented the total isolation of
Iran, as well as securing an Iranian influence in Lebanon. The gains made by Syria
are, however, ambiguous and Asad's main motive for maintaining the alliance seems
to be that it enables Syria to play a leading role in the region.

615 **Iran and Syria: from hostility to limited alliance.**
Shireen T. Hunter. In: *Iran and the Arab world.* Edited by
Hooshang Amirahmadi. New York: St. Martin's Press, 1993,
p. 198-216.

The author analyses the critical role played by Iran in the Middle Eastern region, and
emphasizes its challenge to the Arab world. Its non-Arab, Persian character and close
alliance with the United States and Israel, prior to the revolution of 1979, served to
accentuate the historical differences and antagonisms between Iran and the Arab
world. Although the Islamic revolution brought Iran ideologically closer to the Arab
world, its export of revolution philosophy deepened the sense of hostility between the
two worlds. Hunter examines the competing forces that have contributed to this
hostility and then focuses upon the unique *rapprochement* of Iran and Syria. She
provides an acute insight into the historical development of Syrian-Iranian ties,
stressing their pragmatic nature, which have clearly been dictated by the changes in
the regional and international environments. Hunter opines that the momentum of
Iranian-Syrian relations is dependent on the future of US-Iranian relations and US-
Syrian relations, rather than on ideological interests.

616 **Syria-Iran: a strategic alliance, 1979-1991.**
Christin Marschall. *Orient* (Oplanden), vol. 33, no. 2 (1992),
p. 433-45.

This article provides a useful sketch of Syrian-Iranian relations, and it emphasizes the
strategic, rather than ideological or religious, dimension of the alliance. The durability
of the partnership is examined in five areas: the pre-revolution ties between the Syrian
regime and the Iranian clerics; the Iran-Iraq War; the civil war in Lebanon; resistance

to Western imperialism; and economic ties. In each case, the balance of power in the relationship is tested, and whereas certain conflicts of interests clearly exist, its strategic dimension ensures the triumph of compromise.

617   **Iranian-Syrian relations: between Islam and realpolitik.**
Yosef Olmert.   In: *The Iranian revolution and the Muslim world.*
Edited by David Menashri.   Boulder, Colorado; San Francisco;
Oxford, England: Westview Press, 1990, p. 171-88. (Westview Special
Studies on the Middle East).

Although Olmert's approach to the Syrian-Iranian relationship is chronological, he offers a clear analysis of the dynamics of the alliance. He identifies three stages in the history of Iranian-Syrian relations: 1979-82, years of co-operation on a small scale; 1982-85, years of joint struggle against Israel and the United States; and 1985-90, years of growing friction. Although Syria and Iran have embraced different ideologies, the former secular, socialist-oriented pan-Arabism, the latter 'supranational Islamic revolution', they have co-operated in the fields of economy and politics, and, in particular, in the Iran-Iraq War and the Lebanese civil war. Olmert concludes that the alliance originated in their regional isolation from the late 1970s.

618   **Drawing from the well: Syria in the Persian Gulf.**
Bruce Stanley.   *Journal of South Asian and Middle Eastern Studies,*
vol. XIV, no. 2 (winter 1990), p. 45-64.

Despite considerable political pressure and the loss of financial aid, Syria opposed the wishes of the Arab world and supported Iran in the Iran-Iraq War of 1980-88. The Syrian regime took this unorthodox position for a variety of reasons, receiving as a result a range of material and intangible benefits, but also incurring significant costs. Stanley assesses Syria's Gulf policy in light of the Iran-Iraq War and the Iraqi invasion of Kuwait in 1990, and contends that it is grounded in unchanging contextual factors. In other words, the Persian Gulf is a well from which Asad draws in times of need.

The Kurdish question four years on: the policies of Turkey, Syria, Iran and Iraq.
See item no. 488.

Defence and security policies of Syria in a changing regional environment.
See item no. 624.

Rentierism and foreign policy in Syria.
See item no. 724.

The Arab World

619 Baathi Iraq and Hashimite Jordan: from hostility to alignment.
Amazia Baram. *The Middle East Journal*, vol. 45, no. 1 (winter 1991), p. 51-70.
Despite the disappointing conclusion, which borders on the prophetic, this article demarcates the integral relationship of Jordan, Iraq and Syria. Pressed by geo-strategic concerns, the alienation of Egypt, Syrian-Iranian relations, and the Palestinian *intifada*, King Hussein moved closer to Ba'thist Iraq. Neglecting ideology in favour of pragmatism, the Jordanian and Iraqi leaders consolidated their partnership. Throughout the 1980s, Iraqi-Jordanian relations, based upon economic and political interdependency, reached a stage of *de facto* federation. Baram, however, asserts that Jordan's evolving dependence upon Iraq ensnared it between the competing interests of the Syrians, Palestinians and Israelis.

620 Ideology and power politics in Syrian-Iraqi relations, 1968-84.
Amazia Baram. In: *Syria under Assad: domestic constraints and regional risks.* Edited by Moshe Ma'oz, Avner Yaniv. London: Croom Helm, 1986, p. 125-39.
Baram presents a detailed analysis of Syrian-Iraqi relations. The ideological similarity of their Ba'thist regimes has been an increasing source of friction rather than *rapprochement*. The author notes sharp fluctuations in relations, particularly in the late 1960s and early 1970s. Since 1975, however, the rift has progressively widened. Conflicts over oil royalties, the Iraqi-Syrian pipeline, the allocation of the Euphrates' waters, and the estrangement of the Ba'thist regimes are discussed.

621 La politique régionale de Hafez al-Asad. (The regional politics of Hafiz al-Asad.)
Thierry Bianquis. In: *Damas: miroir brisé d'un orient arabe* (Damascus: broken mirror of an Arab Orient). Edited by Anne-Marie Bianquis, Elizabeth Picard. Paris: Editions Autrement, 1993, p. 154-63. (Série Monde, H.S. no. 65).
As well as being a symbol of Arab civilization, Damascus has always been the natural capital of Bilad al-Sham (Greater Syria). Bianquis argues that this general image is not subscribed to by regional actors, namely, Israel, Jordan, Lebanon and the Palestinians. Bianquis briefly examines Asad's foreign policy with reference to relations with Iraq, Iran, Jordan and Israel. He concludes that Syria's aims to re-create Bilad al-Sham is incompatible with Israel's existence, and that Syria understands that peace is not possible without the evacuation of Israeli and Syrian forces from Lebanon.

622 Asad's Syria and the PLO: coincidence or conflict of interests?
Laurie A. Brand. *Journal of South Asian and Middle Eastern Studies*, vol. XIV, no. 2 (winter 1990), p. 22-44.
Brand challenges the characterization of the Syrian-PLO (Palestine Liberation Organization) relationship as a contradiction between the interests of state and revolution. A more useful characterization is that of a relationship between regional actors, one endowed with stateness and the other in search of statehood. The reader is

introduced to the Syrian-PLO struggles for power in Lebanon, where the rocky relationship reveals a complex story of influence and power struggles. The PLO followed an independent foreign policy, and this enabled it to make and break relations with its Arab partners. As a stateless entity, it was prone to fluctuations of fortune and hence was 'instable' in its relationships. This situation endangers the territorial integrity of the Syrian state, *vis-à-vis* Israel, thus encouraging Syria's desire to constrain and control the Palestinians. Brand concludes that the Syrian regime and the PLO constitute two separate and unequal partners competing in a fractious political arena.

623 **The intifadah and the Arab world: old players, new roles.**
Laurie A. Brand. *International Journal*, vol. XLV, no. 3 (summer 1990), p. 501-28.
The author investigates the impact of the Palestine *intifadah* (uprising) on Egypt, Jordan and Syria. She argues that the *intifadah* led to the 're-empowerment' of the Palestinians and the PLO. A good summary of Syrian-PLO relations from 1970 until the late 1980s is included (p. 512-22).

624 **Defence and security policies of Syria in a changing regional environment.**
Anoushiravan A. Ehteshami. *International Relations*, vol. XIII, no. 1 (April 1996), p. 49-67.
Ehteshami considers the long-term security dilemmas faced by Syria in light of the demise of its superpower patron. The following questions are addressed: how the end of the Cold War has affected Syria's position in the Arab world; what mark, if any, the collapse of European communism has left on the Syrian regime's political ideology; and how Syria has defined and responded to its new security dilemmas and to the post-Cold War crises which have engulfed the Middle East. This piece of work provides a clear account of Syria's security and defence strategies since the 1980s.

625 **Syrian-Iraqi relations during the 1948 Palestine War.**
Michael Eppel. *Middle Eastern Studies*, vol. 32, no. 3 (July 1996), p. 74-91.
The struggle for Syria amongst Hashemite Iraq, Jordan, Saudi Arabia and Egypt impinged upon and exacerbated the fractious nature of Syrian politics during the 1948 Palestine War. In his article, Eppel sheds light on the impact of Iraq's regional ambitions, and examines how they determined Syria's domestic and foreign policy. The intense struggle between the National Bloc, led by pro-Saudi Quwwatli, and pro-Iraqi al-Qudsi, of the People's Party, also indicated the socio-economic orientations of the Damascene and Aleppine politicians. This diversity of approach, symptomatic of a fragmented society, allowed the region's actors a multitude of avenues into Syria.

626   Revisionist dreams, realist strategies: the foreign policy of Syria.
Raymond A. Hinnebusch.   In: *The foreign policies of Arab states: the challenge of change.*   Edited by Bahgat Korany, Ali E. Hillal Dessouki.   Boulder, Colorado: Westview Press, 1991, 2nd rev. ed., p. 374-409.

Hinnebusch argues that Syria is caught between its revisionist dreams of leading the Arab world and its limited capabilities and environment. He examines the environment of Syria in terms of its geography, society and economy and then turns his attention to Syria's military capabilities and its foreign policy in the regional and international spheres. Hinnebusch concludes by looking at the record of Syrian foreign policy under Asad.

627   Whatever happened to the Damascus Declaration': evolving security structures in the Gulf.
Rosemary Hollis.   In: *Politics and international relations in the Middle East: continuity and change.*   Edited by Jane Davis.
Aldershot, England; Brookfield, Vermont: Elgar, 1995, p. 37-60.

This article reviews the text of the Damascus Declaration (a security agreement between Syria and Egypt, with the six Gulf states) and then observes the chasm between intention and implementation. Although Hollis does not offer any deep analysis, the article serves as an introduction to the issues concerning Gulf security, and accounts for the behaviour of the GCC (Gulf Cooperation Council) states, and in particular, Kuwait's predilection towards Western security.

628   From Sykes-Picot through Bandung to Oslo: whither the Arab world?
Atif A. Kubursi, Salim Mansur.   *Arab Studies Quarterly*, vol. 18, no. 4 (fall 1996), p. 1-24.

In this well-researched paper, the co-ordinates of the Middle East, in relation to the configuration of global power, are systematically plotted from the time of the Sykes-Picot Agreement to the New World Order. Using a combination of neo-realist and globalist analysis, Kubursi and Mansur provide an account of the transition from British-led to US-led hegemony in the region. Globalization has exhausted the Westphalian concept of world politics, and the New World Order is perceived as an emerging 'concert' of global powers: the Americas, Europe and East Asia. According to this analysis, although the developing countries are relegated in importance, the Middle East will continue to hold a unique position in the South, as it contains two-thirds of the world's oil reserves. This factor alone has elevated the status of the region, and yet oil is also deemed responsible for constraining sustainable development and a substantive move towards democratization.

629   Contrasting reactions to the Persian Gulf crisis: Egypt, Syria, Jordan, and the Palestinians.
Ann Mosely Lesch.   *The Middle East Journal*, vol. 45, no. 1 (winter 1991), p. 30-50.

Examines the political impact of Iraq's invasion of Kuwait on the Arab world. Prior to the invasion, in the post Iran-Iraq War environment, the Arab world was divided along an Iraq-Jordan-Palestinian and an Egyptian-Syrian-GCC axis; the invasion served to exacerbate the polarization of interests. In this account, Lesch systematically analyses the Egyptian, Syrian, Jordanian and Palestinian response to the invasion.

630   **Gamal Abd-Nasser and an example of diplomatic acumen.**
David W. Lesch.   *Middle Eastern Studies*, vol. 31, no. 2 (April 1995), p. 362-74.

Lesch reviews the role played by Nasser in the Syrian-American crisis of 1957. He contends that the resulting union between Egypt and Syria was the best outcome in order to avoid further 'internal turmoil and external interference'. Although the result brought short-term gains, the additional tension in the Arab cold war served to inflate Nasser's expectations and brought long-term misery upon the Arab world.

631   **The Saudi role in the American-Syrian crisis of 1957.**
David W. Lesch.   *Middle East Policy*, vol. I, no. 3 (1992), p. 33-48.

Lesch focuses on the Saudi role in the Syrian crisis of 1957. The article is based on recently declassified documents from the United States and Britain. Lesch argues that Saudi Arabia played a larger role than was originally thought; moreover, King Sa'ud 'shaped the course of events'.

632   **On a short leash: Syria and the PLO.**
Moshe Ma'oz, Avner Yaniv.   In: *Syria under Assad: domestic constraints and regional risks.*   Edited by Moshe Ma'oz, Avner Yaniv.   London: Croom Helm, 1986, p. 191-208.

Discusses the dramatic fluctuations in Syria's relations with the PLO since the establishment of the terrorist organization al-Fatah in 1964. The authors argue that Syria's support of the PLO hinges on the latter's conformation to Syria's ideological objectives and national interests. Three periods are defined: the formative years (1964-75); the civil war in Lebanon (1975-76); and reconciliation, war and renewed rift (1977-84).

633   **Syrian and Jordan: the politics of subversion.**
Joseph Nevo.   In: *Syria under Assad: domestic constraints and regional risks.*   Edited by Moshe Ma'oz, Avner Yaniv.   London: Croom Helm, 1986, p. 140-56.

Nevo presents an overview of the history of bilateral relations between Syria and Jordan and an analysis of the determinants of Jordanian policy towards Syria. Under King 'Abdullah, Jordan was the dominant party, initiating the Greater Syria scheme for the unity of Syria, Transjordan and Palestine under his rule. Relations improved initially under Hussein but then deteriorated rapidly in the late 1950s. In 1970, Syria invaded northern Jordan in support of the Palestinians. There was a cautious *rapprochement* in the mid-1970s but this was short-lived; when Syria claimed that Jordan was supporting the Muslim Brotherhood, the two countries came close to war in 1980.

634 **The quest for hegemony in the Arab world: the struggle over the Baghdad Pact.**
Elie Podeh.   Leiden, the Netherlands; New York; Cologne, Germany: Brill, 1995. 281p. map. bibliog. (Social, Economic and Political Studies of the Middle East, vol. LII).

Podeh offers the reader a chronological and descriptive history of the Baghdad Pact, a security pact initiated by the British in 1955 which was designed to counter Soviet influence in the Middle East. The book encompasses the text of the agreement (p. 254-56), an organizational chart (p. 257), and an extensive bibliography. The roles played by the Arab states are examined in accordance with British and US archival materials. By utilizing these, Podeh challenges the more familiar thesis that Syria was central to achieving hegemony in the Arab world. He places more emphasis on the significance of other players such as Jordan and Lebanon. He specifically addresses the issue of Syria in chapters six and seven (p. 126-71).

635 **The foreign policy of Syria: goals, capabilities, constraints and options.**
Itamar Rabinovich.   *Survival*, vol. 24, no. 4 (1982), p. 175-83.

Examines Syrian foreign policy under Asad, focusing in particular on the domestic constraints affecting those policies. The same article appeared in *Regional security in the Middle East*, edited by Charles Tripp (New York: published for the International Institute for Strategic Studies by St. Martin's Press, 1984).

636 **Secret war in the Middle East: the covert struggle for Syria, 1949-1961.**
Andrew Rathmell.   London; New York: I. B. Tauris, 1995. 256p. bibliog.

This work complements Seale's classic, *The struggle for Syria* (see item no. 637), but focuses upon the covert operations of foreign actors and Syria's neighbours. The study portrays a state beset with external penetration, where competing foreign powers sought to exploit local rivalries in order to cultivate interest and influence. Relying on the diplomatic archives of the great powers, Rathmell reveals the story as perceived by foreign interests.

637 **The struggle for Syria: a study of post-war Arab politics, 1945-1958.**
Patrick Seale.   London; New York: Oxford University Press, 1965. 344p. maps. bibliog.

The most comprehensive account of the events and trends in Syrian post-war political history, covering the years of independence from 1945 to 1958. The author emphasizes the role of inter-Arab rivalry, particularly between Egypt and Iraq, and the interaction of local and international forces in Syrian political instability during the period. The ousting of the veteran nationalists in the first 1949 *coup d'état* by Husni Za'im and the successive counter-coups of Sami Hinnawi and Adib Shishakli are discussed, and the numerous negotiations for a Syrian-Iraqi union which took place after Za'im's overthrow are examined. Seale also explains the overthrow of the Shishkali's military dictatorship in 1954 and the subsequent rise of the Ba'th and Communist parties, and discusses Syria's reaction to the formation of the Baghdad

Pact in 1955 and to the Suez crisis of 1956. The analysis concludes with a review of events leading to Syria's union with Egypt in February 1958.

638   **Water and politics in the Middle East.**
      Greg Shapland.   In: *Politics and international relations in the Middle East: continuity and change.*   Edited by Jane Davis.   Aldershot, England; Brookfield, Vermont: Elgar, 1995, p. 73-89. 2 maps.
      The article assesses water disputes in three areas: the Nile Basin; Tigris-Euphrates; and water issues pertaining to the Arab-Israeli conflict.

The Kurdish question four years on: the policies of Turkey, Syria, Iran and Iraq.
See item no. 488.

Palestinians in Syria: the politics of integration.
See item no. 508.

Ba'th v Ba'th: the conflict between Syria and Iraq, 1968-1989.
See item no. 529.

Syria, the Kuwait War, and the New World Order.
See item no. 592.

The oldest threat: water in the Middle East.
See item no. 611.

Asad of Syria: the struggle for the Middle East.
See item no. 674.

Rentierism and foreign policy in Syria.
See item no. 724.

The Lebanese crisis

639   **Determinants and characteristics of Syrian policy in Lebanon.**
      As'ad Abukhalil.   In: *Peace for Lebanon? From war to reconstruction.*   Edited by Deirdre Collings.   Boulder, Colorado: Lynne Rienner, 1994, p. 123-35.
      Abukhalil reviews Syria's policy towards Lebanon and opines that neither ideology, nor a Greater Syrian enterprise, motivates the Syrian regime's obsession with Lebanon. Three explanatory paradigms are assessed: Greater Syria; raison d'état; and raison du regime. The author favours the final paradigm endorsing the mosaic approach (looking at the role of ethnicity in politics) to state theory. Despite lacking some breadth, this article offers a succinct and convincing analysis of Syria's Lebanon policy.

640   **Syria and the Shiites: al-Asad's policy in Lebanon.**
As'ad Abukhalil.   *Third World Quarterly*, vol. 12, no. 2 (April 1990),
p. 1-20.
'The Lebanese wounds are self-inflicted, but the "outsiders", as the Lebanese denote
non-Lebanese powers, added salt to these wounds, thereby compounding the pains and
delaying recovery' (p. 1). Abukahlil accounts for Syrian intervention in Lebanon as an
extension of state interest through the services of the Shi'a communities, Amal and
Hizballah. In doing so, he offers an insight into the policies of Asad and the relevance
of Lebanon to Syrian security.

641   **The Syrian involvement in Lebanon since 1975.**
Reuven Avi-Ran.   Boulder, Colorado; Oxford: Westview Press, 1991.
241p. bibliog.
This book is divided into two parts which cover: Syrian intervention in Lebanon
between 1975 and 1981; and Syria's reaction to Israeli intervention from 1982 to
1985. This is a well-informed piece of research, and includes extensive press sources
and a considerable number of interviews with Israeli officials. When first translated
from Hebrew, Avi-Ran's book invited criticism over its transliteration of terms and
occasional factual errors.

642   **Syrian policy in Lebanon, 1976-1984, moderate goals and
pragmatic means.**
Elie Chalala.   *Journal of Arab Affairs*, vol. 4, no. 1 (spring 1985),
p. 67-87.
Chalala argues that Syrian policy towards Lebanon has been dictated by two major
interests. The first interest has been to protect the integrity of the Syrian state; the
second is to maintain the Ba'thist regime, in other words, to strengthen Asad's hold on
power. Chalala divides Syrian policy in Lebanon into three phases: 1976, supporting
Lebanese Christian Rightists against the forces of the Lebanese National Movement
and the Palestinians; 1978, a period of strained relations with the Christian Rightists
and an uneasy alliance with the Lebanese National Movement and the Palestinians;
and 1982-84, providing military and political support for all forces opposing the
Christian Rightists. Asad's policies in Lebanon, Chalala avers, were designed to avoid
confrontation with Israel; however, Syria did resort to force in 1976, 1978 and 1982-
84 when its interests were at stake.

643   **Syria and the Lebanese crisis.**
Adeed I. Dawisha.   London: Macmillan, 1980. 208p. bibliog.
A detailed account of Syria's intervention in the Lebanese civil war of 1975-76,
focusing in particular on Syrian decision-making during the crisis, which was seen to
constitute a major threat to Syrian foreign policy aims. In the introductory chapter, the
author provides the historical and institutional background to Syria's intervention, and
describes the external and internal setting which shaped the Syrian response.
Following chapters constitute a detailed analysis of events and Syrian policy. The final
chapter examines events up to 1979, including the increasing Maronite attacks on pro-
Syrian groups, and the Israeli invasion of March 1978, which demonstrates that Syrian
aims were far from achieved.

644   **The external dimension of the conflict in Lebanon: the role of Syria.**
Marius Deeb.   *Journal of South Asian and Middle Eastern Studies*, vol. XII, no. 3 (spring 1989), p. 37-51.

Deeb underlines the prominent role played by Syria during the Lebanese civil war; indeed, it was often able to prevent other external actors from playing 'any significant role' in Lebanon. Deeb follows the evolution of Syrian intervention from 1976 until 1989. This is a valuable analytical piece of work which offers a quantifiable account of Syria's involvement in Lebanon during the period 1976-78.

645   **Shi'a movements in Lebanon: their formation, ideology, social basis, and links with Iran and Syria.**
Marius Deeb.   *Third World Quarterly*, vol. 10, no. 2 (April 1988), p. 683-98.

Deeb examines the Shi'a movements in Lebanon – namely Amal and Hizballah – and analyses the reasons behind Syrian and Iranian interest in the Shi'a community. The article is divided into three sections, dealing with: Amal; Hizballah; and Amal and Hizballah's links with Syria and Iran. The social basis, organization and ideology of the two movements are discussed in detail.

646   **War and intervention in Lebanon: the Israeli-Syrian deterrence dialogue.**
Yair Evron.   Baltimore, Maryland: Johns Hopkins University, 1987. 246p. bibliog.

Although the existence of Syrian-Israeli dialogue over Lebanon has always been recognized, this is the first systematic study. Evron argues that a clear pattern emerged from 1973 onwards in which Israel succeeded in deterring certain Syrian actions in Lebanon; Syria strictly adhered to the Israeli-set 'red lines', as long as Israel also adhered to them. Even when Syria appeared to be defying Israeli preferences, this resulted from changes in the accepted rules of the 'ballgame' by Israel. The 1982 war destroyed the previous deterrence 'equation', which has since been restored in a modified form.

647   **The Shi'a community of Lebanon: a new assertive political force.**
Mahmud A. Faksh.   *Journal of South Asian and Middle Eastern Studies*, vol. XIV, no. 3 (spring 1991), p. 33-56.

By examining the role of the Shi'a community in Lebanon, Faksh considers the socio-economic, cultural and external factors that led to the prominence of the Shi'a movement. He analyses the Shi'a community's relationship with Syria through the prism of the Syrian-Iranian alliance (p. 47-55). Faksh concludes that the Shi'a community will continue to play a pivotal role in the Lebanese political arena as long as Syria continues to dominate Lebanese politics.

648   **Faces of Lebanon: sects, wars, and global extensions.**
William W. Harris.   Princeton, New Jersey: Markus Wiener, 1997.
354p. maps. bibliog.

Introduces the reader to the geopolitics, domestic politics and neighbourly relations of
Lebanon. Due to the complex relationship between Syria and Lebanon, the former
receives intermittent attention throughout the book, especially in parts two and three,
where the intricacies of the civil war are discussed. The author concludes that
Lebanon is a prisoner to Syrian politics. Although the book offers objective analysis,
the author's passionate appeal in the conclusion reveals his sympathies. Nevertheless,
this is an engaging book which includes data on the state of Syrian-Lebanese relations
up to 1996.

649   **Syrian policy in Lebanon and the Palestinians.**
Raymond A. Hinnebusch.   *Arab Studies Quarterly*, vol. 8, no. 1
(winter 1986), p. 1-20.

Hinnebusch argues that Syrian policy in Lebanon and towards the PLO has been
consistent. Syrian action has been conditioned by the country's historic rejection of
the state system which was imposed after the Arab Revolt, and determined by its
strategy in the wider Arab-Israeli conflict. Syrian policy in Lebanon has been
dominated by fears that a weak and divided Lebanon with a strong Palestinian
presence would be vulnerable to Israeli attack and influence, thus outflanking Syria's
Golan defenders. The author provides a detailed review of Syrian policy in Lebanon
over the period 1975-85, emphasizing the failure of its efforts to build an all-Arab
consensus against Israel.

650   **Syria after Ta'if: Lebanon and the Lebanese in Syrian politics.**
Fida Nasrallah.   In: *Contemporary Syria: liberalization between Cold
War and cold peace.*   Edited by Eberhard Kienle, preface by Patrick
Seale.   London: British Academic Press; New York: St Martin's
Press, 1994, p. 132-38.

Nasrallah examines the Ta'if Accord (which restored a legitimate government in
Lebanon following its civil war). The 'coexistence of two rival governments' in Beirut,
that of General 'Aun and Prime Minister Salim al-Huss, prompted the diplomatic
intervention of Saudi Arabia and Morocco. This article examines the implications of
the Ta'if Accord for the Syrian-Lebanese relationship. Nasrallah observes that the
foreign policy dimension of the treaty indubitably favours, and provides a further
pretext for, a prolonged Syrian intervention. However, she retorts that Syria's second
infitah (Open Door Policy) might lead to a Lebanese 'colonization' of Syria.

651   **The Treaty of Brotherhood, Cooperation and Coordination: an
assessment.**
Fida Nasrallah.   In: *State and society in Syria and Lebanon.*   Edited
by Youssef M. Choueiri.   Exeter, England: Exeter University Press,
1993; New York: St. Martin's Press, 1994, p. 103-11.

Nasrallah offers an historical account of the process that led to the signing of the Ta'if
Accord. The special relationship between Syria and Lebanon is critically examined,
and the author evaluates the main articles of the accord in conjunction with the
hegemonic interests of the Syrian regime.

652 **The changing prism: Syrian policy in Lebanon as a mirror, an issue and an instrument.**
Itamar Rabinovich. In: *Syria under Assad: domestic constraints and regional risks.* Edited by Moshe Ma'oz, Avner Yaniv. London: Croom Helm, 1986, p. 179-90.
Rabinovich presents a useful review of Syrian policy in Lebanon from the military intervention of 1976 to the Israeli invasion of 1982-84. Syria's changing policy in Lebanon is placed in the larger context of shifts in Syrian politics.

653 **Hizb' Allah in Lebanon: the politics of the western hostage crisis.**
Magnus Ranstorp, foreword by Terry Waite. New York: St. Martin's Press; Basingstoke, England: Macmillan Press, 1997. 257p. bibliog.
Ranstorp studies the western hostage crisis in Lebanon and provides a useful historical background to Hizballah. Chapter four, entitled 'The influence of the Syrian-Iranian relationship on Hizballah' (p. 110-33), reviews the Syrian-Iranian relationship from 1982 until 1992. Ranstorp divides the history of the relationship into two phases: Iranian-Syrian co-operation against common enemies (p. 111-19); and rivalry over Hizballah (p. 119-30). He highlights their divergent conceptions over Lebanon's future. He also argues that the abduction of western citizens was motivated either by internal organizational requirements, or in alignment with Syrian and Iranian interests, and that mechanisms for the resolution of the hostage crisis were subject to continuous interaction between Hizballah, Iran and Syria, influenced by internal Lebanese, regional and international events. Ranstorp offers a comprehensive study of Hizballah, together with an incisive analysis of Syrian-Iranian relations.

654 **Dealing with Syria.**
Ze'ev Schiff. *Foreign Policy*, no. 55 (summer 1984), p. 92-112.
An analysis of the complicated situation in Lebanon in which Syria, Israel and the United States were locked in a 'most dangerous bear hug'. After reviewing Israeli interests, Schiff concludes that dialogue with Syria, either directly or through a third party, over security arrangements in southern Lebanon is essential to Israel's security. Without these arrangements, it would be difficult for Israel to avoid an 'all-conflict' with Syria. Schiff opines that the complexion of Lebanon after the war was different to that envisioned by the United States or Israel. The depletion of Christian influence left it more Arab than ever, and the only winners were the Muslim Shi'as.

655 **Hizbuallah, Syria, and the Lebanese elections.**
Graham Usher. *Journal of Palestine Studies*, vol. XXVI, no. 2, issue 102 (winter 1997), p. 59-67.
Usher offers an insight into the Lebanese elections of 1996, and the implications of the results. The 'downsizing' of Hizballah in the 1996 poll and the 'curbing' of elections marked a 'shift in the locus of policy-making away from Beirut and in the direction of Damascus' (p. 60). This event is indicative of Syrian hegemony in Lebanon. Usher remarks that the withdrawal of Syria from Lebanon would be likely to initiate another struggle amongst the numerous religious confessions, due to the current dependence upon Damascus.

656   **Syrian intervention in Lebanon.**
Naomi Joy Weinberger.   New York: Oxford University Press, 1986.
367p. bibliog.
Analyses of Syria's intervention in Lebanon have tended to emphasize one of three topics: a desire to restore stability; the creation of Greater Syria; and Syrian-Palestinian relations. Weinberger subscribes to the theory that the complex relationship between Syria and the Palestinian movement is primarily responsible for Syria's intervention in Lebanon in 1975-76.

Israel, Syria, and Lebanon.
See item no. 672.
Syria's President talks to the American media, 1991.
See item no. 700.

The Arab-Israeli Conflict

657   **Syrian foreign policy at the crossroads: continuity and change in the post-Gulf War era.**
Ghayth Armanazi.   In: *State and society in Syria and Lebanon.*
Edited by Youssef M. Choueiri.   Exeter, England: Exeter University Press, 1993; New York: St. Martin's Press, 1994, p. 112-19.
The author examines how Syria has managed to transform its position from isolation to accommodation with the international community since the collapse of the Soviet Union. Armanazi shows how the Iraqi invasion of Kuwait in 1990 gave Syria the opportunity to adjust its alignment when it provided indispensable support to the Gulf War coalition. Syria's motives for joining the coalition are analysed; Armanazi concludes that Syria has changed the tactics, but not the goals, of its foreign policy.

658   **The Syrian-Israeli border conflict, 1949-1967.**
David Bowen, Laura Drake.   *Middle East Policy*, vol. I, no. 4 (1992), p. 17-28. map.
The authors attribute the outbreak of the 1967 War to the Israeli incursions into the demilitarized zone (DMZ) between the Syrian-Israeli border. The article analyses the struggle over this border between 1948 and 1967, which eventually led to the June War and the occupation of the Golan Heights. The strategic significance of the Golan Heights underlines the premise of this article.

659   **Atlas of the Arab-Israeli conflict.**
Martin Gilbert.   New York: Oxford University Press, 1993. 6th ed.
146p. maps.
Yet another dismal edition of this atlas. This is an unashamedly crude expression of Zionist historiography, lacking the influences of Israeli revisionist historians, and is unsuitable for academic interest.

660   **The Golan Heights: twenty years after.**
      Journal of Palestine Studies, vol. XVII, no. 1, issue 65 (autumn 1988),
      p. 136-43.

A descriptive report that provides an overview of political and economic life in the
Golan Heights, and the status of women, but offers little analysis.

661   **Syria and Israel: keeping the peace in Lebanon.**
      Frederic C. Hof.   *Middle East Policy*, vol. IV, no. 4 (October 1996),
      p. 110-15.

Hof argues that Syria and Israel are both ready to establish a security regime that
would satisfy Syrian, Israeli and Lebanese interests. His argument is based on two
main assumptions: that Israel would like to end its expensive occupation of south
Lebanon 'at the earliest practicable date'; and that, as a condition of its withdrawal,
Israel would establish a 'reliable' security regime in south Lebanon. Hof suggests that
the only way to ensure Syrian co-operation is to involve it in this security regime
without compromising Israel's domestic situation.

662   **The Syrian doctrine of strategic parity.**
      Ahmed S. Khalidi, Hussein Agha.   In: *The Middle East in global
      perspective*.   Edited by J. Kipper, H. Saunders, H. Harold.   Boulder,
      Colorado: Westview Press, 1991, p. 186-218.

Khalidi and Agha review Syria's pursuit of strategic parity in the 1980s. They offer an
account for its development during the post-Camp David period, and then draw the
relevant comparisons with Israel. Despite its intensive drive for parity, Syria was
unable to catch up with the Israelis. Israel's lead in the quality of weapons, in its
training, command and operational techniques, and technological superiority was too
significant for the Syrians. In addition, the qualitative difference in their superpower
relationships gave the Israelis a distinct advantage in terms of technological,
economic, military and psychological support.

663   **Qadīyat al-Jūlān: hadabat al-ishkālīyāt wa-fajawāt al-hulūl al-
      muhtamalah.** (The Golan case: the height of problems and gaps of
      probable solutions.)
      Ma'mun Kiwan, 'Abduh al-Asadi.   Damascus: Dār al-Numayīr, 1991.
      236p. maps. bibliog.

A comprehensive study about the Golan Heights. The authors examine its history,
resources, environment and strategic value. The lives of the Israeli settlers and the
Syrian nationals are also described. After reviewing the recent history of the Golan
Heights, the authors offer a number of possible resolutions to the problem. An
appendix, including the Syrian-Israeli armistice, is included on p. 215-26, and the
demarcation of Syrian-Israeli forces is also provided on p. 227-31.

664   **The limits of mediation: lessons from the Syria-Israel experience, 1974-1994.**
Brian Mandell.   In: *Resolving international conflicts: the theory and practice of mediation.*   Edited by Jacob Bercovitch.   London: Lynne Rienner, 1996, p. 129-49. bibliog.

This article aims to explain the limits of mediation in the development of conflict-management norms. The author argues that conflict management practices fostered by US mediation efforts in the initial Syria-Israel disengagement agreement of 1974 were insufficient for creating new norms, and this precluded further expansion in the domain of politico-military co-operation between the two sides. Although mediation facilitated a negotiation process, and successfully altered the short-term decision calculations of the parties regarding the future of armed conflict, such intervention neither fostered policy co-ordination, strengthened collective expectations about stability, nor engendered shared understandings for durable, peaceful developments.

665   **Syria and Israel: from war to peace-making.**
Moshe Ma'oz.   Oxford: Clarendon Press, 1995. 280p. bibliog.

A comprehensive account of the Syrian-Israeli conflict, as the author swiftly guides the reader through fifty years of modern history. Ma'oz offers a stylized interpretation of Syrian-Israeli history; his accounts of the DMZ problems and his emphasis on Syria's belligerence in 1967 deserve broader discussion. The most important contribution of this book is its coverage of the peace process. Although one may take issue with some of Ma'oz's analysis, he presents the reader with an eloquent and informative depiction of Syrian-Israeli affairs.

666   **Life under occupation in the Golan Heights.**
Tayseer Mara'i, Usama R. Halabi.   *Journal of Palestine Studies*, vol. XXII, no. 1, issue 85 (autumn 1992), p. 78-93.

In a special report, the authors give a descriptive account of life under Israeli occupation in the Golan Heights. They depict the political aspects of life during occupation, and the Israeli policy of counterpoising the Syrian identity with the Druze identity. The article also compares and contrasts the socio-economic services available to the local inhabitants and the Israeli settlers.

667   **The Golan Heights: and obsolete security buffer.**
R. Reuben Miller.   *Mediterranean Quarterly*, vol. 4, no. 2 (spring 1993), p. 121-28.

Miller assesses the strategic value of the Golan Heights. He argues that the Golan no longer serves the doctrine of 'strategic depth', which he describes as an 'outmoded concept' that was argued so convincingly after the 1967 War. The first line of Israel's defence in the 1990s is accurate intelligence; with the advent of sophisticated signal and electronic intelligence, the old threat of deep military penetration across vast territory has passed. Miller opines that the Golan is an economic liability for Israel that should be turned into a political asset.

668   **The Golan: Israel, Syria, and strategic calculations.**
Muhammad Muslih.   *The Middle East Journal*, vol. 47, no. 4 (autumn
1993), p. 611-32.

Muslih examines the Israeli and Syrian positions regarding the DMZs created after the
1948 Palestine War and the issue of the Golan Heights. He analyses these positions
with respect to the political environment in which the Israeli-Syrian conflict emerged
and through the events and policies that gave the conflict its own dynamic. The article
addresses two major questions: what were the immediate and specific actions and
policies that gave rise to the Golan question? What are the strategic considerations
that shape the Israeli and Syrian positions towards the question?

669   **Israel-Syria: conflict at Jordan River, 1949-1967.**
Donald Neff.   *Journal of Palestine Studies*, vol. XXIII, no. 4, issue 92
(summer 1994), p. 26-40.

Neff seeks to challenge the argument that the Golan Heights offer Israel security in its
competition with Syria. He re-examines the reports of the United Nations Truce
Supervision Organization (UNTSO) on the conduct of the Syrian and Israeli
governments with regard to the struggle over the Huleh lakes in the 1950s. Neff
asserts that, contrary to public perception, Israel escalated the conflict over the DMZs
over two separate issues: sovereignty; and the diversion of the Jordan River. These
incursions added to the momentum of the June War of 1967. Drawing on that, Neff
argues that the efficacy of Syrian artillery was not great enough to deter Israel from
taking over the DMZs and the water of the River Jordan, nor to prevent Israel's
capture of the Golan Heights in 1967. In an age where Israel maintains a decisive
military edge over all its neighbours, the issue of the Golan Heights as a security
concern, therefore, seems largely aimed at justifying their retention.

670   **The June War: whose conspiracy?**
Richard B. Parker.   *Journal of Palestine Studies*, vol. XXI, no. 4,
issue 84 (summer 1992), p. 5-21.

Parker examines the familiar conspiracy theory attached to the June War and the
question of whether the Israelis ensnared Nasser. He defines the role played by the
Americans, Egyptians, Syrians and Soviets in the plot portrayed in Heikal's *1967
infijar*. Parker argues that although a conspiracy is conceivable, it cannot be proven.
He offers other explanations for the war, such as: the Arab cold war; the festering
Palestinian issue; and the military miscalculation of Nasser.

671   **Weapons acquisition and arms racing in the Middle East.**
Raymond Picquet.   In: *Change and continuity in the Middle East:
conflict resolution and prospects for peace.*   Edited by M. E. Ahrari.
Basingstoke, England; London: Macmillan Press; New York: St.
Martin's Press, 1996, p. 192-232.

The article is divided into four main sections which deal with: the general acquisition
of non-conventional weapons; the acquisition of non-conventional weapons by Iraq,
Egypt and Iran; Syria (p. 205-07), Libya, Israel and Algeria; and arms racing in the
Middle East region. In the final section, Picquet analyses the Middle Eastern trend of
acquiring weapons of mass destruction.

672   **Israel, Syria, and Lebanon.**
Itamar Rabinovich.   *International Journal*, vol. XLV, no. 3 (summer 1990), p. 529-52.
The author starts by emphasizing the integral nature of Levantine politics; Israel, Syria and Lebanon cannot be separated and deserve equal attention. Rabinovich argues that whereas Syria's position on reaching a settlement has been inconsistent, Israel's position has been determined since 1967. He studies the various phases of Syrian-Israeli policies, and then contemplates the possibilities of: comprehensive peace (p. 541-44); an interim settlement (p. 544-45); military conflict (p. 545); and the resolution of the Lebanese crisis (p. 545-58).

673   **An historical encyclopedia of the Arab-Israeli conflict.**
Edited by Bernard Reich.   Westport, Connecticut: Greenwood Press, 1996. 655p.
Reich attempts to provide detailed information about every aspect of the Arab-Israeli conflict. This volume covers the whole range of the conflict from the adoption of the Palestine partition plan in November 1947 to the Declaration of Principles and the Israel-Jordan peace treaty. Reich claims that this volume is dispassionate and offers a new perspective on the events and individuals in the history and evolution of the Arab-Israeli conflict.

674   **Asad of Syria: the struggle for the Middle East.**
Patrick Seale, with the assistance of Maureen McConville.   London: I. B. Tauris, 1988; Berkeley, California: University of California Press, 1989. 552p. bibliog.
Seale's book has become essential reading for all those interested in Syria. It analyses Syria's domestic, regional and international politics, according to the realist model of international relations theory, since Asad's rise to power. Syria's engagement in Lebanon, the June War (1967), the October, or Yom Kippur, War (1973), Syrian-Iranian relations and the Hindawi affair (in which Syria was implicated in a plot to blow up an aeroplane leaving London Heathrow in 1986) all receive attention. Although Syria is much maligned as a rogue state, its policies, according to Seale, are motivated by national interest and a desire to check Israeli hegemony. However, having based his work on extensive interviews with the Syrian president, Seale has been criticized for apologizing for Asad's excesses. Nevertheless, this is an enlightening, informative and entertaining read. By moving from Asad's childhood psychology to the realms of power politics, Seale breaks the usual academic mold, and aims his book at both academic and non-academic audiences.

675   **Asad's regional strategy and the challenge from Netanyahu.**
Patrick Seale, Linda Butler.   *Journal of Palestine Studies*, vol. XXVI, no. 1, issue 101 (autumn 1996), p. 27-41.
The authors aver that Asad's regional policy has been consistent since 1970. With Netanyahu's ascension to power in 1996, and traditional US hostility towards Syria, peace, it is argued, may not be possible. Asad's change in policy from strategic parity to comprehensive peace shows a consistency in 'containing' Israel. Asad is willing to accept Israel as a player among other regional players, but not as the only player in the region. Netanyahu's attitude towards Syria is characterized as one of mistrust. The

authors conclude that there is no prospect for peace or regional security as long as Israel continues to occupy the Golan Heights, East Jerusalem and the West Bank.

676 **Syria and Israel: the politics of escalation.**
Avner Yaniv. In: *Syria under Assad: domestic constraints and regional risks.* Edited by Moshe Ma'oz, Avner Yaniv. London: Croom Helm, 1986, p. 157-78.

A useful outline of the escalation in the Syrian sector of the Arab-Israeli conflict since 1948. Yaniv argues that the Israeli-Egyptian peace and the 1982 Israeli invasion of Lebanon have brought the Syrian-Israeli conflict to a new level of mutual risk. He discusses the roots of conflict in the 1948 War, the deterioration during the period 1956-67, the June 1967 War, and the effects of the Lebanese conflict.

677 **Domestic politics and the prospects for an Arab-Israeli peace.**
Valerie Yorke. *Journal of Palestine Studies*, vol. XVII, no. 4, issue 68 (summer 1988), p. 3-25.

Yorke argues that the Palestinian *intifada* rendered the environment less favourable for fulfilling the requirements of negotiations. Her article analyses the Israeli attitude towards territorial compromise over the occupied territories. In addition, it emphasizes Syria readiness to conclude peace on its own terms (p. 14-19).

678 **Domestic politics and regional security: Jordan, Syria and Israel. The end of an era?**
Valerie Yorke. Aldershot, England; Brookfield, Vermont: Gower, published for the International Institute for Strategic Studies, 1988. 400p. maps. bibliog.

Discusses the domestic dynamics of Jordan, Syria and Israel throughout the 1970s and 1980s, and projects those dynamics into the inter-Arab and Arab-Israeli arenas. The work is dense, and at times repetitive, yet it remains a solid study. Yorke relies on personal interviews, supplemented by wide-ranging English-language sources, in addition to a handful of Hebrew references. This is a suitable textbook for undergraduate courses examining the Arab-Israeli conflict.

Linkage politics in the Middle East: Syria between domestic and external conflict, 1961-1970.
See item no. 506.

Domestic transformation and foreign steadfastness in contemporary Syria.
See item no. 534.

The superpowers and the Syrian-Israeli conflict: beyond crisis management?
See item no. 580.

Syria and the New World Order.
See item no. 598.

Syrian foreign policy in the post-Soviet era.
See item no. 604.

Turkish-Israeli-Syrian relations and their impact on the Middle East.
See item no. 607.

The intifadah and the Arab world: old players, new roles.
See item no. 623.

Israel and Syria: the search for a risk-free peace.
See item no. 681.

The Israeli-Syrian battle for equitable peace.
See item no. 682.

Why Syria must regain the Golan to make peace.
See item no. 683.

Conflict resolution in the Middle East: stimulating a diplomatic negotiation between Israel and Syria.
See item no. 697.

The Middle East Military Balance.
See item no. 751.

The Middle East in conflict, a historical bibliography.
See item no. 855.

The Peace Process

679   **The peace process and its critics: post-Cold War perspectives.**
M. E. Ahrari.   In: *Change and continuity in the Middle East: conflict resolution and prospects for peace.*   Basingstoke, England; London: Macmillan Press; New York: St. Martin's Press, 1996, p. 21-46. map.
Ahrari examines the activities of the Rejectionist Front during the Cold War era. The Rejectionist Front, according to Ahrari, comprised those countries and organizations who rejected a political solution to the Arab-Israeli conflict, including Iran, Hizballah and Hamas. However, the author does not include Syria due to its decision to engage in dialogue with Israel. Four areas are scrutinized in this article: the peace between the PLO and Israel; the 'off-again-on-again' negotiations between Syria and Israel; the peace treaty signed between Israel and Jordan in October 1994; and the stalled negotiations between Israel and Lebanon. Ahrari emphasizes the centrality of the Palestinians to the peace process by outlining the conflict from the origins of the Israeli state until 1993. Finally, he examines the position of the post-Cold War rejectionists.

680 **Economic interactions among participants in the Middle East peace process.**
Hisham Awartani, Ephraim Kleiman. *The Middle East Journal*, vol. 51, no. 2 (spring 1997), p. 215-29.

The possibilities of economic integration amongst the states of Syria, Egypt, Jordan, the Palestinian Authority and Israel are explored in this article. The authors ascribe to the underlying assumption that economic integration ensures a sustainable peace. However, their observation that the present pattern of trade amongst these states does not constitute a natural trading bloc somewhat obscures the expediency of the premise. By examining the bilateral economic relations between the states, the authors indicate that it is competition rather than complementarity that characterizes their economic and political relationships.

681 **Israel and Syria: the search for a risk-free peace.**
Alon Ben-Meir. *Middle East Policy*, vol. IV, nos. 1 & 2 (September 1995), p. 140-55.

Ben-Meir investigates the 'real and imagined' security problems of Syria and Israel and looks at Israeli and Syrian public perceptions of peace. The article is based upon the author's visits to both countries and his conversations with state officials involved in the peace negotiations. In the case of Syria, peace is perceived in terms of a total Israeli withdrawal from the Golan Heights. From the Israeli perspective, four objections are raised against total withdrawal, namely: Syria's political uncertainty; water; the future of Israeli settlers in the Golan; and the issue of national security. Ben-Meir proposes a more interventionist role for the United States in negotiations, and the resolution of security problems through stationing troops in the Golan. The author offers an objective analysis and this article is recommended to all readers interested in contemporary Syria.

682 **The Israeli-Syrian battle for equitable peace.**
Alon Ben-Meir. *Middle East Policy*, vol. III, no. 1 (1994), p. 70-83.

In his article, Ben-Meir asserts that after a careful examination of the Israeli and Syrian positions, the only viable option for either state is an acceptance of the full withdrawal for peace formula. Israel and Syria will have to compromise. The Syrians are unlikely to recover the Golan Heights unless they opt for full peace, including normalization, and the Israelis, if they wish to continue to prosper, cannot substitute real peace for the strategic advantage of the Golan.

683 **Why Syria must regain the Golan to make peace.**
Alon Ben-Meir. *Middle East Policy*, vol. V, no. 3 (September 1997), p. 104-12.

Ben-Meir explores Asad's reasons for insisting on a full Israeli withdrawal from the Golan Heights. He considers the following factors: strategic relevance; psychology; politics; personality; and history. Ben-Meir argues that prior to creating the necessary psychological and political environment for peace, Syria and Israel should address four crucial issues: the relevance of the Golan; the timetable of withdrawal; Syria's political uncertainty after Asad's death; and the normalization of relations between the two countries.

684 **Have Syria and Israel opted for peace?**
M. Zuhair Diab. *Middle East Policy*, vol. III, no. 2 (1994), p. 77-90.
Diab suggests that Syria's position towards Israel has undergone an incremental change since 1970. Whilst a comprehensive settlement has remained a consistent goal of the Syrian regime, the road to reaching a settlement, and its shape and modalities, have been subjected to variations under the pressure of changing internal, regional and international conditions.

685 **Syria and the Middle East peace process.**
Alasdair D. Drysdale, Raymond A. Hinnebusch.   New York: Council on Foreign Relations, 1991. 244p. maps. bibliog.
Provides prescriptive advice for US policy in the Middle East. Syrian indispensability to the peace process is the cornerstone of this book. The authors argue that to achieve durable peace in the Middle East, the United States must pay homage to Syria's relevance. They build their case upon a review of Syria's recent history, domestic politics and foreign relations.

686 **Fresh light on Syrian-Israeli peace negotiations: an interview with Ambassador Walid al-Moualem.**
Journal of Palestine Studies, vol. XXVI, no. 2, issue 102 (winter 1997), p. 81-94.
Walid al-Mu'allim discusses Syria's role in the bilateral negotiations with Israel. Rabin's commitment to full withdrawal is disclosed, and the significance of the 'Aim and Principles of Security Arrangements' paper is elaborated upon.

687 **The Israel-Syrian track.**
Sami G. Hajjar. *Middle East Policy*, vol. VI, no. 3 (February 1999), p. 112-30.
Hajjar examines the stalled Middle East peace process, focusing on the Israeli-Syrian track. He argues that for ideological and strategic considerations, the Likud government of Netanyahu is unwilling to abide by the 'land for peace' formula established in 1991. Netanyahu and his advisors assume that there is room for flexibility over the issue of the Golan Heights. However, Syria will not agree to any compromises on the Golan Heights; moreover, it refuses to endorse any separate deal between Israel and Syria. Hajjar suggests that without vigorous US involvement, the peace process is deemed to remain on the back-burner.

688 **Does Syria want peace? Syrian policy in the Syrian-Israeli peace negotiations.**
Raymond A. Hinnebusch. *Journal of Palestine Studies*, vol. XXVI, no. 1, issue 101 (autumn 1996), p. 42-57.
Hinnebusch views Syrian policy towards the peace process from a domestic perspective. He indicates that Asad has always been committed to achieving a comprehensive and honourable peace with Israel and that such a peace would be based upon a full Israeli withdrawal from the Golan in exchange for a full peace treaty. Although such a move would deprive Syria of 'front-line' rent, Hinnebusch concurs that regime legitimacy is sufficient to sustain a re-ordering of state-society relations.

689   **The water dimension of Golan Heights negotiations.**
Frederic C. Hof. *Middle East Policy*, vol. V, no. 2 (May 1997),
p. 129-41.
Hof examines the possibility of the Israelis and the Syrians reaching a peace treaty
over the Golan Heights. Whilst the issue of the Golan appears to be insurmountable,
Hof believes that the water issue is not a major obstacle to peace. He offers a
framework for settlement and suggests a multilateral/unified management of
watershed based on a succession of bilateral agreements. As a preliminary, Hof
sketches possible water related issues that could be discussed with the conclusion of
an agreement. Although this article is speculative, it does offer a concise analysis and
constitutes a very useful source.

690   **Keessing's guide to the Mid-East peace process.**
Lawrence Joffe. London: Cartermill, 1996. 436p. map. bibliog.
A handbook to the peace process. It is divided into five parts, covering: historical
background; the timetable of peace; an analysis of the states; biographies of the main
actors; and current developments and the future of the peace process. This is a handy
reference book for students, but cannot act as a substitute for research.

691   **Is Syria ready for peace?**
David W. Lesch. *Middle East Policy*, vol. VI, no. 3 (February 1999),
p. 93-111.
Lesch argues that the question of whether Syria is ready for peace is one of political
economy rather than economics. Although the economy is making progress, the
'ossified business environment' is preventing it from realizing its full potential. He
identifies two obstacles preventing Asad from taking serious liberalization measures:
the issue of succession; and the impasse of Syrian-Israeli negotiations. Economic
reforms, Lesch suggests, can only be introduced if peace is concluded. He argues that
a country is ready for peace when the benefits outweigh the repercussions.

692   **An Israeli-Syrian peace treaty: so close and yet so far.**
James S. Moore. *Middle East Policy*, vol. III, no. 3 (1994), p. 60-82.
This paper assesses the reasons for the lack of significant progress on the Israeli-
Syrian peace track. These are summarized as the nature of peace and the extent of
withdrawal. To help break this deadlock, Moore proposes a possible framework for an
Israeli-Syrian peace agreement, which is based upon a template that seeks to combine
two formal security agreements and the formal peace treaty of Israel and Egypt. This
is a well thought-out paper, which manages to encapsulate the essence of the Israeli-
Syrian conflict, and which offers the student a clear insight into the mechanics of the
peace process.

693   **Syria: not so inscrutable.**
Richard W. Murphy. *The World Today*, vol. 52, no. 8-9 (August-
September 1996), p. 203-05.
Murphy assesses Asad's attitude towards peace, and argues that Asad is prepared
to reach peace when Israel returns to its pre-1967 borders. Murphy analyses the
logic behind Asad's approach. In short, Asad mistrusts Israel's hegemonic
ambitions and requires a total Israeli withdrawal and firm guarantees from the

United States. This article offers a clear political analysis, and is most suited to students of politics/international relations.

694 **Dateline Damascus: Asad is ready.**
Muhammad Muslih. *Foreign Policy*, no. 96 (fall 1994), p. 145-63.
Muslih provides a review of Syrian-US relations under the administrations of Kissinger, Carter, Reagan, Bush and Clinton. His article then follows the peace process from the cessation of the Second Gulf War until 1994. Muslih identifies three distinct phases: the end of the Gulf War until October 1991; the opening of the Madrid Peace Conference until 23 June 1992; and the summer of 1992 with Rabin's declaration that Resolution 242 applied to the Golan Heights. Muslih opines that as far as Asad is concerned, peace has become a strategic option, and, despite the differences between Syria and Israel, the terms of peace are achievable. However, he stresses the importance of the United States in promoting and underpinning peace between the two sides.

695 **Syria beyond the peace process.**
Daniel Pipes. Washington, DC: Washington Institute for Near East Policy, 1996. 110p. (Policy Papers, no. 40).
Daniel Pipes argues that US policy-makers would be wrong to afford Syria, a rogue state, a critical role in the peace process. Although Pipes no longer calls for a US-aided overthrow of Asad's regime, as it has become a bulwark against the Islamic threat, he opines that Syria needs to be coaxed into moderation with sticks instead of carrots. Pipes' chapter on the peace process is measured and useful, and highlights the progress made prior to Rabin's assassination.

696 **The brink of peace: the Israeli-Syrian negotiations.**
Itamar Rabinovich. Princeton, New Jersey: Princeton University Press, 1999. 302p.
As Israel's ambassador to the United States and the chief negotiator with Syria from 1992 to 1996, Rabinovich was ideally placed to provide a record of these talks. The resulting account is as complicated as the talks themselves, whose final results were disappointing. Although Syria surprised all parties by even agreeing to discuss peace with Israel, Rabinovich faults Asad for not following through with this sentiment and for seeming happy to accept a stalemate. This book provides a balanced assessment.

697 **Conflict resolution in the Middle East: stimulating a diplomatic negotiation between Israel and Syria.**
J. Lewis Rasmussen, Robert B. Oakley. Washington, DC: United States Institute of Peace, 1992. 60p. bibliog.
An account of a four-day simulation of diplomatic dialogue, organized by the United States Institute of Peace, between two supposed neighbouring countries that had never had direct, official, bilateral talks. A fundamental purpose of gaming is to encourage creative, innovative thinking about problems that defy treatment with more conventional approaches and methods. The exercise, therefore, was designed to understand the complexities of negotiation and to assist bilateral discussions between Syria and Israel.

698 **Peace with security: Israel's minimal security requirements in negotiations with Syria.**
Ze'ev Schiff.   Washington, DC: The Washington Institute for Near East Policy, 1993. 107p. maps. bibliog. (Policy Papers, no. 34).

A companion to an earlier Washington Institute Policy Paper entitled *Security for peace: Israel's minimal security requirements in negotiations with the Palestinians* (Policy Paper, no. 15). Schiff examines the possibility of concluding peace between Israel and Syria. He gives some background, outlines the geographical constraints, and dwells on the settlements. He argues that peace for Syria is a strategic goal; for Israel, peace would reduce the number of regional threats and create a new buffer against Iran and Iraq. Schiff examines the concept of security for Israel and Syria, and the minimal requirements for peace.

699 **Israel and Syria: peace and security on the Golan.**
Aryeh Shalev.   Boulder, Colorado: Westview Press, JCSS Studies, published for the Jaffee Centre for Strategic Studies, Tel Aviv University, 1994. 228p. maps.

The author examines the prospect of peace between Israel and Syria. The study is divided into five parts, covering: political and historical background (since 1949); major obstacles to peace; topography and balance of forces; security risks for Israel; and security arrangements in a transition period. He argues that Israel will have to insist on security and normalization when engaging in negotiations. The book is based on the supposition that peace negotiations between Israel and Syria will be 'extraordinarily difficult, lengthy and punctuated by frequent crises'. However, Shalev believes that an agreement is possible through painful concessions.

700 **Syria's President talks to the American media, 1991.**
Syrian Arab Republic: Ministry of Information, 1991.

Asad's interviews to the American media were conducted by Lally Graham Weymouth, the Washington Post and Newsweek representative in July 1991, ABC reporter Diane Sawyer in September 1991, and Richard Blystone of CNN in October 1991. The topics discussed include the following: Syria's role in Lebanon; the issue of a Syrian-Israeli peace treaty; the Madrid Peace Conference; and Asad's views on Iraq in the post-Gulf War era. Asad's occasional interviews reveal little information, but they can serve as barometers of incremental change in policy, intention and justification.

701 **Israeli-Syrian peace: the long road ahead.**
Stephen Zunes.   *Middle East Policy*, vol. II, no. 3 (1993), p. 62-67.

Zunes attributes Syria's pursuit of a peace agreement with Israel, during the 1990s, to the divisions amongst the Arab states rather than to the change in the international environment. He outlines the relevance of the Golan Heights to both Syria and Israel, and then contrasts their political postures over its future. Zunes argues that the combination of Israel's reluctance to take the appropriate steps and US timidity in exerting pressure on Israel will consign peace to the distant future.

Syria and the New World Order.
See item no. 598.

Syria and Israel: from war to peace-making.
See item no. 665.

Asad's regional strategy and the challenge from Netanyahu.
See item no. 675.

Economy

702 **Economic policy and class structure in Syria: 1958-1980.**
Syed Aziz al-Ahsan. *International Journal of Middle East Studies*,
vol. 16, no. 3 (August 1984), p. 301-23.

A detailed study of economic policy changes and their impact on Syrian class
structure from the late 1950s to the early 1980s. The first part considers the principal
characteristics of economic policies in five distinct phases: the union with Egypt
(1958-61); traditional civilian rule (1961-63); traditional Ba'th rule (1963-66); radical
Ba'th rule (1966-70); and liberal Ba'th rule (1970-mid-1980s). In each period the
author identifies the main beneficiaries of the economic programme and highlights the
elite's motivation for adopting a particular policy. The second part examines the
impact of these policies on class structure, arguing that the last two decades have seen
the growth of middle-size entrepreneurs and petty bourgeoisie. The author
demonstrates that vertical affiliations, namely religion and regional solidarity, are
emerging as more important than class ties.

703 **The emerging Arab capital markets: investment opportunities in
relatively underplayed markets.**
Henry T. Azzam.   London; New York: Kegan Paul, 1997. 283p.

Azzam claims to offer readily available information pertaining to the region's stocks
and bonds markets. He provides information, which could be useful to investors,
policy-makers, analysts and bankers, on the following Arab stock markets: Saudi
Arabia, Egypt, Jordan, Kuwait, United Arab Emirates, Bahrain, Oman, Lebanon,
Morocco and Tunisia. Issues covering structural economic reforms, privatization and
bond market developments are considered, with Syria's economic reforms receiving
attention on p. 59-61 and p. 257.

704 **The Syrian business community, its politics and prospects.**
Joseph Bahout. In: *Contemporary Syria: liberalization between Cold War and cold peace.* Edited by Eberhard Kienle, preface by Patrick Seale. London: British Academic Press; New York: St Martin's Press, 1994, p. 72-80.

Bahout opines that the Syrian business community is heterogeneous. He classifies the community into four groups: old bourgeoisie; petty bourgeoisie; nouveau riche; and state or bureaucratic bourgeoisie. Bahout examines the composition of the military-mercantile complex that has emerged since the 1970s. He suggests that the alliance between entrepreneurs and the military is essentially dependent upon external factors, namely income from oil, the Arab-Israeli conflict, and developments in Lebanon. In conclusion, he acknowledges that the prospect of further economic liberalization will lead to political liberalization. This article offers a concise analysis of the contemporary business community in Syria.

705 **Economic planning in Syria.**
Muhammad Diab. *Middle East Forum*, vol. 27 (March 1961), p. 20-23, 48.

A review of Syria's first five-year plan for economic development, adopted in 1961, which focused on the exploitation of the country's agricultural potential, and the promotion of agricultural exports.

706 **EEC-Syria Cooperation Agreement.**
Brussels: Commission of the European Community, 1978. 37p. (European Information).

Reviews the objectives and terms of the January 1977 Co-operation Agreement between Syria and the European Community. The agreement covers trade, economic and technical co-operation, and financial aid.

707 **The Syrian economy under the Asad regime.**
Kais Firro. In: *Syria under Assad: domestic constraints and regional risks.* Edited by Moshe Ma'oz, Avner Yaniv. London: Croom Helm, 1986, p. 36-68.

Firro examines economic growth in Syria from 1970 to 1984, on a sectoral basis. He contrasts the achievement in agricultural development, the establishment of new industries and the growth of oil revenues, with growing balance of payments problems and budget deficits. Syria's large defence expenditure and its dependence on foreign aid are highlighted.

708 **Linkages and constraints of the Syrian economy.**
Huda Hawwa. In: *State and society in Syria and Lebanon.* Edited by Youssef M. Choueiri. Exeter, England: Exeter University Press, 1993; New York: St. Martin's Press, 1994, p. 84-102.

Hawwa discusses the concept of 'linkage politics' as applied to the case of Syria. This article focuses upon Syria's economic linkage to the region, and the ensuing benefits. Linkage has given Syria political leverage, both in the domestic and regional domains, thus elevating its regional status. However, it has also acted as a constraint upon

Syria. Growth has remained susceptible to the flow of aid, and this in turn has been determined by the regional contest for influence. In order to appreciate the advantages and the constraints of linkage, the author provides a brief overview of the Syrian economy from 1950 to the 1980s. Tables of economic indicators are also included (p. 96-102).

709 **Liberalization in Syria: the struggle of economic and political rationality.**
Raymond A. Hinnebusch. In: *Contemporary Syria: liberalization between Cold War and cold peace.* Edited by Eberhard Kienle, preface by Patrick Seale. London: British Academic Press; New York: St Martin's Press, 1994, p. 97-113.
Hinnebusch utilizes two models to explain the origins of Syria's economic liberalization, namely Marxism and neo-patrimonialism. The article accounts for the obvious gap between economic and political liberalization in the Third World, and suggests that the political consequences of economic liberalization are dependent upon the maturity of the state building processes.

710 **The political economy of economic liberalization in Syria.**
Raymond A. Hinnebusch. *International Journal of Middle East Studies*, vol. 27, no. 3 (August 1995), p. 305-20.
Hinnebusch applies a political economy approach to Syria's on-going process of economic liberalization. Reconciling opposing economic and political approaches, the author utilizes the neo-patrimonial model of elite political culture and Marxist theories to explain Syria's current economic orientation. However, the Syrian case suggests that neither the Marxist view, where economic crisis and class interest force liberalization, nor the opposing view, where the patrimonial state is incapable of reform, explains the reality.

711 **Syria.**
Raymond A. Hinnebusch. In: *Economic and political liberalization in the Middle East.* Edited by Timothy Niblock, Emma Murphy. London: British Academic Press, 1993, p. 177-202.
Hinnebusch considers the relationship between economic and political liberalization in Syria. Accepting the premise that economic crisis drives change, Hinnebusch analyses the depth of changes taking place within the Syrian political system. Factors which push and resist economic and political reform are examined in light of Investment Law no. 10, which was issued in 1991. The conflicts of class, sectarian and state interests are reviewed. Hinnebusch asserts that economic reform can only proceed at a pace that suits the demands of high politics and regime stability.

712 **Syria: the politics of economic liberalisation.**
Raymond A. Hinnebusch. *Third World Quarterly*, vol. 18, no. 2 (June 1997), p. 249-65.
In a well-argued paper, Hinnebusch asserts that Syria's economic policy is determined by the regime's long-term need to balance political and economic rationality. Accordingly, the Syrian case runs against the more orthodox views accounting for economic liberalization, and the author suggests that the Syrian state retains more

autonomy, even in a situation of economic crisis, than most economic analyses allow for. Assessing the two variables of class interest and the political process, Hinnebusch provides an outline of the conflicting social forces and a snapshot of the political process in the early 1990s.

713 **Step by step to an open economic system: Syria sets course for liberalization.**
Hans Hopfinger, Marc Boeckler. *British Journal of Middle Eastern Studies*, vol. 23, no. 2 (November 1996), p. 183-202.
After summarizing Syria's economic crisis management of the 1970s and 1980s, the authors assert that Syria has now reached a point of no return in its transition towards the market economy. The Investment Law no. 10 of 1991 has sought to transform the economic system, not by revolution but by gradualism. The measures and affects of the Investment Law are assessed with regard to the institutional framework, the strengthening of the private sector, prices and competition, foreign trade, and the monetary system. Although the transformation is far from complete, the authors conclude that the process has gained sufficient momentum to defy a reversal of policy and a return to state socialism.

714 **Contemporary Syria: liberalization between Cold War and cold peace.**
Edited by Eberhard Kienle, preface by Patrick Seale. London: British Academic Press; New York: St Martin's Press, 1994. 187p. bibliog.
Addresses the question of whether economic liberalization will lead to political liberalization within Syria. The work is based on the proceedings of a conference held at the School of Oriental and African Studies (SOAS) in London on 27-28 May 1993. In the introduction (p. 1-13), Kienle discusses whether economic liberalization will lead to more political participation, democratization and a respect for human rights. He examines the links between economic and political liberalization and the various models supported by Ayubi and Heydemann. This is an excellent collection of articles.

715 **Foreign aid and economic development in the Middle East: Egypt, Syria, and Jordan.**
Victor Lavy, Eliezer Sheffer. New York: Praeger, 1991. 163p. bibliog.
Examines the economies of Egypt, Syria and Jordan throughout the 1970s and 1980s. The study is divided into three sections: part one accounts for economic decline throughout the 1980s; part two looks at the obstacles to growth, and in particular heavy military expenditure; and the book concludes with suggestions for economic reform, including the role of foreign aid.

716 **Syria.**
Lloyds Bank Ltd. London: Lloyds Bank, Overseas Division, 1985. 23p. (Lloyds Bank Group Economic Report).
A useful summary and guide to the Syrian economy. The report is divided into five sections, dealing with: the land and people; the domestic economy; the structure of production; the external position; and links with the United Kingdom. It describes changes in monetary and fiscal policies, the balance of payments, trade regime and

policy, exchange rates, foreign investment and foreign debt. A more substantial forty-eight-page report was published in 1981 following the first meeting of the Anglo-Syrian Joint Economic Commission in Damascus in April 1980.

717 Oil in the Middle East: its discovery and development.
Stephen Hemsley Longrigg.   London: Oxford University Press, 1961.
2nd ed. 401p. maps.

Longrigg traces the history of the exploitation of oil resources in the Middle East up to 1960, and includes a useful discussion of the discovery and development of Syria's oil resources. The unsuccessful exploration drilling programme of Petroleum Concession Syria (re-named the Syrian Petroleum Company in 1940) over the period 1938-51 is described. Subsequently the Karachauk field was located in 1956 by J. W. Minhall, an independent Syrian-American drilling contractor, and the Suwaidiya field in 1959 by the Société des Pétroles Concordia. The same year saw the completion of the Homs refinery. In addition to its own oil production, Syria also benefited from transit dues paid on the Iraqi and Saudi Arabian pipelines crossing its territory. The disputes over transit payments and the use of these pipelines are also discussed.

718 The political economy of Syria under Asad.
Volker Perthes.   London; New York: I. B. Tauris, 1995. 298p.
bibliog.

This book offers a synthesis of Perthes' work on Syria up to the mid-1990s. It traces the emergence and on-going transformation of Syria's statist economy towards a more liberal model. Perthes evaluates the dynamic between the interests of economics and politics, and produces a cogent argument that accounts for Syria's snail-pace economic and political reforms. The book offers the student a firm foundation for course work and further economic research.

719 The private sector, economic liberalization, and the prospects of democratization: the case of Syria and some other Arab countries.
Volker Perthes.   In: *Democracy without democrats? The renewal of politics in the Muslim world.*   Edited by Ghassan Salamé.   London; New York: I. B. Tauris, 1994, p. 243-69. bibliog.

The economic crisis of the mid-1980s pushed Syria back towards the path of economic liberalization. Economic reform programmes were implemented, increasing the role of the private sector, and some changes were made in regime structures, in a somewhat half-hearted response towards the global trend for democracy. Perthes analyses the impact of economic liberalization upon the private and public sectors' roles in the making of economic policy. In conclusion, he argues that although economic liberalization and private sector growth can open the door to democracy, the Syrian regime still maintains a monopoly on power.

720   **Stages of economic and political liberalization.**
Volker Perthes.   In: *Contemporary Syria: liberalization between Cold War and cold peace*.   Edited by Eberhard Kienle, preface by Patrick Seale.   London: British Academic Press; New York: St Martin's Press, 1994, p. 44-71.
Perthes compares the depth of the first and second Syrian *infitah*. Furthermore, he looks for the origins of the *infitahs*, and then studies the link between the political and economic restructuring of the early 1970s and 1985-86. Perthes explores the argument that economic and political liberalization are 'interdependent', and concludes that economic liberalization is not necessarily linked to political liberalization. Clear analysis and good sources have been used in this piece of research.

721   **The Syrian economy in the 1980s.**
Volker Perthes.   *The Middle East Journal*, vol. 46, no. 1 (winter 1992), p. 37-58.
In one of many excellent papers, Perthes analyses Syria's economic crisis of the 1980s. Dubbing it as the 'lost decade of development', the author suggests that Syria's economic woes stemmed from its development strategy and the policies of the post-1970 leadership. For the first time since 1970, President Asad and his regime were threatened by a loss of legitimacy as the result of economic rather than political problems.

722   **The Syrian private industrial and commercial sectors and the state.**
Volker Perthes.   *International Journal of Middle East Studies*, vol. 24, no. 2 (May 1992), p. 207-30.
Although the Syrian state is Ba'thist in character, it does not exclude the private sector from participating in economic affairs. In this article, Perthes scrutinizes the relationship between the private sector and the state during the period 1946-72. With the ascension of Asad in late 1970, the private sector was invited to return to economic and political life, albeit closely regulated, with the introduction of *infitah*. The author investigates the newly emerging dynamics between the commercial bourgeoisie and the public sector in an attempt to evaluate the inherent contradiction between state ideology and state policy. Perthes concludes that the public sector is only public in legal terms, but it is private in its 'social content'.

723   **Investment Law no. 10: which future for the private sector?**
Sylvia Pölling.   In: *Contemporary Syria: liberalization between Cold War and cold peace*.   Edited by Eberhard Kienle, preface by Patrick Seale.   London: British Academic Press; New York: St Martin's Press, 1994, p. 14-25.
In relation to the differing and often contradictory investment laws promulgated between 1971 and the late 1980s, Pölling examines private sector investment in tourism, agriculture and manufacturing. Furthermore, she investigates the circumstances which led to the promulgation of Investment Law no. 10 in 1991. The article attempts to assess the impact of the new law upon the structure of the economy, and outlines the future challenges faced by the private sector.

Economy

724 **Rentierism and foreign policy in Syria.**
Leonard Robinson. *Arab Studies Journal*, vol. IV, no. 1 (spring 1996), p. 34-52.
This article argues that the rentierist nature of the Syrian state plays a central role in forming Syria's external behaviour. Robinson examines the relationship between external rent, taxation, state legitimacy and foreign policy in the Middle East through three case-studies: Syria's intervention in Lebanon in 1976; Syria's support for Iran in the Iran-Iraq War; and Syria's participation in the Gulf War coalition in 1990/91.

725 **The economies of the Arab world: development since 1945.**
Yusif A. Sayigh. London: Croom Helm, 1978. 726p.
Chapter six (p. 229-80) is devoted to Syria. It examines in detail economic development and structural change in Syria since independence (and up to 1975), emphasizing the dislocation caused by political instability. The chapter also focuses on economic development under the Ba'th. Four aspects of Ba'th policies for 'socialist transformation' are discussed: agrarian reform; the five-year economic plans of 1960/61-1964/65, 1966-70, and 1971-75; the nationalization of industry, banking, insurance and foreign trade; and the formulation of measures for social justice and egalitarianism.

726 **The crisis of 1986 and Syria's plan for reform.**
Nabil Sukkar. In: *Contemporary Syria: liberalization between Cold War and cold peace.* Edited by Eberhard Kienle, preface by Patrick Seale. London: British Academic Press; New York: St Martin's Press, 1994, p. 26-43.
Sukkar outlines the economic crisis of 1986, reviews the structure of the Syrian economy of the 1970s, and then analyses the factors that led to the foreign exchange crisis. This article presents both a diagnosis and a prescription. Sukkar argues that the crisis was exacerbated by the structure of the economy and the debilitating role played by the public sector. As an antidote, the government applied a set of economic reforms dealing with the role of the private sector, trade, the exchange rate, the liberalization of prices and the reduction of subsidies. The details of these reforms and their implications are explored. Sukkar concludes that more reforms are required to enhance growth and to ensure that Syria keeps pace with its neighbours.

727 **The economies of the Middle East.**
Rodney Wilson. London: Macmillan, 1970. 209p.
In chapter seven (p. 101-18) of this country-by-country examination of the economies of the Middle East, Syria is compared with its Ba'thist neighbour Iraq. Both experienced considerable political upheaval in the 1950s and 1960s with frequent policy changes and uncertainty. Land reform and irrigation projects in the two countries are compared. The development of the Euphrates Dam in Syria has aggravated relations between the two, and other disputes have involved Iraq's royalty payments for its oil shipment pipeline through Syria. Wilson shows that income distribution has changed little under the Ba'thist regimes, despite their commitment to promoting greater equity.

728   **Syrian migration to the Arab oil-producing countries.**
      Onn Winckler.   *Middle Eastern Studies*, vol. 33, no. 1 (January 1997),
      p. 107-18.
Winckler explores the issues surrounding migration from Syria to the oil-producing
countries: Bahrain, Kuwait, Saudi Arabia, United Arab Emirates, Oman, Qatar and
Libya. The author examines the following areas of interest: the effect of migration
upon the Syrian economy between 1970 and 1992; the policy of host countries
towards Syrian workers; and the impact of the Iraqi invasion of Kuwait on migrant
labour. The article offers statistics, supported by clear analysis, and provides tables of
Syrian migrants in oil-producing countries of Middle East, 1970-92 (p. 110), and
workers' remittances and trade exports in Syria, Jordan, and Egypt, 1975-93 (p. 112).

The tariff of Syria 1919-1932.
See item no. 344.

Economic organization of Syria.
See item no. 356.

Monetary and banking system of Syria.
See item no. 357.

Syria and Lebanon under French Mandate.
See item no. 367.

Syria: development and monetary policy.
See item no. 390.

The economic development of Syria.
See item no. 392.

**Social structure and political stability: comparative evidence from the
Algerian, Syrian, and Iraqi cases.**
See item no. 494.

Syria after two years of the March revolution.
See item no. 503.

**Withered socialism or whether socialism? The radical Arab states as
populist-corporatist regimes.**
See item no. 505.

**The political logic of economic rationality: selective stabilization in
Syria.**
See item no. 515.

Syria 1945-1986: politics and society.
See item no. 526.

The return of politics? Scenarios for Syria's second *infitah*.
See item no. 530.

Taxes and investment in the Middle East.
See item no. 569.

Economy

Economic interactions among participants in the Middle East peace process.
See item no. 680.

Is Syria ready for peace?
See item no. 691.

Capitalist agro-business in a socialist country? Syria's new shareholding corporation as an example.
See item no. 736.

Country Report: Syria.
See item no. 837.

Middle East Economic Digest.
See item no. 841.

Middle East Economic Survey.
See item no. 842.

Agriculture

729 Agriculture in the Syrian Arab Republic.
Damascus: Office Arabe de Presse et de Documentation, 1978. 28p. (Série Etudes, no. 178).

The first part of this review examines agrarian reform in Syria since the Ba'thist revolution, and details the restrictions imposed upon the ownership of different types of land. The second part deals with Ba'thist agricultural development strategy, arguing that the changes in agrarian structures, the development of agricultural co-operatives and the achievement of stable government have made higher agricultural growth rates possible. The main features of the fourth five-year plan, (1976-80), as they affect agricultural development, are described.

730 The agricultural system of the Syrian Arab Republic.
M. al-Ashram. Aleppo, Syria: Aleppo University, Faculty of Agriculture, 1985. 41p. bibliog. (Department Information Report/Staff Papers Series, DIR 85-1, SP-2).

A useful report reviewing the main features of the Syrian agricultural sector and evaluating its contribution to the Syrian economy. The areas covered include: levels of production and investment; mechanization; labour; pricing policy; trade; credit; management and administration; soil and water conservation; the organization of the Ministry of Agriculture and Agrarian Reform; and delivery of inputs and services.

731 Public agricultural sector in the Syrian Arab Republic.
M. al-Ashram. Aleppo, Syria: Aleppo University, Faculty of Agriculture, 1985. 43p. bibliog. (Department Information Report/Staff Papers Series, DIR 85-1, SP-5).

Provides an overview of the state agricultural sector in Syria, focusing on its organization, management and production. The author evaluates the state sector's performance and makes recommendations for improvements.

732 **Le développement agricole – ambitions et réalités.** (Agricultural development – ambitions and realities.)
Syrie et Monde Arabe, vol. 39, no. 357 (1983), p. 1-6.

Reviews the achievements of the fourth five-year plan (1976-80) in the agricultural sector, noting particularly the level of investment in agriculture, the intensification of land use, and a reduced trading deficit. The agricultural aims of the fifth five-year plan (1981-85) are listed, and methods of attaining them are discussed.

733 **Land reform in Syria.**
Eva Garzouzi. *The Middle East Journal*, vol. 17, no. 1 (winter-spring 1963), p. 83-90.

Reviews the major phases of the land reform programme in Syria and attempts to assess the results. The 1958 law restricted ownership to 80 hectares for irrigated and 100 hectares for non-irrigated lands. The amendments of 1962, which enabled landowners to disperse ten hectares of irrigated or forty hectares of non-irrigated lands to each dependent, and which raised the size limits of ownership in the Jazira, Euphrates, and Rashid regions, are reviewed. By 1961 some 670,000 hectares had been expropriated, and 175,000 hectares redistributed. The implementation of the land reform programme coincided with three years of drought.

734 **Le monde rural avant les réformes.** (Rural society before the reforms.)
Jean Hannoyer. In: *La Syrie d'aujourd'hui* (Syria today). Edited by André Raymond. Paris: Editions du CNRS, 1980, p. 273-96.

Examines the conditions in, and characteristics of, the Syrian rural sector from the late Ottoman period, through the French Mandate to the early years of independence. It begins by discussing the causes and consequences of rural stagnation during the later years of Ottoman rule. The author divides Syria into three broad zones – marginal areas, plains and oases, and mountainous regions – and examines the characteristics of village society, land tenure, water rights, power structures and the organization of production in each region. The second section examines the rural development policies of the French administration, discussing in particular the question of systematic land registration. The essay concludes with an assessment of Syria's impressive record of growth in the agricultural sector in the first ten years of independence.

735 **Observations sur l'élevage et le commerce du mouton dans la région de Raqqa en Syrie.** (Observations on sheep rearing and trading in the Raqqa region of Syria.)
Jean Hannoyer, J. P. Thieck. *Production Pastorale et Société*, no. 14 (1984), p. 47-63.

Examines the characteristics of sheep-rearing and the production of cheese, wool and other products in the Raqqa region of Syria. Traditional trading relationships, rearing contracts and the role of middlemen in sheep sales are also discussed. The authors examine the impact of contemporary economic change, in particular agricultural mechanization and the role of the state, on traditional production methods, and they consider the implications for the survival of the region's bedouin sheep-herding tribes.

736 **Capitalist agro-business in a socialist country? Syria's new shareholding corporation as an example.**
Hans Hopfinger. *British Society for Middle Eastern Studies Bulletin*, vol. 17, no. 2 (1990), p. 162-70.

Hopfinger examines the success of Syria's new agricultural companies. This type of company was first licensed by Decree no. 10 of 1986, which permitted the establishment of incorporated shareholder companies in Syria's mixed agriculture sector. The author looks at how these companies function in a centrally planned economy. The article is divided into three sections, covering: origin and political background; organization and operational structure; and efficiency and economic success. He concludes that the creation of such companies could be considered a significant step towards economic and political liberalization.

737 **Land reform in Syria.**
Ziad Keilany. *Middle Eastern Studies*, vol. 16, no. 3 (October 1980), p. 209-24.

Keilany describes the background, history and results of the Syrian land reform programme which was introduced in 1958 during the union with Egypt, and which tried to impose Egyptian land reform concepts under very different agricultural conditions. The results of the original reform programme and its revision of 1962 and 1963 are difficult to assess because of climatic conditions, political instability and the 1965 nationalization of foreign trade. Keilany suggests that while the economic success of the reform programme is questionable, it has played a critical role in integrating rural areas with the rest of the country.

738 **La question agraire dans les pays arabes: le cas de la Syrie.** (The agrarian question in the Arab countries: the case of Syria.)
Bichara Khader. Louvain-la-Neuve, Belgium: CIACO Editeur, 1984. 631p. bibliog.

Based on the author's 1979 doctoral thesis, this is a detailed examination of Syria's agricultural sector. Part one presents an historical analysis of Syrian agriculture from antiquity through the early Islamic period to the French Mandate and independence. The second part describes the organization, methods and financing of agriculture in Syria before the agrarian reform. Part three comprises a detailed study of the 1958 agrarian reform programme, its implementation, results and the attitudes of the peasantry. The concluding section examines inter-sectoral relations between agriculture, industry and commerce.

739 **Réforme agraire en Syrie.** (Agrarian reform in Syria.)
Bichara Khader. *Revue Française d'Etudes Politiques Méditerranéenes*, vol. 7/8 (1975), p. 74-86.

A useful summary describing patterns of land-ownership and agricultural income before the first agrarian reform programme of 1958. Syrian agriculture was characterized by 'latifundia' (large rural estates); in 1955 some 49 per cent of landholdings were over 100 hectares, while some 600,000 peasant families were landless. Khader describes the aims, and assesses the progress, of the successive agrarian reform programmes of 1958, 1963 and 1966.

740 **Land reform and class structure in rural Syria.**
Sulayman N. Khalaf. In: *Syria: society, culture, and polity.* Edited
by Richard Antoun, Donald Quataert. Albany, New York: State
University of New York Press, 1991, p. 63-78. (SUNY Series in
Middle Eastern Studies).

This chapter examines the socio-political changes that have occurred in the Euphrates
Valley since the 1940s, paying particular attention to land reform and its effect on
class structure in the rural communities of the Raqqa region. What is especially
attractive about this piece of research is the breadth of fieldwork and the depth of
analysis.

741 **The origins of landownership in Syria.**
Paul J. Klat. *Middle East Economic Papers* (1958), p. 51-66.

Klat traces the history of land-ownership in Syria from the Arab conquest of the 7th
century to 1958, and discusses the various categories of land and land tenure. The
author reviews Islamic concepts of property and the effects of the 1958 union with
Egypt.

742 **Recent agricultural development and bedouin settlement in Syria.**
Adnan Mahouk. *The Middle East Journal,* vol. 10, no. 2 (spring
1956), p. 167-76.

Mahouk examines the question of bedouin settlement in the Euphrates and Jazira
districts of Syria, arguing that recent agricultural developments, in particular the rapid
spread of cotton cultivation, mechanization and land reform, are not fostering a natural
trend towards sedentarization. Government settlement policy, including the allotment
of between ten and fifty hectare plots to bedouin families, is examined. In the Radd
area of Jazira some 100,000 hectares have been allocated to bedouin settlements.

743 **Agricultural development in Syria.**
Ian R. Manners, Tagi Sagafi-Nejad. In: *Agricultural development in
the Middle East.* Edited by Peter Beaumont, Keith McLachlan.
London: John Wiley, 1985, p. 255-78.

An excellent assessment of Syrian efforts to resolve the underlying problems which
are identified as inhibiting Syrian agricultural development. The authors establish
major trends in land and water utilization, and evaluate policies designed to remove
the physical and social constraints on agricultural development. Particular attention is
paid to the development of the Tabqa Dam on the Euphrates. The authors question
whether government preoccupation with large-scale water development schemes,
which have produced only meagre results, has led to the neglect of alternative policy
options, such as improved water management. The decline in cultivated area since the
late 1960s, as marginal lands brought into cultivation have been degraded, prompts the
authors to question the extent to which recent gains in productivity can be sustained.
Historically Syrian agriculture has been geared to survival. Despite low productivity,
this presented a low-risk way of coping with environmental uncertainty, and offered
important lessons for agriculture in the mid-1980s.

744 Land tenure and irrigation projects in Syria: 1948-82.
Françoise Métral. In: *Land tenure and social transformation in the Middle East.* Edited by Tarif Khalidi. Beirut: American University of Beirut Press, 1984, p. 465-81.

Under the influence of the French mandatory authorities, Syrian agricultural policy focused on the control of river water for irrigation. This chapter examines the characteristics of state irrigation schemes, using the Ghab-Asharneh project, which began in 1952, as a case-study. It describes the situation in the Ghab in the 1930s and the subsequent evolution of land tenure and water rights in the area. The centralized organization of production by the autonomous Office of Exploitation of the Ghab and Asharneh, established in 1969, is outlined. Despite state direction of cultivation, there was some room for peasant initiative.

The Middle East: a geographical study.
See item no. 26.

La Ghouta, un paradis entre montagne et steppe. (Ghouta, a paradise between mountain and steppe.)
See item no. 27.

Syria after two years of the March revolution.
See item no. 503.

Authoritarian power and state formation in Ba'thist Syria: army, party, and peasant.
See item no. 516.

Bureaucracy and development in Syria: the case of agriculture.
See item no. 517.

Peasant and bureaucracy in Ba'thist Syria: the political economy of rural development.
See item no. 519.

Agricultural bibliography of Syria, to 1983.
See item no. 859.

Statistics

745 Annual Statistical Bulletin of the Ministry of Social Affairs and Labour.
Damascus: Ministry of Social Affairs and Labour, 1961- . annual.

Presents the results of the Ministry's annual employment survey together with a selection of statistical tables covering the Ministry's various activities in labour relations, social services and community development. The latter includes statistics on: unemployment; minimum wages, factory inspections, accidents at work and union membership; institutions for physically and mentally handicapped people; orphanages; and health centres.

746 Political Risk Yearbook – Middle East and North Africa.
William D. Coplin, Michael K. O'Leary. Syracuse, New York: Political Risk Services, 1987- . annual. maps. bibliog.

Deals with the Middle East and North Africa. It attempts to bridge the gap between academia and the world of politics, government and economics. It provides information about governments and an analysis of policy-making for researchers and students. It has separate country reports that cover geography and history, international relations, social conditions and the different economic sectors. In addition, it provides political and economic forecasts. It is a useful reference work for libraries.

747 Demographic Yearbook.
New York: United Nations, 1948- . annual.

Contains up-to-date demographic statistics from 220 countries, including Syria, on population size and trends in natality, mortality, nuptiality and divorce.

748 Foreign Trade Statistics.
Damascus: Central Bureau of Statistics, 1962- . annual.

Contains annual statistics including time-series data on imports, exports, and transit trade by commodity and countries of origin and destination.

212

749   **International Financial Statistics Yearbook.**
Washington, DC: International Monetary Fund, 1974- . annual.
Provides time-series data on the member states of the International Monetary Fund
(IMF), including Syria, from 1949 onward. The statistical tables included cover:
exchange rates; international liquidity; money and banking; prices; production and
international trade; and balance of payments and national accounts.

750   **The Arab world, Turkey and the Balkans (1878-1914): a handbook
of historical statistics.**
Justin A. McCarthy.   Boston, Massachusetts: G. K. Hall, 1982. 309p.
maps. (International Historical Studies).
Reproduces statistics from Ottoman sources, giving a picture of the Ottoman Empire
during its final years. The coverage includes: climate; population; health; education;
justice; money; government revenue and expenditure; manufacturing; transport;
foreign trade; minerals; and agriculture and animal husbandry. The tables are divided
up by province and include Syria. The introduction comments on the sources and
quality of Ottoman statistics.

751   **The Middle East Military Balance.**
Tel Aviv: The Jaffee Center for Strategic Studies, Tel Aviv University,
1983- . annual.
An annual publication on the Middle East military balance. It includes a collection of
articles, mostly from an Israeli perspective, on the Arab-Israeli conflict, the peace
process, and the regional balance of power. The military balance of Middle Eastern
countries is covered in separate sections. This is a useful statistical tool.

752   **Quarterly Statistical Bulletin.**
Damascus: Central Bank of Syria, Research Department, 1962- .
quarterly.
The Central Bank of Syria's quarterly bulletin is Syria's most up-to-date compendium
of economic statistics. Containing more then sixty-five tables, it is usually available
well in advance of the annual *Statistical Abstract of Syria* (see item no. 753). In
addition to detailed monetary and banking statistics, it provides data on the balance of
payments, foreign trade, government budgets, expenditure, revenue, agricultural and
industrial production, and gross domestic product (GDP). Prior to 1973, it was entitled
the *Periodical Bulletin*.

753   **Statistical Abstract of Syria.**
Damascus: Central Bureau of Statistics, 1947- . annual.
A collection of over 340 statistical tables drawn from the annual reports and surveys
of all the major government departments and ministries. The tables are divided into
sixteen sections: physical; population and demography; manpower and labour force;
agriculture; industry; building and construction; transport and communications;
foreign trade; prices and internal trade; education; health; justice; tourism; co-
operatives and unions; finance; and national accounts.

Statistics

754 **UNESCO Statistical Yearbook.**
Paris: UNESCO, 1963- . annual.
Contains a variety of up-to-date statistics on population, education, science and technology, book production, newspapers, films, and radio and television broadcasting, supplied by over 200 member countries including Syria.

755 **United Nations Statistical Yearbook.**
New York: United Nations, 1948- . annual.
Contains economic statistics from member countries, including Syria, showing data on population, industrial and agricultural production, energy output, trade, transport and communications, and consumption. Summary statistics are provided on balance of payments, wages and prices, national accounts, public finance, and development assistance. The final sections cover social phenomenon, housing, health and education.

756 **UNRWA Statistical Yearbook.**
Vienna: UNRWA, 1964- . annual.
Contains comprehensive statistical data on the UNRWA educational services provided to Palestinian refugee children in Syria, the West Bank, Gaza, Lebanon and Jordan.

757 **The Arab world: an international statistical directory.**
Rodney J. Wilson.   Brighton, England: Wheatsheaf, 1984. 140p.
The introductory section of this work is a guide to the availability in Britain of statistical data on the Arab world. A series of thirty-five inter-Arab tables provide comparative data on trade, banking and finance drawn primarily from international statistical series. The final section of tables provides a guide to the economic structure of each Arab country, including Syria (p. 112-17). On Syria, tables are provided for agricultural production, industrial production, employment and wages in the state sector, major industrial products, labour force, budget and balance of payments. The brief accompanying text is a practical guide to the availability and reliability of Syrian statistical sources.

758 **Yearbook of International Trade Statistics.**
New York: United Nations, 1950- . annual.
Provides detailed country-by-country statistics on trading patterns and the composition of trade and exports.

759 **The Yearbook of Labour Statistics.**
Geneva: International Labour Office, 1935- . annual.
Includes data on economic activity, employment, unemployment, wage rates, labour costs, consumer prices, occupational injuries and industrial disputes for all member countries, including Syria.

760 **Yearbook of National Accounts Statistics.**
New York: United Nations, 1957- . annual.
Includes data on national income and expenditure, capital transactions, GDP by economic activity, domestic factor income, government and private financial

214

consumption expenditure, composition of gross capital formation, and external transactions for all member countries, including Syria.

Report on the commercial statistics of Syria.
See item no. 223.

Education

761 **Islamic benevolent societies and public education in Ottoman Syria, 1875-1882.**
Donald J. Cioeta. *Islamic Quarterly*, vol. 26, no. 1 (1982), p. 40-55.
Examines the role of Islamic benevolent societies in encouraging the spread of education among Syrian Muslims in the late 19th century. Particular attention is paid to the group set up by 'Abd al-Qadir al-Qabbani in 1878, Jam'iyat al-Maqasid al-Khayriyah, which established eight schools in Damascus. By the mid-1880s there were also Islamic education societies in Homs, Latakia and Aleppo. The group's influence with Ahmet Hamdi Pasha, who replaced Midhat Pasha as Governor of Syria in 1880, led to increased government aid for education.

762 **The geography of education in Syria, with a translation of 'education in Syria' by Shahin Makarius, 1883.**
Henry Diab, Lars Wahlin. *Geografiska Annaler*, vol. 658, no. 2 (1983), p. 105-28.
Examines the state of education in geographical Syria in the early 1880s, presenting a translation of an account by Shahin Makarius, first read to members of Beirut's Oriental Scientific Academy in January 1883. The authors check Makarius' figures, which describe the state of education provision in Aleppo, Damascus, Hama, Homs, Latakia, the Hauran and elsewhere, against other contemporary sources. The authors note that there was a significant difference in the level of education between rural and urban areas and among religious sects.

763 **The regional equalization of health care and education in Syria since the Ba'thi revolution.**
Alasdair D. Drysdale. *International Journal of Middle East Studies*, vol. 13, no. 1 (February 1981), p. 93-111.
Drysdale examines the extent to which the Ba'th revolution and the assumption of power by the 'periphery' have led to a reduction in spatial inequalities in health care delivery and education. Although medical students are being recruited from

disadvantaged areas and obligatory rural service programmes for physicians, dentists and pharmacists have been instituted, there has been no real improvement in the distribution of health care services which remain concentrated in a few urban centres. This is largely due to the importance of the private sector in health service provision. The author criticizes the focus on hospital-based curative services. In the education sector, opportunities at the primary level are more evenly distributed but at the intermediate and secondary level results are mixed.

764 **Note sur l'état présent de l'enseignement traditionnel à Alep.**
(Note on the present state of traditional teaching in Aleppo.)
Jean Gaulmier. *Bulletin d'Etudes Orientales*, vol. 9 (1942-45),
p. 1-33.
Describes the administration, teaching methods, materials and curriculum of the traditional Muslim schools – *kuttab* and *madrassa* – of Aleppo in the late 1930s and early 1940s. It provides basic statistics on the numbers of pupils and teachers, and on other characteristics for schools throughout the province of Aleppo.

765 **Ba'thist ideology, economic development and educational strategy.**
Delwin A. Roy, Thomas Naff. *Middle Eastern Studies*, vol. 25, no. 4
(October 1989), p. 451-79.
The authors assert that Syria is facing an impending educational crisis. After years of ideological and central control, the formulation of an educational policy has not accommodated the needs of the Syrian economy. Thus, the Syrian labour force remains critically short of both qualified and semi-skilled workers and, in particular, technicians. Such a shortage necessarily hinders the impact of economic rationalization and liberalization. Accordingly, education has served the political goals of the regime, namely, the disruption of traditional Syrian society, instead of promoting a dynamic national economy. The prescription offered by the authors encompasses the professionalization of the educational establishment, but they also acknowledge that such a move would probably undermine the regime.

766 **Agricultural education in the Syrian Arab Republic.**
T. Shannon, J. D. Stanfield.   Madison, Wisconsin: Wisconsin
University, 1980. 46p. (Working Papers, Human Resources for Rural
Development in the Syrian Arab Republic, no. 8).
Describes the institutions involved in agricultural education, including secondary agrarian schools, post-secondary intermediate institutions and university-level agrarian institutions. The report makes recommendations for achieving greater co-ordination in agricultural education programmes.

767 **American interests in Syria, 1800-1901: a study of educational,
literary and religious works.**
Abdul Latif Tibawi.   London: Oxford University Press, 1966. 333p.
bibliog.
A detailed study of American interests in the Syrian *vilayet* of the Ottoman Empire. These interests were primarily in the cultural and religious fields, and led to the establishment of schools, the Protestant College, and the printing of textbooks in Arabic. Particular attention is given to educational developments that were an

Education

important factor in the evolution of the Arab national movement. The rivalry between Protestant and Catholic missions is also described.

Syria after two years of the March revolution.
See item no. 503.

Syria 1945-1986: politics and society.
See item no. 526.

Arab education 1956-1978: a bibliography.
See item no. 853.

Literature

768 **The old man and the land.**
Mamdouh Adwan, translated by Log Ajjan. Damascus: al-Tawjih
Press, 1971. 71p.
A short story by a Syria poet that focuses on the effects of war on an old farmer. The
novel was inspired by the events of the June 1967 War.

769 **The emancipation of women in contemporary Syrian literature.**
Salih J. Altoma. In: *Syria: society, culture, and polity.* Edited by
Richard Antoun, Donald Quataert. Albany, New York: State
University of New York Press, 1991, p. 79-96. (SUNY Series in
Middle Eastern Studies).
Altoma assesses three studies that have addressed feminism in the Arab world,
namely: *Feminism in Syrian school textbooks*; *The Syrian Arab woman in the
woman's international decade*; and *The structure and functions of the Arab family.*
Altoma's documentation of the emancipation of women, as a literary theme in
contemporary Syrian literature, is based on the works of three Syrians publishing
between 1959 and 1988: Kulit Khuri, Ghadah al-Samman and Bouthaina Sha'ban.
They represent three different approaches to feminism – the rebellious, the
revolutionary and the militant. From these approaches, Altoma concludes that only
Arab women can determine to what extent they can forego traditional values in order
to acquire the status of women in the West.

770 **Mu'jam al-mu'allifīn al-surrīyīn fī al-qarn al-'ishirīn, 1911-1974.**
(Dictionary of Syrian writers in the 20th century, 1911-74.)
'Abd al-Qadir 'Ayash. Damascus: Dār al-Fikr, 1985. 544p.
A biographical dictionary of Syrian authors. The author provides a short biography of
most writers, in addition to a commentary on their most famous works. Entries are
ordered alphabetically according to the authors' popular names.

Literature

771 **Modern Syrian short stories.**
Translated by Michel Azrak, revised by M. J. L. Young. Washington, DC: Three Continents Press, 1988. 131p.
A collection of short stories from the post-Second World War era until the 1980s.

772 **Modern Arab poets, 1950-1975.**
Translated and edited by Issa J. Boullata. London: Heinemann, 1976. 148p.
Four Syrian poets (Nizar Qabbani, Kamal Abu Dib, Muhammad al-Maghut and 'Ali Ahmad Sa'id) are represented in this collection of poems that reflect upon the rapid social and cultural changes which took place within the Arab world from 1950 to 1975. The poems are accompanied by brief biographical notes on each poet.

773 **Women of the Fertile Crescent: an anthology of modern poetry by Arab women.**
Edited by Kamal Boullata. Washington, DC: Three Continents Press, 1978. 253p. bibliog.
This is a collection of poems by thirteen Arab women, written during the period 1948-78. The poems have been translated into English. Syrian women poets are well-represented with twelve poems by 'Asha Arna'ut, three by Samar 'Attar and four by Saniyah Salih.

774 **Arab theatre and Syrian folk culture: comments on the relationship between Syrian dramatic art and the present day public.**
Rosella Dorigo Ceccato. In: *The Arabist Budapest Stories in Arabic 15-16: proceedings of the 14th Congress of the Union Européene des Arabisants et Islamisants, part two Budapest 29 August – 3 September 1988.* Edited by A. Fodor. Budapest: Csoma de Kovas Soc., 1995, p. 101-11.
This article examines the relationship between the audience and the playwright, and also considers the role of theatre in Syrian culture.

775 **Literature for children in Syria.**
Rosella Dorigo Ceccato. *Miscellanea Arabica et Islamica* (1993), p. 186-97.
This article provides an analysis of children's literature in Syria. It examines the texts published for children and the reactions of the local literary critics.

776 **Nizar Qabbani, the poet and his poetry.**
Z. Gabay. *Middle Eastern Studies*, vol. 9, no. 2 (May 1973), p. 208-22.
A biographical study of the Syrian poet Nizar Qabbani. Born into an upper-middle-class Damascene business family in the 1920s, Qabbani grew up in a period of marked social and political change. This was reflected in his early controversial poetry, which

brought to the fore the conflicts between traditional values and Western standards. His first collection was subject to vitriolic attack from conservatives. In the 1940s, Qabbani served in the Syrian foreign ministry, rising to the position of Ambassador to China. During the 1950s, he became more involved in the problems of Syria and the Arab world, joining the staff of the literary *al-Adab* in 1953, and turned to writing nationalist poetry.

777 **Al-masrah al-siyāsī fī Sūrrīyah, 1967-1990.** (The political theatre in Syria, 1967-90.)
Ghassan Ghunaym.   Damascus: Dār 'Alā' al-Dīn, 1996. 320p. bibliog.

The author discusses the rise of political theatre in Syria after 1967. He accounts for its emergence and criticizes its three-dimensional approach in focusing upon the citizen, the nation and the state. Ghunaym analyses the technicalities of the theatre in the third section of the book.

778 **Modern Arabic literature 1800-1970: an introduction, with extracts in translation.**
John A. Haywood.   London: Lund Humphries, 1971. 306p.

This history of modern Arabic literature focuses on the literary renaissance that followed Napoleon's invasion of Egypt in 1798. Forerunners of the literary revival in Syria and Lebanon were the Maronite poet Jabril ibn Faraht, 'Germanos' Bishop of Aleppo, and the Homs poet Sheikh Amin al-Jundi, who produced verse of the *muwashah* type. Two prominent Syrian writers (both from Aleppo) during the renaissance of the late 19th century were Rizqallah Hassun, who founded the first Arabic newspaper in Istanbul (1854) and a bi-monthly in London (1879) entitled *Hall al-Mas'alatain al-Sharqiyya wa al-Misriyya*, and Francis Fathallah Marrash, who wrote on natural history, politics and social problems. The theatrical activities of Ahmad Khalil al-Qabbani in Damascus are also given some attention. Turning to writers of the contemporary period, the author discusses the work of 'Abd al-Salam al-'Ujaili, Fu'ad al-Shaib and Masuf Ahmad al-Arna'ut. An important feature of this book is its inclusion of extensive quotations from many of the authors discussed.

779 **The blood of Adonis.**
Translated by Samuel Hazo.   Pittsburgh: University of Pittsburgh Press, 1971. 54p.

Contains thirty-nine poems in translation by the Syrian poet 'Ali Ahmed Sa'id, widely known as Adonis, who adopted Lebanese citizenship after his education in France. An introduction by Mirene Ghossein describes the life and background of 'Ali Ahmed Sa'id, co-founder of the poetry magazine *Shi'r* and founder of *Mawaqif*. His particular linguistic and stylistic contribution to Arabic poetry is examined in detail.

780 **Lamha 'an al-mawālāt al-sūrrīyah: dirāsah ma' al-nusūs.** (A hint about Syrian mawalat: a study with the texts.)
Ihsan Hindi.   Damascus: Tlasdar, 1991. 329p. bibliog.

The author offers a general definition of the *mawal* (a poetic form), and investigates the time and place of its rise in the Arab world. He examines *mawal* in Syria with an explanation of its interaction with political and social life. He presents a collection of

Syrian *mawalat*, originating from Homs, Hamah, Idlib and Aleppo, in the second part of the book (p. 175-317).

781 **Jamālīyat al-riwāyah: dirāsah fī al-riwāyah al-wāqʻīyah al-sūrrīyah al-muʻāsirah.** (The beauties of the novel: a study of the contemporary Syrian realist novel.)
'Ali Nagib Ibrahim. Damascus: Dār al-Yanābīʻ, 1994. 361p. bibliog.
The author studies the contemporary Syrian realist novel. He opines that the beauty of a novel should be studied from two angles: the theoretical and the artistic reflection of social awareness. The last angle distances the world of the novel from the real world. The author uses these forms to analyse a number of Syrian novels.

782 **Sabriya: Damascus bitter sweet.**
Ulfat Idilbi, translated by Peter Clark. London: Quartet, 1995. 233p.
This novel recounts a woman's life in the Damascus of the 1920s in the form of a diary. It charts the growth of her nationalist and feminist ideas, which are set on a collision course with the society of the time.

783 **Modern Arabic short stories.**
Selected and translated by Denys Johnson-Davies. London: Oxford University Press, 1967. 194p.
A collection of twenty modern Arabic short stories including several by the Syrian authors Walid Ikhlassi (*The dead afternoon*); 'Abdel Salam al-'Ujaili (*The dream*); and Zakariya Tamer (*Summer*). Other short stories by Zakariya Tamer, one of the best-known short story writers in the Arab world, appear in translation by Johnson-Davies in *Arabic short stories* (London: Quartet, 1983. 173p.) and in *Modern Arab stories* (London: Iraqi Cultural Centre, 1980. 132p.).

784 **Al-riwāyah al-nīswīyah fī Bilād al-Shām: al-simāt al-nafsīyah wa-al-faniyah.** (The feminist novel in Bilad al-Sham: the psychological and technical features.)
Iman al-Qadi, introduced by 'Abd al-Karim al-Ashttar. Damascus: al-Ahālī, 1992. 411p. bibliog.
This book examines the place of the feminist novel in Bilad al-Sham (Greater Syria) from 1895 until 1985. Al-Qadi gives a history of the femininist novel in Bilad al-Sham, and then examines the suitability of the term. Psychological features are addressed on p. 53-242 and technical features, such as time, place and symbols, are examined on p. 243-403. The author analyses two types of feminist novels, Colette Kuri's *ayām maʻhu* (Days with him) (p. 313-19) and Hamidah Naʻnaʻs *al-watan fī al-ʻayīnayīn* (The nation in the eyes) (p. 366-88). A bibliography of feminist novels written in Bilad al-Sham is provided.

785 **The development of early Arabic drama 1847-1900.**
Mohamed A. al-Khozai. London; New York: Longman, 1984. 245p. bibliog.
The first part of this book explores the mental, aesthetic, environmental, religious and historical factors that inhibited the development of a true Arab theatre prior to the

mid-19th century. Embryonic and indigenous forms of drama in Arabic culture, such as the *khayal al-zill* (shadow play) and the *ta'ziyah* (passion play), are described. The second, and major, part of the work analyses in detail the extant works of four major Arab playwrights, including Marun al-Naqqash, who wrote and produced the first Arabic plays in Lebanon and Syria, and Ahmad Abu Khalil al-Qabbani, who began his career in Damascus in 1871.

786 **Sufi motifs in contemporary Arabic literature: the case of ibn 'Arabī.**
Alexander Knysh.   *The Muslim World*, vol. LXXXVI, no. 1 (January 1996), p. 33-49.
The article offers a critical analysis of Syria's Muhammad Ghazi 'Arabi, and Egypt's Gamal al-Ghitani's use of ibn 'Arabi's mystical image, the unity of being or *wahdat al-wujud*, in their literary works. Knysh underlines their different approaches to ibn 'Arabi, and includes an analysis of his personality and his mystical doctrine.

787 **An 11th century Muslim's syncretistic perspective of cosmology: Abū al-'Alā' al-Ma'arri's philosophical-poetic reflections in Luzum mā lā yalzm on make-up and dynamics of the universe.**
R. K. Lacey.   *The Muslim World*, vol. LXXXV, no. 1-2 (January-April 1995), p. 122-46.
Lacey traces the dynamics of the universe, the totality of being and creation, as analysed in the philosophical poetry of Abu al-'Ala' al-Ma'arri. This work is intended for students of Islamic studies, philosophy and literature.

788 **The fan of swords: poems.**
Muhammad al-Maghut, translated by May Jayyusi, Naomi Shihab Nye, edited and introduced by Salma Khadra Jayyusi.   Washington, DC: Three Continents Press, 1991. 62p.
Al-Maghut, a Syrian poet born in 1934, started writing in the 1950s. This is a collection of poetry from three volumes of his works: *Sorrow in the moonlight*; *A room with a million walls*; and *Joy is not my profession*.

789 **Walid Ikhlassy: a postmodern Syrian fictionalist.**
John Maier.   *Journal of South Asian and Middle Eastern Studies*, vol. XI, no. 3 (spring 1988), p. 73-87.
This article is most suitable for students of literature and linguistics. It offers a short biography of writer Walid Ikhlassi and a literary criticism of his short story *Such a beguiling return!*

790 **Fragments of memory: a story of a Syrian family.**
Hanna Mina, translated by Olive Kenny, Lorne Kenny.   Austin, Texas: Center for Middle Eastern Studies, The University of Texas at Austin, 1993. 180p.
An autobiographical novel, whose protagonist was born into a poor family in northern Syria. The story is set against the backdrop of political events taking place in Syria during the early 20th century.

Literature

791 **The origins of modern Arabic fiction.**
Matti Moosa. London: Three Continents Press, 1983. 350p.
Traces the evolution and development of Arabic fiction during the 19th and early 20th
centuries, examining the cultural milieu within which new genres of Arabic fiction
emerged. Detailed attention is paid to both the development of Arabic drama in Syria
during the 19th century and to the role of prominent Syrian playwrights, such as
Marun al-Naqqash, Ahmad Abu Kalil al-Qabbani, Sulayman al-Qirdahi and Iskandar
Farah.

792 **Philosophical origins of the Arab Ba'th party: the work of Zaki
al-Arsuzi.**
Saleh Omar. *Arab Studies Quarterly*, vol. 18, no. 2 (spring 1996),
p. 23-37.
Al-Arsuzi's work has received little attention by Middle Eastern scholars, and Omar
seeks to redress this imbalance with an introductory essay on the essence of al-
Arsuzi's philosophy. His contribution, it is argued, lies in his development of a
philosophical foundation for Arab regeneration, which was influenced by Plato,
Plotonius and Bergson. Al-Arsuzi's nationalism was grounded in metaphysics, a
derivational structure in audio-visual form, of the Arabic language.

793 **Al-mūwashāhāt fī Bilād al-Shām mundh nash'ātīhā hatā nihāyt
al-qarn al-thanī 'ashar al-hijjrī.** (The muwashahat in Bilad al-Sham
from its rise until the end of the 12th century AH.)
Miqddad Rahim. Beirut: 'Ālam al-Kūtub, 1987. 528p. bibliog.
A study of the *muwashahat* (a poetic form) in Bilad al-Sham (Greater Syria). The
author uses manuscripts to examine the *muwashahat* in Andalucia and accounts for its
transmission to Bilad al-Sham. This thorough study includes a good bibliography
(p. 423-539).

794 **Al-nns al-ghā'ib: dirāsah fī masrah Sa'dallah Wannūs.** (The absent
script: a study in the theatre of Sa'dallah Wannus.)
Muhammad Mahmud Rahummah. Cairo: Maktabt al-Shabāb, 1991.
476p. bibliog.
The author identifies the major features of Arab theatre by focusing on the works of
Tawfiq al Hakim, Youssef Idris and Ihtifalia in Morocco. He provides a critical study
of Wannus, basing his analysis on the form and content of his theatre. The author
examines Wannus' originality, which springs from an infusion of popular stories,
Syria's cultural heritage and Western influences.

795 **Ughnīyāt al-rahīl al-Wannūsīyah: dirāsah fī masrah Sa'dallah
Wannūs.** (The Wannus departure songs: a study in the theatre of
Sa'dallah Wannus.)
Ahmad Sakhsukh. Cairo: Al-Dār al-Misrīyah al-Lubnānīyah, 1998.
666p. bibliog.
The author analyses the theatre of Wannus, divides it into two distinct stages (p. 21-35,
and p. 37-63) and proceeds to analyse his latest plays. However, the book only
examines the content of the plays, and neglects both form and linguistic analyses.

796 **Ishkālīyat al-mawt fī adab Jūrj Sālim, Ghābriyīl Mārsīl, Albīrt Kāmū.** (The issue of death in the literature of George Salem, Ghabreel Marcel, Albert Kamo.)
Ghassan al-Sayyid. Damascus: Dār Muʿid, 1993. 87p. bibliog.

The author discusses death in human thought. He shows how death has always occupied the human mind and points to religion, the works of ancient civilizations and philosophy as evidence. Al-Sayyid analyses death in the works of George Salem with special reference to *fī al-manfā* (In the exile), and then compares the writing of Ghabreel Marcel with Albert Kamo.

797 **Damascus nights.**
Rafik Schami, translated by Philip Boehm. Cairo: The American University in Cairo Press, 1996. 263p.

Schami draws on the rich heritage of *A thousand and one nights* to tell his magical tales, which include topics ranging from *jinnis* to politics. Depicting and encapsulating the atmosphere of Syrian city life, the tales are elaborately set in contemporary Damascus.

798 **Kings and bedouins in the palace of Aleppo as reflected in Maʿarri's works.**
Pieter Smoor. Louvain, Belgium: University of Manchester Press, 1985. 255p. maps. bibliog. (Journal of Semitic Studies Monograph Series, no. 8).

Smoor's research was conducted at the Suleymaniye library in Istanbul and the library of Ahmet III in Topkapi Saray during the winters of 1973 and 1975. The first part of this book reflects upon Maʿarri's portrayal in his poetry of the balance of power between the Byzantine and the Fatamid Empires and their political struggles for Aleppo. The second part analyses how Maʿarri charts the rise and decline of the bedouin dynasty of the Mirdasids in his poetry.

799 **Musāhamah fī naqd al-naqd al-adabī.** (A contribution to the criticism of literary criticism.)
Nabil Sulayman. Latakia, Syria: Dār al-Hīwar lil-Nashr wa-al-Tawzīʿ, 1986. 2nd ed. 219p. bibliog.

The author analyses literary criticism in Syria. He examines the influence of the social and cultural environment upon literary criticism during the 1960s and 1970s. He offers his own variations on formalism (p. 9-81), selectivism (p. 82-144) and Marxism (p. 145-93).

800 **Daughter of Damascus, ya mal al-Sham.**
Siham Tergeman, English version and introduction by Andrea Rugh. Austin, Texas: Center for Middle Eastern Studies, The University of Texas at Austin, 1994. 202p. (Modern Middle East Literatures in Translation Series).

A personal account of a young Syrian woman living in the *suq sariya* (old city) of Damascus during the first half of the 20th century. The original memoir was entitled *ya mal al-Sham.* It was written as a legacy, designed to preserve the details of an Arab past for a young Syrian audience. The conservative values of Damascus are reflected in the Islamic architecture of the Old Quarter.

801 **Khāmis al-rāshidīn.** (The fifth caliph.)
   'Ali Wannus. Damascus: Wizārat al-Thaqāfah, 1985. 100p. (Silsilat Masrahīyāt 'Arabīyah, no. 4).
A play inspired by the life of Umayyad Caliph 'Umar ibn 'Abd al-'Aziz, otherwise known as the fifth caliph.

802 **Hāmish al-hayāh .. hamish al-mawt.** (The margin of life . . . margin of death.)
   Ghassan Kamilý Wannus. Damascus: Itihād al-Kutāb al-'Arab, 1991. 160p.
A collection of eight short stories by Ghassan Wannus. Throughout the stories, the author focuses upon the essence of the soul. The dreams of the soul amplify the small details of life into events of import and impact.

803 **Hafalat samar min agl 5 hizayīrān.** (An entertainment party for 5 June.)
   Sa'dallah Wannus. Beirut: Dār al-Adāb, 1968. 150p.
A play inspired by the defeat of the June 1967 War.

804 **Malhamat al-sarāb: masrahīyah.** (The epic of the mirage: a play.)
   Sa'dallah Wannus. Beirut: Dār al-Adāb, 1997. 160p.
A modern fable warning against the inducement of material wealth and the duplicitous role of the modern state. The main protagonist enters into a contract with a Satan-like character. As long as he lives and becomes ruthless, he is promised good health. Each time he wishes to renew his health, he is obliged to marry a young woman and then divorce her. The protagonist returns to his village for the third time to marry a young woman, and promises its inhabitants a lucrative future; he awards the father of his desired bride, unknown to either of them, with an investment loan. Faltering and ill-fated projects bankrupt the father, and the daughter is claimed as recompense. The villagers awaken to the mirage of promises and the loss of their precious gifts.

805 **Al-malik huwa al-malik.** (The king is the king.)
   Sa'dallah Wannus. Beirut: Dār ibn Rushd, 1980. 3rd ed. 126p.
This is an overtly political play that considers the constraints of office placed upon a king. Moreover, regardless of the king's personality, the strictures of office will determine his rule and his propensity for repressive measures. Likewise, the king's courtiers will play the same role irrespective of time or location.

806   **Munamnamāt tārīkhīyah: masrahīyah.** (Historical miniatures: a play.)
Sa'dallah Wannus.   Beirut: Dār al-Aādab, 1996; Cairo: Dār al-Hillāl, 1994. 206p.
A play about the defeat of the Muslims by Tamarlane, symbolizing the spiritual and temporal weakness of their leadership. It is divided into three parts: Sahykh Burhān al-Dīn al-Tāzlī / *al-hazīmah* (The defeat) (p. 6-93); Waly al-Dīn 'Abd al-Rahmān ibn Khaldūn / *mahānt al-'ilm* (The humiliation of science) (p. 96-144); and Azdār amir al-qal'ah / *al-majzarah* (The massacre) (p. 146-206).

807   **Nizar Qabbani's autobiography: images of sexuality, death and poetry.**
Stefan Wild.   In: *Love and sexuality in modern Arabic literature.*
Edited by Roger Allen, Hilary Kilpatrick, Edde Moor.   London: al-Saqi, 1995, p. 200-09.
In this essay, Wild analyses Qabbani's autobiography with particular reference to self-image and love. Wild offers a brief resumé of Qabbani's life, and then examines images of him – as 'Rebel', 'Eternal child' and 'Don Juan' – throughout his poetry and autobiography.

Come, tell me how you live.
See item no. 5.

Damascene intellectual life in the opening years of the 20th century: Muhammad Kurd 'Ali and al-Muqtabas.
See item no. 426.

Three approaches, one idea: religion and state in the thought of 'Abd al-Rahman al Kawakibi, Najib 'Azuri and Rashid Rida.
See item no. 433.

Syria 1945-1986: politics and society.
See item no. 526.

Culture

808 **Broadcasting in the Arab world: a survey of radio and television in the Middle East.**
Douglas A. Boyd. Philadelphia, Pennsylvania: Temple University Press, 1982. 278p. bibliog. (International and Comparative Broadcasting Series).

Discusses the developments, characteristics and constraints of radio and television broadcasting in the Arab world as well as international broadcasting to, and within, the region. Syrian radio and television services are discussed in detail on p. 77-84. Even though the Syrian Broadcasting Organization was created in 1946, broadcasting lacked government commitment until the early 1960s. Considerable impetus for the expansion of broadcasting came from Egypt during the union, and television services began in July 1960. The programme characteristics of 'Radio Damascus', 'Voice of the People', and the single national television channel are described.

809 **La cuisine, manger à Damas.** (The cuisine, eating in Damascus.)
Jean-Claude David. In: *Damas: miroir brisé d'un orient arabe* (Damascus: broken mirror of an Arab Orient). Edited by Anne-Marie Bianquis, Elizabeth Picard. Paris: Editions Autrement, 1993, p. 226-39. (Série Monde, H.S. no. 65).

David provides an overview of Damascene cuisine, focusing on home-cooking, but paying some attention to 'street food'. He also examines special foods prepared by Muslims for religious celebrations, as well as foreign foods (macaroni and mortadella from Italy) that have been modified to suit the local taste. This is an engaging and informative article that combines culture, cuisine and custom.

810 **L'impremte de la sainteté.** (The imprint of sanctity.)
Eric Geoffroy. In: *Damas: miroir brisé d'un orient arabe* (Damascus: broken mirror of an Arab Orient). Edited by Anne-Marie Bianquis, Elizabeth Picard. Paris: Editions Autrement, 1993, p. 166-74. (Série Monde, H.S. no. 65).

The author examines the pilgrimage of Syrian Muslims in search of blessings to the tombs of ibn 'Arabi, Sheiykh Arslan and Saydah Zaynab. Geoffroy discusses the religious affinity between Syria's 'Alawis and Iran's Shi'as, and explores the hierarchy of saints and the concept of intercession. He argues that popular religion and pilgrimage to tombs are controlled by religious figures, sheikhs, who guide the masses in their quest for assistance from saints.

811 **Information structures and organizations in the Syrian Arab Republic.**
Yanka Ben Jemia. *Orient* (Oplanden), vol. 25, no. 4 (December 1984), p. 561-81.

Presents a detailed evaluation of the contribution of the broadcasting and print media to information and organization dissemination in Syria. The role of the Ministry of Information and organizations such as the Syrian News Agency (SANA) are discussed, together with an analysis of two programmes on Radio Damascus: 'The Main Programme' and 'The People's Voice'. The political, social and cultural functions of television broadcasting are also examined. The bulk of the article comprises a comprehensive content and style analysis of the three main daily newspapers (*al-Ba'th*, *al-Thawrah* and *Tishrin*), each of which represents a different political tendency within the Ba'th. Other sources of information, including the national unions and professional organizations, are also examined. The author concludes that information structures and organizations in Syria have two basic principles: the promotion of individual responsibility; and individual subordination to society.

812 **Jour de fête au cimetère.** (A feast day at the cemetery.)
Nadia Khost, translated by Aya Sakkal. In: *Damas: miroir brisé d'un orient arabe* (Damascus: broken mirror of an Arab Orient). Edited by Anne-Marie Bianquis, Elizabeth Picard. Paris: Editions Autrement, 1993, p. 196-206. (Série Monde, H.S. no. 65).

An account of a family's feast day at the cemetery which reveals an interesting aspect of Syrian culture. Cemeteries are a place for social gathering, where people talk about their daily lives.

813 **Un zikr chez les soufis.** (A zikr at the Sufis.)
Jean-Yves L'Hôpital. In: *Damas: miroir brisé d'un orient arabe* (Damascus: broken mirror of an Arab Orient). Edited by Anne-Marie Bianquis, Elizabeth Picard. Paris: Editions Autrement, 1993, p. 175-82. (Série Monde, H.S. no. 65).

The author examines the Sufi practice of *zikr* (a meeting of dervishes at which a phrase is chanted rhythmically to induce a state of ecstasy) He explains that *zikr* depends on the *tariqa* of Sufis, which differs from one Muslim country to another, and describes the circle of *zikr*.

814   **The music of Arab Americans: aesthetics and performance in a new land.**
Anne K. Rasmussen.   In: *Images of enchantment: visual and performing arts of the Middle East.*   Edited by Sherifa Zuhur.   Cairo: American University in Cairo Press, 1998, p. 135-56.

This article is based on ethnographic research and fieldwork conducted in 1989. Rasmussen explores the music of Arab emigrants in the United States between 1930 and 1970. Most of the Arab emigrants came from Greater Syria during the late 19th century; musical differences owed their origins to the various village traditions. Rasmussen explains how the music of these 'old timers' has been surpassed by a multinational music industry, thus disrupting a foundation of cultural identity. The *hafla* and *mahrajan*, which served as a basis for social and cultural gatherings, were undermined by the emerging 'night-club scene' in the 1960s. The broad appeal of night-clubs to a multinational youth culture has challenged the musical traditions of the migrant Arab community.

815   **The Arab press: news, media and political process in the Arab world.**
William A. Rugh.   London: Croom Helm, 1979. 205.

A comprehensive analysis of the development, role and characteristics of the Arab news media, focusing on relations between the mass media and the political process. It includes a consideration of the Syrian press, which is ascribed to the 'mobilization press' category, as well as state-controlled radio and television broadcasting. Syria has a long history of newspaper publishing and reading; the first Damascus daily, *Suriya*, appeared in 1865, and newspaper circulation in 1975 was estimated at 134,000 copies per day. The principal characteristics of the 'mobilization press' are its uncritical support for official policy and the national leadership; its lack of diversity; and its use as a tool to mobilize popular support. These principles are seen in the structure and content of the dailies *al-Ba'th* and *al-Thawrah*, published by the Ba'th Party and the Ministry of Information respectively. Other dailies (*al-Fida'*, *al-'Urubah*, *al-Jamahir* and *Tishrin*) are guided by the government-operated Syrian News Agency.

Arabs in tent and town.
See item no. 9.

Nomads and settlers in Syria and Jordan, 1800-1980.
See item no. 14.

Syria today.
See item no. 58.

Ebla: an empire rediscovered.
See item no. 140.

Ebla: a third-millennium city-state in ancient Syria.
See item no. 143.

Syria: society, culture, and polity.
See item no. 491.

'Our Moslem sisters': women of Greater Syria in the eyes of Protestant missionary women.
See item no. 492.

Syria 1945-1986: politics and society.
See item no. 526.

Arab theatre and Syrian folk culture: comments on the relationship between Syrian dramatic art and the present day public.
See item no. 774.

Luth, luthistes et luthiers. (Lute, lutenistes and lute-makers.)
See item no. 817.

Art and Architecture

816　**Vernacular tradition and the Islamic architecture of Bosra.**
　　　Fleming Aalund.　PhD thesis, The Royal Academy of Fine Arts,
　　　Copenhagen, 1991. 101p. maps. bibliog.

A study of the vernacular building tradition of the Hauran and the Islamic architecture of Bosra. Aalund provides some background on the area's geographical and historical setting, and then proceeds to examine the two traditions using the monuments as case-studies. The text is accompanied by extensive maps, site plans and pictures.

817　**Luth, luthistes et luthiers.** (Lute, lutenists and lute-makers.)
　　　Nabil Allao, Anne-Marie Bianquis.　In: *Damas: miroir brisé d'un
　　　orient arabe* (Damascus: broken mirror of an Arab Orient).　Edited by
　　　Anne-Marie Bianquis, Elizabeth Picard.　Paris: Editions Autrement,
　　　1993, p. 219-25. (Série Monde, H.S. no. 65).

The article is divided into two parts. The first is an introduction to Damascene music which highlights the importance of the lute, generally played by amateurs at social gatherings. The second part is an interview with a Damascene *'awwad*, Iyad Haimour, who introduces the lute and identifies its place in the traditional instrument assembly, *takht*. This is an interesting article that introduces the reader to traditions of Damascene music.

818　**Syria: a historical and architectural guide.**
　　　Warwick Ball.　Essex, England: Scorpion, 1994. 216p. maps. bibliog.

This guide accompanies Burns' *Monuments of Syria: an historical guide*. Ball's work provides one with an historical and architectural background to Syria's major archaeological sites and monuments. This is a very accessible book, and is essential for any traveller interested in exploring Syria's considerable architectural past.

819   **La mosaïque romaine et byzantine en Syrie du nord.** (Roman and
Byzantine mosaics in north Syria.)
Janine Balty.   In: *Alep et la Syrie du nord* (Aleppo and northern
Syria).   Edited by Viviane Fuglestad-Aumeunier.   Aix-en-Provence,
France: EDISUD, 1991-94, p. 27-39. bibliog. (La Revue du Monde
Musulman et de la Méditerranée, no. 62).

The author investigates the development of the oriental mosaic during the Byzantine era.

820   **Early churches in Syria: fourth to eleventh centuries.**
Howard Crosby Butler.   Princeton, New Jersey: Princeton University
Press, 1929. 274p. (University Monographs in Art and Archaeology).

A detailed study, by the Director of American and Princeton Archaeological
Expeditions to Syria, which traces the origins, growth and development of
ecclesiastical, church and monastery architecture in Syria. The discussion covers the
characteristics of plan, construction, superstructure, ornamental devices, inscriptions,
origins and influences. The text of each chapter is divided on a geographical basis into
three sections: southern, northern and north-eastern Syria. The work includes more
than 280 illustrations.

821   **Greek and non-Greek interaction in the art and architecture of the
Hellenistic East.**
Malcolm A. R. Colledge.   In: *Hellenism in the East: the interaction of
Greek and non-Greek civilizations from Syria to Central Asia after
Alexander.*   Edited by Amélie Kuhrt, Susan Sherwin-White.
Berkeley, California; Los Angeles: University of California Press,
1987, p. 134-62.

Interaction between Greek and eastern Mediterranean culture existed before the arrival
of Alexander. To appreciate this interaction, Colledge introduces the reader to the
cultural influences of pre-Hellenism before going on to examine the forms of
interaction throughout the four distinct periods of Hellenism.

822   **Beehive villages of north Syria.**
Paul W. Copeland.   *Antiquity*, vol. 29, no. 113 (1955), p. 21-24.

Describes the characteristics, construction techniques, plan and interior arrangement
of the traditional 'beehive' mud-brick housing of villages in the Aleppo-Homs area.

823   **Domaines et limites de l'architecture d'empire dans une capitale
provinciale.** (The domains and limits of empire architecture in a
provincial capital.)
Jean-Claude David.   In: *Alep et la Syrie du nord* (Aleppo and northern
Syria).   Edited by Viviane Fuglestad-Aumeunier.   Aix-en-Provence,
France: EDISUD, 1991-94, p. 169-94. bibliog. (La Revue du Monde
Musulman et de la Méditerranée, no. 62).

An architectural study of Aleppo during the Ottoman period. The author examines two
forms of architecture: domestic (houses), and public buildings (mosques, real estate,
waqfs and *madrassas*). He studies how architecture accommodated local needs;

Ottoman architecture, it is argued, remained distinct and was an expression of power and religion, whilst Mamluk architecture exhibited relative unity. The author examines the architecture of the following buildings: the *waqf* of Hosrow Pasha; the mosque of 'Adliyya; the *waqf* of Mahmud Pasha; the mosque and *waqf* of Baraham Pasha; and the *madrassa* of 'Othamiyya (Rid'iyya).

824 **Reflets de la grande mosquée des Omayyades.** (Reflections of the great mosque of the Umayyads.)
Nikita Elisséeff. In: *Damas: miroir brisé d'un orient arabe* (Damascus: broken mirror of an Arab Orient). Edited by Anne-Marie Bianquis, Elizabeth Picard. Paris: Editions Autrement, 1993, p. 34-39. (Série Monde, H.S. no. 65).

An account of the great mosque, where the Romans first built a temple to Jupiter and, following their conversion to Christianity, transformed it into a church during the 4th century. Christians and Muslims shared it as a place of worship, when Islam entered Syria, until Caliph Walid ibn 'Abd al-Malik replaced it with the mosque in the 8th century. A brief description of the mosque is also provided.

825 **A quarter of Aleppo in the 19th and 20th centuries: some socio-economical and architectural aspects.**
Anette Gangler, Heinz Gaube. In: *Alep et la Syrie du nord* (Aleppo and northern Syria). Edited by Viviane Fuglestad-Aumeunier. Aix-en-Provence, France: EDISUD, 1991-94, p. 159-68. (La Revue du Monde Musulman et de la Méditerranée, no. 62).

The authors offer a preliminary report of the fieldwork, undertaken between 1987 and 1990, in the north-eastern quarters of the old city of Aleppo, east of Bab al-Hadid. The report is divided into two parts, first covering the present and past inhabitants of the houses (p. 159-63), and then providing a chronology of domestic architecture in the quarter (p. 163-68).

826 **Citadel of Damascus: investigation of possible use.**
Hanspeter Hanisch. Damascus: Adnan Dehneh, Syrian Office for Trading and Printing, 1991. 451p.

The publication of a report ordered by the General Directorate of Museums and Antiquities of the Syrian Arab Republic. It provides a detailed study of the medieval citadel of Damascus, which had been used for military purposes until 1985. The author examines the condition of the citadel and makes suggestions for its restoration and future use.

827 **The arts and crafts of Syria.**
Johannes Kalter, Margareta Pavaloi, Maria Zerrnickel. London: Thames & Hudson, 1992. 240p. maps. bibliog.

This book provides an illustrated review of Syria's crafts legacy. With reference to the collections of Antoine Touma and the Linden Museum, Stuttgart, the authors present the handicrafts, ceramics, folk jewellery, textiles and costumes of Syria. Their work also offers an insight into Syria's urban, rural and cultural orientation within the Ottoman Empire.

828   **Towards an archaeology of architecture: clues from a modern Syrian village.**
Kathryn A. Kamp.   *Journal of Anthropological Research*, vol. 49, no. 4 (winter 1993), p. 293-317.

Offers an ethno-archaeological study of a Syrian village, Darnaj. The author suggests eight principles for analysing domestic architecture: functions of the built environment (p. 296-98); ideal characteristics of living spaces and the architectural environment (p. 299-305); interior versus exterior spaces (p. 305); consideration of cost (p. 305-06); benefits of flexibility (p. 306-07); room function versus room use (p. 307-09); effect of changes in room type (p. 309-10); and the symbolism of dwelling places (p. 310-11). The author avers that interpreting architecture is essential to understanding social and political organization. This article is ideal for students of archaeology and anthropology.

829   **Quartiers et paysage.** (Quarters and landscapes.)
Irène Labeyrie.   In: *Damas: miroir brisé d'un orient arabe* (Damascus: broken mirror of an Arab Orient).   Edited by Anne-Marie Bianquis, Elizabeth Picard.   Paris: Editions Autrement, 1993, p. 118-27. (Série Monde, H.S. no. 65).

Labeyrie offers an architectural appreciation of Damascus, considering the old city and Mount Qassioun, and describing the architecture of the ancient and modern parts of Damascus.

830   **Early Abbasid stucco decoration in Bilad al-Sham.**
Michael Meinecke.   In: *Bilad al-Sham during the Abbasid period (132 AH/75 AD – 451 AH/ AD 1059): proceedings of the Fifth International Conference on the History of Bilad al-Sham, 7-11 Sha'ban 1410/4-8 March 1990.*   Edited by Muhammad Adnan Bakhit, Robert Schick.   Amman: University of Jordan Press, 1991, p. 226-67.

Meinecke reflects upon Islamic architecture and its use of stucco decoration during the early 'Abbasid period. After a general introduction, he examines the city of Samarra, founded by Calpih al-Mu'tasim in AD 836, and Harun al-Rashid's palace, built in AD 793, as case-studies.

831   **Coupoles et tombeaux.** (Cupolas and tombs.)
Abd al-Razzaq Moaz.   In: *Damas: miroir brisé d'un orient arabe* (Damascus: broken mirror of an Arab Orient).   Edited by Anne-Marie Bianquis, Elizabeth Picard.   Paris: Editions Autrement, 1993, p. 45-48. (Série Monde, H.S. no. 65).

Moaz describes the numerous mausoleums of Damascus, emphasizing their originality. He focuses on three monuments: the mausoleum of Salah al-Din; the funeral *madrassa* of al-Malik al-'Adil Muhammad (Salah al-Din's brother); and the funeral *madrassa* of al-Malik al-Zahir Baybars (the Mamluk sultan).

832   **Damascus' crowning glory – the Umayyad mosque.**
Habeeb Salloum.   *The Muslim World*, vol. LXXXII, no. 1-2
(January-April 1992), p. 149-52.

In this very brief article, Salloum reviews the history of the Umayyad mosque. The structure and utility of the mosque are described; however, the article falls short of capturing the essence of Damascus' crowning glory.

833   **The Orientalist: Delacroix to Matisse. European painters in North Africa and the Middle East.**
Edited by Mary Anne Stevens.   London: Royal Academy of Arts,
1984. 256p.

This fully-illustrated text on Western art and its encounter with the Orient includes a discussion on several artists who visited and painted in Syria during the 19th century. These include: Gustav Bavernfeind, Léon Belly, Théodore Frère, Edward Lear, Frederic Leighton and David Roberts. Two of Leighton's works on Damascus, which he visited in 1873, are reproduced.

834   **The death of old Damascus.**
Elizabeth Tampier.   *The Middle East*, no. 125 (March 1985), p. 55-57.

Reports on the clearance of several historic *suqs* in 1983-84, such as the wood-turners' *suq* and the 11th-century al-Sadiriyah *madrassa* (school) in the area of the Great Umayyad Mosque. The destruction followed a plan drafted by the French architect Michel Eochard in 1968, when the preservation of historic urban sites was given low priority in Third World planning. Further destruction was prevented by the action of old-city residents.

The Azm Palace of Hama, a historical, architectural, artistic illustrated study.
See item no. 61.

The American archaeological expedition to Syria, 1899-1901.
See item no. 115.

The art of Palmyra.
See item no. 117.

Dura-Europos, a fortress of Syro-Mesopotamian art.
See item no. 126.

Syria: publications of the Princeton University archaeological expeditions to Syria in 1904-05 and 1909, division IV, Semitic inscriptions.
See item no. 139.

Ebla: an empire rediscovered.
See item no. 140.

The art of Dura-Europos.
See item no. 144.

Alep à l'époque Ottomane (xvie-xixe siècles). (Aleppo in the Ottoman era [16th-19th centuries].)
See item no. 282.

The music of Arab Americans: aesthetics and performance in a new land.
See item no. 814.

Periodicals

835 **Arab Studies Quarterly.**
Belmont, Massachusetts: Association of Arab-American University
Graduates, and the Institute of Arab Studies, 1979- . quarterly.
A quarterly journal that deals with history, culture and the institutions of the Arab
world.

836 **British Journal of Middle Eastern Studies.**
Exeter, England: British Society for Middle Eastern Studies, 1973- .
semi-annual.
Published under the title *British Society for Middle Eastern Studies Bulletin* until
1991. The journal publishes articles on the politics, economics, society, literature and
linguistics of the Middle East that range from the end of classical antiquity to
contemporary times. Each issue contains valuable book reviews.

837 **Country Report: Syria.**
London: Economist Intelligence Unit, 1986- . quarterly.
A quarterly review containing a summary of political events and an analysis of
economic trends. An annual supplement is also published. The current title continues
from the *Quarterly Economic Review: Syria, Jordan* (1978-86), the *Quarterly
Economic Review of Syria, Lebanon and Cyprus* (1968-78), and the *Quarterly
Economic Review of Syria, Lebanon, Jordan* (1956-67).

838 **International Journal of Middle East Studies.**
New York: Cambridge University Press, 1970- . quarterly.
A quarterly periodical that covers topics on the Middle East from the 7th century
onwards.

839   Journal of Palestine Studies.
Berkeley, California: University of California Press for the Institute of
Palestine Studies, 1971- . quarterly.
A quarterly journal on Palestine affairs and the Arab-Israeli conflict.

840   Al-Ma'rifah. (The knowledge.)
Damascus: Wizārat al-Thaqāfah, 1966- . monthly.
A monthly review, published by the Ministry of Culture, that covers a wide range of
cultural topics, such as politics, heritage, psychology, poetry and literature.

841   Middle East Economic Digest.
London: Middle East Economic Digest, 1957- . weekly.
A comprehensive weekly account of economic events in the Middle East, with
regional comments and short news items on individual countries, including Syria. It
includes details of contracts together with occasional feature articles and special
reports.

842   Middle East Economic Survey.
Nicosia: Middle East Petroleum and Economic Publications, 1957- .
weekly.
An important weekly review, covering oil, finance and banking, and political
developments in the Middle East region, including Syria.

843   Middle East Insight.
Cleveland, Ohio: International Insight, 1982- . bi-monthly.
Provides analysis on the Middle East and exclusive interviews with US and Middle
Eastern leaders.

844   The Middle East Journal.
Washington, DC: Middle East Institute, 1947- . quarterly.
A social science quarterly, which covers society, politics, religion and government of
the Middle East.

845   Middle East Policy.
Washington, DC: Middle East Policy Council, 1992- . quarterly.
A quarterly periodical that provides a forum for issues relating to US-Middle East
policy.

846   Middle Eastern Studies.
Ilford, England: Frank Cass, 1964- . quarterly.
A quarterly journal that includes articles on the history and politics of the Middle East.

847 **Mijalat Majma' al-Llughah al-'Arabīyah bī-Dimashq.** (Review of
the Arab Academy in Damascus.)
Damascus: Dār al-Ba'th, published for Arab Academy in Damascus,
1921- . quarterly.
A quarterly journal on language and linguistics.

848 **The World of Information: Middle East Review.**
Essex, England: Walden, 1973- . annual.
An economic and business report of Middle Eastern countries. A separate review is
provided for each country. It covers politics, economic sectors, economic indicators in
addition to a country profile. A business guide and business directory are also included
in the country profile.

Bibliographies

849 **Bibliography of Levant geology.**
M. A. Avinmelech.   Jerusalem: Israel Programme for Scientific
Translation, 1965. 192p.

A comprehensive, unannotated bibliography of literature on the geology of the Levant
(Cyprus, Hatay, Israel, Jordan, Lebanon, Sinai and Syria), containing some 4,500
items written between the early 18th century and 1963. There are over 400 references
on Syria arranged by author and divided into six main subject areas: geohistory;
geomorphology; lithology and mineralogy; mineral resources; pedology; and
structural geology. Subject and chronological indexes are provided.

850 **Social stratification in the Middle East and North Africa: a**
bibliographical survey.
Ali Banuazizi.   London; New York: Mansell, 1984. 248p.

An unannotated bibliography of some 1,900 items on the broad theme of social
stratification and inequality. The section on Syria is found on p. 155-60, and includes
sixty-five items. The material is arranged geographically, and subject and author
indexes are provided.

851 **A post-war bibliography of the Near Eastern mandates.**
Edited by Stuart Carter Dodd.   Beirut: American University of Beirut,
1932. 8 vols. (American University Publication of Arts and Sciences,
Social Science Series).

The eight volumes cover material in English, French, German, Italian, Arabic, Hebrew
and miscellaneous Oriental languages. They deal with publications in the period 1918-
29 on the French and British Mandates in Iraq, Palestine, Transjordan and Syria,
covering a wide variety of social, economic and political material.

852 **The Middle East in microform: a union list of Middle Eastern microforms in North American libraries.**
Compiled by Fawzi W. Khoury, Michelle S. Bates.   Seattle, Washington; Washington, DC: University of Libraries, 1992. 377p. bibliog. (Middle East Microform Project).

A useful guide for selecting materials suitable for microfilm. Materials are divided into two categories: the Middle East in general; and the Ottoman Militaria collection in the Hoover Institute. The first edition was entitled the *National union catalog of Middle Eastern microforms.*

853 **Arab education 1956-1978: a bibliography.**
Veronica S. Pantelides.   London: Mansell, 1982. 552p.

A comprehensive, annotated bibliography on education in the Arab world (1956-78) arranged on a country-by-country basis. The section on Syria (p. 416-32) contains over 200 references. A combined author, title and subject index is included.

854 **The Quarterly Index Islamicus: Current Books, Articles and Papers on Islamic Studies.**
Edited by J. D. Pearson.   London: Mansell, 1977- . quarterly.

Contains quarterly supplements to the *Index Islamicus.*

855 **The Middle East in conflict, a historical bibliography.**
Edited by Gail A. Schlachter.   Santa Barbara, California; Denver, Colorado; Oxford: ABC-Clio Information Services, 1985. 301p. (Clio Bibliography Series, no. 19).

Contains over 3,250 annotated items drawn from periodical literature published over the period 1973-82, focusing on 20th-century developments in international relations. The first five chapters are arranged thematically: general works; political integration and co-operation; international relations, aid and trade; the Middle East in the World Wars; and intra-regional wars and conflicts. The latter sections include chapters on each of the Arab-Israeli wars. The remainder of the work is arranged on a country-by-country basis, with Syria being covered on p. 146-49. Author and subject indexes are provided.

856 **Syria.**
Ian J. Seccombe.   Oxford; Santa Barbara, California; Denver, Colorado: ABC-Clio Press, 1987. 341p. map. (World Bibliographical Series).

This comprehensive bibliography of 903 annotated items on Syria was the first edition to the present volume. A combined author, title and subject index is provided.

857 **Middle East bibliography.**
Sanford R. Silverburg.   London; Metuchen, New Jersey: Scarecrow Press, 1992. 564p.

An unannotated bibliography on the Middle East. It includes a list of works on items such as Middle East countries, major cities and minorities, and constitutes a good first search tool.

858　US foreign relations with the Middle East and North Africa – a
　　　bibliography.
　　　Sanford R. Silverburg, Bernard Reich.　London; Metuchen, New
　　　Jersey: Scarecrow Press, 1994. 586p. (Scarecrow Area Bibliographies,
　　　no. 3).
A bibliography of US relations with the Middle East and North Africa since the end of
the Cold War. It builds upon the *US and the Middle East* publication. It includes
books, essays and articles from scholarly publications.

859　Agricultural bibliography of Syria, to 1983.
　　　Edited by A. B. Zahlan.　London: Ithaca Press, 1984. 121p.
An annotated bibliography of some 580 items in Arabic and European languages. The
bibliography is subdivided into ten sections: general works; physical environment;
natural resources; manpower and social organization; transport and mechanization;
research and development, education and extension; agro-industry, packaging and
storage; plant husbandry; animal husbandry; and veterinary medicine. In addition to
books, articles and theses, it includes government publications and Food and
Agriculture Organization (FAO) reports. A combined author and subject index is
provided.

Indexes

There follow three separate indexes: authors (personal or corporate); titles; and subjects. Title entries are italicized and refer either to the main titles, or to other works cited in the annotations. The numbers refer to bibliographical entry rather than page number. Individual index entries are arranged in alphabetical sequence.

Index of Authors

Dodd, Stuart Carter 851
Douwes, Dick 230, 450
Downey, Glanville 171
Drake, Laura 658
Drysdale, Alasdair D.
437-38, 685, 763
D'Suoza, Andreas 209
Dunham, Sally 121
Durgham, Ahmad 547

E

East, Roger 513
Eddé, Anne-Marie 172
Efrat, Moshe 581, 585,
601
Ehteshami, Anoushiravan
419, 613, 624
Eldar, Dan 348
Elisséeff, Nikita 173, 824
Eppel, Michael 625
Epstein, Claire 122
Establet, Colette 231
Evron, Yair 582, 646

F

Faksh, Mahmud A. 439,
583, 647
Farah, Caesar 232
Fargues, Philippe 29
Faroqhi, Suraiya 233
Fawaz, Leila Tarazi
234-35
Finlay, Hugh 63
Firras, Kais M. 458
Firro, Kais 707
Fisher, John 316
Fleischmann, Ellen L. 492
Fodor, A. 774
Frangakis-Syrett, Elena
236
Freedman, Robert O.
584-85
Freeman-Grenville, G. S.
P. 123
Freitage, Ulrike 391
Frey, Wolfgang 90
Freyberger, Klaus Stefan
124
Fuccaro, Nelida 72

Fuglestad-Aumeunier,
Viviane 35, 108, 164,
167, 172, 175, 192, 210,
236, 261, 269, 282, 307,
819, 823, 825

G

Gabay, Z. 776
Gabrieli, Francessco
176-77
Gangler, Anette 825
Garbar, Oleg 125
Garcin, Jean-Paul 57
Gardner, David Pierpont
558
Garfinkle, Adam 349
Garrett, Robert 115
Garzouzi, Eva 733
Gates, Carolyn L. 350
Gates, Marie-Henriette
126
Gaube, Heinz 127, 825
Gaulmier, Jean 764
Gaunson, A. B. 351
Gelvin, James L. 237
Geoffroy, Eric 810
Gervers, Michael 472
Ghafour, Anouar 57
Ghunaym, Ghassan 777
Gibb, H. A. R. 73, 178
Gibb, Hamilton 179
Gil-Har, Yitzhak 352
Gilbar, Gad G. 238
Gilbert, Martin 659
Glazer, Sidney 318
Glubb, John B. 8
Golan, Galia 586
Goldman, Bernard 135
Gombar, Eduard 239
de Gontaut-Biron, Comte
R. 353
Goodich, Michael 202
Goodrich-Freer, A. 9
Gordon, Cyrus H. 410
Gordon, Matthew S. 234,
346
Grainger, John D. 180
Gray-Reddish, Jennifer
604
Greenshields, Thomas H.
463

Gresh, Alain 10, 607
Groom, Nigel 34
Gubser, Peter 440, 459

H

Habashi, F. 46
Haddad, William W. 232,
246
Hajjar, Sami G. 687
Halabi, Usama R. 666
Hall, H. R. 128
Hamadi, Sa'dun 499
Hanihara, Kazuro 129-31
Hanisch, Hanspeter 826
Hannoyer, Jean 734-35
Harel, Yaron 469
Harold, H. 662
Harris, William W. 648
Harrison, David L. 92
Haskins, James 514
Havemann, Axel 181
Hawwa, Huda 708
Hayes, John L. 116
Haywood, John A. 778
Hazo, Samuel 779
Heald, Stephen 354-55
Heller, Peter B. 572
Heltzer, Michael 132-34
Heydemann, Steven 515
Himadeh, Sa'id 356-57
Hindi, Ihsan 780
Hinnebusch, Raymond A.
419, 516-25, 587, 613,
626, 649, 685, 688,
709-12
Hiro, Dilip 11
Hirschfeld, Yair 614
Hitti, Philip Khuri 162,
182-83, 196, 358, 398
Hof, Frederic C. 661,
689
Hollis, Rosemary 627
Holme, Christopher 140
Holod, Renata 125
Holt, P. M. 170, 177,
184-85, 219
Honda, Gisho 93
Hopfinger, Hans 713, 736
Hopkins, Clarke 135
Hopwood, Derek 240,
526

Hourani, Albert Habib 37, 186, 241, 295, 359, 366, 420
Howard, Harry N. 317
Hudson, Michael C. 588-89
Humphreys, R. Stephen 187
Hunter, Shireen T. 615
Hureau, Jean 58
al-Husari, Abu Khaldun Sati 318
Hussein, Lutfi 411
Hütteroth, Wolf-Dieter 242-43
Huxley, Anthony 97

I

Ibrahim, 'Ali Nagib 781
Idilbi, Ulfat 782
Ilawi, M. 42
Ilias, Joseph 527
Imber, Colin 244
International Bank for Reconstruction and Development 392
Irabi, Muhammed Sa'id 61
Isma'il, Munir 455
Ismael, Jacqueline S. 6, 592
Ismael, Tareq Y. 6, 592
Issawi, Charles 376
al-'Itri, 'Abd al-Ghani 12

J

Jackson, D. E. P. 191
Jankowski, James 36
Jayyusi, May 788
Jayyusi, Salma Khadra 788
Jemia, Yanka Ben 811
Jenner, Michael 59
Joffe, Lawrence 690
Joger, Ulrich 94
Johnson-Davies, Denys 783
Jones, Howard 463
Joseph, John 470
Joseph, Tanya 513

K

Kalter, Johannes 827
Kamp, Kathryn A. 828
Kamrava, Mehran 528
Kanya-Forstner, A. S. 311
Karpat, Kemal H. 399
Karsh, Efraim 590-91
Kasmieh, Khairia 319
Kawtharani, Wajih 360
Kayali, Hasan 245
Kazemi, Farhad 297
Kedouri, Elie 320
Keilany, Ziad 737
Kelly, Walter Keating 74
Kenny, Lorne 790
Kenny, Olive 790
Kerner, Susanne 124, 146, 153
Khadduri, Majid 573
Khader, Bichara 738-39
Khairallah, Ibrahim A. 574
Khalaf, Sulayman N. 740
Khalidi, Ahmed S. 662
Khalidi, Rashid 246-49
Khalidi, Tarif 744
Khalidy, Walid 81
Khlusi, Ihsan bint Sa'id 188
Khost, Nadia 812
Khouri, J. 47
Khoury, Fawzi W. 852
Khoury, Philip Shukry 241, 250-51, 361-66
Khoury, Yusuf K. 294
al-Khozai, Mohamed A. 785
Khuri, Fuad I. 441
Khuri, Yusuf 423
Kienle, Eberhard 493, 529-30, 533, 538, 592, 650, 704, 709, 714, 720, 723, 726
Kilpatrick, Hilary 807
Kipper, J. 662
Kirkbride, Alec Seath 321
Kiwan, Ma'mun 663
Klat, Paul J. 741
Kleiman, Ephraim 680
Knustad, James 125
Knysh, Alexander 786
Kobari, I. 152

L

L'Hôpital, Jean-Yves 813
Labeyrie, Irène 829
Lacey, R. K. 787
Lavergne, Marc 35
Lavy, Victor 715
Lawrence, Thomas Edward 323
Lawson, Fred H. 532-37, 594
Layish, Aharon 460
Leary, Lewis Gaston 13
Leca, Jean 494
Legge, Anthony J. 136
Lehmann, Gunnar 137
Lemche, Niels Peter 138
Lesch, Ann Mosely 629
Lesch, David W. 595, 630-31, 691
Levtzion, Nehemia 472
Lewis, Bernard 170, 177, 252, 467, 473
Lewis, Norman N. 14, 230, 450, 452
Lewis, Peter 60
Liebeschuetz, J. 189-90
Little, Douglas 596
Littman, Enno 115, 139
Lloyds Bank Ltd 716
Lobmeyer, Hans Günter 538
Long, David E. 2

Kofsky, Aryeh 416
Kohlberg, Etan 451
Kolkowicz, Roman 438
Korany, Bahgat 626
Korbani, Agnes 531
Korbonski, Andrzej 438
Kren, Karin 482
Kreyenbroek, Philip G. 482-83
Krikorian, Mesrob K. 464
Kubursi, Atif A. 628
Kuhrt, Amélie 193, 821
Kundsen, Erik L. 593
Kuroki, Hidemitsn 471
Kushner, David 608
al-Kuzbari, Salma al-Haffar 322

Picard, Elizabeth 3, 22, 27, 163, 173, 277, 324, 336, 377, 388, 474, 495, 496, 551-52, 609, 621, 809-10, 812-13, 817, 824, 829, 831
Pickthall, Marmaduke 76
Picquet, Raymond 671
Pinault, David 453
Pipes, Daniel 443, 553-54, 597, 695
Pitard, Wayne T. 147
Podeh, Elie 634
Poirier, J. P. 50
Pölling, Sylvia 723
Polunin, Oleg 97
Porath, Yehoshua 375
Porter, Venetia 148
Post, George E. 98
Poujoulat, Baptistin 475
Pouzet, Louis 424
Pranger, Robert 558
Prawer, Joshua 200
Prentice, William 115
Pruser, W. 67

Q

al-Qadi, Iman 784
Qadri, Ahmad 326
al-Qattan, Najwa 476
Quataert, Donald 250, 441, 490-91, 518, 560, 579, 740, 769
Quilliam, Neil 598

R

Rabbat, Nasser O. 201
Rabinovich, Itamar 273, 376, 444, 555, 635, 652, 672, 696
Rabo, Annika 497
Rafeq, Abdul-Karim 274-81, 327
Rahim, Miqddad 793
Rahummah, Muhammad Mahmud 794
Ramet, Pedro 599
Ranstorp, Magnus 653
Rasmussen, Anne K. 814

Rasmussen, Carl G. 425
Rasmussen, J. Lewis 697
Rathmell, Andrew 636
Raymond, André 282, 283, 402, 734
Reeves, John C. 477
Reich, Bernard 2, 544, 673, 858
Reid, Donald M. 478
Reid-Sarkees, Merdith 600
Reilly, James A. 284-90
Richard, Jean 202
Rihawi, Abdulqader 62
Riis, P. J. 149
Roberts, Caroline 148
Roberts, David 556, 601
Robinson, Glenn E. 557
Robinson, Leonard 724
Rodinson, Maxime 29
Rogan, Eugene L. 291
Romanowicz, B. A. 50
Rondot, Pierre 377
Rostovtzeff, Michael I. 203
Rowley-Conwy, Peter A. 136
Roy, Delwin A. 765
Ruete, Emily 77
Rugh, Andrea 800
Rugh, William A. 815

S

Sa'adah, Antun 378
Sachar, Howard M. 379
Sadeque, Syedah Fatima 204
Sadowski, Yahya M. 558-59
Safadi, Chafic 44-45
Sagafi-Nejad, Tagi 743
Sahin, Ilham 292
Saito, Mitsuko 93
Sakaguchi, Yutaka 129
Sakhsukh, Ahmad 795
Sakkal, Aya 812
Salamé, Ghassan 719
Saleh, Samir 576
Salem, Paul 498
Saliba, Najib E. 293, 403
Salibi, Kamal S. 205

Salih, Kamal 294
Salloum, Habeeb 832
Salme, Sayyida 77
Samman, Mouna L. 404
al-Samman, Muti' 394
Sanagustin, Floréal 100
Sanjian, Avedis K. 466
Sasson, Jack M. 138, 143
Satloff, Robert B. 380
Saunders, Bonnie F. 602
Saunders, H. 662
Savory, Roger 376
Sayari, Sabri 610
Sayigh, Yezid 603
Sayigh, Yusif A. 725
al-Sayyid, Ghassan 796
Schaebler, Birgit 381
Schami, Rafik 797
Schatkowski Schilcher, Linda 295-97
Scheffler, Thomas 461
Schein, Sylvia 202
Schick, Robert 161, 830
Schiff, Ze'ev 654, 698
Schlachter, Gail A. 855
Schwartz, Glenn M. 118-19, 150
Seale, Patrick 395, 530, 533, 538, 560, 603, 637, 650, 674-75, 704, 709, 714, 720, 723, 726
Seccombe, Ian J. 856
Segert, Stanislav 412
Seikaly, Samir M. 426-27
Shad, Tahir 604
Shahin, Emad Eldin 428
Shalev, Aryeh 699
Shami, Yahya 40
Shannon, T. 766
Shapland, Greg 638
al-Shatti, Muhammad Jamil 298
Shatzmiller, Maya 206
Shavit, David 605
Sheffer, Eliezer 715
Sherwin-White, Susan 193, 821
Shihade 61
Shimoni, Yaacov 19
Shlaim, Avi 603
Shorrock, William I. 382
Sidahmed, Abdel Salam 419

Index of Titles

S

Index of Subjects

A

'Abbasid
  archaeology 161
  architecture 830
  Damascus 182
  political conditions 183,
    212
  social conditions 161,
    183
  theology 161
Abdulhamid II, Sultan
  266, 304, 473
Abortion 404
Abu Shama 176
Abu Simbel 78
Accommodation 55, 58,
  63
Acre
  conquest 209
  defence against
    Napoleon 304
  socio-political structure
    271
Acropolis 155
al-Adab 776
al-'Adil 187, 831
Adonis 779
'Aflaq, Michel 389, 435,
  498-500, 512, 527
Agha Khan 450
aghas 250
Agrarian reform 503, 577,
  725, 729, 738-39
Agricultural co-operatives
  536, 729
Agricultural development
  707, 729, 732, 742-43
Agricultural policy 744
Agricultural production
  geology 51
  Hama 230
  Ottoman 230, 272
  statistics 755, 757
Agro-business 736
Agro-industry 859

Al-'Ahd al-Iraqi 385
Ahmad Pasha 304
Akkadian
  cuneiform 120
  documents 134
  language 408, 413
  measurements 132
  texts 413
Akkar 374
al-A'laq al-khatira 170,
  198
Aleppo
  11th century 213
  13th century 195
  19th century 307
  1850 riots 258, 469
  administration 192
  archaeology 115
  architecture 175,
    822-23, 825
  Armenians 462-64
  'beehive' villages 822
  Bishopric of Aleppo 466
  capital 182
  consul report 223
  dar al-'adl 201
  death 269
  al-Din, Nur 173
  drought 269
  earthquake 269
  economy 83
  education 761-62, 764
  factory 229, 308
  French Mandate 347, 388
  geography 83
  Hamdanid 164, 182
  herbalists 100
  Islamic education
    societies 761
  Jacobites 470
  Jewish-Christian
    relations 469
  Jewish community 479
  literature 798
  local history writing 170
  majlis 255

Mamluks 192
Mirdasids 164, 213
muwashahat 780
Ottoman 218, 222,
  256-57, 259, 261,
  269, 282-83, 307, 402
plague 269
population 402
religion 68
Saljuq 181
silk trading 229, 308,
  347
Tanzimat reforms 255
trade 236, 308
travel guide 54-55, 58,
  60
travellers' accounts 64,
  66, 68-69, 73, 75, 78
urbanization 35
Alexander the Great 199,
  821
Alexandretta
  Armenians 463, 466
  cession to Turkey 33,
    304, 359, 367, 379,
    609
  communal
    interdependence 380
  crisis 389
  demographic and
    economic change 609
  dispute with Turkey
    489, 608-09
  Franco-Turkish
    agreements 354, 359
  Hatay-Syria boundary 33
  historiography 380
  sanjaq 371, 388
  travellers' accounts 69
Algeria
  acquisition of weapons
    671
  military state 528
  political economy 494,
    504
  society 494, 504

265

Ba'th Party *contd*
  party programme 502
  patronage 504, 515,
    519, 558-60
  recruitment practices
    521
  socialism 535
  society 508, 520, 522,
    524-25
  women 495
Battuta, ibn 66, 73
Baybars, al-Zahir 184,
  204, 831
Beaufort, General de 234
Bedouin
  dynasty 798
  life and customs 14, 65
  settlement 3, 742
  sheep-herding 735
'Beehive' housing 822
Beirut
  consul report 223
  French Mandate 205,
    228, 341, 360
  Ottoman 215, 228, 299
  travellers' accounts 74,
    77
Beqa' 374
Bergson 792
Biogeography 103
Birds 87, 91
Bishopric of Aleppo 466
al-Bitar, 'Abd al-Razzq
  281
al-Bitar, Salah al-Din 389,
  512
Bosra 52, 60, 816
Boundaries
  with Iraq 31
  with Jordan 32
  with Palestine 349
  with Transjordan 333
  with Turkey 33
Bourgeoisie 401, 522, 532,
  557, 702, 704, 722
British Government's Blue
  Book (1916) 462
Broadcasting 754, 808,
  811, 815
Bronze Age
  Damascus 147
  Ebla 140, 145
  Mari 120

Syria-Palestine 138,
  142
Tell Bderi 146
Tell Sukas 149
Tell-Umm al-Marra
  119, 121
*Bughyat al-talab fi tarikh
  Halab* 170, 195
Buqrus 90
Byzantine
  Arab-Byzantine struggle
    197
  economic prosperity 210
  mosaic 819
  period 213, 243, 468,
    798

C

Cairo 167, 201, 330, 426,
  607
Capitalism 261, 284, 535,
  558
Caravan routes 233
Caravan trade 203
Carter 694
Catholic Missions 767
Catholics
  Greek 401
  Ottoman 299
  Syrian 470-71
Catroux, General Georges
  359, 379
Censorship 232
Census 242, 399-400,
  402
Central Bank of Syria 390
Ceramics 112, 118-19,
  122, 148, 155, 827
Chadirji, Kamil 345
Chalcolithic period 122,
  183
Chaqar Bazar 5
Christian Lebanese
  National Movement 374
Christian massacres 300
Christianity
  conversion to 824
  Eastern 468
  in Syria 59, 183, 199
Christianization of Syria
  190

Christians
  baptistery 144
  Catholic 299, 401,
    470-71
  chapel 126, 135
  conversion to Islam
    472
  French Mandate 382
  Greek Orthodox 472
  in Antioch 171
  in Beirut 228
  in Damascus 228, 235,
    474
  in Lebanon 225, 235,
    360, 374, 398, 654
  in Syria 60
  Jacobites 472
  Maronites 283
  migration to United
    States 398, 403
  minority 75
  Orthodox 470-71
  Ottoman 244, 258, 300,
    467, 470
  political and social
    structures 235
  relations with Jews 469,
    473, 480
  relations with Muslims
    469-71, 473, 475
Chronicles
  Crusades 165, 178
Churches
  architecture 59, 820
  Eastern 470
  Presbyterian 492
Circassians 192
Citadel 62, 826
Civil Code 577
Civil council 189
Civil war
  Damascus 187
  Lebanon (1860) 234,
    457
  Lebanon (1975-76) 7,
    616-17, 632, 643-44,
    648
Class structure
  and economic policy
    702
  and land reform 740
  effect of Ba'th 518
Clemenceau, Georges 311

271

Israel *contd*
  Arab-Israeli conflict 7,
    15, 20, 322, 369, 506,
    534, 545-46, 549,
    564, 570, 580, 587,
    589-91, 594, 598,
    601, 604, 607, 619,
    622-23, 636, 638,
    649, 657-78, 681-83,
    697, 751, 855
  Armistice agreement 663
  bombing of Damascus
    551
  courts 460
  dialect 411
  disengagement
    agreement 664
  Druzes 456, 458, 460
  invasion of Lebanon
    612, 641, 643, 652,
    676
  occupation of Lebanon
    621, 641-42, 646,
    654, 661, 672
  occupation of Golan
    649, 658, 669
  peace process 523, 598,
    613, 665, 675,
    670-701
  peace with Egypt 591,
    676, 692
  relations with Iran 615,
    617
  relations with Turkey
    488
  relations with United
    States 580, 599, 602
  Turkey's recognition of
    607-08, 610
*Ittihad al-shabab al-
    thawrri* 521

J

Jabal Amel 374
Jabal al-Druze
  annexation to Jordan 459
  French Mandate 336,
    370, 359
  revolt (1925) 336, 370
  travellers' accounts
    69-70, 75, 80

Jabala 24
Jacobites 470-72
Jadid, Salih 16, 555
*Jam'iyat al-Maqasid al-
    Khayriyah* 761
Janissaries 220, 222, 258,
    261, 274, 283
Japan 25
Jarajima 197
Jazira
  bedouin settlement 742
  Catholics 470
  French Mandate 352, 359
  geology 51
  Jacobites 470
  Kurdish revolt 470
  land tenure 733
  local histories 170
  soil 51
Jerusalem
  biblical land 425
  Crusades 182, 185, 200
  dialect 411
  Israeli occupation 675
  Kingdom of 182, 185,
    200
  money-lending 291
  Ottoman 253, 291
  Patriarchate of 466
  Sadat's trip to 591
  travellers' accounts 69
  'ulama 253
Jews
  Aleppo 75, 469, 479
  archives 375
  Damascus 75, 476, 479
  family life 480
  Ottoman 309, 469, 476,
    479-80
  relations with Christians
    469, 473
  relations with Muslims
    473
  religion 477, 480
Jordan
  Abdullah, King 459
  bibliography 849
  birds 87
  boundary with Syria 32
  caravan trade 203
  conflict with Syria 537
  dialect 411
  domestic politics 678

economic development
    715
economic integration
    680
exports 728
foreign aid 715
geology 849
Greater Syria scheme
    633
historiography 239
history 17
hydro-electric dam 611
identity 273
impact of *intifadah* 623
invasion by Syria 633
life and customs 8
Ottoman 273, 294
Palestinian refugee
    children 756
physical environment 8
political economy 504
property law 577
reaction to Gulf crisis
    629
regional player 634
relations with Iraq 619
relations with Israel 678
relations with Syria 7,
    17, 545-46, 621, 633
ruins 203
social environment 8
society 504
stock market 703
struggle for Syria 625
sultanic regime 528
support for Muslim
    Brotherhood 633
travel guide 63
workers' remittances
    728
Jordan River 669
Jordan Valley 122
Jordanian-Israeli peace
    treaty 570, 673, 679
Judicial accounts 278
Judiciary 192
al-Jundi, Sheikh Amin 778

K

Kalbiyyah 439, 442
Kamo, Albert 796

275

Likud government 687
Limestone formations 44
Lute 817

M

Ma'alula 409
Madrassa 424, 764, 823, 831, 834
Madrid Peace Conference 598, 694, 700
Maktab Anbar 418
Mamluk
  administration 184, 192
  Aleppo 192
  architecture 823, 831
  Circassiene 192
  commercial relations 184
  Damascus 214
  dynasty 159-60, 167, 169, 176, 183-85, 204, 211, 215
Mammals 92
al-Manar 423, 478
Manpower 753, 859
Marcel, Ghabreel 796
Mari
  animals 120, 138, 407
  archives 120
  Bronze Age 120
  cults 120
  currency 120
  division of labour 120
  excavations 59
  exchange rate 120
  food and drink 120
  industrial workshop 120
  transport and communications 120
  warfare and diplomacy 120
  women 120
Maronites
  and Druzes 457
  in Lebanon 643
  Ottoman 283, 457
Marrash, Francis Fathullah 778
Marriage
  between confessions 474

Druzes 460
Jews 480
law of personal status 568
Ottoman 244
Massacres
  Armenians 309, 462
  Damascus (1860) 254, 300, 304
Matar, Ilyas 225
al-Matawirah 436, 439, 442
McMahon 32, 247, 432
Mecca 64, 66, 78, 277, 312, 432
Medina 266, 277
Mediterranean
  culture 821
  flora 97-98
Mesolithic period 136
Mesopotamia
  ancient history 138, 151
  art 126
  biblical land 425
  British policy 316, 320
  desertion 243
  ecology 99
  excavation sites 118-20, 150, 155, 157
  Jews 477
  karst springs 45
Middle East
  arms racing 671
  bibliographies 852, 855, 857-58
  biography 19
  birds 91
  British policy 313, 330
  Christianity 468
  conflict 498, 855
  culture 20, 28, 37, 259
  economy 1, 10, 20, 28, 37, 841-42
  flora and fauna 30, 91, 94
  foreign policy 724
  French Mandate 311, 345, 366
  geography 1, 10, 26, 28, 36, 37
  geology 30
  history 1, 10, 20, 30, 37, 123

Kurds 486
labour migration 728
military balance 751
oil 30, 717
Ottoman 241, 267-68
peace process 489, 669, 685, 680
periodicals 836, 838, 841-46, 848
politics 1, 2, 10, 11, 20, 26, 30, 504, 564, 746
population 1, 10, 28, 37
regional order 607
relations with Soviet Union 586
relations with United States 588-89, 858
snakes 94
society 1, 10,11, 20, 37, 345, 504, 850
state legitimacy 724
struggle for Syria 646
Turkey 607, 610
water 611
Migration
  Armenians 465
  Christians 474
  flow and patterns 406
  to Arab countries 397, 728
  to Egypt 401
  to United States 398, 403
Military
  6th century 190
  agreements between Turkey and Israel 489, 607, 610
  aid to Syria 581, 597, 599, 603-04
  Aleppo 164
  and politics 7, 18, 396, 436, 440, 510-12, 534, 536, 543, 548, 555, 626, 637, 704
  balance in Middle East 751
  biography of leaders 19
  citadel 826
  civil relations 438
  conflict 672
  co-operation with Israel 664

T

Ta'as 90
Tabqa Dam 743
Tadmor see Palmyra
Ta'if Accord 509, 650-51
Takht 817
Takkiya Sulaimaniyya 62
Takritis 445
Tanzimat reforms 216, 245, 253-55, 303-04, 418, 473
Tapu 264, 402, 467
Tauras 98
Taxation 725
   Hama 230
   the Hauran 242
   Ottoman 230, 242, 252
   Palmyra 208
Tectonics 48, 51
Teleilat Ghassul 122
Television 754, 808, 811, 815
Tell Abu Hureyra 136
Tell Ahmar 114
Tell Brak 5
Tell Hariri see Mari
Tell Leilan 112, 155
Tell Mardikh see Ebla
Tell Minus 148
Tell Sabi Abyad 104, 105
Tell Sheikh Hasan 109
Tell Sukas 149
Temple
   Abu Simbel 78
   of Bel 144
   Ebla 143
   Greek 149
   Roman 124
   to Jupiter 825
   Ugarit 133
Textiles 827
   Damascus 285, 288
   Palmyra 117
al-Thawrah 811, 815
Theatre 774, 777, 785, 794-95
Tiglath-pileser I 128
Tiglath-pileser II 128
Tigris River
   hydrobiology 99
   hydrology 99
   water distribution 489, 638

Til Barsib 114
Tischrin 811, 815
Topography 30, 34, 115, 152, 699
Tourism 723, 753
Trade
   1960s 503, 725
   Aleppo 229, 236, 308
   among participants in peace process 680
   ancient history 151
   and agriculture 730
   Beirut 228, 341
   caravan 203
   customs and tariff system 344
   Damascus 75, 284
   exports 728
   foreign 344, 356, 713, 715, 737, 748-49, 752-53
   French Mandate 341, 344, 356
   Ghouta 75
   Lebanon 350
   Levant 259
   Levant Company 229, 308
   Middle East 855
   Ottoman 223, 228-29, 236, 238, 268, 284, 289, 291, 308
   Palmyra 113
   statistics 748, 750, 752-53, 755, 757-58
   Ugarit 132
   under Asad 7, 713, 716, 726
   with Europe 706
   with Iraq 238
   with Soviet Union 581
Trade unions 503, 567
Transjordan
   boundary with Syria 333
   British Mandate 372, 851
   Faysal's campaign 323
   geographical history 242
   Greater Syria scheme 633
   revolution 329

Transport
   agricultural
      bibliography 359
   French Mandate 356
   Mari 120
   Ottoman 750
   statistics 750, 753, 755
   travel guide 55
   travellers' accounts 63
Treaty of Friendship and Alliance 355, 359
Treaty of Sèvres 33
Tribes 220, 385, 442, 482, 735
Tripoli 64, 192, 215, 374
Tunisia
   political economy 504
   society 504
   stock market 703
Turkey
   Alexandretta 304, 367, 379, 609, 611
   Armenians 465
   ancient 151
   boundary with Syria 33
   customs relations with Syria 344
   defeat (1918) 31
   Druzes 457
   Kurds 481, 483, 486-89, 610
   Maronites 457
   nationalism 217, 248
   negotiations with France 382
   Ottoman 245, 302, 327, 457, 473
   relations with Iraq 487, 606
   relations with Iran 487
   relations with Israel 489, 607
   relations with Syria 487-89, 537, 545, 606, 608, 610-11
   relations with the United States 602
   revolution (1908) 225, 464
   rule in Syria 65, 183, 323
   Second World War 372
   statistics 750

Turkey *contd*
  travellers' accounts 64,
    65, 68, 85
  Turkism 246, 302
  water 489, 606, 610-11
Turkish documents 265
Turkish manuscripts 219
Turkish pogroms 466
Tyre 374

U

Ugarit
  archives 133
  commerce 107, 132
  excavations 59
  foreign relations 107
  history 60
  Hittite Empire 107
  internal organization
    133
  royal economy 133
  tablets 410
  texts 410
  trade 132
  villages 134
Ugaritic language 134,
  410, 412
'Ulama 186, 226-27, 253,
  255, 424
Umayyad Mosque 62, 424,
  824, 832, 834
Umayyads
  architecture 59
  dynasty 6, 125, 182-83,
    197
  political conditions 183
  social conditions 183
United Arab Emirates
  (UAE)
  labour migration 728
  political economy 504
  society 504
  stock market 703
United Arab Republic
  (UAR)
  Ba'th Party role 512
  broadcasting 808
  dissolution 7, 394-95,
    608,
  economic development
    393, 702

formation 6, 7, 11, 304,
  322, 630, 637
land reform 737, 741
United Nations Truce
  Supervision
  Organization (UNTSO)
  669
Unites States
  1957 crisis 578, 595,
    602, 607, 631
  and Lebanon 654
  and peace process 594,
    681, 687, 689,
    694-95, 701
  Arab-Israeli conflict
    664
  archives 634
  documents 631
  emigrants to 398, 404,
    814
  impact on education 767
  King-Crane
    Commission 317, 371
  policy towards Middle
    East 589, 600, 685,
    858
  Presbyterian Church 492
  relations with Iran 615
  relations with Israel
    580, 599, 602
  relations with Syria 369,
    546, 582-83, 593,
    596, 600, 675
Urban geography 283
Urbanization 25, 35, 150,
  175
US Department of
  Agriculture 42
US State Department 369
US State Department's
  Terrorist List 587

V

Vegetation 21, 88, 97, 103
  desert 103
  Euphrates Valley 90
  Ghab Valley 102
  Holocene 102
  Lebanon 88
  Mediterranean 97
  Middle East 103

Vichy regime 337, 367,
  372, 379
Villages
  archaeological sites
    104-05
  architecture 124, 822,
    828
  'beehive' housing 822
  dialect 409
  Jabala 24
  music 814
  Neolithic 104-05
  Ottoman 218, 230, 264,
    294
  politics 517
  Raqqa region 497
  Roman 124
  Sabgha 497
  society 734
  Ugarit 134
de Vogüé, Comte
  Melchoir 113
de Volney, Comte 113

W

Wages 347, 567, 745, 755,
  757
al-Walid, Khalid ibn 158
Waqf 221, 823
War
  Arab-Israeli
    1948 322, 625, 658,
      668, 676
    1967 322, 537, 658,
      666-67, 669-70,
      674, 676
    1973 599, 674
  Iran-Iraq War 7, 251,
    296, 311, 316, 321,
    326, 342, 359, 363,
    374, 431-32, 466,
    563, 596, 612,
    616-18, 724
  Second Gulf War 509,
    583, 588, 657
  Second World War 21,
    250, 368, 371, 589,
    605
al-Wardi, ibn 198
Warfare
  Crusades 207
  Mari 120

Map of Syria

This map shows the more important features.

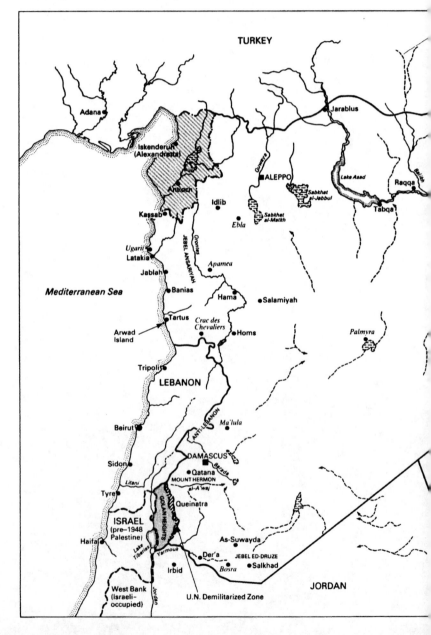

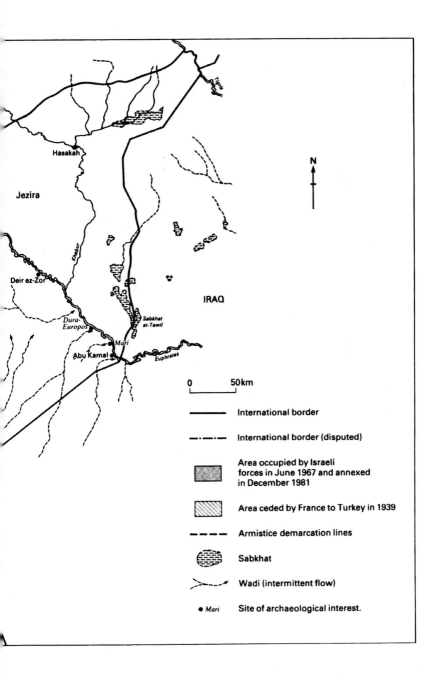

N

Hasakah

Jezira

Deir ez-Zor

Khabur

Tigris

IRAQ

Dura-
Europos

Sabkhat
at-Tawil

Mari

Abu Kamal

Euphrates

0   50 km

International border

International border (disputed)

Area occupied by Israeli
forces in June 1967 and annexed
in December 1981

Area ceded by France to Turkey in 1939

Armistice demarcation lines

Sabkhat

Wadi (intermittent flow)

● Mari   Site of archaeological interest.

INTERNATIONAL ORGANIZATIONS SERIES

Each volume in the International Organizations Series is either devoted to one specific organization, or to a number of different organizations operating in a particular region, or engaged in a specific field of activity. The scope of the series is wide-ranging and includes intergovernmental organizations, international non-governmental organizations, and national bodies dealing with international issues. The series is aimed mainly at the English-speaker and each volume provides a selective, annotated, critical bibliography of the organization, or organizations, concerned. The bibliographies cover books, articles, pamphlets, directories, databases and theses and, wherever possible, attention is focused on material about the organizations rather than on the organizations' own publications. Notwithstanding this, the most important official publications, and guides to those publications, will be included. The views expressed in individual volumes, however, are not necessarily those of the publishers.

VOLUMES IN THE SERIES